Interlinking SDGs and the Bottom-of-the-Pyramid Through Tourism

Marco Valeri
Niccolò Cusano University, Italy

Shekhar
University of Delhi, India

A volume in the Advances
in Hospitality, Tourism,
and the Services Industry
(AHTSI) Book Series

Published in the United States of America by
    IGI Global
    Business Science Reference (an imprint of IGI Global)
    701 E. Chocolate Avenue
    Hershey PA, USA 17033
    Tel: 717-533-8845
    Fax: 717-533-8661
    E-mail: cust@igi-global.com
    Web site: http://www.igi-global.com

Library of Congress Cataloging-in-Publication Data

CIP Data in progress

British Cataloguing in Publication Data
A Cataloguing in Publication record for this book is available from the British Library.

All work contributed to this book is new, previously-unpublished material.
The views expressed in this book are those of the authors, but not necessarily of the publisher.

For electronic access to this publication, please contact: eresources@igi-global.com.

Advances in Hospitality, Tourism, and the Services Industry (AHTSI) Book Series

Maximiliano Korstanje
University of Palermo, Argentina

ISSN:2475-6547
EISSN:2475-6555

MISSION

Globally, the hospitality, travel, tourism, and services industries generate a significant percentage of revenue and represent a large portion of the business world. Even in tough economic times, these industries thrive as individuals continue to spend on leisure and recreation activities as well as services.

The Advances in Hospitality, Tourism, and the Services Industry (AHTSI) book series offers diverse publications relating to the management, promotion, and profitability of the leisure, recreation, and services industries. Highlighting current research pertaining to various topics within the realm of hospitality, travel, tourism, and services management, the titles found within the AHTSI book series are pertinent to the research and professional needs of managers, business practitioners, researchers, and upper-level students studying in the field.

Coverage

- Casino Management
- Customer Service Issues
- Food and Beverage Management
- International Tourism
- Tourism and the Environment

IGI Global is currently accepting manuscripts for publication within this series. To submit a proposal for a volume in this series, please contact our Acquisition Editors at Acquisitions@igi-global.com or visit: http://www.igi-global.com/publish/.

Titles in this Series

For a list of additional titles in this series, please visit:
http://www.igi-global.com/book-series

Dimensions of Regenerative Practices in Tourism and Hospitality
Pankaj Kumar Tyagi (Chandigarh University, India) Vipin Nadda (University of Sunderland, UK) Kannapat Kankaew (Burapha University International College, Thailand) and Kaitano Dube (Vaal University of Technology, South Africa)
Business Science Reference • copyright 2024 • 338pp • H/C (ISBN: 9798369340424) • US $295.00 (our price)

AI Innovations for Travel and Tourism
Ricardo Correia (Instituto Politécnico de Bragança, Portugal & CiTUR, Portugal) Márcio Martins (Instituto Politécnico de Bragança, Portugal and CiTUR, Portugal) and Ruta Fontes (Aveiro University, Portugal and GOVCOPP, Portugal)
Business Science Reference • copyright 2024 • 266pp • H/C (ISBN: 9798369321379) • US $265.00 (our price)

Promoting Responsible Tourism With Digital Platforms
Youssef El Archi (Abdelmalek Essaadi University, Morocco & Hungarian University of Agriculture and Life Sciences, Hungary & Centre for Tourism Research, Development, and Innovation (CITUR), Portugal) Brahim Benbba (Abdelmalek Essaadi University, Morocco) Lóránt Dénes Dávid (John von Neumann University, Hungary & Hungarian University of Agriculture and Life Sciences, Hungary) and Lucília Cardoso (Centre for Tourism Research, Development, and Innovation (CITUR), Portugal)
Business Science Reference • copyright 2024 • 306pp • H/C (ISBN: 9798369332863) • US $295.00 (our price)

For an entire list of titles in this series, please visit:
http://www.igi-global.com/book-series

701 East Chocolate Avenue, Hershey, PA 17033, USA
Tel: 717-533-8845 x100 • Fax: 717-533-8661
E-Mail: cust@igi-global.com • www.igi-global.com

Table of Contents

Detailed Table of Contents

Chapter 1
    Anjali Gupta, University of Delhi, India
    Shekhar, University of Delhi, India
    Marco Valeri, University Niccolo Cusano, Italy

Organizations need a business model that helps them convert opportunities into profitable ventures. Innovating the business models is essential to survive in the dynamic global market. One such business model innovation focuses on the achievement of sustainable development goals and the needs of the Bottom-of-the-pyramid market segment. Integrating the achievement of SDG and the needs of the BoP segment aims to strengthen the competitiveness. Such a strong business model will be very helpful for tourism organizations that continuously strive the achieve a unique positioning. The chapter conceptualizes how a tourism organization, by integrating the SDGs and BoP needs in its business models, can strengthen its competitiveness. The impact of such a model is studied in reference to Porter's Diamond model, which is used in research to assess the competitiveness of the industry, organization, or nation. The findings will be beneficial for the tourism policymakers as they would strengthen their belief in developing business models that focus on both the SDGs and BoP needs simultaneously.

Meenakshi Gupta, Department of Economics, Faculty of Management, Shri Mata Vaishno Devi University, Katra, India

Isha Kumari, Department of Economics, Faculty of Management, Shri Mata Vaishno Devi University, Katra, India

Ajay Kumar Singh, Department of Humanities and Social Sciences, Graphic Era University (Deemed), Dehradun, India

This chapter finds the implication of human capital on SDG1 in selected G20 countries. It uses poverty as a dependent variable, while government spending on health & education, Gini coefficient, and life expectancy at birth as independent variables in the Panel ARDL model. It is noticed that government spending on health and education, Gini coefficient, life expectancy at birth, and total health expenditure has a significant impact on poverty. The presence of cross-sectional dependence indicates the association of these variables within and across economies. The G20 countries should pursue inclusive policy interventions to address the issues of healthcare inaccessibility, income distribution and poverty. Investments in healthcare and education would be useful to reduce poverty and achieve SDG1. Income equality helps to increase the progress of SDGs worldwide. Development of the tourism industry would be effective to reduce poverty and increase human well-being.

Anita Medhekar, Central Queensland University, Australia

Mallika Roy, University of Chittagong, Bangladesh

Chapter provides an overview of the Bangladesh and the Indian economy and the contribution of tourism as an engine of growth to both the countries Both the countries pro-poor tourism development policies to meet United Nations SDGs are presented as a case. The challenges they face for implementing pro-poor tourism policies and opportunities in linking and achieving SDGs by developing and implementing pro-poor tourism policies is discussed amidst the local and global climate change challenges, public health emergencies and supply chain disruptions. The next section will discuss and critique the government policies- if tourism development in both the countries is pro-poor that includes bottom of the economic pyramid people that act as a catalyst for achieving the SDGs, or NOT? with managerial and policy recommendations and a development of an equitable, pro-poor tourism policy/business model, followed by conclusion.

>   *Hulisi Binbasioglu, Malatya Turgut Ozal University, Turkey & Cardiff*
>   *Business School, UK*

The sustainable development goals (SDGs) are a collection of targets that nations must work towards accomplishing by 2030, as mandated by this worldwide action. Tourism, closely tied to the natural, social environment, and economy, contributes significantly to sustainability. As tourism is the world's fastest-growing industry, linking tourism and the SDGs is crucial. Although research on SDGs and tourism has increased, the knowledge level of university students still needs to be adequately addressed. This study aims to assess the level of SDGs knowledge among university students studying in tourism departments. Descriptive and causal-comparative research designs were used. Descriptive statistics were used to determine how familiar the participants were with relevant concepts. The current chapter also provides practical and theoretical implications for tourism educators and researchers.

>   *Ambar Srivastava, Christ University, India*
>   *Ankit Pathania, Eternal University, India*
>   *Geeta Kumari, Malla Reddy College of Engineering and Technology,*
>   *India*

To achieve the sustainable development goals (SDGs) of the 2030 Agenda, which include the goals of gender equality, social inclusion, and women's empowerment, tourism is an essential industry. Gender disparity is a major development barrier in the majority of developing nations. The study aims to explore the challenges women face and gender inequality in tourism industry. The inter-linkage between tourism and SDGs will also be explored. A qualitative research technique was applied, and systematic literature review was based on articles in national and international journals, working papers, etc. explored. The study concluded that restricted opportunities for education, healthcare disparities, economic inequality are among the challenges faced by the women in tourism industry. It is also found that gender inequality in terms of dual presence, discrimination in wages, glass ceiling, sticky floors, etc. are also there. There is a definite linkage between the tourism industry and SDGs.

Ravinay Amit Chandra, Fiji National University, Fiji
Nikeel Niskar Kumar, Royal Melbourne Institute of Technology,
Australia
Jone Toua, Fiji National University, Fiji
Manisha Chand, Fiji National University, Fiji
Pritika Chand, Fiji National University, Fiji
Karishma Kritika Sharma, Fiji National University, Fiji

This study investigates the intricate balance between women's economic empowerment and socio-cultural empowerment within the context of community-based tourism. Specifically, it focuses on the case of Biausevu, Fiji, a community heavily dependent on tourism for its economic sustenance. A survey was executed to gather data, engaging a sample of 32 participants, representing roughly 60 percent of women in the community. Employing logit and Probit regression methodology, the study analyzed the interplay of factors influencing women's empowerment. The findings underscored that income derived from tourism and the resultant enhancement in quality of life significantly contribute to women's economic empowerment. However, it also revealed a potential downside: an over-reliance on tourism could impede socio-cultural empowerment facets. Incorporating insights from sustainable development goal five SDG -5, this study advocates for an integrated approach to women's empowerment. It emphasizes the need for policies that balance economic gains from tourism with preserving and promoting socio-cultural values.

Divya Singh, K.R. Mangalam University, India
Poonam Kumari, K.R. Mangalam University, India
Kristin Sajeev, K.R. Mangalam University, India

The purpose of this research is to perform a comprehensive study of work-family conflict among female employees in the Indian tourist business. It seeks to identify the elements that contribute to work-family conflict, investigate its influence on women's well-being and turnover intentions, and provide strategies to mitigate its effects. The study's findings emphasize the enormous impact of work-family conflict on female employees in India's tourist companies. Long working hours, high job demands, and a lack of workplace assistance are all factors that lead to work-family conflict. The study also outlines methods such as flexible work arrangements, supportive organizational policies, and training programs that might assist reduce work-family conflict, increase women's psychological safety, and reduce turnover intentions.

Chapter 8

Érica Simão, School of Management, Hospitality, and Tourism, University of Algarve, Portugal

Rui Manuel Mendonça-Pedro, School of Management, Hospitality, and Tourism & CinTurs, University of Algarve, Portugal

The chapter intends to reflect on the theoretical role of tourism in reducing inequalities in society (SDG 1 and 16), the supply chain innovations and innovative products in tourism (SDG 8), employment opportunities for marginalised social sectors in tourism (SDG 1 and 8) and the challenges faced by women in tourism (SDG 5). This research aims to analyse the theoretical impacts that the legalisation of prostitution would have on a tourism destination, on the individuals involved, and on contributing to the diversity of tourism products (supply chain innovations). The result of this NLR of the responsibility in tourism in the face of prostitution resulted in the analysis of the impact felt by residents with prostitution. The understanding of the distinction between formal employment and informal employment, thus framing the best position for prostitution. The ethical concerns associated with prostitution are exploitation, trafficking, and prejudgment. The regulation of the demand for sexual services marketed in different political contexts.

Chapter 9

    Arnab Gantait, Independent Researcher, India
    Ravish Mathew, Sri Sri University, Odisha, India
    Prama Chatterjee, Central Tribal University of Andhra Pradesh, India
    Kuldeep Singh, Amity University, Gurugram, India

The evolving global tourism industry increasingly emphasizes sustainable practices benefiting both the environment and local communities. Community-Based tourism (CBT) in the Indian Sundarbans exemplifies this approach, preserving cultural and natural heritage while fostering grassroots socio-economic development. Through qualitative research methods including in-depth interviews, participant observations, and document analysis, this study reveals CBT's positive impact. It showcases successful cultural heritage preservation, community engagement in conservation, local empowerment, and economic diversification through tourism activities. Furthermore, CBT facilitates cultural exchange, education, and responsible tourism practices. This research provides nuanced insights into CBT's multifaceted benefits, offering valuable lessons for sustainable tourism development in ecologically sensitive areas worldwide. By raising awareness among communities, tourism planners, and policymakers, this study aims to support successful implementation of CBT initiatives in diverse tourist destinations.

    Natasha, Amity University, Noida, India
    Kavita Indapurkar, Amity University, Noida, India

Global tourism is becoming progressively acknowledged for its link to the sustainable development goals (SDGs). This study aims to explore how India can meet its sustainable development objectives through religious and wellness tourism. The study explores the effect of push and pull factors on travelers' motivation to travel. The study uses a quantitative and exploratory design, incorporating data gathered from 142 questionnaire responses. Results indicate that independent variables accounted for 38% of the variance in travel motivation, with a R Square value of 0.331. While gender and the cultural significance of the destination are important determinants, other factors may not have as much of an impact on motivation. The study emphasizes how tourism can support sustainable development, especially when it comes to promoting social inclusion, economic growth, and environmental preservation. The research's insights can help location managers, tourist authorities, and legislators create sustainable tourism experiences and regulations that support all-encompassing growth.

Preface

It is with great pleasure that we present this edited reference book, *Interlinking SDGs and the Bottom-of-the-Pyramid Through Tourism*. This volume is the culmination of extensive research and collaboration, aimed at addressing some of the most pressing challenges faced by the global tourism and hospitality industries.

The impetus for this book stems from a recognition of the dual challenges confronting these industries: existing strategies and policies have often fallen short of meeting stakeholder expectations, and the tremendous potential of tourism to contribute to the Sustainable Development Goals (SDGs) has not been fully harnessed. Moreover, the focus on creating value for tourists and other stakeholders at the Bottom of the Pyramid (BoP) has been insufficiently explored within academic circles, despite its critical importance for achieving SDGs.

Tourism holds vast potential to contribute to the SDGs and serve the BoP market. However, this potential remains largely untapped due to limited attention from both academia and industry practitioners. While the SDGs encompass a broad range of social, economic, and environmental objectives, the BoP's focus is predominantly on social and economic goals, making it a crucial sub-strategy for achieving the SDGs.

The studies included in this book aim to design innovative strategies for the tourism industry, emphasizing its potential to generate socio-economic and environmental benefits for BoP stakeholders while advancing the SDGs. The limited knowledge in this area poses significant obstacles to implementing effective strategies that address BoP market needs. Identifying how various SDGs can be targeted through tourism is vital for creating a more equitable and resilient industry.

Integrating SDG strategies into tourism business models has proven to enhance the sector's ability to address the three pillars of sustainable development: economic, social, and environmental. By improving quality of life and well-being, tourism contributes to the economic dimension of the sustainability agenda and has the potential to address SDG 1 (No Poverty), SDG 2 (Zero Hunger), and SDG 8 (Decent Work and Economic Growth). Ensuring the equitable distribution of economic and non-economic resources to all social groups is crucial for achieving

SDG 2 (Zero Hunger), SDG 5 (Gender Equality), and SDG 16 (Peace, Justice, and Strong Institutions).

Additionally, tourism significantly impacts waste generation, particularly in mountainous regions. Practices such as waste reduction and transitioning from a linear to a circular economy in product design can help achieve SDG 12 (Responsible Consumption and Production). Focusing on environmental sustainability, creating shared value (CSV) helps the tourism industry respect socio-symbiotic relationships, targeting SDG 11 (Sustainable Cities and Communities), SDG 13 (Climate Action), SDG 14 (Life Below Water), and SDG 15 (Life on Land). By fostering collaboration among governments, businesses, communities, and NGOs, CSV aligns with the objectives of SDG 17 (Partnerships for the Goals).

Research on making tourism products inclusive for BoP stakeholders is minimal. Literature supports that BoP customers place a stronger emphasis on personalization, product, price, place, and process. Including local stakeholders from the BoP segment in tourism initiatives can effectively interlink tourism and BoP goals. Strategies that combine BoP and SDG approaches will benefit the tourism industry in multifaceted ways. For example, designing affordable and inclusive products and services that address socio-economic and environmental challenges while meeting BoP needs.

Localization of supply chains to include marginalized segments can promote local employment, provide decent work, foster micro-entrepreneurship, and enhance collaboration. Improving the industry ecosystem encourages stakeholder collaboration, leading to better processes and more personalized product development. These approaches significantly contribute to realizing the SDGs.

The chapters in this volume explore diverse facets of how tourism can effectively contribute to achieving Sustainable Development Goals (SDGs) while addressing the needs of the Bottom-of-the-Pyramid (BoP) market segment. From innovative business models and the impact of human capital on poverty reduction to pro-poor tourism policies in Bangladesh and India, each chapter delves into unique challenges and opportunities. The role of tourism in gender equality, community-based initiatives, work-family conflict, and sustainable development through religious and wellness tourism are also examined, offering comprehensive insights for policymakers, educators, and industry practitioners. Together, these chapters present a holistic view of leveraging tourism for sustainable and inclusive growth.

Organizations need business models that convert opportunities into profitable ventures, especially in the dynamic global market. Chapter 1 explores how tourism organizations can innovate their business models to simultaneously achieve the Sustainable Development Goals (SDGs) and meet the needs of the Bottom-of-the-Pyramid (BoP) market segment. By integrating these objectives, tourism organizations can enhance their competitiveness and achieve unique positioning. The chapter conceptualizes the integration of SDGs and BoP needs within tourism business models and assesses the impact using Porter's Diamond model, which evaluates industry, organizational, or national competitiveness. The findings provide valuable insights for tourism policymakers, reinforcing the importance of developing business models that focus on both SDGs and BoP needs.

Chapter 2 examines the implications of human capital on SDG1 (No Poverty) in selected G20 countries. Using a Panel ARDL model, it analyzes poverty as a dependent variable and considers government spending on health and education, Gini coefficient, and life expectancy at birth as independent variables. The findings indicate that government spending on health and education, income equality, and overall health expenditure significantly impact poverty reduction. The chapter underscores the need for inclusive policy interventions in G20 countries to address healthcare inaccessibility, income distribution, and poverty. Investments in healthcare and education are highlighted as crucial for reducing poverty and advancing SDG1, while the development of the tourism industry is identified as a potential driver for poverty alleviation and human well-being.

Chapter 3 provides an overview of the economies of Bangladesh and India, focusing on the contribution of tourism as an engine of growth. It examines pro-poor tourism development policies in both countries as case studies for meeting United Nations SDGs. The chapter discusses the challenges and opportunities in implementing pro-poor tourism policies amid local and global climate change, public health emergencies, and supply chain disruptions. It critiques government policies to determine whether tourism development is inclusive of Bottom-of-the-Pyramid people and acts as a catalyst for achieving SDGs. The chapter concludes with managerial and policy recommendations for developing equitable, pro-poor tourism policies and business models.

The Sustainable Development Goals (SDGs) are a set of targets that nations must achieve by 2030. Given the close ties between tourism and the natural, social environment, and economy, it is crucial to link tourism and the SDGs. Chapter 4 assesses the level of SDG knowledge among university students in tourism departments. Using descriptive and causal-comparative research designs, the study evaluates participants' familiarity with relevant concepts. The chapter offers practical and theoretical implications for tourism educators and researchers, emphasizing the need to enhance SDG knowledge among future tourism professionals.

Achieving the Sustainable Development Goals (SDGs) of gender equality, social inclusion, and women's empowerment is essential, and tourism plays a vital role. Chapter 5 explores the challenges women face and gender inequality in the tourism industry. Through a qualitative research technique and systematic literature review, it identifies barriers such as restricted educational opportunities, healthcare disparities, and economic inequality. The study also highlights gender inequality issues like wage discrimination, glass ceilings, and sticky floors. The chapter concludes that addressing these challenges is crucial for achieving gender equality (SDG 5) and other related SDGs in the tourism sector.

Chapter 6 investigates the balance between women's economic and socio-cultural empowerment within community-based tourism, focusing on Biausevu, Fiji. Using survey data and logit and Probit regression methodologies, the study analyzes factors influencing women's empowerment. Findings show that income from tourism significantly enhances women's economic empowerment, but over-reliance on tourism may impede socio-cultural empowerment. The chapter advocates for integrated policies that balance economic gains with preserving socio-cultural values, aligning with SDG 5 (Gender Equality).

Chapter 7 examines work-family conflict among female employees in the Indian tourism industry. It identifies contributing factors such as long working hours, high job demands, and lack of workplace support, and investigates their impact on women's well-being and turnover intentions. The study proposes strategies to mitigate work-family conflict, including flexible work arrangements, supportive organizational policies, and training programs. The findings emphasize the need to improve women's psychological safety and reduce turnover intentions, contributing to a more inclusive and supportive work environment.

Chapter 8 reflects on the theoretical role of tourism in reducing societal inequalities and promoting SDGs. It examines supply chain innovations, employment opportunities for marginalized sectors, and the challenges faced by women in tourism. The research analyzes the potential impacts of legalizing prostitution on tourism destinations and the ethical concerns associated with it. The chapter provides a nuanced understanding of formal and informal employment in tourism and the implications for achieving SDGs, particularly in terms of social and economic inclusion.

The evolving global tourism industry increasingly emphasizes sustainable practices benefiting the environment and local communities. Chapter 9 explores Community-Based Tourism (CBT) in the Indian Sundarbans, highlighting its role in preserving cultural and natural heritage while fostering socio-economic development. Through qualitative research methods, the study reveals the positive impact of CBT on cultural heritage preservation, community engagement, and economic diversification. The chapter offers valuable lessons for sustainable tourism development in ecologically sensitive areas and provides insights for tourism planners and policymakers to support successful CBT initiatives.

Chapter 10 explores how India can meet its sustainable development objectives through religious and wellness tourism. It examines the influence of push and pull factors on travelers' motivation to travel, using data from 142 questionnaire responses. The study finds that gender and the cultural significance of destinations are important determinants of travel motivation. The chapter emphasizes the role of tourism in promoting social inclusion, economic growth, and environmental preservation, providing insights for location managers, tourism authorities, and legislators to create sustainable tourism experiences and policies that support comprehensive growth.

In essence, tourism business models that cater to BoP needs and enhance industry practices can serve as catalysts for achieving the SDGs. Tourism offers governments an opportunity to interlink BoP initiatives with SDGs. For instance, business models integrating people from the BoP can target SDG 1. Food tourism can promote traditional crops, benefiting poor farmers and raising awareness about food waste, thus addressing SDG 2. Community tourism in hilly and tribal areas has empowered women by providing decent job opportunities, targeting SDGs 5 and 8.

We hope this book provides valuable insights and strategies for harnessing the potential of tourism to achieve the SDGs while serving the BoP market. By creating shared value, the tourism industry can ensure equitable benefits for all stakeholders, paving the way for a sustainable and inclusive future.

Marco Valeri
Niccolo Cusano University, Italy

Shekhar Asthana
University of Delhi, India

Chapter 1
Assessing the Perception of Tourism Managers on Tourism Business Models Integrating SDGs and BoP Needs

Anjali Gupta
University of Delhi, India

Shekhar
https://orcid.org/0000-0002-7329-2994
University of Delhi, India

Marco Valeri
https://orcid.org/0000-0002-9744-506X
University Niccolo Cusano, Italy

ABSTRACT

Organizations need a business model that helps them convert opportunities into profitable ventures. Innovating the business models is essential to survive in the dynamic global market. One such business model innovation focuses on the achievement of sustainable development goals and the needs of the Bottom-of-the-pyramid market segment. Integrating the achievement of SDG and the needs of the BoP segment aims to strengthen the competitiveness. Such a strong business model will be very helpful for tourism organizations that continuously strive the achieve a unique positioning. The chapter conceptualizes how a tourism organization, by integrating the SDGs and BoP needs in its business models, can strengthen its competitiveness. The

DOI: 10.4018/979-8-3693-3166-8.ch001

impact of such a model is studied in reference to Porter's Diamond model, which is used in research to assess the competitiveness of the industry, organization, or nation. The findings will be beneficial for the tourism policymakers as they would strengthen their belief in developing business models that focus on both the SDGs and BoP needs simultaneously.

INTRODUCTION

Innovative business models are drivers for organizational profitability in the modern era. Organizations tend to innovate their business models to not only gain financial advantages, but rather they aim to gain sustainable and long-term competitiveness over their rivals (Latifi et al., 2021; Saqib & Satar, 2021). One such strategy of business is market segmentation, i.e. serving a targeted group of customers selected based on certain homogeneous characteristics (Dolnicar et al., 2018). While segmenting customers based on income group is a followed segmentation technique, businesses often rely on serving middle-income or higher-income groups and neglect the lower-income groups because of the additional challenges they create for the business. However, studies have empirically highlighted that the people at the Bottom of the Pyramid (or BoP from hereon) can effectively serve as a market segment for organizations. Nevertheless, limited efforts are made by the organizations to target such groups.

Another emerging issue globally, that has required innovation in business models is the Sustainable Development Goals (SDGs). These are the set of 17 goals established by the United Nations, that the participant nations have to try to achieve to make the world a better place to live (UN DESA, 2019). These goals impact the social, environmental, and economic aspects of humans and aim to address major issues that harm human development (Kumar et al., 2018). Organizations make several efforts in their operations, product development, marketing, and Human Resource policies to try to achieve these goals, however, reports indicate that the efforts in this regard are not sufficient. In developing nations, the efforts need to be more holistic as organizations tend to engage in cherry-picking easily attainable goals (Bradley et al., 2021).

An exploration into the needs of the BoP market segment and the targets laid down in the SDGs highlights overlapping. Studies also recommend that instead of taking them as two separate issues, organizations can innovate their business models to achieve them together as these needs are interrelated and interdependent (Van Tulder et al., 2021). This approach seems logical as the BoP market faces the issue of affordability in products. They are unable to consume these products because they do not have higher purchasing power. Such issues are more visible in health products as they have bad health because of higher medicine and healthcare prices. Organizations working on these issues can simultaneously contribute to SDG 1 (No poverty), SDG 2 (No Hunger), and, SDG 3 on Universal Health Coverage. It will also be beneficial for the organization as it will increase its potential market size. Furthermore, if organizations start working on these issues early, they can gain a decisive competitive advantage over their rivals. Thus the present study aims to assess the impact of the business model integrating SDGs and BoP needs in reference to the Porter Diamond model, which is a model to determine the competitiveness of an organization.

LITERATURE REVIEW

Business Models

A business model is defined as……..

" a representation of a firm's underlying core logic and strategic choices for creating and capturing value within a value network." (Shafer et al., 2005)

It reflects how businesses generate, provide, and retain value and explains the reasoning behind how a company generates, provides, and retains value in various economic, social, cultural, and other situations. It captures the core of a business venture, detailing its plan for long-term success and financial sustainability. It delineates the interplay between various components such as the value proposition, customer segments, revenue streams, and cost structure, and lays the foundation of a strategy that helps an organization achieve its vision.

Poter Diamond Model

The Porter Diamond model was given by Micheal Porter to assess the competitiveness of nations in particular industries (Porter, 1990). This model has been widely used in research to assess the competitiveness of an organization or an industry. For instance, Tiwari *et al.* (2023) applied the model to assess the competitiveness of tea tourism in India and Sri Lanka. Similarly, authors have used this model to assess to competitiveness of other industries such as medical and wellness tourism in India (Joseph, 2017). This model suggests that a nation's competitiveness in a certain industry depends on four key determinants, which collectively form a diamond-shaped framework. The first determinant is *Factor Conditions* which comprise of nation's natural resources, human resources, capital resources, infrastructure, and technological capabilities. A favorable, replenishing, and ever-evolving pool of factor conditions is conducive to the development of industries and provides an edge over competitors (Tsai et al., 2021). These resources affect productivity and thus their presence is crucial for an industry to thrive. They often provide industries and organizations with a competitive advantage that is valuable and relevant (Fainshmidt et al., 2016). The second determinant is *Demand Conditions* which represent the nature and size of the domestic market demand for products and services (Öz, 2002). A huge population means a ready market for the product and the potential for an organization to capture the market and become profitable (Kharub & Sharma, 2017). Good demand conditions are crucial for an industry as they ensure that economic gains are continuously reaped by the stakeholders. Also, informed customers often push organizations to innovate, which can become a strong competitive advantage. The third determinant is the *presence of related and supporting industries* (Chung, 2016). Strong support from the allied industries can boost the organization's competitive advantage. They offer unique resources, technology, and talented workers, leading to higher levels of creativity and productivity across the entire supply chain. The last determinant is the *Firm Strategy, Structure, and Rivalry* which encompasses the industry structure, competition between the firms, corporate governance mechanisms, and possibilities of international expansion to create a competitive advantage (Waverman, 1995). The relationship and connection between these four factors form a constantly changing environment that influences the competitive advantage of organizations. Through studying these elements, decision-makers, companies, and other interested parties can pinpoint strengths and weaknesses and devise plans to improve the competitiveness of their industries on a global scale

Objectives of Various SDGs

Table 1 lists the seventeen sustainable development goals released by the United Nations along with the targets covering economic, social, and environmental aspects to be achieved by 2030. In SDG 1 of no poverty, the target is to eradicate extreme poverty globally (Küfeoğlu, 2022). It also envisions providing vulnerable people, equal access to economic resources. SDG 2 aims for zero hunger with the key targets of ending hunger and access by all people to safe, nutritious, and sufficient food (Gil et al., 2019). There are also provisions to increase the investments in developing rural infrastructure primarily agriculture infrastructure to ensure that food production and supply remain continuous. The next SDG 3 aims to promote good health and well-being, by targeting to end the epidemics such as AIDS, tuberculosis, malaria, and other communicable diseases (Seidman, 2017). It also aims to prepare the countries for an efficient health system through early warning signals, risk reduction, and management (Fong & Law, 2021). The SDG 4 of quality education targets to ensure that everyone has access to free, equitable, and quality primary and secondary education (Saini et al., 2023). It also works to ensure that youths achieve literacy and numeracy. SDG 5 of gender equality targets ending all forms of discrimination among women and ensuring their full participation in leadership roles in the public and private sectors (Filho et al., 2023). The SDG 6 of clean water and sanitation aims to achieve universal access to safe drinking water and ensure equitable access to sanitation and hygiene for all (Biswas et al., 2022). SDG 7 of clean and sustainable energy aims for affordable, reliable, and modern energy services by increasing the share of renewable energy (Mawla & Khan, 2020). SDG 8 aims to provide economic growth through decent work opportunities. It targets to achieve at least seven per cent growth in per capita national income, after factoring in national circumstances (Kreinin & Aigner, 2022). SDG 9 of fostering innovation and industrial infrastructure development promotes inclusive and sustainable industrial development and builds quality and resilient infrastructure (Singh & Ru, 2023). SDG 10 aims to reduce inequalities in society by targeting to sustain income for the bottom 40 per cent of society (Roy & Roy, 2019). SDG 11 of sustainable cities and communities aims to ensure affordable housing for all and protect the cultural and natural heritage (Koch & Krellenberg, 2018). SDG 12 of responsible consumption and production patterns targets sustainable use of natural resources and reduces waste generation through implementing the 3Rs (reduce, reuse, and recycle) (Gasper et al., 2019). SDG 13 aims at climate action targeting building capacity for tackling climate hazards and developing climate-change integrated policies, plans, and strategies (Purnell, 2022). SDG 14 to protect life below water aims to minimize marine pollution, save aquatic life, and reduce exploitation (Haas, 2023), and SDG 15 Life on Land targets desertification, land erosion, and mountain ecosystem conservation (Krauss, 2022). SDG 16 of peace, justice, and strong institutions targets reducing violence, war, and crimes globally (Milton, 2021). It promotes global access to justice for all. SDG 17 of partnership for all targets effective public, public-private, and civil society partnerships for sustainable development (Halkos & Gkampoura, 2021).

There are two key observations from the above discussion. First, the goals of SDG are interrelated i.e., targeting one goal may lead to the achievement of another goal. For instance, targeting SDG 1 of no poverty may directly influence achieving SDG 2 of zero hunger. Similarly, SDG 13 of climate action will impact SDG 14 and SDG 15. Realizing this, Kumar et al. (2018) carried out a study to determine the interrelationship between these SDGs through interpretive structural modelling and observed that SDG 4 of quality education channelizes the framework to achieve SDG 17 of partnership for all. Second, although the SDGs have been formulated for almost a decade, there have been reports that globally we are very much behind the desired targets. It is because the efforts to achieve these goals have been individualistic and there is a lack of common industry that could be targeted globally to achieve these goals. Furthermore, several reports have suggested that developed and developing countries equally lag in several of these goals because it conflicts with their economic interests. Furthermore, the emergence of the pandemic pushed back the progress made by the countries in several of these goals.

Table 1. Key targets and indicators for SDGs

SDG No.	Goal	Key Targets
1	No Poverty	• By 2030, eradicate extreme poverty for all people; • Ensure that all men and women, in particular the poor and the vulnerable, have equal rights to economic resources, as well as access to basic services
2	Zero Hunger	• By 2030, end hunger and ensure access by all people to safe, nutritious, and sufficient food all year round • Increase investment, including through enhanced international cooperation, in rural infrastructure
3	Good Health and Wellbeing	• By 2030, end the epidemics of AIDS, tuberculosis, malaria, and other communicable diseases • Strengthen the capacity of all countries, in particular developing countries, for early warning, risk reduction, and management of national and global health risks
4	Quality Education	• By 2030, ensure that all girls and boys complete free, equitable, and quality primary and secondary education • By 2030, ensure that all youth and a substantial proportion of adults, both men and women, achieve literacy and numeracy
5	Gender Empowerment	• End all forms of discrimination against all women and girls everywhere • Ensure women's full and effective participation and equal opportunities for leadership
6	Clean Water and Sanitation	• By 2030, achieve universal and equitable access to safe and affordable drinking water for all • By 2030, achieve access to adequate and equitable sanitation and hygiene for all
7	Clean and Sustainable Energy	• By 2030, ensure universal access to affordable, reliable, and modern energy services • By 2030, increase substantially the share of renewable energy in the global energy mix
8	Economic Growth and Decent Work	• Sustain per capita economic growth in accordance with national circumstances (at least 7 percent) • By 2030, achieve full and productive employment and decent work for all women and men
9	Innovation and Infrastructure	• Develop quality, reliable, sustainable, and resilient infrastructure • Promote inclusive and sustainable industrialization
10	Reduced Inequalities	• By 2030, progressively achieve and sustain income growth of the bottom 40 percent of the population • Adopt policies, especially fiscal, wage, and social protection policies, and progressively achieve greater equality

continued on following page

Table 1. Continued

SDG No.	Goal	Key Targets
11	Sustainable Cities and Communities	• By 2030, ensure access for all to adequate, safe, and affordable housing and basic services • Strengthen efforts to protect and safeguard the world's cultural and natural heritage
12	Responsible Consumption and Production	• By 2030, achieve the sustainable management and efficient use of natural resources • By 2030, substantially reduce waste generation through prevention, reduction, recycling, and reuse
13	Climate Action	• Strengthen resilience and adaptive capacity to climate-related hazards and natural disasters in all countries • Integrate climate change measures into national policies, strategies, and planning
14	Life Below Water	• By 2025, prevent and significantly reduce marine pollution of all kinds • Minimize and address the impacts of ocean acidification
15	Life on Land	• By 2030, combat desertification, restore degraded land and soil • By 2030, ensure the conservation of mountain ecosystems, including their biodiversity
16	Peace, Justice, and Strong Institutions	• Significantly reduce all forms of violence and related death rates everywhere • Promote the rule of law at the national and international levels and ensure equal access to justice for all
17	Partnership for All	• Enhance the Global Partnership for Sustainable Development, complemented by multi-stakeholder partnerships • Encourage and promote effective public, public-private, and civil society partnerships

Source: Compiled from United Nations Statistics Division. (2017). SDG Indicators — SDG Indicators. https://unstats.un.org/sdgs/indicators/indicators-list/

ISSUES IN SERVING THE BoP MARKET SEGMENT

Literature brings about several apprehensions of businesses in serving the BoP market. Most business organizations tend to avoid the BoP market because they believe that the current cost structures do not make them their potential customers as the prices are higher and the BoP segment can not afford products at such prices. Also, managers have the viewpoint that they need to develop new products for BoP as their needs are different and they can not afford the products that are being sold in the developed markets because of their low purchasing power. The businesses rationalize the higher prices for their products on their expenditure incurred in Research and Development. They have a viewpoint that they need to recover their R&D costs and remain operationalized. Thus, they need to charge a price premium to justify their efforts, which unfortunately makes products unaffordable for people at BoP. Another issue highlighted by the literature is that serving BoP markets is not in the best interests of the organizations in the long run. As these markets have an impact on economic performance, businesses tend to lose more than they earn which impacts their survival. Further, the BoP market brings out new challenges for the managers which makes it difficult for them to strategise. These new challenges make decision-making problematic and thus managers are not very keen on serving the BoP market. At last, the literature highlights that this market segment does not excite the managers and thus they tend to avoid the BoP market.

METHODOLOGY

The study adopts an exploratory approach to test the competitiveness of business models focusing on SDGs and BoP needs. A semi-structured interview is conducted with the senior management executives of ten private business organizations engaged in the tourism and hospitality sector and five managers in Destination Management Organizations (DMOs) in India. These organizations were selected based on their contribution to tourism development. DMOs were selected based on the ranking of states. Managers from five Indian states, Uttar Pradesh, Uttrakhand, New Delhi, Maharashtra, and Madhya Pradesh were selected. It should be noted that DMOs include all those organizations that are responsible for managing tourism and engaging in policy-making related to tourism, irrespective of the name they are called. The managers were contacted at their workplace and an interview was fixed with them at their convenience. They were explained the purpose of their data collection and their consent for participation and recording of interviews were formally obtained in writing. The questions in the interview primarily focused on the viewpoint of the managers towards the potential of the business models integrating SDGs and BoP needs in increasing the competitiveness of the organization. The authors visited the offices and conducted interviews that lasted from 35 minutes to 55 minutes. Interviews were conducted in English and the data collection was carried out from December 2023 to February 2023. The interviews were transcribed manually by one of the authors and checked for any inconsistencies and biases by the other authors. For any clarification, the authors reapproached the respondents and gave them final transcripts for reading and approval. The data was analyzed using *NVivo*.

FINDINGS

The interview transcripts were coded using NVivo to identify the major themes in the responses. The descriptive results of the interview were as follows: Eighty percent of respondents were male and the rest female; age-wise, respondents fell in the category of 40-50 years of age with 15+ years of experience. Since the study does not intend to capture the influence of demographics on the responses, the demographics are not presented separately. The study utilizes the exact responses from the respondents to validate the findings. Grammatical inconsistencies in the quotes are however corrected by the authors without changing the meaning of the response. The respondent having the opinion is denoted by the number ahead of the quote. If multiple respondents had similar views, the authors phrased them in a meaningful sentence, combining the elements of every opinion. The results were categorized into five themes, each related to an aspect of the Porter Diamond model.

Impact On Firms' Strategy, Rivalry, And Structure

CSV can have a significant influence on the firm's strategy and its rivalry. First, it provides a competitive advantage over rivals, beating them through enhanced brand reputation, customer loyalty, and market positioning. CSV can also bring changes to a firm's strategy of conducting business. It could encourage focusing more on innovation and building a unique proposition for product, service, and the organization itself. One of the respondents noted,

"If I can address environmental and social issues better than competitors, who treat it as mere responsibility and make business out of it, I will gain the confidence of customers." (R3).

CSV helps maintain stronger relationships with the stakeholders such as customers, suppliers, government, employees, and society. These relationships are a competitive advantage for the organization. A respondent opined,

"CSV can help us make our supply chain strong, which would be tough to replicate. If we are the first choice for our stakeholders, we will dominate the market." (R5)

CSV can also impact the structure of the industry. Since it is not about just competing and beating everyone, organizations often co-create with the competition to make the industry grow and satisfy customer needs. There are numerous examples of competitors merging for a product or component. Sharing knowledge is one of the most important components of CSV. A senior respondent noted,

"We have to often share knowledge with other hotels regarding carrying capacity issues, bookings, and pricing decisions. It helps us to serve tourists better." (R1)

However, respondents were also concerned about knowledge sharing that there is a chance to lose the competitive advantage they have over rivals (R2 and R6). They also keep brainstorming to remain competitive even after knowledge sharing.

Impact on Demand Conditions

As already discussed, demand conditions mean that domestic demand for products and services is huge giving an advantage over rivals. CSV can positively influence the domestic demand for the products and services. It can help tourism organizations to better understand and flexibly adapt to their changing needs. Since the needs are ever-evolving, it helps co-creating products with customers. Thus, there is not much concern about their satisfaction once the needs are identified and applicable. To ensure customers remain loyal to the destinations, CSV helps service providers develop avenues in congruence with tourist needs. One respondent noted,

"Tourists are not well aware of their needs. But after they visit and realize that they do not need what they are offered, they start to complain virtually everywhere, and we lose customers. If we get to know before about their needs, we will be better prepared." (R12 and agreed by R4)

CSV also helps in creating differentiation in the market which ensures that demand for the products and services continues. Sometimes, new products can be created or new destinations can be developed to ensure demand continues (R3 and R7).

The respondents were also positive about the potential of serving the Bottom of the pyramid customers in tourism. They opined that till now, the focus is on high-earning tourists, a niche segment, but highly profitable. Therefore, there are instances where they have to compromise on sustainability. However, when the customer pool is large, we could focus on affordable products, without creating lavish infrastructure and damaging the natural heritage (R13 and R1).

Impact on Related and Supporting Industries

CSV can help in removing the quality uncertainty component from an industry. For the tourism industry, it would mean that if DMOs and other tourist organizations start implementing CSV, then they would ensure that everything is as per the quality standards, meeting all the ethical norms, and thus remove any doubt from the minds of the upcoming tourists. A good and flourishing tourism industry will also help businesses for cab drivers, shopkeepers, and souvenir sellers in that region. They need not make provision for marketing. If they tie up with the nig players, they can ensure the continuity of business during tourist seasons. During the off-season, they could engage in the work of big players not directly related to tourists. For the industries run by small enterprises and marginalized communities, if big organizations, through CSV, can promote their products and services, it would help them in activities that are beyond themselves.

"If I could convince tourists that they will not feel unsatisfied after the visit, I have already won in marketing. The small-scale restaurants and cab-owners need not to work too hard to market themselves." (R8)

Impact on Factor Conditions

CSV helps in the development of factors of production and stakeholders in the delivery of service. It includes the development of employees and workers, infrastructure development, infusion of technology and innovation within the industry, training of suppliers, and community development. CSV initiatives like education and training programs, workforce development, and health and wellness initiatives can help companies improve the skills, knowledge, and well-being of their employees. Big organizations can improve transportation, communication, energy, and other essential facilities to reduce logistical costs, improve access to markets, and create a more conducive environment for business operations and growth.

"We need more trained workers in rural tourism. If we implement CSV, we can have better trained and skilled workers who can also participate as stakeholders in the tourism industry." (R15 and R11)

"Tourism is an infrastructure-dependent industry. We can not create on our own, but together we can build it and help in maintenance. We also require big players to do more for it." (R11 and R10)

Tourism needs suppliers to be well trained, skilled, and have skills to meet international standards. As a lot of foreign tourists arrive in India, the service delivery needs to be at par with the international quality. However, this is a problem as in tier II and tier III cities and rural areas, such facilities are not found due to a lack of infrastructure and also because of the lower educational level of suppliers. CSV involves training and educating the suppliers for conducive industry operations and for the development of the suppliers also

"We have invested so much in teaching English to our suppliers. Today we welcome so many tourists from non-English-speaking countries. To welcome them, we have started training our staff in other languages too. They also provide services as translators during the off-season to earn more income." (R9)

DISCUSSION

CSV-led business model focusing on BoP needs and SDGs will be beneficial for all as it might influence the competitiveness of the industry by creating favourable circumstances for growth and expansion. However, there exists very little empirical research to prove that integrating the three concepts could provide the tourism industry with a competitive advantage. Thus, future studies could assess the implications of such business models focusing on SDG and BoP on the competitiveness of the industry or the organization to determine whether the model would be a success or not. For this, we propose that scholars test whether the said business models would help in improving competitiveness by assessing the impact based on the Porter Diamond model (Figure 4). The said model has six determinants of competitiveness and the interaction between them generates scenarios that determine the competitiveness of the nation or the business and suggests whether the business would flourish or not. By working on these determinants businesses and nations enhance their competitiveness. Future scholars could empirically test whether CSV-integrated business models focusing on SDG and BoP together could potentially influence these determinants in favour of the nation or business.

Impact On Firms' Strategy, Rivalry, And Structure

CSV promotes collaboration which could be extended to making collaborative decisions on pricing, market, and product differentiation. Also, CSV does not align with the principle of enjoying a dominant position at the expense of social and environmental welfare. It also intends to reduce price wars and advertisement battles and promote innovation in products. All these benefits from CSV help the BoP market as they require innovative products at a low price which is possible only when industries forego their dominant position in the market and consider social welfare as a business practice. Similarly, by reducing price wars, it reduces the wastage of resources and the possibility of over-consumption which are crucial SDGs. Thus, a business model that integrates the CSV, SDG, and BoP will make a favourable change in the determinant of competitiveness and tourism practitioners could leverage it to competitively position themselves in the market.

P1. CSV-integrated business models focusing on SDG and BoP will influence the firm strategy, rivalry, and structure.

Impact on Demand Conditions

Much of the demands of the BoP market are unmet although they have huge market potential. Similarly, SDG implementation also opens up opportunities for the development of new sustainable products and markets. CSV requires businesses and industries to continuously monitor the unmet needs of society while addressing social needs. A business model integrating the three concepts will allow businesses to effectively identify the untapped markets stemming from the unmet needs of BoP and SDG implementation, allowing the businesses to gain more market. For example, a tourist destination has a famous religious site that is underdeveloped, and rural people do not have the resources to develop it. The absence of infrastructure causes a lack of revenue generation which would otherwise be very beneficial for the locals in the regions and will ensure development. Similarly, excessive tourism at a destination causes a crowding-out effect for the poor people who cannot compete economically for the resources. Tourism operators could ensure destination discontinuity or transfer burden from one destination to another to ensure that BoP people do not suffer and sustainability is not compromised. Thus, we make the following proposition.

P2. CSV-integrated business models focusing on SDG and BoP will influence the demand conditions in the domestic market.

Impact On Related and Supporting Industries

The developed business model has the potential to positively influence the growth and development of the supporting and allied industries. A few of the ways in CSV are to share knowledge with the allied industries, develop infrastructure that supports the growth of MSMEs, and share resources with industries that could not afford them. All these practices contribute to the growth of supporting industries in the domestic market. Furthermore, organizations could share strategies to achieve the SDGs without compromising on profitability. Similarly, the marketing insights on the BoP market could help the allied industries to align their interests and serve them effectively and efficiently. For instance, if a tourism organization through marketing analytics could identify the changing BoP consumer pattern, it may share the information with the allied hospitality sector so that they may make suitable changes in their operations. Such knowledge sharing will ensure responsible consumption and production patterns which is an essential SDG. Thus, we make the following proposition.

P3. CSV-integrated business models focusing on SDG and BoP will influence the development and growth of allied and supporting industries.

Impact on Factor Conditions

Factor conditions are one of the most significant determinants of competitiveness. CSV-led business models could be leveraged to develop products or services that address societal issues. Since most of the societal issues are covered in the SDGs and BoP product designing strategies, therefore, such a business model that integrates all three concepts will not only ensure optimum usage, but will also improve factor conditions by upskilling labour resources, upgrading technology, and responsible usage of natural resources. For instance, upgrading technology will have a role in reducing the cost and improving the quality of the products, which is a basic need of the BoP market. Similarly, it might also help in reducing resource consumption and waste generation. Thus, by improving a factor through creating shared value, businesses can achieve SDG targets and fulfil the needs of the BoP market. Therefore, we make the following proposition.

P4. CSV-integrated business models focusing on SDG and BoP will influence the factor conditions in the domestic market.

Impact on Government

One of the arguments in Porter's diamond model is the active role of the government in supporting the industries. It requires businesses and industries to engage in partnerships and collaborations with governments, NGOs, and other stakeholders to leverage their expertise and resources in achieving goals which could be SDGs or serving the BoP market. However, industries often find it difficult to engage with the stakeholders because of a lack of common goals and a suitable platform. CSV provides the platform for fostering such collaboration as it requires continuous collaboration between the stakeholders to attain the goals. Similarly, the government will also have an interest in the businesses and industry if they are also sharing the equitable value derived from the businesses. Thus, we make the following proposition.

P5. CSV-integrated business models focusing on SDG and BoP will influence the role of the government in enhancing competitiveness.

Figure 1. Proposed model of implication of business model integrating CSV, SDG, and BoP on industry competitiveness

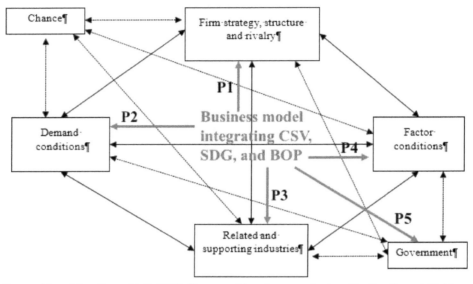

Source: Adapted from Porter, M. E. (1990). The competitive advantage of nations. The Free Press. A Division of Macmillan Incorporation.

STUDY IMPLICATIONS

The study offers theoretical implications by contributing to the theory of creating shared value and also offers managerial implications. One of the issues highlighted in the BoP literature is the manager's resistance to engaging in CSV because they find it less profitable. However, the present study highlights that the managers feel that engaging in BoP and SDG together can create business models that provide a competitive advantage to the organizations. Thus, it might help them in reducing the negative attitude of the managers. Furthermore, businesses often find it difficult to justify their actions to other stakeholders for working towards SDGs attainment and finding business among the BoP. The study highlights that such business models improve the competitiveness of organizations and if well implemented, can help organizations succeed over competition. BoP segments occur mostly in developing and underdeveloped countries. Also, these countries have huge populations that can serve as potential markets. Organizations that face maturity in their market or declining market share can get a first-mover advantage by serving these customers and adding SGS into their operation and business model would further validate their *licence to operate* in the market.

CONCLUSION

The present study was undertaken to understand the perspective of tourism managers about the business models that are developed integrating the needs of the BoP market, SDGs, and also the concept of creating shared value. The impact of such business models was assessed on their impact on industry and organization competitiveness using the Porter Diamond framework. the data was obtained from managers in tourism organizations through semi-structured interviews. The literature review helped in understanding the issues of the BoP market and, the goals of several SDGs that can be addressed through Tourism. The findings reveal that policymakers have a favorable attitude towards such business models as they believe that implementing them will provide them with a competitive advantage. The results further reveal that such business models will improve the demand conditions by extending the market, enhance factor conditions by developing infrastructure and training the stakeholders, improve the firm's positioning against their rivals, and also have a positive impact on the supporting and allied industries. The study then provides a framework to enhance competitiveness which could be empirically tested in future research.

REFERENCES

Biswas, S., Dandapat, B., Alam, A., & Satpati, L. (2022). India's achievement towards sustainable Development Goal 6 (Ensure availability and sustainable management of water and sanitation for all) in the 2030 Agenda. *BMC Public Health*, 22(1), 2142. 10.1186/s12889-022-14316-036414936

Bradley, M., Fraioli, C., & Osusky, D. (2021). *SDG Insights Report*.

Chung, T. W. (2016). A Study on Logistics Cluster Competitiveness among Asia Main Countries using the Porter's Diamond Model. *The Asian Journal of Shipping and Logistics*, 32(4), 257–264. 10.1016/j.ajsl.2016.12.010

Dolnicar, S., Grün, B., & Leisch, F. (2018). Market Segmentation. Springer. 10.1007/978-981-10-8818-6

Fainshmidt, S., Smith, A., & Judge, W. Q. (2016). National Competitiveness and Porter's Diamond Model: The Role of MNE Penetration and Governance Quality. *Global Strategy Journal*, 6(2), 81–104. 10.1002/gsj.1116

Fong, B. Y. F., & Law, V. T. S. (2021). *Sustainable Development Goal 3*. Routledge. 10.4324/9781003220169

Gasper, D., Shah, A., & Tankha, S. (2019). The Framing of Sustainable Consumption and Production in <scp>SDG</scp> 12. *Global Policy*, 10(S1), 83–95. 10.1111/1758-5899.12592

Gil, J. D. B., Reidsma, P., Giller, K., Todman, L., Whitmore, A., & van Ittersum, M. (2019). Sustainable development goal 2: Improved targets and indicators for agriculture and food security. *Ambio*, 48(7), 685–698. 10.1007/s13280-018-1101-430267284

Haas, B. (2023). Achieving SDG 14 in an equitable and just way. *International Environmental Agreement: Politics, Law and Economics*, 23(2), 199–205. 10.1007/s10784-023-09603-z

Halkos, G., & Gkampoura, E.-C. (2021). Where do we stand on the 17 Sustainable Development Goals? An overview on progress. *Economic Analysis and Policy*, 70, 94–122. 10.1016/j.eap.2021.02.001

Joseph, S. (2017). Sustainable Medical Tourism Model - A Case Study of Kerala, India. *Asia-Pacific Journal of Innovation in Hospitality and Tourism*, 6(1), 77–98.

Kharub, M., & Sharma, R. (2017). Comparative analyses of competitive advantage using Porter diamond model (the case of MSMEs in Himachal Pradesh). *Competitiveness Review*, 27(2), 132–160. 10.1108/CR-02-2016-0007

Koch, F., & Krellenberg, K. (2018). How to Contextualize SDG 11? Looking at Indicators for Sustainable Urban Development in Germany. *ISPRS International Journal of Geo-Information*, 7(12), 464. 10.3390/ijgi7120464

Krauss, J. E. (2022). Unpacking SDG 15, its targets and indicators: Tracing ideas of conservation. *Globalizations*, 19(8), 1179–1194. 10.1080/14747731.2022.2035480

Kreinin, H., & Aigner, E. (2022). From "Decent work and economic growth" to "Sustainable work and economic degrowth": A new framework for SDG 8. *Empirica*, 49(2), 281–311. 10.1007/s10663-021-09526-5

Küfeoğlu, S. (2022). SDG-1 No Poverty. In *Emerging Technologies* (pp. 191–208). Springer. 10.1007/978-3-031-07127-0_3

Kumar, P., Ahmed, F., Singh, R. K., & Sinha, P. (2018). Determination of hierarchical relationships among sustainable development goals using interpretive structural modeling. *Environment, Development and Sustainability*, 20(5), 2119–2137. 10.1007/s10668-017-9981-1

Latifi, M.-A., Nikou, S., & Bouwman, H. (2021). Business model innovation and firm performance: Exploring causal mechanisms in SMEs. *Technovation*, 107, 102274. 10.1016/j.technovation.2021.102274

Leal Filho, W., Kovaleva, M., Tsani, S., îrcă, D.-M., Shiel, C., Dinis, M. A. P., Nicolau, M., Sima, M., Fritzen, B., Lange Salvia, A., Minhas, A., Kozlova, V., Doni, F., Spiteri, J., Gupta, T., Wakunuma, K., Sharma, M., Barbir, J., Shulla, K., & Tripathi, S. (2023). Promoting gender equality across the sustainable development goals. *Environment, Development and Sustainability*, 25(12), 14177–14198. 10.1007/s10668-022-02656-136124160

Mawla, M. R., & Rahman Khan, M. Z. (2020). A Study on Sustainable Development Goal 7: Future Plan to Achieve the Affordable and Clean Energy-Bangladesh Perspective. *2020 IEEE Region 10 Symposium (TENSYMP)*, (pp. 421–426). IEEE. 10.1109/TENSYMP50017.2020.9230795

Milton, S. (2021). Higher education and sustainable development goal 16 in fragile and conflict-affected contexts. *Higher Education*, 81(1), 89–108. 10.1007/s10734-020-00617-z

Öz, Ö. (2002). Assessing Porter's framework for national advantage: The case of Turkey. *Journal of Business Research*, 55(6), 509–515. 10.1016/S0148-2963(00)00167-3

Porter, M. E. (1990). The Competitive Advantage of Nations. *Harvard Business Review*, 68(2), 73–93.

Purnell, P. J. (2022). A comparison of different methods of identifying publications related to the United Nations Sustainable Development Goals: Case study of SDG 13—Climate Action. *Quantitative Science Studies*, 3(4), 976–1002. 10.1162/qss_a_00215

Roy, R. P., & Sinha Roy, S. (2019). SDG 10—A Probe into the Factors Underlying Differences in Inequality: Evidence at the Sub-national Level in India. In *2030 Agenda and India: Moving from Quantity to Quality* (1st ed., pp. 149–164). Springer. 10.1007/978-981-32-9091-4_7

Saini, M., Sengupta, E., Singh, M., Singh, H., & Singh, J. (2023). Sustainable Development Goal for Quality Education (SDG 4): A study on SDG 4 to extract the pattern of association among the indicators of SDG 4 employing a genetic algorithm. *Education and Information Technologies*, 28(2), 2031–2069. 10.1007/s10639-022-11265-435975216

Saqib, N., & Satar, M. S. (2021). Exploring business model innovation for competitive advantage: A lesson from an emerging market. *International Journal of Innovation Science*, 13(4), 477–491. 10.1108/IJIS-05-2020-0072

Seidman, G. (2017). Does SDG 3 have an adequate theory of change for improving health systems performance? *Journal of Global Health*, 7(1), 010302. 10.7189/jogh.07.01030228567275

Shafer, S. M., Smith, H. J., & Linder, J. C. (2005). The power of business models. *Business Horizons*, 48(3), 199–207. 10.1016/j.bushor.2004.10.014

Singh, S., & Ru, J. (2023). Goals of sustainable infrastructure, industry, and innovation: A review and future agenda for research. *Environmental Science and Pollution Research International*, 30(11), 28446–28458. 10.1007/s11356-023-25281-536670221

Tiwari, S., Mohanty, P. P., Fernando, I. N., Cifci, I., & Kuruva, M. B. (2023). Bridging tea with tourism: Empirical evidence from India and Sri Lanka. *Tourism Review*, 78(1), 177–202. 10.1108/TR-06-2022-0280

Tsai, P.-H., Chen, C.-J., & Yang, H.-C. (2021). Using Porter's Diamond Model to Assess the Competitiveness of Taiwan's Solar Photovoltaic Industry. *SAGE Open*, 11(1), 215824402098828. 10.1177/2158244020988286

UN DESA. (2019). *The Sustainable Development Goals Report 2019*.

Van Tulder, R., Rodrigues, S. B., Mirza, H., & Sexsmith, K. (2021). The UN's Sustainable Development Goals: Can multinational enterprises lead the Decade of Action? *Journal of International Business Policy*, 4(1), 1–21. 10.1057/s42214-020-00095-1

Waverman, L. (1995). A critical analysis of Porter's framework on the competitive advantage of nations. In *Beyond The Diamond* (pp. 67–95). Elsevier. 10.1016/S1064-4857(95)05004-3

Chapter 2
Impact of Human Capital on SDG1 in Selected G20 Countries

Meenakshi Gupta
https://orcid.org/0000-0002-7866-4961

Department of Economics, Faculty of Management, Shri Mata Vaishno Devi University, Katra, India

Isha Kumari

Department of Economics, Faculty of Management, Shri Mata Vaishno Devi University, Katra, India

Ajay Kumar Singh
https://orcid.org/0000-0003-0429-0925

Department of Humanities and Social Sciences, Graphic Era University (Deemed), Dehradun, India

ABSTRACT

This chapter finds the implication of human capital on SDG1 in selected G20 countries. It uses poverty as a dependent variable, while government spending on health & education, Gini coefficient, and life expectancy at birth as independent variables in the Panel ARDL model. It is noticed that government spending on health and education, Gini coefficient, life expectancy at birth, and total health expenditure has a significant impact on poverty. The presence of cross-sectional dependence indicates the association of these variables within and across economies. The G20 countries should pursue inclusive policy interventions to address the issues of healthcare inaccessibility, income distribution and poverty. Investments in healthcare and edu-

DOI: 10.4018/979-8-3693-3166-8.ch002

cation would be useful to reduce poverty and achieve SDG1. Income equality helps to increase the progress of SDGs worldwide. Development of the tourism industry would be effective to reduce poverty and increase human well-being.

INTRODUCTION

Sustainable development (SD) is essential to meet the diverse needs of the present and future population without harming the ecosystem services and natural services (Singh & Kumar, 2022). Therefore, sustainability of ecosystem services would be effective to meet the requirement of raw materials for the production sector in the long-term. Subsequently, it would play a significant role to develop an important path to enhance all drivers of SD. It, therefore, is true that production activities of any sector cannot be sustained without ecosystem services. Thus, researchers, scientists and international organizations are developing a scientific and digital platform to maintain the productivity and efficiency of factors of production to increase sustainable development (Singh et al., 2021). Although, the key agenda of SD is not new in the academic literature and how to achieve SD is a global agenda since 1972. The main focus of SD is to ensure the sustainable future of everyone in the world.

Sustainable future of an individual depends on economic and social development, and a clean environment (Singh et al., 2019). Hence, SD is a combination of the above-mentioned indicators of development (Zile, 2016; Pradhan et al., 2023; Singh et al., 2023a). Accordingly, most scholars included diverse indicators in the domain of social, economic, environmental, technological, financial and human development to explain the performance of global countries in SD (Guijarro & Poyatos, 2018). Also, the scientific research community realizes that SD is only a way to increase the well-being of the coming generation (Zile, 2016; Singh et al., 2020; Jin et al., 2020). The well-being of people depends on several variables that are essential to increase sustainability in energy, water, air, environmental, education, health, technological, financial, and other sectors (Yang et al., 2020). It is also evident that maintaining sustainability in livelihood security associated sectors would promote SD in the long-run. The SD works in multiple ways to improve the production, productivity and efficiency of the system and increase the quality of ecosystem services (Singh & Jyoti, 2023).

Sustainable development (SD) covers a broad range of indicators which help to reduce poverty, income inequality, gender diversity, and increase quality of education and health of the people (Guijarro & Poyatos, 2018; Gaspar et al., 2019; Prasetyanto & Sari, 2021). Conversely, low quality of education is responsible for high poverty and inequality (Moyo et al., 2022). Although, scientific research could not develop a uniform measurement of SD (Koirala & Pradhan, 2019). Education and health are worthy drivers to increase social development, and it also maintains the economic and cultural prosperity of the people (Jin et al., 2020). Therefore, SD is a scientific process to maintain the sustainability of resources in the domain of social, economic, financial, human, environmental and technological sectors (Kumar et al., 2016). SD, thus, nurtures an appropriate ecosystem in multiple ways to ensure the future of the present and coming generation. Without achieving the path of SD, it is difficult to meet the diverse needs of people in future (Singh et al., 2023a).

The global countries are growing very fast due to several reasons such as rising population, infrastructural development, industrialization, and urbanization (Singh et al., 2023b). High growth of industrialization and infrastructural development are helping to increase social and economic, and technological development across counties (Singh et al., 2023a). Despite that, poverty eradication is a significant challenge for policy makers in many countries. Poverty is a challenge in many regions (Gaspar et al., 2019). At global level, the existence of poverty is significantly increased after COVID-19 (Arora & Sarker, 2022). Existence of chronic poverty is creating a barrier to achieve various goals of SDGs that are prescribed by UNDP (Gaspar et al., 2019). SDGs are also targeted to reduce inequality, conflict and conserve natural resources (Yang et al., 2020). It is also noticed that poverty has a significant and negative impact on all components including education, health, basic amenities, social equity and inclusion, social justice, food security etc. (Singh & Sharma, 2018). While these are essential to increase SD (Pradhan et al., 2023).

At the same time there are many factors like income inequality, high unemployment, low education level, poor medical facilities, poor infrastructural development, low market accessibility, social inequality, cultural diversity, traditional occupation, crime, black marketing, high food prices, and ineffective policy mechanism that cause to increase chronic poverty (Ghosh et al., 2002; Ghosh, 2010; Ighodalo, 2012; Arora & Sarker, 2022; Singh & Jayaram, 2020). In contrast, employment, effective market, perfect competition in the market, appropriate health facilities, quality education and food security play a positive role to reduce poverty and income inequality (Singh et al., 2022b). The development of tourism also plays a significant role to reduce poverty and achieve the first goal of SDGs. Although, this sector also needs sustainable practices to increase SDGs (Khizar et al., 2023). Previous studies also noticed a positive impact on the tourism industry on poverty and income inequality (Kc et al., 2021). Thus, the development of the tourism sector may be an alternative to achieve SDGs. Tourism industry helps to promote cultural diversity and economic growth (Moslehpour et al., 2023). Also, the scientific research community is searching for a link between tourism and SDGs (Kc et al., 2021).

Eradication of poverty and income inequalities are the crucial goals of the SDG1 (Kumar et al., 2016). There may be multiple negative implications of poverty and income inequality on social, economic and environmental development (Gaspar et al., 2019; Prasetyanto & Sari, 2021). Highly educated people may be more conscious of maintaining a clean environment. Education, therefore, plays a positive role to reduce environmental degradation (Prasetyanto & Sari, 2021). Further, the existence of chronic poverty is also creating an obstacle to achieve SD (Ighodalo, 2012). While poverty is a significant cause to reduce social and economic development, and human wellbeing (Singh et al., 2021; Pradhan et al., 2023). It also hampers the decision-making capacity and psychological well-being of people and reduces their contribution in social and economic development (Ighodalo, 2012). Thereupon, it may produce a negative impact on food and health security (Singh et al., 2022b). Subsequently, poverty, food insecurity and hunger create several restrictions to achieve the SDGs (Singh et al., 2022b). Therefore, there is a slower progress of the developing countries to achieve many goals of SDGs by 2030 than developed countries. For instance, poverty has moved in many developing countries after COVID-19 pandemic (Singh et al., 2022b; Arora & Sarker, 2022).

No poverty is the 1st goal of SDGs and it was proposed by UNDP in 2015 (Pradhan et al., 2023). It is also a main target of SDG1 to make the world free from poverty (Singh & Jayaram, 2020). Poverty is a main cause that also creates multiple obstacles to achieve other goals of SDGs i.e., zero hunger, income equality, social equality, social justice, wealth and well-being, economic empowerment, gender equality, self-reliance, environmental sustainability, etc. Rising unemployment and low efficiency of resources are the main causes for poverty (Singh et al., 2022a). Low capital efficiency, low productivity of resources, low quality of education, low technological skills of people are also accountable for poverty. Therefore, social capital may be supportive to reduce poverty (Li et al., 2024). Education, health and welfare schemes are essential to increase social capital (Li et al., 2024). Creation of social capital would develop a platform to reduce poverty and income inequality. Poverty also creates numerous barriers to meet the basic requirements of human livelihood like food, cloth, water, education, social freedom, etc.

Moreover, poor people cannot meet the calorie intake requirement to improve their health and well-being. Thus, poverty may be caused to increase mental disability among the people. There is also increased spiritual poverty in the society and people do not complete the requirement of good thinking in many countries. It also reduces the involvement of people in the political system. Also, poor people are not involved in social activities. While there is high diversity in the existence of poverty and income inequality in developed and developing countries. Accordingly, there are many factors that lead to decrease poverty and income inequality. One of these factors is tourist inflow in the respective economies. As the tourism sector grows, the employment opportunities for the local people increases (Moslehpour et al., 2023). The local people already engaged in the tourism sector upgrade their skills that allow them to seek employment not only in this sector but also in its allied sectors. This increases the overall income level of the local community. Besides, the revenue generated through tourism can be used to develop human capital by investing in education and health infrastructure. Thus, it helps to increase the accessibility of quality education and health services (Jin et al., 2020).

Tourism industry also enhances regional entrepreneurship and generates foreign revenue in a country (Moslehpour et al., 2023). Thus, the development of the tourism industry may be effective to reduce poverty at a substantial level (Khizar et al., 2023). Limited accessibility of education, inappropriate infrastructure and poverty have a negative impact on human skills (Bekele et al., 2014). This will ultimately lead to better educational and health outcomes which are the determining factors of poverty reduction. Quality education and good health through government expenditure on health and education is essential for improving the living standard of local people and it contributes towards the attainment of SDG1. It is also positive to increase financial development and SD (Li et al., 2024).

India is the most populated country in the world, with one-sixth of the world's population. All states of the country are endowed with good natural resources which are suitable for better growth of agriculture and its allied sectors. Also, a large part of the population depends on the agriculture sector for their daily livelihood in India. Furthermore, India achieved better economic growth in the last decades among the G20 countries. However, poverty and income inequality are still being a critical challenge for Indian policy makers. The government's estimates indicate a decline in poverty over the past two decades in India, while International Organizations (like Asian Development Bank, World Bank) have reported that poverty has increased in India. Still, there are severe regional disparities and inter-state differences in poverty and income inequality across Indian states and within states. Many states like Gujarat, Maharashtra, Kerala, Punjab and Haryana achieved effective growth in social, economic, technological and infrastructure (e.g., roads, electricity, railway, and telecommunication) sectors in the past two decades. While some states like Bihar, Uttar Pradesh, Orissa, Andhra Pradesh and Madhya Pradesh have lagged behind in growth patterns in various sectors.

Moreover, there is no appropriate facility of clean water, electricity, clean environment, road connectivity and low education facilities in rural India. Many government initiatives were taken for poverty eradication, to increase socio-economic development and to reduce high income inequalities across India states. However, effectiveness of these initiatives is always questioned and in some instances these initiatives might have significant contributions to increase income inequality and poverty across Indian regions. India has a target to reduce poverty rate from 21.29% to 10.95% by 2030s under SDGs (Singh & Jayaram, 2020). Further, it has been proved that income inequality and poverty have a negative implication on living standard and socio-economic development of people in many G20 countries like Brazil,

China, Indonesia, Russia Federation and South Africa. While most countries from the EU have created an effective ecosystem to reduce poverty and income inequality.

Income inequality and poverty are also caused to create several obstacles on the path of social and economic development in many G20 countries. In aforementioned perspective, previous studies have given a confirmation that income inequalities have once again stated to move in an upward direction in most developing economies due to several reasons like high population growth, high inflation, decreasing employment opportunities, decreasing education level, human migration from rural to urban area, extensive capitalization, ineffective role of government policies, and others (Gaspar et al., 2019; Koirala & Pradhan, 2019). Thus, rising new forms of income inequality and poverty will be hampering the development path of most developing economies including India. Hence, it is essential for academicians and existing researchers to give more attention to assess the crucial determinants of new forms of income inequality and poverty in the era of digitalization and technological advancement (Singh et al., 2019).

A substantial fraction of people in developing nations including India still live in poverty due to which they have limited access to basic healthcare facilities and education (Singh et al., 2022b). Reducing poverty, and income disparity and promoting sustained economic growth largely depends on fostering human capital (Bekele et al., 2014). Further, it would be positive to increase various goals of SDGs. Appropriate health and quality of education are important components of human capital formation. Since the beginning of the 1960s, the human capital has been considered as crucial to increase economic development (Moyo et al., 2022). Public education spending develops human capital, which may then support economic expansion (Gaspar et al., 2019). Further, capital expenditure is supportive to create new assets and more employment opportunities (Singh & Kumar, 2022). Thus, it may help to reduce poverty. Besides this, the expenditure on research and development (R&D) also contributes to economic expansion (Romer, 1990). R&D expenditure is also vital to increase technological progress and innovation.

Numerous studies also urged that earnings are related to education and vice-versa (Hanushek & Wossmann, 2007; Psacharopoulos & Patrinos, 2004). Investment in education develops a path to increase human skills and economic development (Psacharopoulos & Patrinos, 2004). Educational attainment, therefore, promotes income, employment, and economic growth are also necessary to increase SDGs (Barro & Lee 2013; Singh & Jyoti, 2023). Therefore, the economic growth of a nation is highly dependent on the educational attainment of its dweller (Ghosh & Cheruvalath, 2007). Income and employment opportunities help to achieve various goals (e.g., no poverty, zero hunger, well-being, decent work, reduce inequality, inclusive economic growth, self-reliance, etc.) of SDGs (Kumar et al., 2016; Pradhan et al., 2023). SDGs are expected to increase equity, human rights and non-discrimination

(Kumar et al., 2016). Besides, it also creates awareness among people regarding their health that is also a crucial goal of SDGs (Currie & Moretti, 2003; Singh et al., 2019). Health security is a crucial agenda to increase well-being (Zile, 2016).

Howitt (2005) argued about the positive impacts of health on income, employment and economic growth. Thus, economic growth and employment are essential to increase the health security of people. Earlier studies also highlighted that the expenditure on the education and health sector fosters human capital formation and stimulates economic growth (Lee and Barro, 2001; Moyo et al., 2022). Moreover, education creates awareness towards healthcare among individuals and communities. This awareness increases availability and accessibility of health care services among the people. Further, it helps to improve life expectancy and reduce infant mortality, and many other health issues (Singh & Jyoti, 2023). The availability and accessibility to health care facilities and education requires infrastructure development in the social sector (Singh et al., 2019). This can be supported by the fact that practically all economies, especially those in their early phases of development, spend more on the health and education sectors and thus significantly contribute to the course of economic growth through human capital formation (Bekele et al., 2014).

Moreover, expenditure on health and education is one of the major national expenditures, so health care and educational costs are significant for economies. However, there exists variation in allocations to these sectors across different economies which may be attributed to divergent national priorities. It also doesn't mean that high spending in these sectors can always assure quality outcomes, but it often indicates a commitment to well- being. Against this backdrop, the present study tries to examine the trends of variables viz., poverty level, government spending on health & education, income inequality (Gini Coefficient) and life expectancy at birth in selected G20 countries. Further, in this study an attempt is made to find the impact of government spending on health & education, Gini coefficient, life expectancy at birth on poverty in selected economies of G20 groups. The reason for choosing these economies is that this international forum brings together the world's major economies. Most G20 counties are taking effective initiatives to achieve certain goals of SDGs. The group of G20 countries contribute a significant share of GDP, human resources, youth population, technology, foreign trade, etc. in the world. Moreover, it offers a platform for discussion and cooperation as it primarily addresses the major challenges that are encountered in the global economy (Yadav et al., 2024). Moreover, prior studies have low attention to examine the impact of human capital on poverty reduction in India and other G20 countries.

LITERATURE REVIEW

Most scholars examined the significance of education and health expenditure, and life expectancy in the G20 countries. For instance, poverty and inequality have a major impact on health and education and both are affected by existing levels of health and education (Singh et al., 2019). Several studies also investigated the relationship between poverty and inequality (Chelliah & Shanmugam, 2007). An unhealthy, uneducated and food insecure person contributes very little to society (Singh & Sharma, 2018). Therefore, investing in effective health and education sectors help to reduce mortality rate, and it also increases the number of people in the workforce. Spending on healthcare has a direct relationship with per capita income and it ensures the living standards of people (Balaji, 2011; Azam & Awan, 2022). The government expenditure is also essential to increase money flow in the market and it also helps to maintain the aggregate demand and supply. Subsequently, unemployment is expected to decline due to increase in aggregate demand and supply. Moreover, government expenditure on road construction and agricultural R&D are very effective for reducing poverty.

Bloom et al. (2004) claimed that individuals with good health have better ability to learn new things and, as a result, are more productive. Some studies are attempted to assess the relationship between population health and overall economic performance and reported that improvements in population health led to increased production, given labour and capital (Bhargava et al., 2001; Balaji, 2011; Dias & Tebaldi, 2012; Bedir, 2016). A higher income leads to better health status via access to improved health services. Expenditure on health and education determines higher efficiency, and it is important to reduce poverty (Nurudeen & Usman, 2010; Ghosh, 2010). Al-Yousif (2008) reported a significant impact on education expenditure on economic growth in GCC countries. It would also be positive to increase economic growth (Ghosh et al., 2002). The government expenditure in the health sector is also helpful to increase health security, productivity and efficiency of people. Health expenditure also prepares a path for economic growth in the long-term (Bedir, 2016).

Income equality is also strongly associated with life expectancy. Although high income inequality may also increase social crime and black marketing, thus, it may not be appropriate social development and justice. There is a negative relationship between income inequality and life expectancy. The government should increase per capita health expenditure to increase life expectancy, and to reduce poverty. Recent studies also claimed a positive contribution of life expectancy on economic development (Singh et al., 2023a). Health expenditure also helps to increase well-being of people and nurture an ecosystem to increase SD (Ullah et al., 2021). Mehrara (2011) analysed the relationship between expenditures on health and economic development in Iran. The finding of this study suggests that education, real GDP, healthcare expense, stock of capital, and gasoline earnings all exhibit a co-integrated relationship. Ogungbenle et al. (2013) employed an autoregressive vector model to analyse the correlation between Nigeria's economic growth, health-related spending, and longevity. The study reveals no direct correlation between life expectancy and public health expenditure (PHE).

However, it is also observed a direct link between PHE and economic development. Singh et al. (2023a) also noted a positive impact of life expectancy rate on economic development. Gebrehiwo (2016) revealed that good health and education signify the better performance of human capital. Both have a significant impact on real GDP per capita growth. Wahab et al. (2018) used data from the Organisation of Islamic Cooperation (OIC) nations to study the dynamic relationship between healthcare and education spending and economic development. The study analysed the data from 1990 – 2015 using the Pool Mean Group (PMG) technique. The analysis demonstrates a strong long-run co-integrating link between economic growth and spending on health care, education, research, and development. The short-term benefits for education spending and research and development (technology) have been found negligible in OIC. It is also established that expenditure on health and education is generally found positively related to economic growth.

Furthermore, numerous scholars reported significant implications of government expenditure on poverty eradication in India. Pradhan et al. (2023) examined the association between expenditure in the social sector and multidimensional poverty index in Odisha state of India. It reported that public spending is useful to reduce poverty. Therefore, extensive investment is required in the social sector to achieve SDGs. It is also essential to invest in education to achieve SDG4 (Saini et al., 2023). The above-mentioned literature claimed that government expenditure on health and education, life expectancy and total health expenditure have a significant contribution in poverty eradication. However, existing studies could not examine the impact of these variables on poverty in selected G20 countries. Accordingly, most studies also explore the link between poverty and SD. For example, Ighodalo (2012) explains the association of poverty and sustainable social and economic development in Nigeria.

Guijarro and Poyatos (2018) explained the role of SDGs in social-economic development in EU countries. Ullah et al. (2021) noted that social and economic promoting indicators create a path of sustainable development (SD). Therefore, education and health expenditure would assist to increase human skills and human well-being. Moyo et al. (2022) examined the impact of education attainment on poverty and income inequality in Eastern cape provinces in the long-run. It claimed that poverty is likely to be decreased as education attainment increases, while human capita is caused to increase income inequality. Human capital may also lead to increased inequality in economic opportunities and the education system. Further, human skills and quality education lead to decreased poverty (Bekele et al., 2014).

Therefore, Bekele et al. (2014) suggested that sustainable economic development can be achieved through improving quality education and human skills. Kc et al. (2021) explained the role of the tourism industry in SDGs in Nepal. Moslehpour et al. (2023) observed the role of the tourism sector in SDGs in Indonesia. This study reported a significant impact of the tourism sector on multiple goals of SDGs including poverty and income inequality.

Previous studies have also estimated the determinants of economic growth and their association with income inequalities and poverty at micro and macro level in India and other G20 countries. However, very few studies could deceive attention to estimate the association between economic growth and poverty. Although, previous studies could not provide the significant association of income inequality and poverty in India and the G20 countries. Also, limited studies could assess the determinants of poverty and income inequality. Furthermore, earlier studies could not consider the most factors which might be having significant association with income inequality and poverty. Hence, this chapter is a research attempt to examine the impact of government expenditure in the health and education sectors, income inequality, and life expectancy rate on poverty in selected G20 countries.

DATA AND RESEARCH METHODOLOGY

Explanation of Variables and Its Sources

The state of poverty can be detected by many methods. For instance, relative poverty measures the income inequality in the society. While absolute poverty is based on calorie intake availability. It can also be observed with the help of the Lorentz curve that shows the income inequality in the society. Poverty headcount ratio at $2.15/day used as a dependent variable in this chapter. It is the ratio of total poor population to total population. Hene, it is best representative of overall poverty in a country (Subramanian, 2005). While independent variables consisted of various socio-economic indicators listed as, government spending on health & education, Gini coefficient, life expectancy at birth, and total health expenditure. Many studies such as Al-Yousif (2008); Nurudeen and Usman (2010); Ghosh (2010); Gebrehiwo (2016) also used government spending on health & education, and total health expenditure as independent variables in poverty affecting factors. Moyo et al. (2022) also used education attainment as a proxy variable for human capital to assess its impact on poverty. Gini coefficient is a statistical measurement of income and wealth distribution inequality in the society. It is a useful indicator to measure the income inequality in the society and it has a crucial impact on poverty. Life expectancy is also a useful variable that has a negative impact on poverty. Also, high life expectancy refers to a better health infrastructure.

The statistical data of the above-mentioned variables were derived from reputable sources like Our World in Data (https://ourworldindata.org) & sustainable development report (https://dashboards.sdgindex.org/). The chapter selected countries from G20 as per the availability of statistical information of the above-mentioned variables during 2000 – 2019. Following countries from the G20 are included in this chapter: Argentina, Australia, Brazil, Canada, China, France, Germany, India, Indonesia, Italy, Japan, Mexico, Russia Federation, South Africa, Turkiye, United Kingdom, United States. The statistical and empirical investigations were performed utilizing E-Views 12 statistical software.

Methodology

The study employed the Panel Autoregressive Distributed Lagged (ARDL) Co-Integration approach to examine the impact of stated underlined explanatory variables on poverty head count ratio in selected G20 countries. The model is used by Mehrara (2011); Akinwale (2021) in the associated field. Nurudeen and Usman (2010) applied a co-integration and error-correction model to examine the impact of government expenditure on economic growth in Nigeria. Ogungbenle et al. (2013) examined the association of economic growth with government expenditure and longevity in Nigeria using the ARDL model. Gebrehiwo (2016) also observed the implications of health and education on real GDP per capita in Ethiopia using the ARDL model. Singh et al. (2023b) develop ARDL model to observe the interconnection of SD and its other dimensions with green entrepreneurship. Moyo et al. (2022) also developed a pooled mean group estimator to examine the impact of human capital on poverty in Eastern Cape province. This approach allowed for both long-term and short-term analyses of this study. The functional form of dependent and independent variables is defined as:

$$PHR = f\,(GSHE,\ GC,\ LE,\ THE) \qquad (1)$$

Here, *PHR* is poverty head count ratio, *GSHE* is government spending on health & education, *GC* is Gini coefficient, *LE* is life expectancy at birth, and *THE* is total health expenditure in equation (1). To estimate the effect of various socio-economic indicator components over the PHR2.15, the equation is used as:

$$PHR_{it} = \beta_0 + \beta_1\,GSHE_{it} + \beta_2\,GC_{it} + \beta_3\,LE_{it} + \beta_4\,THE_{it} \qquad (2)$$

Here, β_0 is the intercept; β_1, β_2, β_3, and β_4 are the parameters of associated variables that to be estimated in equation (2). According to Pesaran and Shin (1995), the equation (2) can be converted in following ARDL form (Singh et al., 2023b):

$$\Delta PHR_{it} = \alpha_0 + \sum_{j=0}^{p}\varphi j\Delta\, GSHE_{it-j} + \sum_{j=0}^{p}\emptyset j\Delta\, GC_{it-j} + \sum_{j=0}^{p}\gamma j\Delta\, LE_{it-j} + \sum_{j=0}^{p}\delta j\Delta\, THE_{it-j} +$$

$$\beta_1\, GSHE_{it} + \beta_2\, GC_{it} + \beta_3\, LE_{it} + \beta_4\, THE_{it} \tag{3}$$

Here, $\emptyset, \varphi, \gamma, \delta$ refer to short-run; β_1 to β_4 long-run parameters; Δ is the difference of corresponding variables; i is specific country and t is time period in country-wise panel; and t-j are various lags of dependent and independent variables in equation (3). The null hypothesis of no cointegration is: $H_0 = \beta_1 = \beta_2 = \beta_3 = \beta_4 = 0$ against alternative hypothesis is $H_1 = \beta_1 \neq \beta_2 \neq \beta_3 \neq \beta_4 \neq 0$ (Singh et al., 2023b).

The ARDL specification of short-run dynamics is investigated using the ECM version of the ARDL model of the following:

$$\Delta PHR_{it} = \alpha_1 + \sum_{j=0}^{p+1}\varphi j\Delta\, GSHE_{it-j} + \sum_{j=0}^{p+1}\emptyset j\Delta\, GC_{it-j}$$

$$+ \sum_{j=0}^{p+1}\gamma j\Delta\, LE_{it-j} + \sum_{j=0}^{p+1}\delta j\Delta\, THE_{it-j} + \upsilon ECT + \varepsilon_{it}$$

$$\tag{4}$$

Here, ECT is error component term that is measured the stability between explanatory and dependent variables in equation (4).

TREND IN THE VARIABLES

This section describes the emerging trends of the variables that are included in this the study and later discusses the findings of the studies.

Trends in Poverty in the Selected G20 Economies

Among the selected economies, it was observed that South Africa and India were the economies that possess the lowest poverty headcount ratio. It is clearly showing that, in these economies the fraction of people living below the poverty line are smaller as compared to other economies. India has extreme poverty due to large population size, high dependency of population on the agricultural sector, low education level, low employment opportunities, and low entrepreneurial skills of people (Singh et al., 2022b). The manufacturing sector could also not create additional jobs for agricultural workers in India. Macroeconomic policies are also responsible for poverty and high-income inequality in India. Further, it is also attributed that these countries should implement better poverty reduction measures. Accordingly, India would be able to eradicate poverty through the process of structural transformation of the economy.

India should focus integrated policies to reduce poverty, income inequality, and to improve the social welfare of people. Tourism industry may be an option to create capital infrastructure, jobs and more occupation resources for the local community in India. Thus, the G20 countries should promote the tourism industry to increase regional entrepreneurship and human well-being of the rural community. The poverty headcount ratios of other groups of economies like Canada, United Kingdom, United States, Germany, France, Australia and others is high. Thus, the trends in selected economies highlight the discrepancies in poverty. It emphasizes the need for continued efforts to address the issue of poverty on a global scale. Otherwise, most countries in the G20 group would not achieve SDG1 by the 2030s. Also, high poverty would create diverse problems to attain other goals of SDGs like no hunger, good health and well-being, and social justice in G20 countries in future.

Trends in Government Spending on Health and Education in Sectors (As a Percentage of GDP) in the Selected G20 Economies

It is discernible from the data of the selected economies that France, the United States and Japan allocate a relatively higher proportion of government spending on health and education. Therefore, these countries could create better technical skills among the people. Also, France, the United States and Japan have high per capita income as compared to other countries in the G20 group. Whereas China and India allocate significantly lower percentages to government spending on health and education (WDI, World Bank, 2023). Both countries are unable to increase health security of people and could not create human skill development. China also made significant progress in the health care sector to reduce poverty (Yang et al., 2020). However, China has a better position in technological development, technology transfer, creation of high-tech products as compared to other countries in the G20 group. This variation in the allocations of health and education expenditure exists due to divergent national priorities, economic and social structure across G20 countries. However, it doesn't mean that high spending in these sectors can always assure quality outcomes, but it often indicates a commitment to well- being. Hence, G20 countries should increase a large share of their GDP in education and health sectors to improve technical skills of people, education quality, and technological development. It would also enhance the technological and digital literacy of people to be active in social and economic activities in G20 countries.

Trends in Gini Coefficients and Life Expectancy in the Selected G20 Economies

The data on Gini coefficients highlights disparities among the countries. Thus, it also provides insight into the distribution of income within each country and areas for potential policy interventions. The disparities in income are due to variation in education quality, technological skills of people, technological development, employment level, social and financial inclusion, social-economic development related policies across G20 countries. It is also discernible from the data that Japan is the leading economy in life expectancy at birth. It indicates that Japan has advanced healthcare system and a high standard of living for people. Japan has more focus on the health and wellness of people as compared to other G20 countries. Indonesia also could also improve life expectancy rate by increasing accessibility of clean water, sanitation, electricity and educational attainment (Gaspar et al., 2019).

It is followed by countries like Australia, Italy and France, highlighting the availability of strong healthcare infrastructures and quality of life in the G20 economies. The United States falls slightly below the above-mentioned economies which may possibly due to disparities in healthcare access and lifestyle factors. South Africa has the lowest life expectancy which may be prevailing challenges such as high rates of infectious diseases, poverty, and healthcare accessibility issues. India, with a life expectancy at birth of 70 years, also faces significant health challenges which may be due to widespread poverty, limited healthcare access in rural areas and a high burden of infectious diseases. India has low life expectancy due to poor infrastructure of health facilities, low diet pattern, low food security, and low nutritional quality of food, and low availability of food-grain products (Singh et al., 2022b).

DISCUSSIONS ON EMPIRICAL RESULTS

This study investigates the relationship between the poverty headcount ratio and key socio-economic indicators such as government spending on health & education, Gini coefficient, life expectancy at birth, and total health expenditure across various G20 nations during 2000 – 2019. The results indicated that all variables are found stationary at the first difference (Table 1). It implies that an order of integration of I(1) (Bhat & Jain, 2004). Cross-sectional dependence tests including the Breusch-Pagan LM, Bias-Correlated Scaled LM, and Pesaran CD & LM reveal significant findings (Singh et al., 2023b). It is also suggesting a strong indication of cross-section dependence, particularly for the poverty headcount ratio and the Gini coefficient in G20 countries. However, the Pesaran CD test results showed a potential lack of cross-section dependence for the poverty headcount ratio. The long-run relationship between variables is examined using the Kao-cointegration test. It reveals no significant linear relationship between the poverty headcount ratio and the independent variables at the 0.05 significance level.

A panel ARDL model is estimated, indicating a positive and significant relationship between the socioeconomic indicators and the poverty headcount ratio at $2.15/day (except for total health expenditure). Total health expenditure indirectly contributes to poverty alleviation through other socioeconomic factors. However, most variables are not significant individually, suggesting the complexity of poverty dynamics in the short-run equation. The results claimed that there is needed targeted interventions are needed to reduce poverty in the G20 countries. Disparities in poverty levels among countries underscore the necessity for continued efforts to address poverty globally. Furthermore, analysis of government spending on health and education as a percentage of GDP reveals varying allocations across countries. Similarly, Gini coefficients highlight disparities in income inequality, with Japan leading in life expectancy, and the United States exhibiting a slightly lower figure possibly due to healthcare access disparities. Overall, the data underscores the complex interplay of socio-economic factors in determining poverty levels and highlights the need for comprehensive policy interventions to address disparities and improve well-being globally (Refer Geographical Region data in Appendix I).

Preliminary Tests

Stationarity tests: Based on the below estimation, it appears that both the test statistics, namely ADF and PP-test statistics, suggest that all the variables are stationary at the first difference (Table 1). Additionally, the Gini coefficient analysis indicates stationarity both at the first differences level. Therefore, every variable in the model exhibits the same order of integration, namely I(1). Consequently, we would proceed to run our model while retaining all the variables based on the results.

Table 1. Tests for stationarity

	ADF test Statistics				PP test statistic	
		Level	1st Difference		Level	1st Difference
continued on following page						

Table 1. Continued

	ADF test Statistics				PP test statistic	
Poverty Headcount Ratio at $2.15/day		0.9266	0		0.8998	0
Government Spending on Health & Education		0.4665	0		0.0535	0
Gini Coefficient		0.120.7	0		0.0181	0
Life Expectancy at Birth	ADF – Fisher Chi-square	1	0	PP – Fisher Chi-square	1	0
Total Health Expenditure		1	0		0.9493	0

Source: Author's estimation using E-views12 statistical software.

Test for checking cross sectional dependence: The presence of cross-sectional dependence has a significant impact on panel data, as it indicates that the units in the cross-section are all interconnected (Table 2). Neglecting to address this issue can lead to serious consequences, such as decreased estimator reliability and inaccurate test measurements. Therefore, it is crucial to thoroughly examine cross-sectional dependence before conducting a data analysis. This review employs several tests, including the Bresusch-Pagan LM, Bias-Correlated Scaled LM, Pesaran CD and LM test to evaluate cross-sectional reliance. The results of these tests are analysed below:

H_0 = There is no cross-section dependence among variables.

H_1 = There is cross- section dependence among variables.

The provided findings present the outcomes of cross-section dependence tests across various variables, for the poverty headcount ratio at $2.15/day and the Gini coefficient reveals significant findings across various statistical measures. Firstly, when considering the Breusch-Pagan, Pesaran scaled, and Bias correlated tests for both variables, all these tests demonstrate significance in terms of statistical measures (p-values) as well as the test statistics themselves. This implies a strong indication of cross-section dependence for both the poverty headcount ratio and the Gini co-efficient. It is obvious that poverty is a significant cause for income inequality and vice-versa. However, a noteworthy contrast emerges when examining the Pesaran CD test results. For both variables, a negative correlation is observed in terms of the test statistics, suggesting a potential lack of cross-section dependence. Yet, when considering the probability values, only the Gini coefficient exhibits significance with a value below 0.05. This discrepancy implies that while there might be some indication of cross-section dependence for the Gini coefficient according to Pesaran CD, it's less pronounced or not present for the Poverty Headcount ratio. In contrast to these findings, the rest of the variables under examination show significant results in both probability & statistical measures. This suggests a consistent presence of cross-section dependence across these additional variables.

Table 2. Results of cross-section dependence test

Variables/Tests	Breusch-Pagan LM		Pesaran scaled LM		Bias-corrected scaled LM		Pesaran CD	
	Statistics	Prob.	Statistics	Prob.	Statistics	Prob.	Statistics	Prob.
Poverty headcount ratio at $2.15/day	1264.474	0.0000	68.42379	0.0000	67.97642	0.0000	-1.8631	0.0624
Government spending on health & education	1315.596	0.0000	71.52351	0.0000	71.07614	0.0000	26.05091	0.0000
Gini coefficient	687.3540	0.0000	33.43075	0.0000	32.98338	0.0000	-2.4334	0.0150
Life expectancy at birth	2553.183	0.0000	146.5633	0.0000	146.1159	0.0000	50.4600	0.0000
Total health expenditure	2564.136	0.0000	147.2274	0.0000	146.7800	0.0000	50.62799	0.0000

Source: Author's estimation using E-views12 statistical software.

Kao-Cointegration Test: The long-run relationship among variables is examined using the cointegration test (Table 3). The study used the Kao-Cointegration test to examine the co-integration between the variables. The results are given below:

H0 = There is no Long – Run Co-integration among the series.

H1 = There is Long – Run Cointegration among the series.

The results of t- statistic reveal that the coefficient for one of the independent variables is about 1.49 standard errors away from zero. The outcome of the analysis suggests that there may not be a significant linear relationship between the poverty headcount ratio at $2.15/day and the independent variables at the 0.05 significance level. However, it is significant at 0.10 significance level.

Table 3. Kao-Cointegration test (having poverty as dependent)

ADF	t-statistics -9.287152	Prob. Value (0.10 significance level) 0.0000
Residual Variance	0.780885	
HAC Variance	1.322595	

Source: Author's estimation using E-views12 statistical software.

Panel ARDL Test: After conducting unit root, cross-section dependence, and Kao-Cointegration tests, the panel ARDL model is estimated (Table 4). It enables the estimation of long-run relationships in a panel data context while controlling for individual and time-specific effects, making it valuable for analysing the effects of policies or shocks across various countries or regions over time.

Table 4. Estimates of panel ARDL test

Variables	Coefficient	Std. Error	t-statistics	Prob.*
Long Run Equation				
Government_Spending_on_Healt...	0.423325	0.129587	3.266730	0.0014
Gini_Coefficient ...	0.618952	0.077885	7.947037	0.0000
Life Expectancy At Birth...	0.869277	0.069410	12.52382	0.0000
Total_Health_Expenditure...	-0.018705	0.002285	-8.186525	0.0000
Short Run Equation				
Cointeq01	-0.046129	0.039671	-1.162779	0.2468
D (Poverty Headcount Ratio At...	-0.135619	0.152123	-0.891508	0.3741
D (Government_Spending_On_Healt...	-0.026976	0.020646	-1.306612	0.1934
D (Government_Spending_On_Healt...	-0.009630	0.016424	-0.586350	0.5585
D(Gini_Coefficient)	0.004733	0.017602	0.268867	0.7884
D (Gini_Coefficient (-1))	-0.034591	0.028249	-1.224494	0.2227
D (Life_Expectancy_At_Birth)	-0.076598	0.038941	-1.967029	0.0510
D (Life_Expectancy_At_Birth (-1))	0.004495	0.026498	0.169638	0.8655
D(Total_Health_Expenditure)	0.002727	0.002381	1.145347	0.2539
D (Total_Health_Expenditure (-1))	0.000232	0.004831	0.047932	0.9618
Constant term	-0.325769	0.570616	-0.0570908	0.5689
Root MSE	0.294120	Mean dependent var		0.159758
S.D. dependent var	0.900994	S.E. of regression		0.444294
Akaike info. Criterion	-0.773609	Sum Squared resid		29.41218
Schwarz criterion	1.377358	Log-likelihood		322.5135
Hannan-Quinn criteria	0.083460			

Source: Author's estimation using E-views12 statistical software.

Following hypothesis are tested under ARDL test in this chapter:

H_0 = There does not exist long run relationship between dependent and independent variables.

H_1 = There exists long run relationship between dependent and independent variables.

The results of a regression analysis that investigate the relationship with key socioeconomic indicators including government spending on health and education, Gini coefficient, life expectancy at birth, & total health expenditure against poverty headcount ratio at \$2.15/day is provided in Table 4. The long-run equation reveals that there is a positive and significant relationship between the variables of socio-economic indicators against the poverty headcount ratio at \$2.15/day except for total health expenditure. Moyo et al. (2022) also reported a two-ways causal relationship between poverty and human capital. While both coefficient and *t*-statistics are negative but prob. value shows a significant impact over the factor on poverty which means that it indirectly contributes to poverty alleviation through other socioeconomic factors not captured in the model. In the long run, the government expenditure has a positive impact (with coefficient value 0.42) on reducing poverty headcount ratio while it has a negative impact (with coefficient value -0.13, -0.03, -0.009) at different time lags. This indicated that the government investment in health and education may need more time to get better education and health outcomes that may reduce the poverty head count ratio. It means the government investment in the health and education sector would be effective to reduce poverty after long-time. Therefore, the government should allocate huge funds in both the sectors for poverty eradication.

The coefficients for life expectancy and Gini coefficient are 0.61 and 0.87 in the long run, while the respective values are different at different time lags. The short-run equation reveals that none of the variables appeared significant to poverty headcount ratio at \$2.15/day either in terms of prob. value (except life expectancy at birth or in terms of statistics) While Gini coefficient, total health expenditure, and lagged value of life expectancy at birth and total health expenditure reveals their statistically significant correlation with poverty. The estimates suggest that most variables might not individually explain changes in poverty at \$2.15/day. Factors related to health, income distribution (as measured by the Gini Coefficient), and previous periods' health expenditure levels play crucial roles in determining poverty levels at the \$2.15/day. While other variables included in the model might not have significant direct effects on poverty at this specific threshold. It suggests the complexity of poverty dynamics and the need for targeted interventions addressing healthcare access, income distribution, and their long-term impacts on poverty alleviation.

CONCLUSION

The findings suggested that government spending on health and education, the Gini coefficient, life expectancy at birth and total health expenditure have a significant impact on poverty. The findings emphasise the need for inclusive policy measures that address the issue of investment in human capital, i.e. healthcare and education, income distribution and sustaining economic growth by focussing on poverty eradication in the G20 countries. This study highlighted the need to focus on solutions to fight poverty globally in a customized manner as there are disparities in life expectancy. The government spending on health and education would lead to reducing poverty and income inequality across different economies. Therefore, the study recommends that to tackle the problem of poverty, there is a requirement to focus on developing the human capital for the well-being of people in different economies (Bekele et al., 2014). Therefore, the said economies must develop a comprehensive approach that integrates health, education and poverty reduction strategies for promoting sustainable development (SD) and to achieve SDGs by the 2030s.

POLICY IMPLICATIONS

This study concluded that poverty and income inequality have a causal association in the G20 countries. Further, income inequalities and poverty have a complex association with socio-economic factors and other policy factors. It delivers several practical and viable policy suggestions to eradicate poverty and to reduce income inequalities in the G20 countries. Income-based taxation policies, more job opportunities to low income-group communities, control inflation, trade openness, and conductive policies for small and medium farmers would be useful to increase economic capacity of the people, and reduce income inequality. Education and employment levels also seemed significant factors to reduce poverty and income inequality in the G20 countries. Thus, the G20 countries need to reinforce the education quality of their populations to increase human skill development and make them economically and socially productive. High population growth is a significant cause for increasing income inequality and poverty in many countries. Thus, policy makers are needed to control high population growth with greater priority to increase human well-being.

India is a largely agriculture intensive economy, therefore to increase the share of this sector in India's GDP which may be effective to control income inequality and poverty. Mallick (2009) also suggested that government expenditure in the agricultural sector would be crucial to reduce rural poverty in largely agricultural intensive countries like India, Brazil and China. The government should increase public spending in education and health sectors to increase life expectancy of people to achieve SDG1 in the G20 countries (Yang et al., 2020). The G20 countries should also increase extensive investment in the social sector to achieve SDGs (Pradhan et al., 2023). The development of the tourism industry would bring multiple opportunities to create sources of livelihood security of the local people (Khizar et al., 2023). However, extensive development of the tourism industry may be accountable to increase resource depletion (Moslehpour et al., 2023). Hence, the tourism industry may not be conducive to improving all components and drivers of SDGs. Hence, the G20 countries should promote the tourism industry for poverty eradication and to reduce income inequality in G20 countries.

SIGNIFICANCE AND INNOVATION OF THE CHAPTER

The current chapter examines the impact of certain independent variables (i.e., government expenditure in health, public spending in education, total health expenditure and life expectancy at birth) on poverty in selected G20 countries. For this investigation, it uses the ARDL model and explains the association of poverty with government spending in health and education sectors, income inequality, total health expenditure and life expectancy in short-run and long-run. Thereupon, it highlights that capital expenditure is essential to reduce poverty and income inequality. Accordingly, capital expenditure would be useful to increase life expectancy, health quality and well-being of people. Hence, it attracts the attention of policy makers from the G20 countries to increase public spending to reduce poverty, and to achieve SDG1. Therefore, the chapter makes a significant contribution in the existing literature.

LIMITATIONS AND FURTHER RESEARCH DIRECTIONS

The chapter used limited variables in the empirical investigation. However, poverty depends on multiple variables like food security, agricultural production, employment opportunities, trade openness, foreign direct investment, technological change, digitalization, etc. These variables play a significant role in increasing social and economic development in multiple ways. Also, many goals of SDGs like no poverty, zero hunger, women empowerment, technological development, quality education and literacy etc. can be attained as including above-mentioned indicators in policy formulation. However, these variables could not be included in the empirical investigation of this chapter. Hence, further study can consider underlined indicators for increasing SD across countries. Furthermore, there are many measures of poverty like relative and absolute measure of poverty, cultural poverty, political poverty, etc. However, this chapter could consider the head count ratio as the best measurement of poverty. Thus, the above-mentioned points are the limitations of this chapter.

Further study can also examine the impact on multiple indicators on various forms of poverty.

Nowadays, global countries are giving more priority to tourism to enhance infrastructural development and social welfare. Development of tourism industry would work as a great driver to create jobs for local people, physical infrastructure, and generate foreign revenue (Kc et al., 2021). Further, the tourism industry would be supportive to increase per capita income, social welfare, and social equity. Also, it would be effective to reduce poverty and income inequality (Khizar et al., 2023). Thus, it would also play a positive role to increase SD. However, the present study could not examine the impact of the tourism industry on SDG1 (no poverty). Existing researchers, therefore, can also examine the role of the tourism industry for promoting local development, environmental development and social welfare of the people in the next study. Further study can also be considered to examine the impact of poverty on quality of life across countries. Also, further study can be devoted to assess the impact of inequalities in human, environmental, social and public resources on poverty in G20 countries. Most specifically, the research community can assess the interconnection of various SDGs with poverty in global countries. Existing researchers also observe the impact of poverty alleviation programs on chronic poverty and other SDGs.

REFERENCES

Akinwale, Y. O. (2021). Energy consumption, trade openness and economic growth: Empirical evidence from Nigeria. *International Journal of Energy Economics and Policy*, 11(6), 373–380. 10.32479/ijeep.11617

Al-Yousif, Y. K. (2008). Education expenditure and economic growth: Some empirical evidence from the GCC countries. *Journal of Developing Areas*, 42(1), 69–80. https://www.jstor.org/stable/40376194. 10.1353/jda.0.0025

Arora, R., & Sarker, T. (2022). Financing for sustainable development goals (SDGs) in the era of COVID-19 and beyond. *European Journal of Development Research*, 35(1), 1–19. 10.1057/s41287-022-00571-936620200

Azam, M., & Awan, A. M. (2022). Health is wealth: A dynamic sur approach of examining a link between climate changes and human health expenditures. *Social Indicators Research*, 163(2), 505–528. 10.1007/s11205-022-02904-x

Balaji, B. (2011). Causal nexus between public health expenditure and economic growth in four southern Indian states. *The IUP Journal of Public Finance, IX*(3), 7–22. https://ideas.repec.org//a/icf/icfjpf/v09y2011i3p7-22.html

Barro, R. J., & Lee, J. W. (2013). A new data set of educational attainment in the world, 1950–2010. *Journal of Development Economics*, 104, 184–198. 10.1016/j.jdeveco.2012.10.001

Bedir, S. (2016). Healthcare expenditure and economic growth in developing countries. *Advances in Economics and Business*, 4(2), 76–86. 10.13189/aeb.2016.040202

Bekele, M., Sassi, M., Jemal, K., & Ahmed, B. (2024). Human capital development and economic sustainability linkage in Sub-Saharan African countries: Novel evidence from augmented mean group approach. *Heliyon*, 10(2), 1–14. 10.1016/j.heliyon.2024.e2432338293427

Bhargava, A., Jamison, D. T., Lau, L. J., & Murray, C. J. L. (2001). Modeling the effects of health on economic growth. *Journal of Health Economics*, 20(3), 423–440. 10.1016/S0167-6296(01)00073-X11373839

Bhat, R., & Jain, N. (2004). *Time series analysis of private health care expenditures and GDP: Co-integration results with structural breaks* [Working Paper]. https://vslir.iima.ac.in:8443/xmlui/handle/11718/1954

Bloom, D. E., Canning, D., & Sevilla, J. (2004). The effect of health on economic growth: A production function approach. *World Development*, 32(1), 1–13. 10.1016/j.worlddev.2003.07.002

Chelliah, R. J., & Shanmugam, K. R. (2007). Strategy for poverty reduction and narrowing regional disparities. *Economic and Political Weekly*, 42(34), 3475–3481. https://www.jstor.org/stable/4419942

Currie, J., & Moretti, E. (2003). Mother's education and the intergenerational transmission of human capital: Evidence from college openings. *The Quarterly Journal of Economics*, 118(4), 1495–1532. 10.1162/003355303322552856

Dias, J., & Tebaldi, E. (2012). Institutions, human capital, and growth: The institutional mechanism. *Structural Change and Economic Dynamics*, 23(3), 300–312. 10.1016/j.strueco.2012.04.003

Gaspar, V., Amaglobeli, D., Garcia-Escribano, D., Prady, D., & Soto, M. (2019). *Fiscal policy and development: human, social, physical investment for SDGs*. IMF Staff Discussion Note. https://www.imf.org/en/Publications/Staff-Discussion-Notes/Issues/2019/01/18/Fiscal-Policy-and-Development-Human-Social-and-Physical-Investments-for-the-SDGs-46444

Gebrehiwo, K. G. (2016). The impact of human capital development on economic growth in Ethiopia: Evidence from ARDL approach to co-integration. *Bahir Dar Journal of Education*, 16(1), 1–23. https://www.ajol.info/index.php/bdje/article/view/249033

Ghosh, J. (2010). *Poverty reduction in China and India: policy implication and trends*. (DESA Working Paper No. 92, ST/ESA/2010/DWP/92).

Ghosh, P., & Cheruvalath, R. (2007). Indian female entrepreneurs as catalysis for economic growth and development. *International Journal of Entrepreneurship and Innovation*, 8(2), 139–147. 10.5367/000000007780808048

Ghosh, P. K., Shariff, A., & Mondal, S. K. (2002). *Indian public expenditure on social sector and poverty alleviation programmes during the 1990s*. (Working Paper 169). National Council of Applied Economic Research Human Development Division, Overseas Development Institute, Westminster, London, UK.

Guijarro, F., & Poyatos, J. A. (2018). Designing a sustainable development goal index through a Goal programming model: The case of EU-28 countries. *Sustainability*, 10, 1-17.

Hanushek, E. A., & Woessmann, L. (2007). *The role of education quality for economic growth* (SSRN Scholarly Paper 960379). https://papers.ssrn.com/abstract=96037910.1596/1813-9450-4122

Howitt, P. (2005). Health, human capital, and economic growth: A schumpeterian perspective. In López-Casasnovas, G., Rivera, B., & Currais, L. (Eds.), *Health and Economic Growth* (pp. 19–40). The MIT Press., 10.7551/mitpress/3451.003.0005

Ighodalo, A. (2012). Poverty and sustainable socio-economic development in Africa: The Nigeria experience. *European Scientific Journal, 8*(26), 51-65. chrome-extension://efaidnbmnnnibpcajpcglclefindmkaj/https://core.ac.uk/download/pdf/236412432.pdf

Jin, H., Qian, X., Chin, T., & Zhang, H. (2020). A global assessment of sustainable development based on modification of the human development index via the Entropy method. *Sustainability (Basel), 12*(8), 1–20. 10.3390/su12083251

Kc, B., Dhungana, A., & Dangi, T. B. (2021). Tourism and the sustainable development goals: Stakeholders' perspectives from Nepal. *Tourism Management Perspectives,* 38(1), 1–13. 10.1016/j.tmp.2021.100822

Khizar, H. M. U., Younas, A., Kumari, S., Akbar, A., & Poulova, P. (2023). The progression of sustainable development goals in tourism: A systematic literature review of past achievements and future promises. *Journal of Innovation & Knowledge,* 8(4), 12–23. 10.1016/j.jik.2023.100442

Koirala, B. S., & Pradhan, G. (2019). Determinants of sustainable development: Evidence from 12 Asian countries. *Sustainable Development (Bradford),* 28(3), 1–7. 10.1002/sd.1963

Kumar, S., Kumar, N., & Vivekadhish, S. (2016). Millennium development goals (MDGs) to sustainable development goals (SDGs): Addressing unfinished agenda and strengthening sustainable development and partnership. *Indian Journal of Community Medicine,* 41(1), 1–4. 10.4103/0970-0218.17095526917865

Lee, J., & Barro, R. J. (2001). Schooling quality in a cross-section of countries. *Economica,* 68(272), 465–488. https://www.jstor.org/stable/3549114. 10.1111/1468-0335.00257

Li, C., Zhao, G., Koh, K. P., Xu, Z., Yue, M., Wang, W., Tan, Y., & Wu, L. (2024). Impact of China's financial development on the sustainable development goals of the Belt and Road Initiative participating countries. *Humanities & Social Sciences Communications,* 11(294), 1–12. 10.1057/s41599-024-02791-2

Mallick, S. (2009). Macroeconomic policy and poverty reduction in India. *IGIDR Proceeding/Project Report Series.*

Mehrara, M. (2011). Health expenditure and economic growth: An ardl approach for the case of Iran. *Journal of Economics and Behavioral Studies*, 3(4), 249–256. https://ideas.repec.org//a/rnd/arjebs/v3y2011i4p249-256.html. 10.22610/jebs.v3i4.277

Moslehpour, M., Firman, A., & Lin, C. H. (2023). The moderating impact of government support on the relationship between tourism development and growth, natural resources depletion, sociocultural degradation, economic environment, and pollution reduction: case of Indonesian economy. *Environmental Science and Pollution Research, 30*(1), 56863–56878. 10.1007/s11356-023-26231-x

Moyo, C., Mishi, S., & Ncwadi, R. (2022). Human capital development, poverty and income inequality in Eastern cape province. *Development Studies Research*, 9(1), 36–47. 10.1080/21665095.2022.2032236

Nurudeen, A., & Usman, A. (2010). Government expenditure and economic growth in Nigeria, 1970-2008: A disaggregated analysis. *Business and Economics Journal*, 4(1), 11. https://www.hilarispublisher.com/abstract/government-expenditure-and-economic-growth-in-nigeria-19702008-a-disaggregated-analysis-29819.html

Ogungbenle, S., Olawumi, O. R., & Obasuyi, F. O. T. (2013). *Life expectancy, public health spending and economic growth in nigeria: A vector autoregressive (Var) model*. CORE. https://core.ac.uk/display/236408152?utm_source=pdf&utm_medium=banner&utm_campaign=pdf-decoration-v1

Our world in data. (2023). Our World in Data. [Online]. https://ourworldindata.org

Pesaran, M. H., & Shin, Y. (1995). *Autoregressive distributed lag modelling approach to cointegration analysis*. (DAE Working Paper Series No. 9514). Department of Economics, University of Cambridge, Cambridge.

Pradhan, B., Yadav, S., Ghosh, J., & Prashad, A. (2023). Achieving the sustainable development goals (SDGs) in the Indian states of Odisha: Challenges and opportunities. *World Development Sustainability*, 3(1), 43–52. 10.1016/j.wds.2023.100078

Prasetyanto, P. K., & Sari, F. (2021). Environmental Kuznets curve: Economic growth with environmental degradation in Indonesia. *International Journal of Energy Economics and Policy*, 11(5), 622–628. 10.32479/ijeep.11609

Psacharopoulos, G., & Patrinos, H. A. (2004). Returns to investment in education: A further update. *Education Economics*, 12(2), 111–134. 10.1080/0964529042000239140

Romer, P. M. (1990). Endogenous technological change. *Journal of Political Economy*, 98(5), 71–102. 10.1086/261725

Saini, M., Sengupta, E., Singh, M., Singh, H., & Singh, J. (2023). Sustainable development goal for quality education (SDG 4): A study on SDG 4 to extract the pattern of association among the indicators of SDG 4 employing a genetic algorithm. *Education and Information Technologies*, 28(2), 2031–2069. 10.1007/s10639-022-11265-435975216

Singh, A. K., Issac, J., & Narayanan, K. G. S. (2019). Measurement of environmental sustainability index and its association with socio-economic indicators in selected Asian economies: An empirical investigation. *International Journal of Environment and Sustainable Development*, 18(1), 57–100. 10.1504/IJESD.2019.098641

Singh, A. K., & Jyoti, B. (2023). *Impact of digitalization on global sustainable development across countries*. Green and Low-carbon Economy., 10.47852/bonviewGLCE32021482

Singh, A. K., Jyoti, B., Kumar, S., & Lenka, S. K. (2021). Assessment of global sustainable development, environmental sustainability, economic development and social development index in selected economies. *International Journal of Sustainable Development and Planning*, 16(1), 123–138. 10.18280/ijsdp.160113

Singh, A. K., & Kumar, S. (2022). Exploring the impact of sustainable development on social-economic, and science and technological development in selected countries: A panel data analysis. *Society & Sustainability*, 4(1), 55–83. 10.38157/ss.v4i1.405

Singh, A. K., Kumar, S., & Jyoti, B. (2022b). Impact of the COVID-19 on food security and sustainable development goals in India: Evidence from existing literature. GNOSI: An *Interdisciplinary Journal of Human Theory and Praxis*, 5(2), 94-109. http://gnosijournal.com/index.php/gnosi/article/view/196/225

Singh, A. K., Kumar, S., Sharma, A. K., & Sinha, S. (2022a). Does green entrepreneurship have an association with sustainable development and its components? Evidence from a country-wise panel data investigation. In Magd, M., Singh, D., Spicer, D., & Syed, R. T. (Eds.), *International Perspectives on Value Creation and Sustainability Through Social Entrepreneurship* (pp. 132–172). IGI Global. https://www.igi-global.com/gateway/chapter/30982910.4018/978-1-6684-4666-9.ch008

Singh, A. K., Sharma, A. K., & Jyoti, B. (2023a). Does economic development have a causal relationship with environmental degradation? Experience from different income group countries. In Sart, G. (Ed.), *Considerations on Education for Economic, Social, and Environmental Sustainability* (pp. 300–333). IGI Global. 10.4018/978-1-6684-8356-5.ch015

Singh, A. K., & Sharma, P. (2018). Implications of climatic and non-climatic variables on food security in developing economies: A conceptual review. *MOJ Food Processing & Technology*, 6(1), 1–12. 10.15406/mojfpt.2018.06.00138

Singh, A. K., Sharma, S. K., & Lenka, S. K. (2023b). Causality between green entrepreneurship and sustainable development: A cross-country analysis using ARDL model. *The IUP Journal of Applied Economics*, 22(1), 5–38.

Singh, A. K., Singh, B. J., & Negi, V. (2020). Does sustainable development have a causal relationship with environmental development? Evidence from a country-wise panel data analysis. *International Journal of Technology Management & Sustainable Development*, 19(2), 147–171. 10.1386/tmsd_00020_1

Singh, S., & Jayaram, R. (2020). Attainment of the sustainable development goal of poverty eradication: A review, critique, and research agenda. *Journal of Public Affairs*, 22(1), 1–10. 10.1002/pa.2294

Subramanian, S. (2005). *Headcount poverty comparisons*. International Poverty Centre (United Nations Development Programmes) (IPC) SBS – Ed. BNDES, Brasilia, Brazil. http://www.ipc-undp.org/pub/IPCOnePager18.pdf

Ullah, A., Pinglu, C., Ullah, S., & Hashmi, S. H. (2021). Nexus of regional integration, socioeconomic determinants and sustainable development in belt and road initiative countries. *PLoS One*, 16(7), 1–29. 10.1371/journal.pone.025429834242342

Wahab, A. A. A. O., Kefeli, Z., & Hashim, N. (2018). *Investigating the dynamic effect of healthcare expenditure and education expenditure on economic growth in organisation of Islamic countries (Oic)* [MPRA Paper]. https://mpra.ub.uni-muenchen.de/90338/

Yadav, N., Gupta, M., Sharma, V., Yadav, D. K., & Sharma, A. K. (2024). How can the G-20 enhance its accountability and effectiveness? a comparative analysis of existing and proposed mechanisms. *Academy of Marketing Studies Journal*, 28(S3), 1-11. chrome-extension://efaidnbmnnnibpcajpcglclefindmkaj/https://www.abacademies.org/articles/how-can-the-g20-enhance-its-accountability-and-effectiveness-a-comparative-analysis-of-existing-and-proposed-mechanisms.pdf

Yang, S., Zhao, W., Liu, Y., Cherubini, F., Fu, B., & Pereira, P. (2020). Prioritizing sustainable development goals and linking them to ecosystem services: A global expert's knowledge evaluation. *Geography and Sustainability*, 1(4), 321–330. 10.1016/j.geosus.2020.09.004

Zile, S. (2016). Sustainable development goals challenges and opportunities. *Indian Journal of Public Health*, 60(4), 247–250. 10.4103/0019-557X.19586227976644

Chapter 3
Linkage Between Pro–Poor Tourism Development and Sustainable Development Goals:
Case of Bangladesh and India

Anita Medhekar
https://orcid.org/0000-0002-6791-4056
Central Queensland University, Australia

Mallika Roy
https://orcid.org/0000-0002-5854-5084
University of Chittagong, Bangladesh

ABSTRACT

Chapter provides an overview of the Bangladesh and the Indian economy and the contribution of tourism as an engine of growth to both the countries Both the countries pro-poor tourism development policies to meet United Nations SDGs are presented as a case. The challenges they face for implementing pro-poor tourism policies and opportunities in linking and achieving SDGs by developing and implementing pro-poor tourism policies is discussed amidst the local and global climate change challenges, public health emergencies and supply chain disruptions. The next section will discuss and critique the government policies- if tourism development in both the countries is pro-poor that includes bottom of the economic pyramid people that act as a catalyst for achieving the SDGs, or NOT? with managerial and policy

DOI: 10.4018/979-8-3693-3166-8.ch003

recommendations and a development of an equitable, pro-poor tourism policy/business model, followed by conclusion.

INTRODUCTION

Tourism sector can be used as an engine of growth for pro-poor economic development and power of pro-poor tourism development is under-estimated to achieve numerous United Nations Sustainable Development Goals (UN-SDGs) such as SDG-1 no poverty, SDG-2 no hunger, SDG-3 reduce inequality, SDG-6 clean water and sanitation, SDG-11 sustainable cities and communities, and SDG-8 decent work/employment creation for the poor to meet socio-economic goals (United Nations, 2024). In many developing countries, poor or 'Bottom of the Economic Pyramid' (BoEP) people have been excluded (invisible people) from the tourism economy, as consumers, producers, employers, or employees. Tourism can play a significant role in targeting pro-poor tourism development in rural areas to reduce poverty, promote equity, employment creation and improve supply chains and contribute to UN-SDGs (Chok *et al.*, 2007; Gantait *et al.*, 2021; Jeyacheya & Hampton 2020; Roy *et al.*, 2010; Spenceley, 2022; Soliman, 2018; Suntikul *et al.*, 2009). In populated developing countries of Bangladesh and India in the South Asian region involving BoEP people in tourism policy-making and development, employment, and micro-entrepreneurship, will empower the most vulnerable and create value by achieving SDGs and providing net benefits. Roy *et al.* (2020), in their study, suggest that through self-help and tourism-related employment, poor-people development should be promoted to effectively participate in their own development process and improve their socio-economic status.

Poverty is defined by the Asian Development Bank (ADB, 1999) "deprivation of essential assets and opportunities to which every human is entitled". Therefore, poverty is where a person's lack access to basic needs of nutritious food, clean drinking water, sanitation, clothing, shelter, health-care, education, and employment opportunities. Pro-poor development of tourism and linking it to SDGs could provide local poor living around the centuries old heritage tourism sites and places of worship with government employment opportunities in the tourism sector such as cleaners, gardeners, interpreters, tour guides, sales-persons at tourist's retail food and souvenirs shops and tourist first-aid and wheelchair support. The role that tourism can play in pro-poor economic development is under-estimated in developing countries, which is linked to achieving numerous SDGs by including the marginalized sections of society. This is only possible according to Adie *et al.* (2022) through parentships between various stakeholders.

Therefore, pro-poor tourism-led economic growth in developing countries is the driver of bringing about a positive social, economic, and environmental sustainability, including poor people's empowerment, by changing the perception and involving the local poor in tourism policy development and ownership of their local heritage monuments, sites, people, and places of worship and contributing to uplift their own wellbeing and generating economic benefits for themselves, households, society, and the economy, in Bangladesh and India. It is therefore imperative for these counties to not only reduce poverty by adopting por-poor inclusive economic development and growth strategies but also achieve sustainable development gaols.

In the 21st century poor people in Africa, Bangladesh, India, and the world over are still facing barriers and challenges in terms of inclusive pro-poor economic development due to infrastructure bottlenecks and lack of education which hinders their inclusion in various sectors of the formal economy (Medhekar & Roy, 2010). Therefore, linking SDGs with pro-poor tourism development in both countries will be an essential strategy for pro-poor development of tourism policy and business models. For pro-poor tourism development public-private partnerships (PPPs) and government promotion like 'Incredible India Campaigns,' to attract foreign direct investment (FDI) in related businesses via SWOT analysis is essential in both the countries (Medhekar, 2022; Roy, 2021).

The seventh five-year plan strategy paper (2016-2020) of Bangladesh highlighted three different types of tourism: nature, culture, and religion (Government of Bangladesh, 2016). Whereas India's 12th Five-Year Plan (2012-2017) clearly outlines promoting brand "Incredible India" and sustainable pro-poor tourism economic development, which us tourism-led for employment creation for inclusive growth (Government of India, 2012; Gaur & Koltru, 2018; Pérez-Rodríguez *et al.,* 2021; Rauniyar & Kanbur, 2006). Government of India has under-incredible India campaign, (https://www.incredibleindia.org/content/incredible-india-v2/en.html) has developed various niche tourism types such as Sustainable Tourism, Eco- and Wildlife, wellness and medical, Cruise, Golf, Polo, Dolphin, Desert, MICE (meetings, incentives, conferences, and exhibitions) and Wedding Destinations, Train, Heritage and Spiritual/Religious tourism.

The introductory section of the chapter provides an overview of the Bangladesh and Indian economy and the contribution of tourism to both the countries. This is followed by a literature review on pro-poor tourism development to meet UN-SDGs. Tourism development policies related to Bangladesh and India are presented as a case. The challenges they face for implementing pro-poor tourism policies and opportunities in linking and achieving SDGs by developing and implementing pro-poor tourism policies is discussed amidst the local and global climate change challenges, public health emergencies and supply chain disruptions. The next section will discuss and critique the government policies- if tourism development in both countries is pro-poor that includes BoEP people that act as a catalyst for achieving the SDGs, or NOT? with managerial and policy recommendations and development of an equitable, pro-poor tourism policy/business model, followed by a conclusion.

LITERATURE REVIEW

Tourism and Developing Countries

In developing countries and island economies pro-poor tourism-led economic growth is the key pillar of economic development and growth, as it can significantly reduce poverty, hunger by providing job opportunities and empowering the poor to improve their livelihood (Boonsiritomachai & Phonthanukitithaworn, 2019; Eluwole et al., 2022). Over the past decade, developing countries have experienced rapid expansion within the global tourism industry. This growth can be attributed to various factors including rising economic prosperity, increased disposable income and leisure opportunities, enhanced political stability, and proactive tourism promotional efforts. Despite facing numerous challenges in the realm of tourism, developing countries boast a multitude of advantages in terms of tourism destinations generating significant revenue for the countries.

According to Gomes (2020), a study in Cox's Bazar Bangladesh, the two main factors that determine the contribution of the pro-poor tourism value chain to poor households' income are from the (i) extent of linkages in supply chains, and (ii) the number of poor people directly employed in businesses. Whereas Ara et al (2021) study found that poor people in Cox Bazar, Kuakata, and Rangamati areas were not aware that tourism can improve their livelihood and provide employment opportunities. Roy and Roy (2015) mentioned that Bangladesh cannot attract tourists due to few limitations. Roy et al. (2020) conducted a study on the economic contribution of tourism in Bangladesh and found that tourism investment contributes to economic growth and recommended focusing on capital investment in tourism in Bangladesh.

Roy (2010) applied the multiple regression for panel data for examining the relationship between tourism, poverty, and per-capita income to study the relationship. Findings of this empirical study is that the net-benefit of Indian tourism development did not trickle down to the poorest of poor, which is contrary to the empirical evidence for other developing countries. Developing countries need empirical government data as evidence to prove that the net-benefits of tourism-led economic growth are trickling down (Singh, 2022).

Ashley *et al.* (2001) provided a conceptual idea of discussing the important role played by different stakeholder's that is pro-poor tourism partnerships between public, private, non-government organisations, and target group of poor-people for achieving the objective of pro-poor tourism development projects based on destinations. Goodwin (2006) studied the different ways of measuring the local economic impact of tourism on poverty reduction and meeting the World Trade Organisations Millennium Development Goal (MDGs), in the developing countries of Egypt to agricultural communities, market access to workers from the informal sector in Gambia, and coffee farmers in Tanzania. Goodwin (2006) concludes that it is difficult to measure the trickle-down net benefits to the local poor community.

Pro-Poor Tourism Development Theories

Pro-poor tourism development strategies aim is to have all-inclusive development by increasing the net benefit for the poor population and empower them to meet 17- SDGs and uplift them out of poverty. Pro-poor tourism development refers to tourism projects and programs that are developed in a way that aims to alleviates poverty and provides tangible benefit to the poorest segments of society, including opportunities for employment, income generation, uplifting their socio-economic living standards and empowerment.

The two terms 'pro-poor inclusive growth' and 'pro-poor inclusive development' are used interchangeably or are complimentary strategies applied by the developing countries to reflect the socio-economic realities of the poor-people of their country. Asian Development Banks (1999) poverty reduction by inclusive growth strategy can be interpreted "either narrowly or broadly" (p1). That is a narrow definition of pro-poor inclusive growth is applied if the focus is placed on economic growth. In this context Sen (1999) mentions that human capabilities are instruments as driving tools to accelerate economic growth. The economic indicators used to measure growth are demand-side factors and depends on people's employment, income, and distribution of income (through fiscal policies such as tax system).

The broader definition of pro-poor inclusive development places greater value on non-income measures of development such as access to (basic-capabilities) education, health housing, nutritious food, credit/finance, and infrastructure facilities. This border definition is led by the supply-side factors to determine whether – (i) the poor people have the basic human capabilities that are available and accessible to them to be capable to be employed and can socially participate in the society in a productive manner for social inclusion, and secondly (ii) other (non-basic) capabilities exist that would lead to being gainfully employed and productive outcomes for the individual, society, and the economy.

Three theoretical domains underlying tourism in developing countries can be applied: (i) pro-poor tourism development approach (Spenceley, 2022), (ii) capability approach (Sen, 1999), (iii) tourism development, poverty reduction, and empowerment approach (Timothy, 2007)

(i) Tourism has the potential to redistribute wealth by generating income and employment opportunities for local communities in impoverished regions, because tourism serves as a significant source of foreign exchange earnings for many of the poorest countries, contributing to their economic development and sustainability (Spenceley & Meyer, 2012; Spenceley, 2022).

(ii) The capability approach, introduced by economist and philosopher Noble laureate Amartya Sen, has been extensively utilised to assess development and well-being across various fields including philosophy, law, health, education, and sociology (Alkire & Deuneulin, 2009). This approach emphasizes the importance of individuals' capabilities and freedoms in assessing their well-being, rather than solely focusing on material wealth or utility. Sen's contributions have "shifted the focus of economics and development studies from an overemphasis on growth towards considerations of individual well-being, agency, and freedom" (Clark, 2005, p. 1340).

(iii) Sen has highlighted the important role of social, political, and economic factors in expanding or restricting individuals' capabilities, and advocates for policies and interventions that enhance people's freedom to lead lives they value. Sen argues that people's capabilities, or their real opportunities to achieve valuable functioning, should be the central focus of development efforts. The capability approach has been applied to analyse poverty, inequality, social justice, and public policy, providing a nuanced understanding of human development beyond traditional economic measures (Deneulin & Shahani, 2009).

However, particularly since the pandemic and post-pandemic, there is a shift of focus for all sectors of the economy from MDGs to achieving United Nations seventeen SDGs. As sustainable use of resources and achieving the 17 Goals are the key for the current and the future generations to survive. Table-1 illustrates how the principles of pro-poor tourism development can be applied in the context of developing countries like Bangladesh and India to promote sustainable and inclusive tourism-led economic growth. Investments in physical and human capital in developing the skills and capabilities of local communities to actively participate in pro-poor policy making and benefit from tourism activities, fostering sustainable development and tourism-led pro-poor economic growth.

Table 1. Examples and principles of pro-poor tourism development

Principles of Pro-Poor Tourism Development	Description	Application in Developing Countries	References
Community Participation	Involving local communities in tourism planning, decision-making, and management processes.	Engaging communities in the development of tourism initiatives to ensure their active involvement and ownership.	Rahman et al., 2022; Sharma, 2011.
Equitable Distribution of Benefits	Ensuring that the benefits generated by tourism are fairly distributed among all stakeholders, poor and marginalized.	Promoting economic opportunities and social benefits from tourism for marginalized communities.	Islam & Carlsen, 2016; Werner, 2009.
Capacity Building	Providing training and skills development opportunities for residents to participate in and benefit from tourism activities.	Offering capacity-building programs to equip communities from developing nations with the skills needed to engage in tourism-related ventures.	Pandey, 2011; Yamashita, 2011.
Sustainable Resource Management	Promoting sustainable practices to minimize negative impacts on natural resources, cultural heritage, and the environment.	Implementing measures to preserve natural beauty and cultural heritage of developing countries while promoting responsible tourism practices.	Aayog, 2018; Hoang, 2021.
Empowerment and Inclusivity	Empowering marginalized groups by creating opportunities for entrepreneurship, leadership, and social inclusion within the tourism sector.	Supporting initiatives that empower women, youth, and indigenous communities to actively participate in and benefit from tourism.	Aayog, 2018; Rahman et al., 2022; Rhaman, 2016.

Source: Developed by authors based on empirical studies

Sustainable Development Goals (SDGs)

Tourism development can contribute to achieving few of the seventeen SDG, by strategically developing and implementing programs for pro-poor development, and environmental conservation and sustainability.

Vinodan *et al*. (2022) study identified that the sustainability facets of pro-poor tourism development in developing countries have five distinct facets such as (i) cultural heritage, (ii) environmental, (iii) societal, (iv) monetary, and (v) governance, which can achieve various SDGs. Various UN-SDGs can be achieved by pro-poor tourism development. Such as SDG-1: No poverty, SDG-2→Zero Hunger, SDG-5→Gender Equality, SDG-8→Decent Work and Economic Growth, SDG-14→ Life below Water, SDG-15→ Life on Land, and SDG-17→ Partnerships for Goal (United Nations, 2024).

Therefore, to develop programs which are Pro-Poor Tourism Development to achieve SDGs should be the objective of government department of tourism. Figure -1 provides the linkages between pro-poor tourism development and UN-SDGs and economic growth.

Figure 1. Pro-Poor tourism development, UN-SDGs, and economic growth linkage

In the context of developing countries, pro-poor tourism development focuses on leveraging the country's natural and cultural assets to create sustainable livelihoods and improve living standards for marginalized communities. This may entail initiatives such as grass-root participation for community-led tourism projects, ecotourism ventures, and cultural heritage preservation efforts that actively involve and benefits host-countries residents. Community engagement led policy development is a vital aspect of rural tourism development, contributing to the sustainability and success of tourism initiatives and empowerment in rural areas (Malek et al., 2017). Involving residents in the planning stages of rural tourism projects ensures that their perspectives, needs, and concerns are considered. This participatory tourism-led pro-poor development approach helps create sustainable tourism experiences that are authentic and reflective of the community's identity (Garrod, 2003).

The advancement of sustainable tourism in a developing country such as Bangladesh and India present a multifaceted challenging factor, demanding a whole-of-the-government approach to a comprehensive strategy. Table 2 outlines and compares various aspects of tourism and sustainability in Bangladesh and India.

Table 2. Aspects of tourism and sustainability in Bangladesh and India

Principles of Pro-Poor Tourism Development	Description	Application in Developing Countries	References
Community Participation	Involving local communities in tourism planning, decision-making, and management processes.	Engaging communities in the development of tourism initiatives to ensure their active involvement and ownership.	Rahman et al., 2022; Sharma, 2011.
Equitable Distribution of Benefits	Ensuring that the benefits generated by tourism are fairly distributed among all stakeholders, poor and marginalized.	Promoting economic opportunities and social benefits from tourism for marginalized communities.	Islam & Carlsen, 2016; Werner, 2009.
Capacity Building	Providing training and skills development opportunities for residents to participate in and benefit from tourism activities.	Offering capacity-building programs to equip communities from developing nations with the skills needed to engage in tourism-related ventures.	Pandey, 2011; Yamashita, 2011.
Sustainable Resource Management	Promoting sustainable practices to minimize negative impacts on natural resources, cultural heritage, and the environment.	Implementing measures to preserve natural beauty and cultural heritage of developing countries while promoting responsible tourism practices.	Aayog, 2018; Hoang, 2021.
Empowerment and Inclusivity	Empowering marginalized groups by creating opportunities for entrepreneurship, leadership, and social inclusion within the tourism sector.	Supporting initiatives that empower women, youth, and indigenous communities to actively participate in and benefit from tourism.	Aayog, 2018; Rahman et al., 2022; Rhaman, 2016.

Among the seventeen SDGs, Bangladesh has made remarkable strides in combating extreme poverty and poverty in general, through various initiatives aimed at fostering rapid economic growth while concurrently adopting strategies and policies to ensure inclusivity, responsiveness, and adaptability throughout the transformation process (Ashraf et al., 2019). According to the World Bank Bangladesh Poverty Assessment report, Bangladesh has made remarkable strides in combating extreme poverty and poverty in general to achieve SDG-1. The incidence of absolute poverty declined from 19.6% to 11.3% between 2010 and 2019, while the proportion of the population living below the national poverty line decreased from 31.5% in 2010 to 21.6% in 2018. The coverage of social safety nets witnessed a substantial increase, reaching 58.1% in 2019 compared to 24.6% in 2010 (World Bank, 2019). However, resource mobilization, particularly from external sources, and the persistent challenge of frequent natural disasters remain significant hurdles in achieving these poverty reduction goals.

Whereas India plays a crucial role in shaping the global success of the SDGs through various strategies (Mishra & Maheshwari, 2020). The sustainability of pro-poor tourism strategies has been explored, with a focus on monetary, environmental, societal, cultural heritage, and governance factors (Vinodan et al., 2022). India's efforts towards achieving SDG-1, which focuses on eradicating poverty in all its forms, entail a multifaceted approach aimed at reducing poverty levels across the country (Ahamad & Narayana, 2020). World Bank's most recent estimates suggest that the percentage of the population living below the international poverty line of $1.90 per day decreased from 21.6% in 2011 to 9.2% in 2020 (Hasell, 2022). This indicates a substantial reduction in the incidence of extreme poverty. However, it's important to note that poverty statistics can vary depending on the measurement method used.

CASE STUDY: BANGLADESH AND INDIA

Bangladesh

Tourism in Bangladesh is a significant and diverse industry that plays a crucial role in the country's economy, contributing to foreign exchange earnings, employment generation, and regional development. The seventh five-year plan strategy paper (2016-2020) of Bangladesh highlighted three different types of tourism: nature, culture, and religion (Government of Bangladesh, 2016). National Tourism Policy, 2010 of Bangladesh focused on physically challenged people, disabled, and women. The tourism industry has the potential to significantly contribute to the country's economy (Hafsa, 2020; Sultana, 2016).

Bangladesh boasts diverse natural landscapes, including the Sundarbans mangrove forest, Cox's Bazar beach, and numerous rivers and hills (Polash & Habeb, 2020). Ahmed et al. (2010) underscores the importance of natural beauty in the selection of tour destinations. The attractiveness of these destinations plays a significant role in attracting tourists (Biswas et al., 2020). While destinations with natural attractions such as Cox's Bazar, St. Martin's Island, and Bandarban offer satisfactory accommodation options for tourists, other historically and archaeologically significant sites lack comparable facilities (Akhy & Roy, 2020).

Nonetheless, the sector encounters obstacles including insufficient research, ineffective marketing strategies, and the absence of a comprehensive tourism policy (Roy & Roy, 2015; Alauddin et al., 2014). Despite these challenges, the industry has been gradually growing and has the potential to contribute significantly to the country's economy (Alauddin et al., 2014). A range of factors influences tourism behaviour and satisfaction in Bangladesh. Several researchers have focused on natural beauty, transportation, and accommodation facilities, safety and security, and costs (Ahmed et al., 2010; Akhy & Roy, 2020; Roy et al., 2016).

The international tourist arrival numbers in Bangladesh according to World Tourism Organization, Yearbook of Tourism Statistics from 1995 to 2019, pre-covid showed a steep increase from 156,000 to 271,000 thousand in 2014 and falling to 200,000 in 2016. Between the period from 2006 to 2009 showing a steep increase to 467, 000 international visitor and falling in 2010 to 139,000, due to the Global Financial Crisis (GFC) and then and then a steep fall in 2013 to 104,000 and steadily rising in 2019 to 323,000 arrivals (WTO, 2019). Bangladesh experienced a significant decline in international tourist arrivals in 2020 due to the pandemic. The data suggests potential challenges in consistently attracting significant tourism spending, influenced by factors such as infrastructure limitations, marketing efforts, and global economic conditions.

Efforts to enhance tourism infrastructure, promote Bangladesh as a tourist destination, and address any underlying constraints may be necessary to bolster tourism spending, employment creation and its contribution to the economy. In Bangladesh, the occupation of tour guide has gained popularity as an early-career employment option. Presently, over 10,000 tour guides and more than 200 travel and tourism companies are actively engaged in providing tourism services (Airways office, 2019). In the fiscal year 2013-14, tourism made a direct contribution of approximately 2.1 percent to Bangladesh's GDP and employed 1.3 million individuals (Planning Commission, 2015, Table 5.3, p. 270).

Further, WTO (1995-2020) data shows that from 1995, there has been a steady increase in the foreign exchange revenue earned from international tourism expenditure from US$ 251,000,000 to US$ 471, 000,000 in the year 2000, a positive trajectory with occasional fluctuations. Further steadily increasing to US$ 735,000,000 in 2008 and falling due to GFC in 2008 to US$ 651,000,000 and thereafter peaking in 2013 to US$ 1.31 billion. And again, due to domestic reasons falling to US$-782,000,000. Given the drop in the number of arrivals, the international tourism expenditure plummeted and steeply dropped from US$1.39 billion in 2019 to US$ 659,000,000 in 2020, due to the impact of the pandemic-associated border closures and travel regulations.

India

India's tourism sector continues to evolve, driven by a combination of cultural richness, natural beauty, and government initiatives. India's 12th Five-Year Plan (2012-2017) clearly outlines pro-poor tourism economic development and employment creation for inclusive growth (Gaur & Koltru, 2018). In the 21st century, tourism is becoming one of the key economic sectors for India under the current governments innovative railway reforms, which promotes inclusive development (Medhekar, 2023). Mishra *et al.* (2011) investigated the dynamics of causal relationship between tourism and economic growth in India. Venugopalan and Kumar (2017) focused on sustainable development through sustainable tourism based on the case study of Kerala. Saad (2021) explored that tourism supports SDGs based on the case study of culture and handicraft tourism in India.

India has centuries old rich cultural and spiritual heritage, diverse landscapes, historical monuments, and a variety of cuisines and languages, which attract millions of tourists from around the world each year for niche tourism segments such as culinary, golf, mountain, coastal, Rajasthan desert, spiritual, wellness, and medical (Kaushal & Yadav, 2021; Medhekar & Haq, 2020). Despite its immense potential, tourism in India faces challenges such as infrastructure bottlenecks, safety concerns, and environmental sustainability issues (Haq & Medhekar, 2019; Roy & Saxena, 2020). However, concerted efforts have been made since -2019 to overcome these challenges by the government incredible India campaigns, infrastructure development, private partnerships, and Indian railways to further boost domestic and inbound tourism sector in India (Medhekar, 2023).

According to The World Bank, Tourism Organization, Yearbook of Tourism Statistics from 1995 to 2019, the international tourists' numbers in India pre-covid showed a steep increase from 2,124, 000 million to 2,726,000 million in 2003 and steadily rising to 5,283, 000 in 2008. Slightly falling due to the GFC to 5,168000 and rising to 5, 968,000 million in 2013. Thereafter in 2014 showing a steep increase to13,107,000 million international visitors to 17, 914, 000 in 2019 (WTO, 2019). Due to pandemic driven travel restrictions and health regulations to stop the spread of the virus, the international tourist arrivals dropped all over the world. Despite these recent setbacks, the overall trend suggests a growing interest in India as a tourist destination over the past two decades, indicating potential for recovery and continued growth in the post-pandemic era due to government policy to encourage domestic tourism by Bharat Gaurav Tourists Train packages, which are also attracting overseas India diaspora for toruisnm in India (Medhekar, 2023).

The WTO international tourist expenditure data for India is available from year 2000 onwards showing a steady increase in the foreign exchange revenue from a low of US$ 3.69 billion in year 2000, and peaking to US$ 12.08 billion in 2008 to US$ 14.11 billion in 2012 showing an increase by approximately US$ 2 billion in international tourists expenditure, probably due to being an affordable destination for foreign tourists earning in Dollars, Euros, and Pounds, during the GFC period, and thereafter peaking in 2020 to US$ 17.58 billion, until the international border closed due to the Global pandemic by the end of March-2020. Despite this setback, the overall trend highlights substantial growth over the years, with earnings increasing steadily, indicating the growing importance of tourism as a revenue generator for the country. The percentage change in earnings fluctuates annually, reflecting both internal and external factors influencing tourism trends, such as economic conditions, government policies, and global events as Terrorism, GFC and the Pandemic. Nonetheless, the data underscores the resilience and potential of the tourism sector in contributing to economic growth and development.

While both countries grapple with income inequality, Bangladesh's index suggests a slightly more equitable distribution of income compared to India, albeit within the context of their respective socio-economic landscapes, despite numerous national and World Bank programs to alleviate poverty. In 2022, Bangladesh recorded a Gini-Index of 33.4, indicating a lower level of income inequality compared to India, which reported a Gini-Index of 35.9 in 2017 and dropping to Gini-Index of 32.8 in 2021 (World Bank, 2024). Income inequality in Bangladesh has worsened over the past six years. According to the Bangladesh Bureau of Statistics (2023) Household Income and Expenditure Survey - 2022, the Gini Coefficient concerning income increased to 0.499 in 2022, marking an uptick from 0.482 in 2016 and 0.458 in 2010. Bharati et al. (2024) World Inequality Lab study findings call it a rise of the "Billionaire Raj" in India, where post-independence inequality in India declined until early 1980s, after which since the 2000 it increased steeply until 2023 due to income (22.6%) and wealth (40.15%) share concentration in top 1% of the population. They conclude that this is due to regressive income tax, rise of corporate businesses, and lack of transparency. However, further analysis considering additional factors such as population size, economic development, and policy frameworks would provide a more comprehensive understanding of the nuances in income inequality between the two nations.

Opportunities and Challenges for Bangladesh and India in Linking SDG and Pro-Poor Tourism and Economic Development

The United Nations SDGs provide a global framework for addressing various social, economic, and environmental challenges. As Bangladesh and India navigate their developmental trajectories, a critical avenue for inclusive growth emerges in the form of pro-poor tourism, and both have shown commitment to achieving the SDGs and recognise the importance of integrating these (Figuire-1), goals into their national Pro-poor tourism development agendas.

Challenges

The Bangladesh and Indian government have taken various measures to promote pro-poor tourism led development and economic growth. Previous research demonstrates that not all tourism-led pro-poor development and poverty alleviate programmes have reduced poverty and achieved net-benefit for local communities and UN- SDGs, due to the problems encountered in implementing tourism policies and not clearly defined roles and responsibilities of tourism development stakeholders which could impact on the efficiency and effectiveness of implementing pro-poor tourism programs to provide employment, alleviate poverty and reduce income inequality (Chok et al., 2007; Goodwin, 2006; Luo & Bao, 2019; Rendon & Bidwell, 2015).

Tourism is overly sensitive and vulnerable to cultural, social, economic, terrorism, natural disasters, pandemic, virus, wars, and global events, which can impact on in-bound and out-bound tourism numbers and the livelihood of people depending on tourism as a source of income. Terrorism and Global pandemic have demonstrated how tourism can negatively impact on the individuals, business, society, and the economy causing unemployment, inequality, poverty, and recession. Although tourism-led economic development can create employment opportunities for the poor, but these low paying jobs as gardeners, cleaners, kitchen hands, tour guides, souvenir or fast-food vendors are poorly paid and depend on tips, given by the tourists thereby limiting opportunities for poverty alleviation, and pro-poor economic development to achieve UN-SDGs. Further, remoteness and difficult geographical landscape can be an obstacle to development of reliable transportation and supply-chain networks which can weaken pro-poor tourism sustainable tourism development and economic growth.

The following challenges can be encountered in implementing pro-poor tourism-led development strategies.

1. *Cultural differences:* Pro-poor tourism development in developing countries could result in a clash of cultural differences between host country's people (Asian or African developing countries) and tourist from western developed countries are seen as barriers to capacity-building between the different stakeholders for pro-poor tourism development.

2. *Lack of education and training*: Lack of opportunities for the poor people to invest in their human capital, resulting in low literacy rate and employment. They lack respectful language skills and could be difficulty to communicate in a respectful way with the domestic and international tourists.

3. *Poor infrastructure facilities:* In countries, centuries old heritage tourism sites in rural regional areas do not have proper infrastructure road, rail or even hotels and restaurants for the tourists, to support pro-poor tourism projects and programs.

4. *Lack of government programs*: To support pro-poor tourism development, there is lack of programs in both the countries to create jobs and involve the real homeless poor people by training them as gardeners, cleaners, and security guards, and proving meals on wheels and hotel type accommodation.

5. *Lack of access to finance*: Lack of access to credit, makes it difficult for the poor-people to engage in any small business related to tourism. Therefore, PPP is required to support micro- business enterprises to empower the poor-people for tourism related jobs.

6. *Lack of BoEP entrepreneurs*: Lack of entrepreneur ability and capacity from BoEP population to establish, own, and operate micro-enterprises and social enterprises facilities. This includes providing access to finance, technical assistance, market linkages, and mentorship to promote entrepreneurship and income generation.

7. *Lack of BoEP community participation:* BoEP people to collaborate with local communities and other key stakeholders to implement grassroots projects, advocacy campaigns, and capacity-building activities. Non-Government Organisations can mobilize resources, provide technical assistance, and monitor the impact of pro-poor tourism interventions.

Opportunities

Since the beginning of this century, the governments of Bangladesh and India have achieved remarkable progress in developing domestic and international tourism. This has resulted in an increase in the tourism revenue and providing economic and social development opportunities for pro-poor tourism development as a tool for achieving the SDGs of poverty reduction, employment generation, and inclusive economic growth. However, the potential for tourism development of the Eastern states of India is severely restricted by its geographical mountainous terrain, insufficient and poor infrastructure -road, rail and tourism facilities and services.

Both Bangladesh and India, can capitalise on their existing tourism related natural, cultural and heritage assets and explore potential areas to leverage their respective strengths in tourism-led pro-poor tourism development, to foster travel and tourism between the two countries, mutual economic development and achieve shared SDG target. Business opportunities can be tapped for BoEP poor population, as collectively four billons of poor constitute a large market share for goods and services that are affordable, accessible, and tailored to their needs. But to generate demand from BoEP poor people one needs to first provide pro-poor tourism-led economic development opportunities and PPP partnerships, to provide net benefits and improve the livelihood of the poor people.

The following business opportunities can be generated via tourism-led projects and programmes to have a net- benefit impact and achieve the SDGs.

1. *Education:* Providing tourism relate hands-on basic education and training for tour guides, gardeners, security, first-aid, and interpreters to build capacity.
2. *Employment:* Employing poor people in tourism related enterprises and related businesses on the government tourism sites registered with the archaeological society of the two countries. Such as cleaning the tourism sites, gardening, security, cleaning washroom facilities, first-aid counter, interpreting services, coolies, locker room security, food, and souvenir shops.
3. *Micro- Social Enterprises*: Small and mediums tourism business enterprises can play an important role to alleviate poverty via pro-poor sustainable development (Zeng, 2018) and supply goods and services and traditional handicrafts and artifacts made by the poor people such as arts and craft work, pottery, jewellery, and local embroidery items. Macro-Business enterprises corporate social enterprise objectives could donate money, invest and support to bring together poor-people to start a micro-business- run by the poor, for the poor, with could employ the poor people who have traditional skills to produce these goods for tourism related souvenir shops.
4. *Empowerment and Poverty reduction*: Employment opportunities in micro-business enterprises of goods and services, will provide direct income to the individuals and the households, thus reducing poverty and improving their lives.
5. *Access to fiancé or micro-credit facilities:* Poor entrepreneurs with small enterprises such as candle making, incense sticks making or tourism related souvenirs- can be provided with micro credit facilities for the poor, who can work from home and supply them to the shops.

6. *Private Multinational Business Corporation (MNC):* India and Bangladesh have famous or Multinational Business Corporation large business houses can play an important role to fulfill their corporate social responsibility and support scholarship and entrepreneurship initiatives for the poor, and partner with the government for planning and implementing pro-poor development projects and programs in tourism to alleviate poverty and create wealth. For example- in India (Adita Birla Group, Bajaj, Adani, Ambani, Tata, Infosys, and Wipro). Bangladesh MNC (Abul Khair Group, Bashundhara Group, BEXIMCO, Meghna Group, Pran Group, and City Group). This will not only preserve heritage monuments, environment and places but also meet the various UN-SDGs through pro-poor tourism development.

DISCUSSION AND RECOMMENDATIONS

International organisations (e.g. World Tourism Organsiation) WTO tourism researchers, historians, poor-people, and local community residents need to come together in order to develop projects and activities for investing in pro-poor tourism development programs for their region, which requires long-term funding needs and keeping in mind the cultural sensitivity of the regions. Pro-poor tourism-led development requires cooperation and collaboration between various stakeholders and poor-people themselves (Suntikul *et al.,* 2009), for long-run stainability of net-benefits flowing from tourism-led pro-poor economic development and growth projects and programs.

It is essential that public-and private sector tourism stakeholders adopt a pro-poor tourism business model integrating the SDGs to meet the needs of the Bottom of the Economic Pyramid (BoEP) with a public-private partnership (PPP) model –to involve the key stakeholders' role in pro-poor tourism development to achieve inclusive growth. Managerial implications for prop-poor development strategy in the 21st century is necessary to fully understand the realistic demands of different tourism related stakeholders so that they have a common goal of pro-poor tourism development strategy. The three levels of government (local, state, and central) and distinct government departments (tourism, transport, archaeology, forestry, environment, and natural resource management) can effectively link with the key stakeholders - private tourism businesses, non-government organisations (NGOs), Aid agencies, and philanthropist.

Therefore, planned, and tailor-made tourism initiatives taken by both the countries align with specific SDGs as identified. UN-SDGs can be achieved by pro-poor tourism development. Such as SDG-1: No poverty, SDG-2→Zero Hunger, SDG-5→Gender Equality, SDG-8→Decent Work and Economic Growth, SDG-14→ Life below Water, SDG-15→ Life on Land, and SDG-17→ Partnerships for Goal (United Nations, 2024). Figure 2 illustrated that to meet the SDGs, public-and private partnerships are essential between all the stakeholders to have a trickle-down net benefit impact from pro-poor tourism-led development projects and programs.

Figure 2. Public-Private partnerships, pro-poor tourism-led development and SDGs

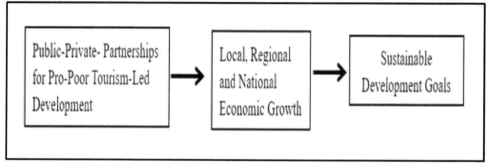

Source: Developed by authors

Similarities and Dissimilarities Between Bangladesh and India

The following can be summarised in context of pro-poor tourism-led economic development and growth, which can be an enabling factors or barriers to achieving pro-poor tourism-led development objective for both countries.

Similarities: Both Bangladesh and India with shared common history possess rich cultural heritage, diverse landscapes, and centuries old historical sites, which offer immense potential for pro-poor tourism development initiatives. These initiatives aim to create opportunities for marginalized communities, promote inclusive growth, and alleviate poverty by involving locals in tourism activities. Both the countries aim for sustained economic growth and development. They can foster peace and mutual trust and understanding, to encourage travel, and tourism opportunities cross-border, for economic development, growth, and prosperity of its citizens and nation. Particularly pro-poor tourism activities and potential can be harnessed to contribute significantly to this goal by generating employment, fostering entrepreneurship, and promoting infrastructure development in rural and remote areas across borders.

Dissimilarities: India's economy is significantly larger and more diverse in terms of economy, geography, population, toruisnm policy, with a diverse industrial base and higher per-capita income and population, with significant economic disparities with Bangladesh. Consequently, India's tourism sector is more developed, offering a wider range of opportunities and challenges compared to Bangladesh. India has a well-developed tourism infrastructure facility compared to Bangladesh, including transportation networks by air, road, and Bharat Gavrav tourists-train, accommodation facilities, and centuries old UNESCO heritage attractions. This infrastructure divide presents different challenges and opportunities for implementing pro-poor tourism initiatives in each country.

Further, whilst, both countries have policies promoting sustainable tourism development policies, but the implementation and enforcement mechanisms may vary. India being vast geographically with 28 States and their 28 official languages, diversity of geography, climate and cultures, bureaucratic complexities, financial and regulatory hurdles can pose challenges for pro-poor tourism initiatives at a national and a state level, to have a whole-of-the- government approach for por-poor tourism development tragedy, compared to Bangladesh, which may have a more streamlined policy environment in some cases given one state, with one language and culture. However, Bharat Gaurav Tourists Train packages launched from 2021, by the Ministry of Indian Railways Catering & Tourism Cooperation at a national level for the whole country, is an excellent example to create employment opportunism for the youth as well as for small businesses at the railway platforms (Medhekar, 2023).

Furthermore, India's vast and diverse geographical expanse encompasses a wide range of ecosystems, climates, and cultural landscapes, offering diverse opportunities for tourism development. In contrast, Bangladesh's geography is more compact, which was with a focus on riverine landscapes and coastal areas, presenting different opportunities and challenges for pro-poor tourism initiatives. While Bangladesh and India share common economic goals of achieving sustainable development through pro-poor tourism development and economic growth; their socio-economic contexts, tourism infrastructure, and policy environments differ, leading to variations in the implementation and impact of initiatives aimed at linking SDGs, pro-poor tourism, and economic development. Understanding these similarities and dissimilarities is crucial for designing tailored strategies to harness the potential of tourism for inclusive growth and poverty reduction in both countries.

Sustainable Development Goads and Pro-Poor Tourism-Led Development

It is important to stocktake poor-peoples potential and accordingly provide, necessary education and training to empower them in tourism related activities. By integrating the principles of sustainability, inclusivity, and partnership, this pro-poor tourism business model aims to harness the potential of tourism as a driver of poverty reduction and sustainable development, while advancing progress towards the SDGs. By working together in a PPP model all stakeholders can promote the successful tourism-led inclusive economic development of pro-poor tourism, so that the net-benefits from tailor-made tourism development programs reaches the poor sections of the society and be instrumental to achieve the following UN-SDGs.

1. *No Poverty (SDG-1):* Pro-poor tourism development programs can reduce and alleviate poverty by engaging grass root poor-people living around the tourist attractions and giving them job training to be tour guides, learning interstate or a foreign language, cleaning, garden maintenance, security, and setting up small souvenir and food stalls.

2. *Zero Hunger (SDG-2):* Tourism related employment opportunities for the poor ensure food security to combat hunger and malnutrition of poor families.

3. *Gender Equality (SDG-5):* Tourism development in rural remote areas can empower poor-women to own food, souvenir stalls, and encourage gender equality. They can be trained in handling food in a hygienic manner and cooking healthy food catering to the tourists and other tourism-related businesses and jobs on tourism sites related to security check, cleaning, and gardening.

4. *Decent Work and Economic Growth (SDG-8):* Pro-poor tourism related job opportunities and on the field training programmes should be provided to the local poor living around the tourism sites. Given their local knowledge for sustainable income and pro-poor tourism-led economic development and growth, poor people can play a participatory role in engaging with the stakeholders for developing pro-poor tourism-led development programs.

5. *Life below Water (SDG-14):* By targeting poor-people living around the water resources, such as lakes, rivers, and oceans sites, and harnessing their local knowledge and history of the marine life can be an important strategy for pro-poor tourism development and promoting sustainable use of water, lookout for protected water species, and those plants and animals along the river banks to preserve biodiversity and thus conserve and promote sustainable use of ocean, sea, and marine resources for future generations and for responsible tourism activities.

6. *Life on Land (SDG-15):* By targeting poor-people living around the tourism sites, and harnessing their local knowledge related to national parks, forests and having local Indigenous knowledge of plants, birds and animal life can be an important strategy to for pro-poor tourism development. Local people can be trained and educated as tourists guides given their local knowledge in protecting, restoring, and promoting sustainable use of natural resources, manage forest resources, efficient use of water, lookout for protected species of wildlife, combat land degradation and loss of biodiversity.

7. *Partnerships for Goal (SDG-17):* Partnership between government tourism department, department of forestry, private sector tourism organisations, archaeological societies, tourism research institutions, philanthropic organisations

and local poor-people is essential to establish initiative programs to provide opportunities and recognise inclusive pro-poor tourism-led development strategies, and tailor-made tourism education, training, and employment programs to achieve UN-SDGs.

Recommendations

The following recommendations are outlined below to engages the BoEP people for tourism-for Pro-poor Tourism-led development strategy to achieve the SDGs.

1. *Local Community Engagement:* Engage local communities in tourism development processes, ensuring their active participation and ownership. This involves capacity building, cultural preservation, and empowerment initiatives to enhance their socio-economic well-being.

2. *Education and Training:* Provide training and skill development programs tailored to the needs of BoEP communities, focusing on areas such as hospitality, tourism services, crafts, and sustainable agriculture. This empowers individuals with the necessary skills to access employment opportunities within the tourism sector.

3. *Infrastructure Investment*: Invest in infrastructure development projects that benefit BoEP communities, such as improving road connectivity, water supply, sanitation facilities, and renewable energy solutions. This enhances their quality of life and enables them to participate more effectively in tourism-related activities.

4. *Promote Sustainable Tourism Practices:* Environmental conservation and sustainable tourism practices needs to be promoted in collaboration with local communities. This involves implementing waste management systems, biodiversity conservation initiatives, and eco-friendly tourism operations to preserve natural resources and enhance resilience to climate change.

5. *Provide Policy Support*: Important to establish policy and regulatory frameworks, and financial incentives to promote pro-poor tourism-led initiatives and programs. This includes creating an enabling environment for private sector investment, facilitating land use planning, and ensuring equitable distribution of tourism benefits.

6. *Invest in Tourism Infrastructure:* Public-private partnerships for tourism infrastructure facilities should be adopted for tourism facilities and marketing initiatives while adhering to responsible business practices. Private sector partners play a crucial role in providing funding, expertise, and innovation to drive pro-poor tourism development.

7. *Tourism Planning and Implementations*: BoEP people need to be invited to actively participates in active partners in tourism planning, decision-making, and implementation processes. Communities contribute local knowledge, cultural assets, and labour to tourism activities, while benefiting from employment opportunities, income generation, and social development initiatives.

8. *Facilitate Inclusive Pro-poor Policy*: Coordinate inter-sectoral collaboration, and allocate resources for pro-poor tourism development, by promoting inclusive tourism planning, monitor progress towards SDG targets, and ensure equitable distribution of tourism benefits.

9. Invest in inclusive business models, engage in sustainable value chains, and adopt responsible tourism practices. Private sector stakeholders have a responsibility to respect human rights, support local procurement, and contribute to community development through corporate social responsibility (CSR) initiatives.

10. Engage in tourism planning processes, voice their concerns, and actively participate in project implementation and monitoring. Communities should be empowered to negotiate fair and equitable partnerships with external stakeholders, ensuring that tourism benefits are shared inclusively and sustainably.

CONCLUSION

Tourism-led economic development and growth plays an important role in developed and developing countries to create job opportunities and improve the livelihood of the people for inclusive growth. However, tourism development must be inclusive, and tailor made to include marginalised poor people and achieve the UN-SDGs though public-private partnerships. Developing countries with large percentage of poor population such as India and Bangladesh can create and provide government funded opportunities for tourism related education, employment, and pro-poor tourism development by involving the poor-people to improve their livelihood, through health, education and create employment opportunities in tourism related jobs. Pro-poor economic development and growth requires strategic planning and sustained action by the government and PPPs in both the countries to encourage domestic as well as cross-border tourism.

Future research agenda can focus on empirically testing with actual data based on various program outcomes and collecting qualitative interview data from the key stakeholders to explore the linkages between the pro-poor tourism development → UN-SDGs → and economic growth. To explore via qualitative interviews what are the cultural, social, political, financial, and economic factors that hinder or drive this pro-poor tourism development and economic growth to achieve the UN-SDGs.

REFERENCES

Adie, B. A., Amore, A., & Hall, M. C. (2020). Just Because It Seems Impossible, Doesn't Mean We Shouldn't At Least Try: The Need for Longitudinal Perspectives on Tourism Partnerships and the SDGs. *Journal of Sustainable Tourism*, 30(10), 2282–2297. 10.1080/09669582.2020.1860071

Ahamad, T., & Narayana, A. (2020). Eradicating Poverty & Approach to Sustainable Development with Special Emphasis to Millennium Development Goal-1: An Indian Perspective. *International Journal of Scientific & Technology Research*, 9(1), 51–57.

Ahmed, F., Azam, M., & Bose, T. K. (2010). Factors affecting the selection of tour destination in Bangladesh: An empirical analysis. *International Journal of Business and Management*, 5(3), 52.

Airways office. (2019). *Top 10 Travel Agency in Bangladesh*. Airways Office. https:// airwaysoffice. com/top-10-travel-agency-in-bangladesh/

Akhy, A. A., & Roy, M. (2020). Socio-economic impacts of accommodation on tourism development: Bangladesh perspective. In *Tourism marketing in Bangladesh* (pp. 51–71). Routledge. 10.4324/9781003007241-7

Alauddin, M., Shah, M. F., & Ullah, H. (2014). Tourism in Bangladesh: A prospects analysis. *Information and Knowledge Management*, 4(5), 67–73.

Alkire, S., & Deneulin, S. (2009). The human development and capability approach. In *An introduction to the human development and capability approach* (pp. 22–48). Routledge.

Ara, A., Hussain, M. E., & Sardar, S. (2020). An exploratory Approach to Pro-Poor Tourism and Poverty Alleviation in some Selective Tourism Destinations of Bangladesh. *Journal of Business Studies*, 13(1), 1–17.

Ashley, C., Roe, D., & Goodwin, H. (2001). *Pro-poor tourism strategies: Making tourism work for the poor: A review of experience* (Pro-poor Tourism Rep. No. 1). Nottingham: The Russell Press.

Ashraf, M., Ullah, L., Shuvro, M. A., & Salma, U. (2019). Transition from millennium development goals to sustainable development goals: Blueprint of Bangladesh for implementing the sustainable development goals 2030. *Medicine Today*, 31(1), 46–59. 10.3329/medtoday.v31i1.40323

Asian Development Bank. (1999). *Fighting Poverty in Asia and the Pacific: The Poverty Reduction Strategy*. ADB.

Bangladesh Bureau of Statistics. (2023). *Household Income and Expenditure Survey, Bangladesh.* BBS. https://bbs.portal.gov.bd/sites/default/files/files/bbs.portal .gov.bd/page/57def76a_aa3c_46e3_9f80_53732eb94a83/2023-04-13-09-35-ee 41d2a35dcc47a94a595c88328458f4.pdf

Bharati, N. K., Chancel, L., Piketty, T., & Somanchi, A. (2024). *Income and wealth Inequality in India, 1922-2023: The Rise of the Billionaire Raj.* (Working paper No. 2024/09). World Inequality Lab, Paris.

Biswas, C., Omar, H., & Rashid-Radha, J. R. R. (2020). The Impact of Tourist Attractions and Accessibility on Tourists' satisfaction: The Moderating Role of Tourists' age. *Geo Journal of Tourism and Geosites*, 32(4), 1202–1208. 10.30892/ gtg.32402-558

Boonsiritomachai, W., & Phonthanukitithaworn, C. (2019). Residents' support for sports events tourism development in beach city: The role of community's participation and tourism impacts. *SAGE Open*, 9(2), 2158244019843417. 10.1177/2158244019843417

Chok, S., Macbeth, J., & Warren, C. (2007). Tourism as a tool for poverty alleviation: A critical analysis of "pro-poor tourism" and implications for sustainability. *Current Issues in Tourism*, 10(2-3), 144–165. 10.2167/cit303

Clark, D. (2005). Sen's capability approach and the many spaces of human well-being. *The Journal of Development Studies*, 41(8), 1339–1368. 10.1080/00220380500186853

Deneulin, S., & Shahani, L. (Eds.). (2009). *An introduction to the human development and capability approach: Freedom and agency.* IDRC. 10.4324/9781849770026

Eluwole, K., Bekun, F. V., & Lasisi, T. T. (2022). Fresh insights into tourism-led economic growth nexus: A systematic literature network analysis approach. *Asia Pacific Journal of Tourism Research*, 27(4), 374–410. 10.1080/10941665.2022.2075775

Gantait, A., Mohanty, P., Singh, K., & Sinha, R. (2021). Pro-Poor Tourism Development in India: Reality or Hyperbole! *Psychology and Education*, 58(2), 9672–9682.

Garrod, B. (2003). Local participation in the planning and management of ecotourism: A revised model approach. *Journal of Ecotourism*, 2(1), 33–53. 10.1080/14724040308668132

Gaur, V. S., & Koltru, R. (2018). *Sustainable Tourism in the Indian Himalayan Region. NITI Aayog Report-II.* Government of India.

Gomes, B. (2021). *The tourism value chain and the prospect of pro-poor tourism in Cox's Bazar, Bangladesh.* [Unpublished Thesis]. https://eprints.bournemouth.ac .uk/35140/

Goodwin, H. (2006). *Measuring and reporting the impact of tourism on poverty.* University of Surry, UK. Chrome. https://www.haroldgoodwin.info/resources/ measuring.pdf

Government of Bangladesh. (2016). *Tourism Master Plan of Bangladesh.* Seventh Five-Year Plan 2016-2020, Ministry of Civil Aviation & Tourism, Planning Commission, Dhaka. https://file.portal.gov.bd/uploads/8ef2a505-c131-4a8f-b6d0 -2ac4760cc936//631/6c4/06a/6316c406a9807875210649.pdf

Government of India. (2012). *12th Five Year Plan (2012-2017) Report on Tourism.* Government of India. https://tourism.gov.in/sites/default/files/2019-10/ 020220120146055.pdf

Hafsa, S. (2020). Economic contribution of tourism industry in Bangladesh: At a glance. *Global Journal of Management and Business Research*, 20(1), 29–38. 10.34257/GJMBRFVOL20IS1PG29

Haq, F., & Medhekar, A. (2019). Challenges for 'innovative transformation' in heritage tourism development in India and Pakistan. In Srivastava, S. (Ed.), *Conservation and Promotion of Heritage Tourism* (pp. 127–154). IGI Global. 10.4018/978-1-5225-6283-2.ch006

Hasell, J. (2022). *From $1.90 to $2.15 a day: the updated International Poverty Line.* Our World in Data. https://ourworldindata.org/from-1-90-to-2-15-a-day-the -updated-international-poverty-line

Jeyacheya, J., & Hampton, M. P. (2020). Wishful thinking or wise policy? Theorising tourism-led inclusive growth: Supply chains and host communities. *World Development*, 131, 104960. 10.1016/j.worlddev.2020.104960

Kaushal, V., & Yadav, R. (2021). Understanding customer experience of culinary tourism through food tours of Delhi. *International Journal of Tourism Cities*, 7(3), 683–701. 10.1108/IJTC-08-2019-0135

Luo, X., & Bao, J. (2019). Exploring the impacts of tourism on the livelihoods of local poor: The role of local government and major investors. *Journal of Sustainable Tourism*, 27(3), 344–359. 10.1080/09669582.2019.1578362

Medhekar, A. (2022). Australia's Bilateral and Multilateral Health Sector Partnership with South Asian Nations: Opportunities and Challenges. In Medhekar, A., Saha, S., & Haq, F. (Eds.), *Strategic Cooperation and Partnerships Between Australia and South Asia: Economic Development, Trade, and Investment Opportunities Post-COVID-19*. (pp. 1-21). Pennsylvania USA: IGI Global.

Medhekar, A. (2023). The Economic Dimensions of Indian Railways 'Bharat Gaurav' Pilgrimage Routes. In V.J.P. Domingues Martinho *et al.,* (Eds.), *Experiences, Advantages, and Economic Dimensions of Pilgrimage Routes,* (pp. 306- 327). Pennsylvania USA: IGI Global.

Medhekar, A., & Haq, F. (2020). Cross-Border Cooperation for Bilateral Trade, Travel and Tourism: A Challenge for India and Pakistan. In Castanho, R. A. (Ed.), *Cross-Border Cooperation Strategies for Sustainable Development.Chapter10* (pp. 168–191). IGI Global. 10.4018/978-1-7998-2513-5.ch010

Medhekar, A., & Roy, K. (2010). Public and private sector partnerships for correcting infrastructure bottleneck in India. In Roy, K. C., Medhekar, A., & Chittoo, H. (Eds.), *Globalization and Development: Country Experiences* (pp. 15–30). Nova Science.

Mishra, P. K., Rout, H. B., & Mohapatra, S. S. (2011). Causality between tourism and economic growth: Empirical evidence from India. *European Journal of Soil Science*, 18(4), 518–527.

National Tourism Policy. (2010). Ministry of Civil Aviation and Tourism. Peoples Republic of Bangladesh. In *National Tourism Policy Report* (pp. 1-17). National Tourism Policy. http://parjatan.portal.gov.bd/sites/default/files/files/parjatan.portal .gov.bd/policies/401cea95_b71f_4591_a77d_81eb95e689f6/2020-06-21-12-42-ab 744be9913f6906fce79ecee1354d9a.pdf

Pérez-Rodríguez, J. V., Rachinger, H., & Santana-Gallego, M. (2021). Testing the validity of the tourism-led growth hypothesis under long-range dependence. *Current Issues in Tourism*, 24(6), 768–793. 10.1080/13683500.2020.1744537

Planning Commission. (2015). *Seventh Five Year Plan FY 2016- FY 2020, Accelerating Growth, Empowering Citizens.* Dhaka: Bangladesh.

Polash, A. K., & Habeb, A. (2020). Ecotourism: A new door to possibilities for Bangladesh. *International Journal of Advances in Engineering and Management*, 2(8), 121–132.

Rauniyar, G., & Kanbur, R. (2006). *Inclusive Growth and Inclusive Development: A Review & Synthesis of Asian Development Bank Literature.* (Occasional Paper, No.8).

Rendon, M. L., & Bidwell, S. (2015). Success in progress? Tourism as a tool for inclusive development in Peru's Colca Valley. In Panosso Netto, A., & Trigo, L. (Eds.), *Tourism in Latin America* (pp. 207–233). Springer. 10.1007/978-3-319-05735-4_12

Roy, B., & Saxena, A. K. (2020). Destination competitiveness, tourism facilities and problems in promoting Uttarakhand as a tourism destination. *Journal of Tourism. Hospitality & Culinary Arts*, 12(2), 1–20.

Roy, D., Dhir, M. G. M., & Ahsan, M. K. (2016). Factors affecting tourist satisfaction: A study in Sylhet Region. *ABC Research Alert*, 4(3), 9–20. 10.18034/abcra.v4i3.307

Roy, H. (2010). The Role of Tourism to Poverty Alleviation. 10.2139/ssrn.1599971

Roy, M. (2021). Tourism Industry in Bangladesh: An Assessment of advanced SWOT Model and TOWS Matrix. In Hasan, A. (Ed.), *Tourism in Bangladesh Investment and Development Perspectives* (pp. 279–310). Springer. 10.1007/978-981-16-1858-1_18

Roy, M., Yajing, F., & Biswas, B. (2020). Economic contribution of tourism in Bangladesh: Capital investment perspective. In *Tourism Marketing in Bangladesh* (pp. 223–237). Routledge. 10.4324/9781003007241-22

Roy, P. B., Roy, T. B., & Saha, S. (2010). Pro-Poor Tourism as an Approach towards Community Development: A Case Study. *South Asian Journal of Tourism and Heritage*, 3(2), 90–98.

Roy, S. C., & Roy, M. (2015). Tourism in Bangladesh: Present status and future prospects. International. *Journal of Management Science and Business Administration*, 1(8), 53–61.

Saad, S. (2021). *Culture and Handicraft Tourism in India: Tourism supporting sustainable development goals. Master's Dissertations*. Auckland University of Technology.

Sen, A. (1999). *Development as Freedom*. Harvard University Press.

Singh, S. (2022). Do indexes assess poverty? Is tourism truly pro-poor? *Journal of Ekonomi*, *07*, 06-13 https://dergipark.org.tr/ekonomi

Soliman, M. S. (2015). Pro-poor tourism in protected areas– opportunities and challenges: "The case of Fayoum, Egypt.". *Anatolia*, 26(1), 61–72. 10.1080/13032917.2014.906353

Spenceley, A. (2022). Pro-Poor Tourism's Evolution and Implications Arising from the COVID-19 Pandemic. *Tourism Planning & Development*, 19(1), 13–25. 10.1080/21568316.2021.2021470

Spenceley, A., & Meyer, D. (2012). Tourism and poverty reduction: Theory and practice in less economically developed countries. *Journal of Sustainable Tourism*, 20(3), 297–317. 10.1080/09669582.2012.668909

Sultana, R., Pala, S. S., Mohammad, A., & Tasnim, T. (2023). Achieving SDGs in Bangladesh: A meta-analysis on challenges and opportunities. *Journal of Bangladesh Institute of Planners*, 16, 77–104.

Sultana, S. (2016). Economic contribution of tourism industry in Bangladesh. *Journal of Tourism. Hospitality and Sports*, 22(2), 55–54.

Suntikul, W., Bauer, T., & Song, H. (2009). Pro-poor Tourism Development in Viengxay, Laos: Current State and Future Prospects. *Asia Pacific Journal of Tourism Research*, 14(2), 153–168. 10.1080/10941660902847203

Timothy, D. J. (2007). Empowerment and stakeholder participation in tourism destination communities. In Church, A., & Coles, V. T. (Eds.), *Tourism, power, and space* (pp. 203–216). Routledge.

Venugopalan, T., & Kumar, D. (2017). Sustainable development through sustainable tourism in India-A case study of Kerala tourism. *Asian Journal of Research in Business Economics and Management*, 7(12), 10–27. 10.5958/2249-7307.2017.00189.X

Vinodan, A., Sethumadhavan, M., & Manalel, J. (2022). Exploring sustainability facets of pro-poor tourism programs in India. *Enlightening Tourism: A Pathmaking Journal,* 12(2), 732-766. https://doi.org/10.33776/et.v12i2.7235

World Bank (2019). *Bangladesh Poverty Assessment. Bangladesh Poverty Assessment*. World Bank.

World Bank. (2024). *Gini Index*. World Bank. https://data.worldbank.org/indicator/SI.POV.GINI

World Tourism Organisation. (2019). International Tourism Number of Arrivals. *Statistical Yearbook 1995-2019*. WTO. https://data.worldbank.org/indicator/ST.INT.ARVL

World Tourism Organisation. (2019). *International Tourism Expenditure. Statistical Yearbook 1995-2019*. WTO. https://data.worldbank.org/indicator/ST.INT.XPND.CD

Yunis, E. (2004). *Tourism and poverty alleviation, Chief Sustainable Development of Tourism*. World Tourism Organization. www.rete.toscana.it/sett/turismo/euromeeting _2004/ eng_yunis.pdf

Zeng, B. (2018). How can social enterprises contribute to sustainable pro-poor tourism development? *Zhongguo Renkou Ziyuan Yu Huanjing*, 16(2), 159–170. 10.1080/10042857.2018.1466955

ADDITIONAL READINGS

Balsalobre-Lorente, D., Driha, O. M., Bekun, F. V., & Adedoyin, F. (2021). The asymmetric impact of air transport on economic growth in Spain: Fresh evidence from the tourism-led growth hypothesis. *Current Issues in Tourism*, 24(4), 503–519. 10.1080/13683500.2020.1720624

Khan, H. R., Zaman, K., Yousaf, S. U., Shoukry, L. M., Gani, S., & Sharkawy, A. S. (2019). Socio-economic and environmental factors influenced pro-poor growth process: New development triangle. *Environmental Science and Pollution Research International*, 26(28), 29157–29172. 10.1007/s11356-019-06065-2

Rasool, H., Maqbool, S., & Tarique, M. (2021). The relationship between tourism and economic growth among BRICS countries: A panel cointegration analysis. *Future Business Journal*, 7(1), 1. 10.1186/s43093-020-00048-3

Rogerson, C. M. (2011). Pro-Poor local economic development in South Africa: The role of pro-poor tourism. *Local Environment*, 11(1), 37–76. 10.1080/13549830500396149

Winfred, A.Jr. (2006). Pro-poor economic growth: Role of small and medium sized enterprises. *Journal of Asian Economics*, 17(1), 35–40. 10.1016/j.asieco.2006.01.005

Wu, L., Zhang, J., Lu, Q., & Rahman, A. S. (2017). Tourist adaptation behavior in response to climate disasters in Bangladesh. *Journal of Sustainable Tourism*, 25(2), 217–233. 10.1080/09669582.2016.1195837

KEY TERMS AND DEFINITIONS

Bottom of the Economic Pyramid (BoEP): The bottom of economic pyramid, term was coined by the US President Franklin D. Roosevelt during the great depression of 1932. BoEP refers to the poorest of poor socio-economic group of approximately four billion global population living on $2.50 a day in the developing countries of African continent, South American countries, Bangladesh, China, India, and Indonesia.

Capacity Building: Capacity for any organisations is based on the concept of six capitals: intrinsic, financial, human, political, physical, community social capital.

Inclusive Development: Inclusive development means developing a region harmoniously, to reduce poverty and including bottom of the economic pyramid people in socio-economic development opportunities for pro-poor development strategies.

Pro-poor Economic Empowerment: Pro-poor economic empowerment means to have all-inclusive economic growth, which enables the poor to actively participate in and significantly benefit from any economic activity. All-inclusive pro-poor economic growth is a major departure from the trickle-down development approach.

Pro-poor Tourism Development: Pro-poor tourism development is a responsible tourism development strategy to reduce poverty by generating benefits for the poor through collaboration and involving the poor in local development of tourism services and products and generating employment opportunities.

Sustainable Development: Sustainable development is defined as the type of economic development that meets the needs of the present generation, by using and managing scarce economic resources in a sustainable manner and not depleting them fully, so that resources are also left for the future generations, and therefore not compromising the ability of future generations to meet their own needs.

Tourism-Led Economic Growth: Tourism development can stimulate investments in new infrastructure projects like rail, road, hotels, restaurants, museum, and airports. This has a multiplier effect in terms of creating new jobs in tourism related activities, goods, and service provision, resulting in economics growth.

Chapter 4
Tourism Students' Level of Knowledge Regarding Sustainable Development Goals

Hulisi Binbasioglu
https://orcid.org/0000-0001-7488-8450
Malatya Turgut Ozal University, Turkey & Cardiff Business School, UK

ABSTRACT

The sustainable development goals (SDGs) are a collection of targets that nations must work towards accomplishing by 2030, as mandated by this worldwide action. Tourism, closely tied to the natural, social environment, and economy, contributes significantly to sustainability. As tourism is the world's fastest-growing industry, linking tourism and the SDGs is crucial. Although research on SDGs and tourism has increased, the knowledge level of university students still needs to be adequately addressed. This study aims to assess the level of SDGs knowledge among university students studying in tourism departments. Descriptive and causal-comparative research designs were used. Descriptive statistics were used to determine how familiar the participants were with relevant concepts. The current chapter also provides practical and theoretical implications for tourism educators and researchers.

INTRODUCTION

Sustainability is crucial for the international growth and development of tourism (Roxas et al., 2020), and starting from this consideration, tourism plays a significant role in promoting sustainable development. The United Nations officially designat-

DOI: 10.4018/979-8-3693-3166-8.ch004

ed the 2030 Agenda for Sustainable Development in September 2015. Sustainable Development Goals (SDGs) are a universal call to action that include goals aimed at being achieved by United Nations member states by the end of 2030. The purpose of this Agenda is to achieve a comprehensive set of 17 SDGs (see Table 1) that will result in a better future for all nations (UN, 2015). Two global organisations, the UNWTO and UNDP, have made the decision to promote collaboration and leadership to enhance tourism's influence on the SDGs, especially in light of the UN General Assembly's designation of 2017 as the International Year of Sustainable Tourism for Development, which gives the tourism sector an ideal opportunity to reflect on its role and embark on a collective journey towards 2030 (UNWTO, 2017).

As the importance of sustainable development in a global context rises, numerous issues and concepts are discussed. Yet, knowledge of the SDGs is limited. Individuals who claim to have a considerable understanding, or even knowledge, of the SDGs are relatively uncommon (8%), according to an international study investigating awareness of the SDGs by 56,409 respondents from 24 countries (Lampert & Papadongonas, 2016). Furthermore, a global survey was conducted on approximately 27,000 individuals worldwide, and the findings revealed that only a small proportion of respondents are familiar with the SDGs and know their meaning (Globalsurvey-SDGs, 2020). However, a global survey shows that 92% of respondents in Turkey are aware of the SDGs (Tedeneke, 2019). Another research indicates that global awareness of the SDGs has increased during the years between 2017 and 2023, and Turkey's awareness has risen from 32% to 60% during this period (Globescan, 2023). However, according to the overall performance of the SDG index, Turkey's country score ranks 71st among 163 countries with a score of 70.4 (Sachs et al., 2022).

Education is the initial step to implementing sustainability or sustainable tourism, and this is considered to facilitate the achievement of all the SDGs (Boluk et al., 2019). Some research reveals a gap in knowledge among students studying tourism at university about the SDGs in an innovative, feasible, and compelling manner (Manolis & Manoli, 2021). SDGs in tourism studies focus on issues of society, business models, and policy implications (Rosato et al., 2021). There is a rising interest in tourism research within education to support the achievement of the SDGs. This has led to a demand for critical and practical approaches to be integrated into curricula and classrooms (Boluk et al., 2019; Cotterell et al., 2019). Therefore, it is crucial to examine how efficiently these practical attempts raised knowledge of the SDGs among university students (Manolis & Manoli, 2021). University students catalyze addressing global sustainability action. Due to their adaptability, expertise, creativity, and environmental concerns, young people are the most influential stakeholders for sustainable concepts (Varah et al., 2021). UNESCO recognizes education as a crucial objective in relation to other SDGs and underlines the need to integrate education with these objectives. Currently, the starting point of the present study is target 4.7, as highlighted by UNESCO below:

"By 2030, ensure that all learners acquire the knowledge and skills needed to promote sustainable development, including, among others, through education for sustainable development and sustainable lifestyles, human rights, gender equality, promotion of a culture of peace and non-violence, global citizenship and appreciation of cultural diversity and of culture's contribution to sustainable development (UNESCO, 2017, p. 2)."

In recent years, the tourism research field has reached a growing number of studies related to the SDGs in tourism. Numerous studies have emphasised the necessity of perspectives from different stakeholders approaches to the SDGs in the tourism industry (Raub & Martin-Rios, 2019; Izurieta et al., 2021; KC et al., 2021; Özgit & Zhandildina, 2021; Scheyvens & Cheer, 2022; Vrontis et al., 2022). However, there isn't much research available that aims to understand the students' level of knowledge regarding the SDGs. The results highlight the necessity for further research and discourse on significant matters and their consequences for the education of sustainable development in the tourism industry (Hall et al., 2023). Starting from these considerations, in the current research, the concept of tourism students' level of awareness of SDGs serves this purpose. This article bridges the gap in the existing literature regarding the knowledge of the SDGs among Turkish university students studying tourism. This is one of the first studies to offer empirical findings and discussions on tourism students' knowledge level of the SDGs.

LITERATURE

The 17 Sustainable Development Goals and 169 goals set in 2015 reflect the scope of a universal Agenda. These goals aim to expand on the Millennium Development Goals, recompense for their failures, realise human rights, gender equality, and empower women and girls within the framework of economic, social, and environmental sustainability (UN, 2015). Besides that, tourism's contribution to attaining these 17 goals may be greatly enhanced when sustainable development becomes a collective duty within the tourism industry. Tourism and the Sustainable Development Goals seek to educate, equip, and motivate stakeholders involved in tourism to implement measures that would expedite the shift towards a more sustainable tourism industry. This involves aligning regulations, corporate practices, and investments with the SDGs (UNWTO, 2017). Considering achieving the Sustainable Development Goals, there are possible tourism-specifics to attain them. The following samples are provided in Table 1 (UN, 2015, p:18; Siakwah et al., 2020, p:359-360; Buhalis et al., 2023, p:306):

Table 1. The 17 sustainable development goals and their link to tourism

Sustainable Development Goal	Explanation	Possible tourism-specifics
1. No poverty	End poverty in all its forms everywhere.	Pro-poor tourism, volunteer tourism
2. Zero hunger	End hunger, achieve food security and improved nutrition and promote sustainable agriculture.	Agri-tourism
3. Good health and well-being	Ensure healthy lives and promote well-being for all at all ages.	Medical and health tourism, tourists' physical and mental health
4. Quality education	Ensure inclusive and equitable quality education and promote lifelong learning opportunities for all.	Tourism in-house training courses and skills development of local communities
5. Gender equality	Achieve gender equality and empower all women and girls.	Inclusive tourism
6. Clean water and sanitation	Ensure the availability and sustainable management of water and sanitation for all.	Responsible tourism
7. Affordable and clean energy	Ensure access to affordable, reliable, sustainable and clean energy for all.	Alternative tourism
8. Decent work and economic growth	Promote sustained, inclusive and sustainable economic growth, full and productive employment and decent work for all.	Local economic development through tourism, inclusive tourism
9. Industry, innovation and infrastructure	Build resilient infrastructure, promote inclusive and sustainable industrialization and foster innovation.	Infrastructure upgrades and renovation, smart destinations
10. Reduced inequalities	Reduce inequality within and among countries.	Inbound and outbound tourism, inclusive tourism, pro-poor tourism
11. Sustainable cities and communities	Make cities and human settlements inclusive, safe, resilient and sustainable.	Urban tourism, community-based tourism, inclusive tourism
12. Responsible consumption and production	Ensure sustainable consumption and production patterns.	Responsible tourism, green tourism
13. Climate action	Take urgent action to combat climate change and its impacts.	Ecotourism
14. Life below water	Conserve and sustainably use the oceans, seas and marine resources for sustainable development.	Aqua-tourism

continued on following page

Table 1. Continued

Sustainable Development Goal	Explanation	Possible tourism-specifics
15. Life on land	Protect, restore and promote the sustainable use of terrestrial ecosystems, sustainably manage forests, combat desertification, and halt and reverse land degradation and halt biodiversity loss.	Sustainable tourism, Ecotourism
16. Peace, justice and strong institutions	Promote peaceful and inclusive societies for sustainable development, provide access to justice for all and build effective, accountable and inclusive institutions at all levels.	Inclusive tourism, peace through tourism, justice tourism, solidarity tourism
17. Partnerships for the goals	Strengthen the means of implementation and revitalize the global partnership for sustainable development.	Justice tourism, collaborative community-based tourism

Tourism encompasses a diverse group of individuals and organisations, each with its own goals, plans, and concerns that shape its growth and progress (Roxas et al., 2020). SDGs with a high priority for educational institutions, companies, civil society, local authorities, and non-governmental organizations. Reaching consensus on sustainability development goals may be challenging, as various stakeholder values are discussed and criticized (Robert et al., 2005). Understanding the perspectives of all relevant and essential stakeholders is crucial if the SDGs are to be achieved through tourism. Figure 1 demonstrates the relationships between the three dimensions of sustainability within the tourism sector and the relevance of each dimension to SDGs.

Figure 1. Tourism 2030: SDG interconnections with tourism

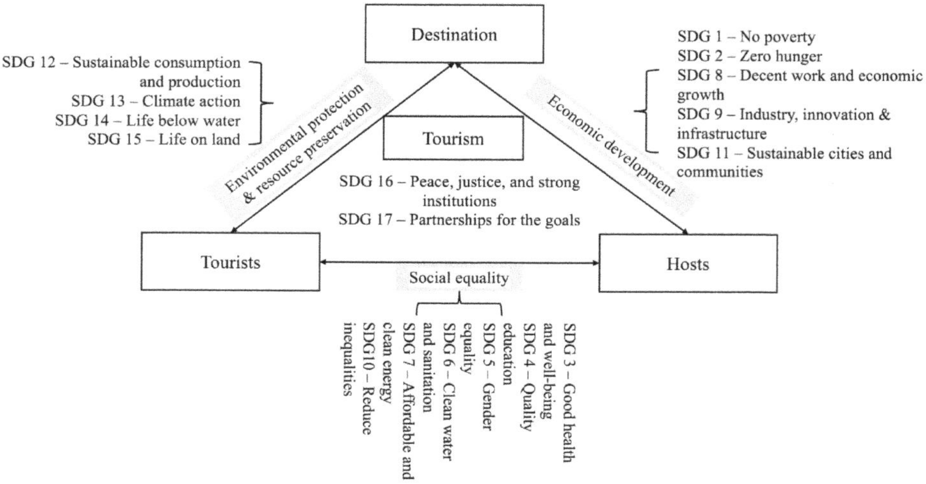

Source: Buhalis et al. (2023). Tourism 2030 and the contribution to the sustainable development goals: the tourism review viewpoint. Tourism Review, 78(2), p. 294.

In the figure above, SDGs 1, 2, 8, 9, and 11 relate to the economic development element of sustainability, which is regarding hosts and destinations. SDGs 3, 4, 5, 6, 7, and 10 link to social equality, namely in association with tourists and hosts. SDGs 12, 13, 14, and 15 are all connected to the environmental protection & resource preservation aspect of sustainability, particularly in relation to tourists and destinations. SDGs 16 and 17 emerge as common dimensions of tourism and sustainability.

The marketing and management of tourism and hospitality services and destinations rely on a skilled and competent workforce because the tourism industry is a labour-intensive one (Buhalis et al., 2023). An appropriately educated and trained workforce yields favourable outcomes by expediting the implementation of the SDGs (KC, 2024). Integrating Education for Sustainable Development (ESD), target 4.7 as highlighted by UNESCO, into the tourism education system is crucial to ensuring that upcoming tourism professionals possess sufficient understanding of sustainable development and environmentally conscious ways of living (UNWTO, 2023). ESD should be integrated into national education policy, curricula, teacher training, and student assessment. There is a framework of ESD implementation in schools in Figure 2.

Figure 2. The framework of ESD implementation

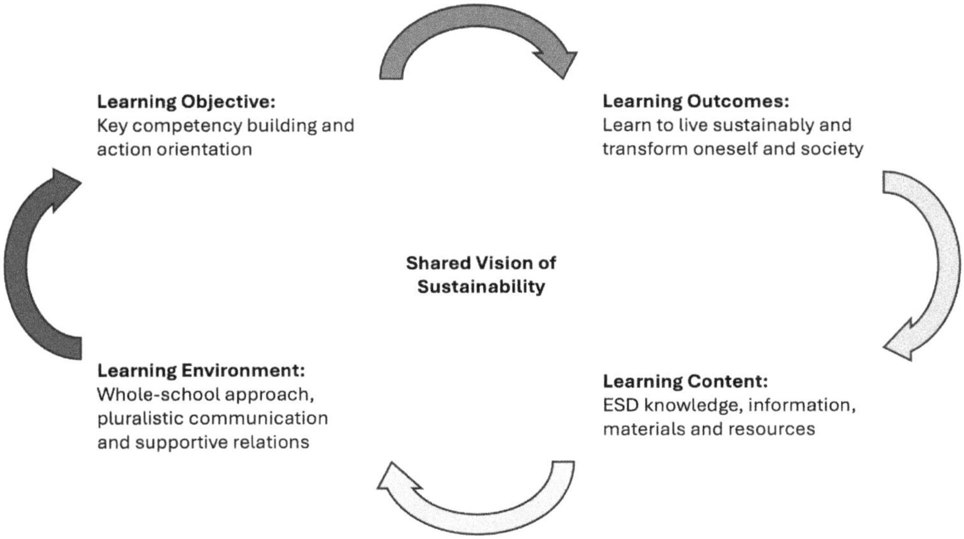

Learning Objective:
Key competency building and
action orientation

Learning Outcomes:
Learn to live sustainably and
transform oneself and society

**Shared Vision of
Sustainability**

Learning Environment:
Whole-school approach,
pluralistic communication
and supportive relations

Learning Content:
ESD knowledge, information,
materials and resources

Source: Yuan et al. (2021). Awareness of sustainable development goals among students from a Chinese senior high school. Education Sciences, 11, 458, p. 5.

According to Figure 2, the shared vision of sustainability depends on the relationship and integration of learning objectives, outcomes, content, and environment for the schools. Yuan et al. (2021) reveal that knowledge of SDGs among the students had a significant positive impact on the impact of personal life on SDGs. It can be considered that the students believe SDG knowledge has an important influence on their personal lives. Furthermore, students possessing this ability will have the opportunity to enhance their level of competitiveness through the cultivation of global attention (de Lange, 2013). Investing in education and vocational training in the tourism industry not only addresses SDG 4, but also serves as the foundation for quality employment and entrepreneurship (UNWTO, 2017). Tourism offers opportunities as an educational tool for creating a sustainable tourism world (Pritchard et al., 2011).

According to the findings, the primary and most significant source of information regarding sustainability and sustainable development is the coursework that students undertake at the university (Camargo & Gretzel, 2017). Thus, students play a crucial role as significant stakeholders in a sustainable workforce. Several countries have invested in formal and informal tourism education, including undergraduate, graduate, vocational, and professional development programs in tourism and hospitality, to meet the continued growth of tourism (Airey, 2020). For example, globally, there is a 'The World's Largest Lesson' program that is delivered in partnership with

UNICEF and UNESCO to promote the use of the Sustainable Development Goals in learning so that children and young people can contribute to a better future for all (Worldslargestlesson, 2023).

Higher education fosters inventive and critical thinking and plays a crucial role in advancing and supporting the achievement of the SDGs (Leon-Gomez et al., 2023). By emphasizing higher education for SDGs, the integration of SDGs in research methodology may be further enhanced, leading to their application in future initiatives (Manolis & Manoli, 2021). Nevertheless, studies indicate that tourism students lack comprehensive sustainability knowledge due to course structures that prioritize less robust sustainability principles and do not encourage holistic, critical, and systemic thinking (Cotterell et al., 2019). By encouraging sustainable habits among young people, who are the target group for tourism activities, it is crucial to assess their knowledge on this matter and identify the specific information they require (Frick et al., 2004).

Based on the literature above, the research question of the current study to be examined is as follows: What is the knowledge level among Turkish university students studying in tourism departments regarding the Sustainable Development Goals (SDGs)?

METHOD

Descriptive statistics (percentage and frequency) calculations were made on the data obtained to determine how familiar the students were with the concepts related to SDGs. The study group of the research consists of 51 students studying at the Faculty of Tourism of Bolu Abant Izzet Baysal University in the spring semester of the 2022-2023 academic year who voluntarily participated in the research. Data was obtained online between the 26th and 29th of February 2023. Students were asked to rate their familiarity with SDGs concepts. This was assessed through a 5-item scale from not familiar at all (1) to very familiar (5). The distribution of the participants according to their gender is female 54,9% (28), male 44,1% (23). Their departments are tourism and hotel management 37,3% (19), gastronomy and culinary arts 35,3% (18), and tourism guiding 27,5% (14).

RESULTS

A questionnaire survey-based study was used to ask university students studying tourism in Turkey about their individual knowledge level related to the 17 SDGs. The questionnaire consisted of two sections. The objective of the first part was to collect the demographic information of university students, and the second part was about their knowledge of the SDGs. Table 1 displays the mean of each SDG categorised by gender.

Figure 3. Gender-based histogram of the mean of each SDGs

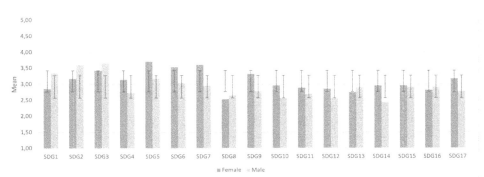

According to Figure 3, the mean score of SDG8 was around the median value of "2,5" (5-point scale), while the values of the other SDGs were higher than 2,5 for the female students. The mean score of SDG5 was the highest. For the male students, the mean score of SDG10, SDG12, and SDG14 were around and lower than the median value 2,5. The mean score of SDG3 was the highest. In Table 2, university students' familiarity with SDGs were shown.

Table 2. Students' familiarity with SDGs

SDGs Concepts	% of Respondents									
	Not familiar at all		A little familiar		Moderately familiar		Quite familiar		Very familiar	
	F	M	F	M	F	M	F	M	F	M
1. No poverty	**39,3**	13,0	3,6	13,0	17,9	30,4	10,7	13,0	28,6	30,4
2. Zero hunger	35,7	8,7	7,1	17,4	3,6	17,4	10,7	17,4	**42,9**	**39,1**
3. Good health and well-being	25,0	4,3	7,1	17,4	10,7	26,1	14,3	13,0	**42,9**	**39,1**
4. Quality education	32,1	**34,8**	7,1	4,3	10,7	30,4	14,3	13,0	**35,7**	17,4
5. Gender equality	21,4	17,4	3,6	8,7	14,3	**30,4**	3,6	26,1	**57,1**	17,4
6. Clean water and sanitation	10,7	21,7	17,9	8,7	17,9	**39,1**	14,3	4,3	**39,3**	26,1

continued on following page

Table 2. Continued

SDGs Concepts	% of Respondents									
	Not familiar at all		A little familiar		Moderately familiar		Quite familiar		Very familiar	
	F	M	F	M	F	M	F	M	F	M
1. No poverty	**39,3**	13,0	3,6	13,0	17,9	30,4	10,7	13,0	28,6	30,4
7. Affordable and clean energy	10,7	8,7	21,4	30,4	7,1	**34,8**	17,9	8,7	**42,9**	17,4
8. Decent work and economic growth	**32,1**	**34,8**	28,6	13,0	10,7	26,1	10,7	4,3	17,9	21,7
9. Industry, innovation and infrastructure	21,4	21,7	14,3	**26,1**	14,3	21,7	10,7	13,0	**39,3**	17,4
10. Reduced inequalities	**28,6**	**39,1**	14,3	4,3	10,7	34,8	25,0	4,3	21,4	17,4
11. Sustainable cities and communities	**25,0**	17,4	**25,0**	30,4	10,7	**34,8**	14,3	0,0	**25,0**	17,4
12. Responsible consumption and production	**32,1**	**39,1**	21,4	13,0	7,1	17,4	7,1	13,0	**32,1**	17,4
13. Climate action	**32,1**	21,7	17,9	13,0	14,3	**34,8**	14,3	13,0	21,4	17,4
14. Life below water	21,4	**34,8**	7,1	13,0	**39,3**	34,8	17,9	8,7	14,3	8,7
15. Life on land	21,4	21,7	10,7	13,0	**35,7**	34,8	14,3	13,0	17,9	17,4
16. Peace, justice and strong institutions	**35,7**	30,4	14,3	4,3	10,7	**30,4**	10,7	13,0	28,6	21,7
17. Partnerships for the goals	21,4	21,7	14,3	17,4	17,9	**34,8**	17,9	13,0	**28,6**	13,0

According to results, most female students are not familiar with the SDGs including No poverty, Decent work and economic growth, Reduced inequalities, Sustainable cities and communities, Responsible consumption and production, Climate action, and Peace, justice and strong institutions while they are familiar with concepts related to Zero hunger, Good health and well-being, Quality education, Gender equality, Clean water and sanitation, Affordable and clean energy, Industry, innovation and infrastructure, and Partnerships for the goals.

However, most male students are not familiar with the SDGs concepts including Quality education, Decent work and economic growth, Reduced inequalities, Responsible consumption and production, Life below water, and Peace, justice and strong institutions while they are familiar with concepts related to No poverty, Zero hunger, Good health and well-being. They are moderately familiar with Gender equality, Clean water and sanitation, Affordable and clean energy, Sustainable cities and communities, Life below water, Life on land, Peace, justice and strong institutions, and Partnerships for the goals.

CONCLUSION

The present study examined the knowledge level of university students related to the SDGs. The result of this study reveals that gender equality has the highest mean score for female students, while good health and well-being have the highest score for male students. Female students are most unfamiliar with the SDG of no poverty and very familiar with gender equality. However, male students are most unfamiliar with the goals of reduced inequalities and responsible consumption and production while being very familiar with the zero hunger and good health and well-being goals. This suggests prioritising these comparatively unknown goals, particularly in both formal and informal educational attainment contexts. Considering the lack of an equivalent study, the findings of comparable research and studies are acknowledged.

Global awareness of the SDGs was initially limited but has shown growth over time in several surveys. The concern for sustainability among the young, particularly university students, has been present for a considerable period of time (Cini et al., 2015; Camargo & Gretzel, 2017). Cotterell et al. (2019) state that more robust conceptualizations and sustainability abilities are crucial for sustainability pedagogy and practices in tourism courses. Young people (under the age of 30) those who have higher education are more inclined to be knowledgeable of the SDGs (Globescan, 2023).

According to a global survey, the top-five SDGs in terms of perceived significance are: (1) zero hunger, (2) clean water and sanitation, (3) good health and well-being, (4) affordable and clean energy, (5) life below water, and the lowest-five are: (1) gender equality, (2) reduced inequality, (3) industry, innovation and infrastructure, (4) responsible consumption and production, (5) peace, justice and strong institutions (Tedeneke, 2019).

Without addressing gender equality effectively, the potential of tourism to contribute to the SDGs would be diminished, and sustainable tourism would remain difficult to achieve (Alarcón & Cole, 2019). However, there was no significant difference in the awareness of sustainable development between male and female students (Yuan et al., 2021).

Besides, according to Rasoolimanesh et al. (2023), decent work and economic growth, and life on land goals are the most used in articles, while goals of no poverty, zero hunger, peace and justice strong institutions, and partnerships to achieve the goals are notable for being largely understudied areas of papers. The primary reason for this can be attributed to the fact that the majority of the articles predominantly concentrate on environmental and economic issues.

When the SDG level of Turkey is analysed, major challenges remain to the goals of good health and well-being, gender equality, decent work and economic growth, industry, innovation and infrastructure, reduced inequalities, responsible consumption and production, climate action, life below water, life on land, and peace, justice and strong institutions, while the others remain challenges and significant challenges (Sachs et al., 2022).

This study can provide a basis for potentially assisting tourism educators and researchers in gaining a deeper understanding of how tourism students can contribute to addressing the SDGs. The practical implications of this research provide valuable insights for higher education institutions having a great deal of responsibility in arranging their curricula. Elective courses related to SDGs and the relevance of the other courses to the SDGs can be added to the curriculum in all tourism departments at universities. However, global projects and programmes such as ESD and the world's largest lesson should adopt the curricula to enhance students' awareness and knowledge about the SDGs. The current studies have several limitations. Using students was suitable for this tourism-related research, but generalizing to the full population should be avoided. Future studies should employ a sample that is more representative of the full population of the target group, and the adoption of various research methodologies would enhance the progress of scientific understanding on the relationship between the SDGs and students studying tourism. Studies on this topic that can offer guidelines on modifying university curricula is crucial for intellectual and future advancement.

ACKNOWLEDGMENT

This paper is a revised and expanded version of a paper entitled 'The Knowledge Level of University Students Towards Sustainable Development Goals' presented at the 4th Conference on Managing Tourism Across Continents (MTCON23) on March 15-18, 2023, in İstanbul, Türkiye.

REFERENCES

Airey, D. (2020). Education for tourism: A perspective article. *Tourism Review*, 75(1), 260–262. 10.1108/TR-02-2019-0074

Alarcón, D. M., & Cole, S. (2019). No sustainability for tourism without gender equality. *Journal of Sustainable Tourism*, 27(7), 903–919. 10.1080/09669582.2019.1588283

Boluk, K. A., Cavaliere, C. T., & Duffy, L. N. (2019). A pedagogical framework for the development of the critical tourism citizen. *Journal of Sustainable Tourism*, 27(7), 865–881. 10.1080/09669582.2019.1615928

Buhalis, D., Leung, X. Y., Fan, D., Darcy, S., Chen, G., Xu, F., Wei-Han Tan, G., Nunkoo, R., & Farmaki, A. (2023). Tourism 2030 and the contribution to the sustainable development goals: The tourism review viewpoint. *Tourism Review*, 78(2), 293–313. 10.1108/TR-04-2023-620

Camargo, B. A., & Gretzel, U. (2017). What do tourism students know about sustainability and sustainable tourism? An exploratory study of Latin American students. *Journal of Teaching in Travel & Tourism*, 17(2), 101–117. 10.1080/15313220.2017.1294038

Cini, F., Van der Merwe, P., & Saayman, M. (2015). Tourism students' knowledge and tenets towards ecotourism. *Journal of Teaching in Travel & Tourism*, 15(1), 74–91. 10.1080/15313220.2014.999737

Cotterell, D., Hales, R., Arcodia, C., & Ferreira, J.-A. (2019). Overcommitted to tourism and under committed to sustainability: The urgency of teaching "strong sustainability" in tourism courses. *Journal of Sustainable Tourism*, 27(7), 882–902. 10.1080/09669582.2018.1545777

de Lange, D. E. (2013). How do universities make progress? Stakeholder-related mechanisms affecting adoption of sustainability in university curricula. *Journal of Business Ethics*, 118(1), 103–116. 10.1007/s10551-012-1577-y

Frick, J., Kaiser, F. G., & Wilson, M. (2004). Environmental knowledge and conservation behavior: Exploring prevalence and structure in a representative sample. *Personality and Individual Differences*, 37(8), 1597–1613. 10.1016/j.paid.2004.02.015

Globalsurvey-SDGs. (2020). *Report of results global survey on sustainability and the SDGs - awareness, priorities, need for action. Hamburg.* Global Survey. https://www.globalsurvey-sdgs.com/wp-content/uploads/2020/01/20200205_SC_Global_Survey_Result-Report_english_final.pdf

Globescan. (2023). *Growing awareness of the SDGs*. Globescan. https://globescan.com/2023/11/22/growing-awareness-of-the-sdgs/

Hall, C. M., Seyfi, S., & Koupaei, S. N. (2023). Politics and the sustainable development goals: Tourism Agenda 2030 perspective article. *Tourism Review*, 78(2), 314–320. 10.1108/TR-10-2022-0498

Izurieta, G., Torres, A., Pati, J., Vasco, C., Vasseur, L., Reyes, H., & Torres, B. (2021). Exploring community and key stakeholders' perception of scientific tourism as a strategy to achieve SDGs in the Ecuadorian Amazon. *Tourism Management Perspectives*, 39, 100830. 10.1016/j.tmp.2021.100830

Kc, B., Dhungana, A., & Dangi, T. B.KC. (2021). Tourism and the sustainable development goals: Stakeholders' perspectives from Nepal. *Tourism Management Perspectives*, 38, 100822. 10.1016/j.tmp.2021.100822

Kc, B.KC. (2024). Pedagogy in operationalizing sustainable development goals. *Journal of Hospitality, Leisure, Sport and Tourism Education*, 34, 100476. 10.1016/j.jhlste.2023.100476

Lampert, M., & Papadongonas, P. (2016). *Towards 2030 without poverty*. Amsterdam: Glocalities. https://www.glocalities.com/reports/towards-2030-without-poverty.html

León-Gómez, A., Forero, J. A. M., & Santos-Jaén, J. M. (2023). A bibliometric analysis of sustainability education in tourism universities. *SAGE Open*, 13(3), 1–20. 10.1177/21582440231193215

Manolis, E. N., & Manoli, E. N. (2021). Raising awareness of the Sustainable Development Goals through Ecological Projects in Higher Education. *Journal of Cleaner Production*, 279, 123614. 10.1016/j.jclepro.2020.123614

Özgit, H., & Zhandildina, D. (2021). Investigating stakeholder awareness of the sustainable development goals and tourism stakeholder collaboration: The case of North Cyprus. *Worldwide Hospitality and Tourism Themes*, 13(4), 498–509. 10.1108/WHATT-02-2021-0027

Pritchard, A., Morgan, N., & Ateljevic, I. (2011). Hopeful tourism: A new transformative perspective. *Annals of Tourism Research*, 38(3), 941–963. 10.1016/j. annals.2011.01.004

Rasoolimanesh, S. M., Ramakrishna, S., Hall, C. M., Esfandiar, K., & Seyfi, S. (2023). A systematic scoping review of sustainable tourism indicators in relation to the sustainable development goals. *Journal of Sustainable Tourism*, 31(7), 1497–1517. 10.1080/09669582.2020.1775621

Raub, S. P., & Martin-Rios, C. (2019). "Think sustainable, act local" – a stakeholder-filter-model for translating SDGs into sustainability initiatives with local impact. *International Journal of Contemporary Hospitality Management*, 31(6), 2428–2447. 10.1108/IJCHM-06-2018-0453

Robert, K. W., Parris, T. M., & Leiserowitz, A. A. (2005). What is sustainable development? Goals, indicators, values, and practice. *Environment*, 47(3), 8–21. 10.1080/00139157.2005.10524444

Rosato, P. F., Caputo, A., Valente, D., & Pizzi, S. (2021). 2030 Agenda and sustainable business models in tourism: A bibliometric analysis. *Ecological Indicators*, 121, 106978. 10.1016/j.ecolind.2020.106978

Roxas, F. M. Y., Rivera, J. P. R., & Gutierrez, E. L. M. (2020). Framework for creating sustainable tourism using systems thinking. *Current Issues in Tourism*, 23(3), 280–296. 10.1080/13683500.2018.1534805

Sachs, J. D., Lafortune, G., Kroll, C., Fuller, G., & Woelm, F. (2022). *Sustainable Development Report 2022 - From Crisis to Sustainable Development: the SDGs as Roadmap to 2030 and Beyond*. Cambridge University Press., 10.1017/9781009210058

Scheyvens, R., & Cheer, J. M. (2022). Tourism, the SDGs and partnerships. *Journal of Sustainable Tourism*, 30(10), 2271–2281. 10.1080/09669582.2021.1982953

Siakwah, P., Musavengane, R., & Leonard, L. (2020). Tourism governance and attainment of the sustainable development goals in Africa. *Tourism Planning & Development*, 17(4), 355–383. 10.1080/21568316.2019.1600160

Tedeneke, A. (2019). *Global survey shows 74% are aware of the Sustainable Development Goals*. WeForum. https://www.weforum.org/press/2019/09/global-survey -shows-74-are-aware-of-the-sustainable-development-goals/

UN. (2015). *Transforming our world: The 2030 agenda for sustainable development*. UN. https://sustainabledevelopment.un.org/content/documents/21252030%20 Agenda%20for%20Sustainable%20Development%20web.pdf?_gl=1*1l9w1zc* _ga*NDQzNTgyMjEwLjE3MTcxOTY1OTTg.*_ga_TK9BQL5X7Z*MT cxNzE5NjU5Ny4xLjEuMTcxNzE5NzUxMy4wLjAuMA

UNESCO. (2017). *Measurement strategy for SDG Target 4.7*. UNESCO. https://uis .unesco.org/sites/default/files/documents/gaml4-measurement-strategy-sdg-target4 .7.pdf

UNWTO. (2017). *Tourism and the sustainable development goals – journey to 2030*. UNWTO. https://www.e-unwto.org/doi/epdf/10.18111/9789284419401

UNWTO. (2023). *Achieving the sustainable development goals through tourism*. UNWTO. https://tourism4sdgs.org/tips_indicators/

Varah, F., Mahongnao, M., Pani, B., & Khamrang, S. (2021). Exploring young consumers' intention toward green products: Applying an extended theory of planned behavior. *Environment, Development and Sustainability*, 23(6), 9181–9195. 10.1007/ s10668-020-01018-z

Vrontis, D., Christofi, M., Giacosa, E., & Serravalle, F. (2022). Sustainable development in tourism: A stakeholder analysis of the Langhe Region. *Journal of Hospitality & Tourism Research (Washington, D.C.)*, 46(5), 846–878. 10.1177/1096348020982353

Worldslargestlesson (2023). *World's largest lesson*. World's Largest Lesson. https:// worldslargestlesson.globalgoals.org/about-us/

Yuan, X., Yu, L., & Wu, H. (2021). Awareness of sustainable development goals among students from a Chinese senior high school. *Education Sciences*, 11(9), 458. 10.3390/educsci11090458

Chapter 5
Women and Tourism:
A Study on Gender Equality, Social Inclusion, and Empowerment

Ambar Srivastava
https://orcid.org/0000-0002-7334-3421
Christ University, India

Ankit Pathania
https://orcid.org/0000-0003-2643-9743
Eternal University, India

Geeta Kumari
https://orcid.org/0000-0002-2115-7408
Malla Reddy College of Engineering and Technology, India

ABSTRACT

To achieve the sustainable development goals (SDGs) of the 2030 Agenda, which include the goals of gender equality, social inclusion, and women's empowerment, tourism is an essential industry. Gender disparity is a major development barrier in the majority of developing nations. The study aims to explore the challenges women face and gender inequality in tourism industry. The inter-linkage between tourism and SDGs will also be explored. A qualitative research technique was applied, and systematic literature review was based on articles in national and international journals, working papers, etc. explored. The study concluded that restricted opportunities for education, healthcare disparities, economic inequality are among the challenges faced by the women in tourism industry. It is also found that gender inequality in terms of dual presence, discrimination in wages, glass ceiling, sticky floors, etc. are also there. There is a definite linkage between the tourism industry and SDGs.

DOI: 10.4018/979-8-3693-3166-8.ch005

INTRODUCTION

One of the most important and fastest-growing service sectors today is tourism. The tourism and hospitality sectors are vital to an economy and influence the course of the country (Aslam et al., 2014). It has a favourable effect on the social, economic, cultural, political and educational facets of development. In many nations, tourism generates jobs and opens up markets for the employment of women (Aytug and Mikaeili, 2017; Hafci, 2018). The industry has enormous potential for growth and diversification and employs both qualified and untrained personnel. Apart from delivering economic benefits, tourism plays a key role in fostering gender equality, social inclusion and women empowerment. Women's participation is a crucial aspect of tourism. Women are an integral part of society and cannot be excluded from any definition of development that is deemed appropriate. Women have the potential and right to engage in tourism activities as members of society. Gender inequality in development can be lessened by women's participation in the tourism industry. One of the goals of Agenda 2030 is to advance women's empowerment and equality. To maximize development, efforts must be taken to expand the capacity and engagement of currently available resources. As resources in society, men and women fundamentally have equal opportunities to contribute to progress. But the proportion of women working in this field is significantly lower, necessitating special consideration. Eliminating inequality and dominance is a prerequisite for sustainable growth in all domains.

To achieve the Sustainable Development Goals (SDGs) of the 2030 Agenda, which include the goals of gender equality, social inclusion and women's empowerment and leaving no one behind, tourism is one of the essential industry which has the potential to help in achieving these SDGs. Without establishing gender equality and women's empowerment, half of humanity would not have the rights and opportunities that are necessary for progress and sustainable development. That is the exact reason, it is included in the 2030 Agenda's list of SDGs: Goal 5: Empower all women and attain gender equality. Gender equality is also essential for achieving other SDGs like SDG 8 on decent work and economic growth and SDG 10 on reduced inequalities (The 2030 Agenda for Sustainable Development).

Although women make up 54% of the workforce in the tourism industry worldwide, there exist salary differences (World Tourism Organization, 2019). In underdeveloped nations, the inequality is more pronounced. Inequalities affect women in the job market at both horizontal and vertical levels (Rinaldi & Salerno, 2020). Gender disparity is a major development barrier in the majority of developing nations. One of the most crucial things to do in order to accomplish the SDGs by 2030 will be to attempt to close the gender gap in terms of abilities, opportunities and resource accessibility and vulnerability to violence and conflict. The development of tourism is one area where gender (inequalities) issues might be crucial (UNWTO, 2006). Given that numerous studies on tourism highlight the critical connection between tourism, local development and women's empowerment, the UN's commitment to addressing these challenges has generated a significant political agenda for more study and investigation of these topics. For this reason, at the most recent ITB in Berlin, the UNWTO unveiled an Action Plan for women's empowerment through tourism. The Action Plan's main objectives are to reduce poverty and improve women's status and contribution to the workforce (UNWTO, 2006).

STATUS OF WOMEN IN TOURISM SECTOR

One of the most well-known segments of India's services industry is the travel and hospitality sector. The Ministry of External Affairs claims that tourism is not only India's third-largest source of foreign exchange earnings globally, but also a vital growth driver. From 2013 to 2023, the economy is predicted to develop at an annual rate of 7.8% in terms of its contribution to the GDP. The World Travel and Tourism Council (WTTC) reports that India's tourism earnings increased by 5.1 percent in 2013 and are expected to increase to 8.2 percent by the end of 2014. The percentage of women working in the tourist industry is 59%; this figure is considerably higher for the hospitality industry (61%) and travel agencies (64%). In the food service and lodging sectors in the EU, 53% of unregistered workers are women. Women are disproportionately impacted by variables such as part-time labour, seasonality, unpredictable contracts and frequent job rotation in this industry compared to men. For example, men tend to work in more established tourist destinations where they receive better compensation among other benefits. Even though women in the tourism industry have higher educational levels than males, there is a 14.7 percent pay gap because of the horizontal and vertical segregation that they face. Despite performing the same work, they are paid less than their colleagues, and as education levels improve, the gender pay gap is growing. Despite data showing that companies with female managers outperform those without, men continue to hold the majority of managerial roles.

Women are limited to lower-level jobs, concentrating on specific job sectors that are frequently associated with an increase in responsibilities, such as cooking, cleaning staff, crew labour and so on, if they are able to secure those positions. The fact that women make up over 79 percent of airline employees in the US, or over 5% of flight crews and 1.43 percent of leaders, is indicative of this concentration. Due to prejudice and gender stereotypes, women are less likely to advance in life and are often excluded from social networks that contribute to the segregation of genders. While women continue to make up the majority of portion agreements, males opt for part-time job to conduct research or training, which leaves a dearth of full-time employment options. A study by Travel & Tourism, 2013 Traveling Economic Effect Report states that over 101 million jobs, or 3.4% of labour, were entirely supported by tourism. According to industry projections for 2023, the tourist sector supports one in every eleven jobs globally, including occupations that are indirectly supported by businesses.

A woman's presence on a flight is typically regarded as that of an air hostess in the tourist sector. In the early 1970s, when the tourism sector was just getting started, it was believed that women should only work in a select few fields. However, she now has a number of posts, such as minister in several states that have promoted tourism. Bureaucrats in government tourism departments, chairmen and management committees, large hotel operations, airline marketing, travel and visa administration, holiday package creation and implementation and so forth. It is astounding how many Indian women are employed in foreign tourism industries.

REVIEW OF LITERATURE

This section of literature review is segregated into three parts based on the objectives of the study.

Challenges Faced by Women in Tourism

Women-owned businesses encounter difficulties obtaining finance (International Finance Corporation 2011) whereas the social networks of women are less advanced. Carvalho et al (2019) demonstrated that, despite the fact that prejudice against women is still prevalent but less overt, they are still viewed as less suitable for executive positions in the travel and tourism industry. As a result, the widely acknowledged "glass ceiling" effect is more subtly reinforced by the stereotype that women are less capable and unsuited for managerial roles (Acker, 1998; Bruni; Patterson et al., 2012). Based on many data sources, present a more nuanced picture of how male and female-owned businesses in Sub-Saharan Africa differ in their access to financial resources. When actual statistics are analyzed, it frequently seems that female-owned businesses face the same constraints as male-owned businesses, particularly when it comes to smaller businesses. According to Van der Merwe's (2003) findings, obstacles that female entrepreneurs encounter include inadequate financial backing, absence of familial support, unfavourable societal perspectives and insufficient self-assurance. Fried (1989) found that while the majority of working-age women are still single, the majority of female entrepreneurs are married. Married women have greater difficulties running their enterprises than single, unmarried women do since they have to give their spouses and kids more time.

Gender Inequality in Tourism

Bardasi et al. (2011) study was among the first to examine the problem of gender disparities in productivity between businesses run by different genders in a sample of emerging nations on various continents. The 2010 Global Report on Women in Tourism by the United Nations World Tourism Organization (UNWTO) stated that "women in tourism are still underpaid, under-utilized, undereducated and under-represented". Boluk et al. (2019) emphasize the significance of gender parity for the growth of environmentally friendly travel, as also mentioned by the UNWTO in a 2017 statement. The purpose of this declaration is to promote tourism as a means of achieving the 17 Sustainable Development Goals (2015–2030) (SDGs) and 169 goals of the worldwide 2030 Agenda for Sustainable Development. Recent research has shown that there is a gender gap in leadership roles (Munar et al, 2015; Pritchard and Morgan, 2017). Reaching the Third Millennium Development Goal and empowering women could be facilitated by the tourism industry (Ferguson, 2010). Despite their great projected potential, economic policy interventions targeted at promoting female employment, ownership and management are still in their infancy. Women make up over 46% of the workforce globally, however they are still subjected to occupational and sectoral discrimination in this field (Rinaldi and Salerno, 2010). For example, women are more likely to work in hospitality, cleaning, and cooking than in more specialized fields (Purcell, 1997; Campos-Soria et al., 2011). Santero-Sanchez et al. (2015) provides evidence for the lower quality level of occupations held by women utilizing their work quality index. In the fields of tourism economics and management, the presence of a glass ceiling effect a wider disparity at the top end of the salary distribution—has long been recognized (Cotter et al., 2001). Islam et al. (2019) have discovered that the kind of law and its capacity to ensure gender equality are important. Furthermore, in the sample of nations taken into consideration, legal gender gaps disempower women in the private sector through property ownership, labour market limits, financing availability and business registration.

Sustainable development and progress are impossible without gender equality and women's empowerment, as half of humankind would be denied rights and opportunity (United Nations. Transforming Our World: The 2030 Agenda for Sustainable Development). Due to gender stereotypes, discrimination and women's exclusion from unofficial networks that support gender segregation, women have less prospects for advancement (Kogovsek and Kogovek, 2012).

Tourism and Sustainable Development Goals (SDGs)

For a considerable time, the tourism industry's sustainable development has been supported by policy and research (UN WTO, 2017, 2012; Buckley, 2012). The United Nations World Tourism Organization (UN WTO) started a dialogue about the tourism industry's alignment with the Sustainable Development Goals in 2017 through collaborative research conducted with the United Nations Development Program. This study looked at the benefits and drawbacks of the sector.

Several scholars have recently highlighted the necessity for the tourism industry to establish policies for the Sustainable Development Goals (Boluk et al., 2019; Hall, 2019; Scheyvens and Hughes, 2019). Furthermore, the industry has a complex impact on the areas in which it works because it has brought new philanthropic endeavours, such building roads, infrastructure and other structures. The varied economic and cultural backgrounds of the local populations influence how they will accept these investments (Lenao, 2015; Scheyvens and Hughes, 2019). However, prior studies have demonstrated that the impact of tourism on natural resources is one of the main reasons for concern (Manomaivibool, 2015). It can, however, also have a detrimental effect on the ecosystem because it can deteriorate both renewable and non-renewable natural resources (Lacitignola et al., 2007). Notably, there has been an increasing amount of attention paid to the potential consequences of tourism enterprises transitioning to more ecologically friendly business models (Boluk et al., 2019; Gossling and Michael, 2019; Niaia et al., 2010). Further investigation has been conducted to explore potential links between the expansion of sustainable practices and the overall health of nearby communities. People's quality of life has been improved and poverty has decreased as indicators of this wellbeing (Boluk et al., 2019; Hall, 2019; Scheyvens and Hughes, 2019).

In the tourism sector, partnerships are frequently intricate, multifaceted matters governed by numerous regulatory frameworks and governance structures (Scheyvens and Cheer, 2021). The integration of the Sustainable Development Goals (SDGs) into the tourism industry will center around six key issues, namely: gender in the SDGs, indigenous perspectives, degrowth and the circular economy, governance and planning, and ethical consumption (Boluk et al., 2019). There is a misperception that increasing effort and efficiency will solve all of the problems with sustainable tourism. This misperception necessitates a re-evaluation of the interactions between people and their surroundings (Hall, 2019). The topic of governance is sometimes overlooked (Rasoolimanesh et al. 2020). The tourism and hospitality industries' most prosperous companies are in a great position to significantly advance the Sustainable Development Goals (SDGs) (Jones et al. 2017). The community is involved at every stage, with the ultimate aim of enabling them to take ownership of the interventions so that they can continue to benefit from their involvement long after the project and relationship have ended (Adie et al., 2014). Governmental administrations must encourage safe and respectable employment opportunities and the reduction of the current gender pay gap in addition to raising public awareness of the principles of the tourism industry (Pena-Sanchez et al., 2020). Redefining sustainable tourism development indicators is a direct result of the mindset, values and attitudes of decision-makers (Glyptou et al. 2022).

Rinaldi and Salerno (2019) provided proof that the number of women running and owning tourism businesses is rising sharply across the globe, especially in developed nations like the EU. Even yet, there are still a lot of distinctions and country-specific empirical data can help determine how this issue has developed. It is anticipated that legislative initiatives designed to increase the number of women working in, managing and owning tourism-related businesses will be more successful (Ferguson, 2010) considering that the services, hospitality, event planning and other related industries do offer a competitive advantage to women. Amin and Islam (2014) confirm that women typically run businesses in the service sector, especially in the retail rather than the wholesale sector, based on an empirical analysis pertaining to over 90 developing nations. Additionally, businesses run by women typically have a modest workforce and are located in smaller cities.

OBJECTIVES OF THE STUDY

a) To understand the challenges faced by the women engaged in the tourism industry.
b) To find out the areas for gender inequality in tourism.
c) To explore the interlinkage between tourism and SDGs.

RESEARCH METHODOLOGY

A qualitative research technique was applied in this study. With a focus on academics and practitioners, the researcher offers an informative and well-organized overview of the literature on current trends in the study area which were based on articles in national and international journals, magazines, working papers, etc. gathered and analyzed to achieve the research objective. The Scopus database, google scholar, web of sciences database was used for in-depth review.

CHALLENGES FACED BY WOMEN IN TOURISM INDUSTRY

a) **Restricted Educational Opportunities:** Girls confront numerous obstacles to education in rural areas, including long commutes to school, subpar facilities, early marriage and cultural traditions that place a higher value on a boy's education. Approximately 132 million females between the ages of 6 and 17 were not attending school in 2020, according to UNESCO, with a large majority living in rural areas.

b) **Disparities in Health:** Occupational risk is the probability of experiencing any harm while working, such as a sickness, accident, or injury. Gender-based job allocation determines which tasks are assigned to men and which to women in the tourism industry. In relation to that, women typically labor under less favorable circumstances in terms of pay, advancement chances and degree of responsibility. Higher rates of maternal mortality and fewer alternatives for reproductive health result from rural women and girls' frequent lack of access to high-quality healthcare facilities. The majority of these deaths more than 800 women every day occur in rural regions and are connected to pregnancy and childbirth-associated avoidable causes, according to the World Health Organization.

c) **Economic Inequality:** Women frequently work in informal jobs or subsistence farming, where they frequently face low wages, restricted access to financing and limited ownership of productive assets. The Food and Agriculture Organization (FAO) estimates that if women and men had equal access to resources, agricultural output could rise by 20–30%, potentially ending hunger for 100–150 million people.

d) **Violence against Women:** Due to poor law enforcement and restricted access to support services, women and girls living in rural areas are more vulnerable to gender-based violence.

Around 35% of women globally have suffered physical or sexual violence, with rates of abuse being greater in rural regions, according to UN Women.

e) **Sexual Harassment:** Sexual harassment is classified as a type of discrimination and includes solicitations for sexual favours, unwanted sexual innuendos and other verbal or physical acts that have a sexual overtone. Sexual harassment typically happens when situations like these arise, either overtly or covertly, as a result of accepting or rejecting such behaviour: Affectation regarding safety and career advancement; psychological and emotional damage that could hinder one's ability to work or maintain one's well-being, such as stress or low self-esteem and the creation of an intimidating, offensive, or hostile work environment (Theocharous and Philaretou, 2009). Harassment can have negative effects on one's psychological and physical health in addition to at work (Cho,

2002). They can also have long-term effects or short-term ones and they have an impact on the affected person's surroundings (Theocharous and Philaretou, 2009). Sexual harassment can be made easier in the tourism business by factors including extended work hours, high levels of social interaction at work and direct client contact, among others (Cho, 2002). These working settings might encourage situations of exploitation, sexual harassment among them, in addition to the high standard of care that must be provided to tourists (Dyer et al., 2010). Because of their enthusiasm and kindness, certain jobs in the tourism industry like those of receptionists, housekeepers, flight attendants, nightclub waitresses, or entertainers are more vulnerable to harassment situations, like innuendos and sexual demands from patrons (Cabezas, 2006).

f) **Sexual Exploitation:** In tourist studies, sexual exploitation is a common and contentious topic. It is defined by the World Health Organization (2020) as the attempt or abuse of a position of power, trust, or vulnerability for sexual objectives, including but not limited to the use of another person's sexual exploitation for one's own economic, social, or political gain. Nonetheless, conceptual misunderstandings frequently hinder the generation of new knowledge. It's important to distinguish sex tourism from its counterpart, human trafficking for the purpose of exploitation. Concurrently, it's important to distinguish human trafficking from irregular migrants who cross borders in order to become prostitutes.

g) **Social and Family Opposition to Work:** The resistance of family and society to getting a career is one entry hurdle for women. Women rely heavily on their spouses and in-laws because historically, men were expected to provide the household money. Women were only allowed to work in jobs that their husbands had previously approved of, therefore it was expected that they would contribute to the household economy. In addition, women experience a lack of social support because their families want them to fulfill the conventional position of mother and all of its responsibilities. Married women who enter the workforce, especially those who work in the tourism industry or on their own projects, may experience stress or domestic disputes, particularly with their spouses (Getz et al., 2004).

GENDER INEQUALITY IN TOURISM INDUSTRY

Achieving inclusive growth and sustainable development requires gender equality as well as the empowerment of women and girls. Despite tremendous advancements over time, women and girls still confront particular difficulties that limit their access to economic opportunities, healthcare, education and decision-making authority.

The tourism industry employs far more women than males, but there is still a significant gender wage gap and many women still experience discrimination in the workplace. According to UNWTO, the tourism industry has an excellent opportunity to rethink gender balance in light of the terrible effects of the COVID-19 epidemic. It is impossible to discuss women's rights, status and working conditions in the workplace without mentioning men's; in fact, women's active participation in the workforce is regarded as one of the most revolutionary developments of the past century. Although women and men are protected under the rules that they should have equal rights both in social life and in business life, it is noticed that gender-based discrimination is regularly made in business life. It has been established that discrimination in the workplace, which exists in both developed and developing nations, is the product of numerous intricate factors, such as social, cultural and economic ones. The travel and tourism sector is one of the most significant areas where gender-based discrimination occurs in the workplace. The causes and practices of gender discrimination in business life and the tourism industry are provided in this part.

- **Dual presence:** Across the globe, women have generally been subjected to a number of traditional gender-based duties that assign them the responsibility of taking care of the elderly, the family, childcare and home tasks. This creates a barrier for women to pursue professional professions known as "dual presence," which is defined as the requirement to balance the demands of both paid employment and taking care of one's home and family at the same time (Moreno et al., 2010). The requirement to fulfill these obligations may have a variety of consequences on the personal life of the employees. They have little time or energy left over for personal devotion, leisure, or rest because of the amount of time and effort they spend on paid job and housework. Furthermore, this burden may put workers' health at danger by depleting their mental and physical well-being and producing stress-related behavioral and cognitive symptoms.

- **Gender and Race-Based job segmentation:** The gender-based divide of the workforce is reflected in the activities associated with either feminine or masculine values. As a result, the societal disparity is seen as normalized prejudice and becomes naturalized. Precarious employment, variable contracts, lengthy and irregular work hours and exploitation techniques are all linked to the tourism industry. Immigrant laborers are typically affected by these situations, particularly women (Rydzik and Anitha, 2019). Women are underpaid and in low-categorized roles in the tourism business. In addition, people of immigrant backgrounds face disadvantages because of their unfamiliarity with the workforce, small social circles and underappreciated qualifications (Dyer et al., 2010).

- **Discrimination in wages:** For the most part, workers in the tourism industry earn poor wages on average and suffer unfavourable working conditions. Gender discrimination, which is defined as the devaluation of feminized employment and reflected in remuneration, contributes to these impacts. The researcher examined the sociological and cultural elements that influence this salary disparity, which is purportedly caused by prejudice against men and women based on their respective productive potential. Among these, the female group has less work experience, which is made worse by the fact that women are typically responsible for taking care of their families and homes. Men are frequently perceived as having to support their families financially, with women working to augment their husbands' incomes, which is socially viewed as a priority.

- **Glass Ceiling:** In the United States, the phrase "glass ceiling" first appeared in the 1970s to refer to the intangible, man-made obstacles that keep women out of leadership roles due to bias in both behavioural and organizational bias (Wirth, 2001). In other words, these are the barriers that women who possess the necessary training and personal and professional skills must overcome to advance into roles with greater management and responsibility. Women's advancement to managerial positions is impeded, in part, by the demands and compromises that these roles entail, which are deemed incompatible with their obligations as homemakers. Furthermore, in a workplace that is still dominated by men, women who advance to executive positions nonetheless use their professional and personal authority. However, their leadership is linked to characteristics that are similar to the stereotype of a traditional gender, like relationship thinking, teamwork, inclusive communication, emotion, empathy and the ability to multitask.

- **Sticky Floor:** "A metaphor used to denote a discriminatory employment pattern that keeps working women at the lowest levels of the occupational pyramid, with scarce mobility and invisible barriers to their professional improvement," is the definition of "sticky floor". The sticky floor concept is closely related to the glass ceiling concept; however, rather than signifying the challenge of reaching higher positions, these are either non-existent or extremely unlikely to be held because of the nature of the work, which hinders employees' ability to advance in their careers and improves their working conditions and skill set. This issue is caused by the majority of management and senior positions in the hierarchy being imposed on men, as well as the fact that many feminized vocations have a relatively short professional scale or evolve very seldom. The majority of women working in the hospitality or catering industries, particularly as housekeepers, hotel cleaners, or kitchen staff, exhibit few opportunities for advancement, which keeps them in a stagnant position.

LINKAGE BETWEEN SDGS AND TOURISM

The United Nations 2030 Agenda for Sustainable Development has significant implications for tourism theory, practice and policy. Notably, unsustainable growth can have detrimental effects on a nation, a community and the world at large, which is why the UN introduced the SDG framework. The UN underlined that all member nations should work towards achieving the SDGs and protecting the environment and natural resources for coming generations (Pachot and Patissier, 2023). The tourist sector has embraced sustainable practices to control its effects on the environment, economies and society. Sustainable tourism has the ability to boost global peace, ecological security, cultural diversity and economic growth in addition to enhancing people's quality of life. Additionally, it can directly or indirectly support each of the SDGs in the areas of the economy, society and environment. Similarly, the SDG framework supports the tourism industry's future growth and offers a safe and sustainable business model. In order to achieve "decent work and economic growth" (SDG 8), "responsible consumption and production" (SDG 12) and "life below water" (SDG 14), tourism has an important role to play. Sustainable tourism and "gender equality" (SDG 5) are related, but advancing gender equality through tourism begins with an understanding of existing tourism development strategies.

CONCLUSION

The study aims to reflect the challenges faced by the women in tourism industry. It also aims to reflects areas of gender inequality. Lastly to explore the interlinkage between Tourism and SDGs. After going through the literature review of earlier studies and various articles, it was concluded that women face challenges in the tourism industry in term of restricted educational opportunities, disparities in healthcare, economic inequality, financial inequality, violence against women, sexual harassment, sexual exploitation and social and family opposition to work. These challenges are not the exhaustive areas, there are various other challenges they faced while working in the tourism industry. In terms of gender inequality, the areas found are dual presence, gender and race-based job segmentation, discrimination in wages, glass ceiling and sticky floor. The last conclusion is related to the interlinkage between tourism and SDGs. There are various targets under the SDGs which are directly or indirectly related to tourism industry. Whether it is gender equality, life below water, economic growth, etc. It shows a definite linkage between the tourism and SDGs.

Gender is becoming more and more recognized in the tourism industry as an important factor. It is crucial to recognize that, despite the fact that tourism is frequently promoted as a way to give women flexible and varied work options, research warns that, by providing temporary and part-time jobs in fields that are typically associated with one gender, it may also serve to reinforce traditional gender roles. Women are committed to being successful in the tourism industry and think they are well-suited for the role due to their training and background. There is an unofficial role for women in tourism. Low-paying jobs are held by women. Due to several issues, women are also limited in their ability to perform their jobs. The situation surrounding women's empowerment through tourism is complicated, with opportunities and difficulties that are inextricably linked. Indeed, opportunities have been greatly expanded by tourism and problems can be solved by incorporating them into the ordering process to create innovative tourism. These innovations will include opening doors and providing creative spaces for women to start and run tourism initiatives that simultaneously tackle major global issues.

SUGGESTIONS FOR ACHIEVING GENDER EQUALITY, SOCIAL INCLUSION AND EMPOWERMENT

For social progress and sustainable development, rural women and girls must receive equitable treatment and empowerment. By tackling the obstacles they encounter and seizing chances for self-determination, we may establish a more comprehensive and just community. To ensure a better future for future generations, governments, civil society organizations and international entities must collaborate to develop focused policies and initiatives that improve the lives of rural women and girls.

i) **Education and Skill Building:** Encouraging women and girls in communities to participate in education and skill-building initiatives is essential to their empowerment. The lack of adequate educational resources and infrastructure in many rural communities makes it challenging for females to attend school on a regular basis. We may establish a supportive atmosphere for education and individual growth by making investments in schools and career training facilities. Having access to a high-quality education gives women and girls the knowledge and skills they need to take advantage of greater economic opportunities. Women with education have a higher chance of landing steady jobs, launching their own enterprises, and making significant contributions to the advancement of their communities. This in turn has the potential to end the poverty cycle and raise rural residents' level of living in general.

ii) **Enhancing Healthcare Services:** The lack of proper healthcare facilities in remote locations frequently has a disproportionately negative impact on women's health and wellbeing. In order to lower the rate of maternal mortality and guarantee improved general health outcomes for women, it is imperative to fill the gaps in rural healthcare. Telemedicine and mobile clinics can greatly increase the accessibility of healthcare in remote places. Mobile clinics can provide necessary medical treatments and preventive care to areas where access to healthcare institutions is restricted. Without requiring travel, telemedicine can facilitate virtual consultations with medical specialists, providing medical guidance and assistance. By running health-related awareness programs, women might gain the confidence to make decisions regarding their own and their families' health. In rural communities, promoting health behaviours including family planning, hygiene and prenatal care can improve health outcomes.

iii) **Economic Empowerment:** One of the main forces behind women's autonomy and gender equality is economic empowerment. Women can manage their finances, launch enterprises and make investments in ventures that generate revenue with the assistance of financial services and training. Microfinance programs provide women with access to loans, enabling them to start or grow small companies that contribute to economic growth and the alleviation of poverty. Women's cooperatives can encourage group decision-making and resource sharing, resulting in an atmosphere that is beneficial for female entrepreneurs. Women's economic empowerment depends on promoting the ownership of productive resources like land and property. Women's bargaining power within homes and communities can be increased by land ownership, which can give them a source of income and financial security.

iv) **Legal Reforms and Gender Awareness:** It is imperative to fortify legal safeguards against gender-based violence in order to establish a secure atmosphere for females. Legal changes ought to concentrate on resolving problems like child marriage, sexual harassment and domestic abuse. Programs that promote gender sensitization can combat damaging societal norms and prejudices that support gender inequity. These initiatives support societal shifts in attitudes and behaviors by increasing knowledge of women's rights and equality. Raising awareness of equality and women's rights can enable women to speak up for these rights and take part in societal and local decision-making. This understanding may result in a more inclusive society and more women holding leadership roles.

v) **Increase women's participation in decision-making:** Foster an atmosphere that supports the greater involvement of rural women in fora for decision-making by offering child care during meetings and scheduling them at times that work for families. Create and promote leadership, public speaking, decision-making and self-assuredness training programs for rural women. Open up new avenues for women to participate in decision-making by endorsing participatory methods and integrating women's associations and groups in all tiers of decision-making. Promote communication and the establishment of connections between rural development organizations and authorities and local women's networks and associations.

vi) **Social equality and cultural revival:** Make sure women are treated equally to urban women in terms of access to social institutions and services. Encourage and spread knowledge within rural communities and between these and metropolitan centers about the rich and varied rural cultural legacy and the role that women play in preserving it. Encourage programs that will give women and girls living in rural areas fulfilling options for how to spend their free time.

REFERENCES

Acker, J. (1998). The future of "gender and organizations": Connections and boundaries. *Gender, Work and Organization*, 5(4), 195–206. 10.1111/1468-0432.00057

Adie, B. A., Amore, A., & Hall, C. M. (2020). Just because it seems impossible, doesn't mean we shouldn't at least try: The need for longitudinal perspectives on tourism partnerships and the SDGs. *Journal of Sustainable Tourism*, 1–16. 10.1080/09669582.2020.1860071

Amin, M., & Islam, A. (2014). Are There More Female Managers in the Retail Sector? Evidence from Survey Data in Developing Countries. *Journal of Applied Econometrics*, 17(2), 213–228.

Aslam, M. S. M., Awang, K. W., & Othman, N. B. H. (2014). Issues and Challenges in Nurturing Sustainable Rural Tourism Development. *Tourism. Leisure and Global Change*, 1, 75–89.

Aytug, H. K., & Mikaeili, M. (2017). Evaluation of Hopa's Rural Tourism Potential in the Context of European Union Tourism Policy. *Procedia Environmental Sciences*, 37, 234–245. 10.1016/j.proenv.2017.03.039

Bardasi, E., Sabarwal, S., & Terrell, K. (2011). How Do Female Entrepreneurs Perform? Evidence from Three Developing Regions. *Small Business Economics*, 37(4), 417–441. 10.1007/s11187-011-9374-z

Boluk, K. A., Cavaliere, C. T., & Higgins-Desbiolles, F. (2019). A critical framework for interrogating the United Nations Sustainable Development Goals 2030 Agenda in tourism. *Journal of Sustainable Tourism*, 27(7), 847–864. 10.1080/09669582.2019.1619748

Bruni, A., Gherardi, S., & Poggio, B. (2004). Entrepreneur-mentality, gender and the study of women entrepreneurs. *Journal of Organizational Change Management*, 17(3), 256–268. 10.1108/09534810410538315

Buckley, R. (2012). Sustainable tourism: Research and reality. *Annals of Tourism Research*, 39(2), 528–546. 10.1016/j.annals.2012.02.003

Cabezas, A. L. (2006). The Eroticization of Labor in Cuba's All-Inclusive Resorts: Performing Race, Class and Gender in the New Tourist Economy. *Social Identities*, 12(5), 507–521. 10.1080/13504630600920092

Campos-Soria, J., Marchante-Mera, A., & Ropero-García, M. (2011). Patterns of occupational segregation by gender in the hospitality industry. *International Journal of Hospitality Management*, 30(1), 91–102. 10.1016/j.ijhm.2010.07.001

Carvalho, I., Costa, C., Lykke, N., & Torres, A. (2019). Beyond the Glass Ceiling: Genderism Tourism Management. *Annals of Tourism Research*, 75, 79–91. 10.1016/j. annals.2018.12.022

Cho, M. (2002). An Analysis of Sexual Harassment in Korean Hotels from the Perspective of Female Employees. *Journal of Human Resources in Hospitality & Tourism*, 1(3), 11–29. 10.1300/J171v01n03_02

Cotter, D. A., Hermsen, J. M., Ovadia, S., & Vanneman, R. (2001). The glass ceiling effect. *Social Forces, 80*(2), 655–682.

Dyer, S., McDowell, L., & Batnitzk, A. (2010). The impact of migration on the gendering of service work: The case of a west London hotel. *Gender, Work and Organization*, 17(6), 635–657. 10.1111/j.1468-0432.2009.00480.x

Ferguson, L. (2010). Promoting gender equality and empowering women? Tourism and the third Millennium Development Goal. *Current Issues in Tourism*, 14(3), 235–249. 10.1080/13683500.2011.555522

Fried, L.I. (1989). *A new breed of entrepreneur-women.*

Getz, D., Carlsen, J., & Morrison, A. (2004). *The family Business in Tourism and Hospitality. Trowbridge*. Cromwell Press. 10.1079/9780851998084.0000

Glyptou, K., Amore, A., & Adie, B. A. (2022). From aspirations to applications: The SDGs and the role of indicators in the measurement of sustainable tourism. In A. Farmaki, L. Altinay, & X. Font (Eds.), *Planning and Managing Sustainability in Tourism, Hospitality and Events* (pp. 13-25). (Tourism, Hospitality & Event Management). Springer. 10.1007/978-3-030-92208-5_2

Gossling, S., & Michael Hall, C. (2019). Sharing versus collaborative economy: How to align ICT developments and the SDGs in tourism? *Journal of Sustainable Tourism*, 27(1), 74–96. 10.1080/09669582.2018.1560455

Hafci, B. (2018). Could Rural Tourism be a Good Generator of Women Work-force?: The Case of Kirazli Town. *International Rural Tourism and Development Journal, 2*(2).

Hall, C. M. (2019). Constructing sustainable tourism development: The 2030 agenda and the managerial ecology of sustainable tourism. *Journal of Sustainable Tourism*, 27(7), 1044–1060. 10.1080/09669582.2018.1560456

Hansen, H., & Rand, J. (2014). Estimates of Gender Differences in Firm's Access to Credit in Sub-Saharan Africa. *Economics Letters*, 123(3), 374–377. 10.1016/j. econlet.2014.04.001

International Finance Corporation (2011). *Strengthening Access to Finance for Women-Owned SMEs in Developing Countries*. IFC.

Islam, A., Muzi, S., & Amin, M. (2019). Unequal Laws and the Disempowerment of Women in the Labour Market: Evidence from Firm-Level Data. *The Journal of Development Studies*, 55(5), 822–844. 10.1080/00220388.2018.1487055

Jones, P., Hillier, D., & Comfort, D. (2017). The sustainable development goals and the tourism and hospitality industry. *Athens Journal of Tourism*, 4(1), 7–18. 10.30958/ajt.4.1.1

Kogovsek, M., & Kogovsek, M. (2012). Hospitality and Tourism Gender Issues Remain Unsolved: A Call for Research. *Quaestus*, 6, 194–203.

Lacitignola, D., Petrosillo, I., Cataldi, M., & Zurlini, G. (2007). Modelling socio-ecological tourismbased systems for sustainability. *Ecological Modelling*, 206(1), 191–204. 10.1016/j.ecolmodel.2007.03.034

Lenao, M. (2015). Challenges facing community-based cultural tourism development at Lekhubu Island, Botswana: A comparative analysis. *Current Issues in Tourism*, 18(6), 579–594. 10.1080/13683500.2013.827158

Manomaivibool, P. (2015). Wasteful tourism in developing economy? A present situation and sustainable scenarios. *Resources, Conservation and Recycling*, 103, 69–76. 10.1016/j.resconrec.2015.07.020

Moreno, N., Moncada, S., Llorens, C., & Carrasquer, P. (2010). Double presence, paid work, and domestic-family work. *New Solutions*, 20(4), 511–526. 10.2190/NS.20.4.h21342873

Munar, A. M., Biran, A., Budeanu, A., Caton, K., Chambers, D., Dredge, D., Gyimothy, S., Jamal, T., Larson, M., Nilsson Lindstrom, K., Nygaard, L., & Ram, Y. (2015). The Gender Gap in the Tourism Academy: Statistics and Indicators of Gender Equality. Copenhagen: While Waiting for the Dawn.

Niäiä, M., Ivanovic, S., & Drpic, D. (2010). Challenges to sustainable development in Island tourism. *South East European Journal of Economic Business*, 5(2), 43–53. 10.2478/v10033-010-0014-3

Pachot, A., & Patissier, C. (2023). *Towards Sustainable Artificial Intelligence: An Overview of Environmental Protection Uses and Issues*. Green and Low-Carbon Economy., 10.47852/bonviewGLCE3202608

Patterson, N., Mavin, S., & Turner, J. (2012). Envisioning female entrepreneur: Leaders anew from a gender perspective. *Gender in Management*, 27(9), 395–416. 10.1108/17542411211269338

Pena-Sanchez, A. R., Ruiz-Chico, J., Jimenez-García, M., & Lopez-Sanchez, J. A. (2020). Tourism and the SDGs: An analysis of economic growth, decent employment, and gender equality in the European Union (2009–2018). *Sustainability (Basel)*, 12(13), 5480. 10.3390/su12135480

Pritchard, A., & Morgan, N. (2017). Tourism's lost leaders: Analysing gender and performance. *Annals of Tourism Research*, 63, 34–47. 10.1016/j.annals.2016.12.011

Purcell, K. (1997). Women's employment in UK tourism: Gender roles and labour markets. In Sinclair, M. (Ed.), *Gender, work and tourism* (pp. 33–56). Routledge.

Rasoolimanesh, S. M., Ramakrishna, S., Hall, C. M., Esfandiar, K., & Seyfi, S. (2020). A systematic scoping review of sustainable tourism indicators in relation to the sustainable development goals. *Journal of Sustainable Tourism*, 1–21. 10.1080/09669582.2020.1775621

Rinaldi, A., & Salerno, I. (2020). The tourism gender gap and its potential impact on the development of the emerging countries. *Quality & Quantity*, 54(5-6), 1465–1477. 10.1007/s11135-019-00881-x

Rose, C. (2007). Does Female Board Representation Influence Firm Performance? The Danish Evidence. *Corporate Governance*, 15(2), 404–413. 10.1111/j.1467-8 683.2007.00570.x

Rydzik, A., & Anitha, S. (2019). Conceptualising the Agency of Migrant Women Workers: Resilience, Reworking and Resistance. *Work, Employment and Society*, •••, 1–17.

Santero-Sanchez, R., Segovia-Perez, B., Castro-Nunez, C., Figueroa-Domecq, P., & Talón-Ballestero, P. (2015). Gender Differences in the Hospitality Industry. *Tourism Management*, 51, 234–246. 10.1016/j.tourman.2015.05.025

Scheyvens, R., & Cheer, J. M. (2021). Tourism, the SDGs and partnerships. *Journal of Sustainable Tourism*, 1–11. 10.1080/09669582.2021.1982953

Scheyvens, R., & Hughes, E. (2019). Can tourism help to "end poverty in all its forms everywhere"? The challenge of tourism addressing SDG1. *Journal of Sustainable Tourism*, 27(7), 1061–1079. 10.1080/09669582.2018.1551404

Theocharous, A., & Philaretou, A. G. (2009). Sexual Harassment in the Hospitality Industry in the Republic of Cyprus: Theory and Prevention. *Journal of Teaching in Travel & Tourism*, 9(3-4), 288–304. 10.1080/15313220903445306

UNWTO. (2017). *Discussion paper on the occasion of the international year of sustainable tourism for development*. UNWTO.

Van der Merwe, M. (2003). *Women Entrepreneurs in South Africa*.

Wirth, L. (2001). *Breaking through the glass ceiling: Woman in management*. International Labour Office.

World Tourism Organization. (2019). *Global Report on Women in Tourism* (2nd ed.). UNWTO. 10.18111/9789284420384

Chapter 6
Obstacles Faced by Women Entrepreneurs in Community–Based Tourism:
Insights From Economic and Socio–Cultural Empowerment Lenses

Ravinay Amit Chandra
Fiji National University, Fiji

Nikeel Niskar Kumar
Royal Melbourne Institute of Technology, Australia

Jone Toua
Fiji National University, Fiji

Manisha Chand
Fiji National University, Fiji

Pritika Chand
Fiji National University, Fiji

Karishma Kritika Sharma
Fiji National University, Fiji

ABSTRACT

This study investigates the intricate balance between women's economic empowerment and socio-cultural empowerment within the context of community-based tourism. Specifically, it focuses on the case of Biausevu, Fiji, a community heavily dependent on tourism for its economic sustenance. A survey was executed to gather data, engaging a sample of 32 participants, representing roughly 60 percent of women in the community. Employing logit and Probit regression methodology, the study analyzed the interplay of factors influencing women's empowerment. The

DOI: 10.4018/979-8-3693-3166-8.ch006

findings underscored that income derived from tourism and the resultant enhancement in quality of life significantly contribute to women's economic empowerment. However, it also revealed a potential downside: an over-reliance on tourism could impede socio-cultural empowerment facets. Incorporating insights from sustainable development goal five SDG -5, this study advocates for an integrated approach to women's empowerment. It emphasizes the need for policies that balance economic gains from tourism with preserving and promoting socio-cultural values.

INTRODUCTION

In Small Islands Developing States (SIDs) such as Fiji tourism has emerged as the primary driver of economic growth and women represent a large volume in the tourism sector (Kumar et al., 2021). Women in rural areas were introduced to entrepreneurship after seeing the economic benefits of tourism. Valeri and Katsoni (2021) highlight that women have played a central role in an economic and social transformation that has significantly reshaped the tourism environment. However, in SIDs the literature has focused on coastal and maritime regions, with less attention diverted to inland communities reliant on tourism development (Morais et al., 2005). Inland communities are often neglected in tourism policymaking and development, and due to the lack of concentration on community-based tourism (CBT), the economic and social hardships are further exacerbated (Butlera, 2017; Bakas, 2017; Farrelly, 2011). Tran and Walter (2014) Higgins-Desbiolleset et al. (2019) identified by linking the objective of women empowerment and tourism and hidden agendas there is a need to analyze the impacts from a critical point of investigation. On the other hand, policies that govern women's empowerment have been criticized for being an "instrumentalist" approach to the relationships between gender equality and development (Cotterell et al., 2020; Rasoolimanesh, 2020). Despite progress in recent years, achieving United Nations Sustainable Development Goal 5 - "achieving gender equality and empowerment of all women and girls" - remains a challenge, as highlighted by contemporary research (Khoo et al.,2019). In achieving sustainability in the context of tourism development other forms of tourism were identified including CBT. Moreover, recognizing the outcome of CBT is an alternative approach to trickle down poverty level and empowering the poor which also entails numerous benefits to the host community (Butlera, 2017; Saarinen & Rogerson, 2014; Tavakoli et al., 2017; Vongvisitsin et al., 2024). However, Dolezal and Novelli (2020) underscore that CBT initiatives have the potential to foster the expression of villagers' agency, self-organization, and autonomy, thereby reinstating equilibrium on an island where extensive tourism has disrupted the harmony among the human, natural, and spiritual realms. Yet this statement is undermined with lack of concentration on women empowerment and the issues they face while achieving the aspects of SDG 5.

Tourisms contributions to development and poverty reduction were highlighted under the MDGs (Ferguson & Alarcón, 2015; Jeffrey, 2017). Yet, less attention was paid to gender equality and women empowerment (Cave & Kilic, 2010). Nonetheless Kato (2019) identified areas of women empowerment include equal participation, opportunities, rights, and decision-making. However, research on women empowerment requires a critical re-investigation with clear objectives and methods due to the gender "greenwashing" prevalent in the tourism industry (Jeffrey, 2017; Tucker & Boonabaana, 2012; Figuero-Domecq et al., 2015; Bakas, 2017b). By employing the Logit Regression method, we identify the relationship between tourism and women's economic empowerment while quantifiable variables analyze the transformation of women's livelihood and power relations through tourism data. As Khoo (2019) proposes that researchers in the tourism field should employ a range of methodological approaches to expand the discourse and enhance understanding of tourism-related issues The identification of the variables is drawn from Goal 5 UNWTO (2017) and Movono and Dales (2017) which contribute towards women's economic and socio-cultural empowerment. Thus, significantly this research seeks to answer the question *is there a balance approach between women's economic empowerment and socio cultural empowerment while promoting CBT.* While the empirical results shed light on the role of tourism in promoting women's economic empowerment and improvement in the quality of life. Similarly it has caused hinderance towards achieving socio cultural empowerment. In policy recommendations we propose a holistic based approach towards tourism development and women empowerment that caters for a balanced relationship. Issues also surround gender, empowerment, and achieving sustainability due to the changes in tourism development. Currently, there is less debate in overall achieving sustainable tourism from a gender-based perspective. Sustainability and gender can be achieved if there are strong links between policy and practice with a clear vision of empowerment and underlying factors of economic and social complexities within the marginalized in community-based tourism (Tucker & Boonabaana, 2012; Cotterell et al., 2020).

In country specific study Fiji is highly dependent on tourism for its development purposes, yet the literature is limited towards finding obstacles faced by women in relations to socio-cultural and economic empowerment. In response to the above the objective of this paper is to investigate the problems faced by rural women directly and indirectly involved in tourism development. Also drawing insights from SDG 5 we further advance our research on women's socio cultural and economic empowerment, particularly on the socio cultural aspect linked to decision-making, involvement, quality of life and education. Findings from the data will be utilized on the effectiveness of tourism development and how it affects women of Biausevu

Thus, the relationship between tourism and women in the host community is observed through economic dependency, and importantly the need to conserve culture and traditions. The contributions are reflected in the findings that tourism development positively affects women's economic empowerment by promoting entrepreneurial activities in rural areas. Given the limitation of obstacles related studies to women empowerment, this study aims to enrich the existing literature by integrating socio-cultural empowerment and economic empowerment viewpoints of CBT. This study introduces a model to deepen understanding of women empowerment in the context of urban CBT, providing actionable insights for policymakers, practitioners, and urban communities.

The remainder of the study is set as follows. Part 1 includes the literature that includes an evidence-based approach towards community tourism development and women empowerment from different country perspectives. Parts 3 and 4, cover empirical findings and discussion from the selected community. In the concluding part, the study is based on policy recommendations and further research.

THEORETICAL SETTING

Empowerment in the Tourism Context

In the early research of empowerment theory Dolezal and Novelli (2020) presented the notion of "empowerment" on the possibilities and increasing a person's ability without diminishing other abilities. Cornwall (2016) studied the context of empowerment and deliberated that empowerment is a process of the existing power while gaining dominance or control over the source of power. Developer studies in gender and tourism have found the difference in a social structure, which explores the division of men and women in terms of labor output and gender stereotyping in tourist destinations. Harvey et al. (1995) identified the viewpoints of men and women in the early stages of tourism development where women perceived more negativity towards tourists. Wilkinson and Pratiwi (1995) commented on tourism and women empowerment with critical insights and viewpoints of the feminist approach. They concluded the need to identify power relationships and understanding the social constructs of gender. Pritchard and Morgan's (2005) study concerning women in tourism, pointed out how the power of marketing creates a patriarchal construct that introduced a male tourism construct. Still there is existence of power imbalance among men and women created by tourism (Dolezal & Novelli, 2020).

The identification of potential policy intervention was through the introduction of the Millennium development goal 3: to promote gender equality and empower women (Hughes & Scheyvens, 2016). The outcome of projects on policy intervention that led to tourism as described by argument prescribed moving one-dimensional thought of and less consideration on cultural intricacies and restraints of gender norms that affects sustainable development (Scheyvens & Russell, 2012).

Following the failure of MDGs, the UN has called for a much-anticipated way of looking into tourism development and its effects (Alarcón & Cole, 2019). The argument is backed up with re-organizing women empowerment-related policy under a new paradigm that can overcome inequality in gender, however, Liu et al. (2020) underscored that development regarding women empowerment has been uneven. In terms of theoretical contribution on women empowerment and tourism was based on the feminist theory of Women in Development (WID) and Gender and Development (GAD) (Ferguson, 2011). Following the SDGs from a perspective of gender are one of a robust framework designed to ensure that improved outcome is achieved in relations to (Kato, 2019). Gentry (2007) described the relationship between and tourism development by focusing on gender identities. This was further explored by Figueroa-Domecq and Perez (2020) with the critical focus of power-play amongst structural sex groups, as gender is viewed as a system of culturally constructed identities and expressed in terms of masculinity and femininity (Butlera, 2017; Cave & Kilic, 2010). It also depends on the adaptation of women moving forward with the changes in tourism development due to hegemonic tourism discourse by the interaction of host and guest partisanship, manifestation, and bias symbolic gender illustration through post structuralism tourism study (Panta & Thapa, 2018).

Women's Socio-Cultural Empowerment in CBT Setting

According to Chilufya et al (2019), women's socio-cultural empowerment is differentiated in countries that consist of a strong dominance by men who have still been unnoticed due to the fact of game-changers and power play by the opposite gender. Women are also part of a larger community that derives social cohesions and hold a symbolic attachment that ties the socio-cultural aspect of a rural community (Jeffery, 2018). A sense of belonging encourages women to actively participated in tourism-related activities with indigenous rituals and cultural traits and customary beliefs that are portrayed for marketing purposes (Costa et al., 2016) however, in Taiwan socio-cultural heritage associated with is exploited in sexualized terms and used in tourism marketing (Panta & Thapa, 2018; Kimbu & Ngoasong, 2016). Socio-cultural pointers act as an agent of growth and development for women who perceive tourism as a tool for development. Social construction within communities was questioned due to the unequal power structure that undermined the true potential of women, which binds the social fabric of communities (Imbaya et al., 2019). In rural areas where strong culture is maintained with avenues of tourism, women are seen as keeps of tradition that have been inherited from passing generation (Pierre

Walter, 2011). However, the change in lifestyle from the host community because of modernization can influenced women to change. On this same note Ditta-Apichai et al. (2023) identified that women in the mange their business in informal sectors have limited access to training and education affecting social capital cause by indifference in social and cultural standards.

Empowerment through the socio-cultural aspect is considered as a human right, which gives women in the community to adapt to tourism centric impacts (Bakas, 2017), understanding social empowerment accounts for improved social standards, opportunities to capitalize on decision making, self-fulfillment, and improvement on the quality of women's life (Alarcón & Cole, 2019; Aghazamani et al., 2020). Socio-cultural empowerment accounts for the right to known and heard for self-being society adapting to women's image without any form of prejudice. Unfolding the development issues regarding women's socio-cultural empowerment and UN SDG 5 was one a key highlight the claims of inequality, discrimination, and unjust behaviors (Boluk et al., 2019a). Key finding from Bali in the content of womens ablitity to make decision is understood that women are part of decision making on the income genreated. The authority of womens decision making shed light on social cohesion and increased family well being. Thus, there is a clear indication womens ability on decision making is only for the family and not on herself (Doneys et al., 2020). Alternatively, there are mixed views of SDGs concerning women empowerment, as is a need for education on the vigorous living experience of women's livelihood (Figueroa-Domecqa et al., 2020). In destinations such as Iran women who in a position of perceiving a positive outcome of socio-cultural empowerment will identify themselves as holding positions in society and attain goals for future education and balance their commitment towards society norms (Aghazamani et al., 2020). The success of community-based tourism and socio-cultural empowerment is measured through a social system that works best with a communal objective (UNWTO, 2010). According Ribeiro et al. (2021) women entrepreneurs are more prone to challengers faced by social ties affecting women being less aggressive and competitive towards social obligations of the society. Moreover, Pecotv et al. 2024 found that gendered social innovation emergers as a disruptive force and a strong sense towards social transformation shifting powers.

Changes in socio-cultural tradition and practice affecting authenticity and commodification as in the PICs, women hold special skills and practices that are only women-centric. This practice is sought to have mutual benefit to the wider community's social value and benefit tourism for attraction purposes (Vujko et al., 2019). Göreme is one of a rural village in Turkey where women were least suitable for tourism, as over time the development of social change allowed women to participate in tourism (Tucker & Boonabaana, 2012;Walter, 2018). Tourism development communal identities and norms were being practiced within patriarchal and hierarchical dimensions that had control over women. With culture, tourism has a significant relationship with women empowerment, but debatable to the extent and nature of empowerment.

Women's Economic Empowerment in CBT Setting

The typology of women's economic empowerment conceptualizes into categories, such as general understanding of improvements in capital reproduction, entrepreneurship opportunities, and income generation, self-confidence, and self-esteem (Kimbu & Ngoasong, 2016; Prasad Acharya & Halpenny, 2013). Women's economic empowerment also considers the regularity and predictability of income and flows of resources that ensures women engaging in security plans for present and future (Conrnwall, 2016). The instrumentalist approach urges to move ahead of simplistic and ascertain thoughts of women's economic empowerment while also advocating the thoughts of cultural complexities (World Tourism Organization, 2019). Ideology in women's economic empowerment can define women's role in materialist nature but shifting ideas that impact all aspects of life (Gentry, 2007), while shifting margins of tourism has resulted in greater participation of women into entrepreneurship activities (Ling et al., 2013; Kimbu & Ngoasong, 2016). Women entrepreneurship is one of the key parts of community-based tourism, which involves women being independent in managing business and making independent decisions (Figueroa-Domecqa et al., 2020; Costa et al., 2016). The significance of women managing her own business is purely justified if the money generated into the business is controlled by her own (Surangi, 2018; Bakas, 2017). This include womens ability of making her own deciosn on the income earned from tourism. In Belize, women were able to introduce themselves as holistic members of the community, as women taking part in economic activities saw great potential in gendered based entrepreneurship (Gentry, 2007). Hence, in destinations such as Laos although women have attained benefits from economic empowerment but constrain socio-cultural barriers that deprive women to take up a leadership role in the higher level of community setting (Phommavong & Sörensson, 2014; Boluk et al., 2019b). In developing countries such as the Dominican Republic problem of lack of participation from donor agencies and government to overcome problems of implementing policies faced by women in communities (Duffy et al., 2015).

Tourism has also benefited women in terms of improvement in livelihood through earnings from homestays in Nepal and Malaysia even though of outliers in the tourism development process and potential challenge women face. (Birendra KC, 2020; Tavakoli et al., 2017). Furthermore, a study by Aghazamani et al. (2020) in Iran highlighted the importance of financial stability and independence where women would question the framework of inequality and lack of power. Butlera (2017) highlighted the importance of rural tourism projects in Siberia but failed to recognize women's roles as it was seen as a supplementary income . According to Vujko et al., (2019) the inclusiveness of women in community-based tourism was in terms of poverty reduction and contribute growth towards tourism development in rural parts of Sweden (Pettersson & Cassel, 2014; Pierre Walter, 2011). The inclusion of women to participate in tourism for economic gains is grouped with patriarchal power, where men have persuaded, allowed freely, or by forcefully is still contested with contrast to control over women's economic gains (Kling et al., 2020) The significance of studying links between economic empowerment and still needs to be explored with competent evidence and combination, which is sufficient to establish a fact-based presumption (Ling et al., 2013). In addition to empowerment economic gain and entrepreneurship involvement is in contrast with neoliberal discourse as the main objectivity and motivation of the self-interest of women (Costa et al., 2016; Cave & Kilic, 2010). The problem of limited conceptualization of women's economic empowerment fails to capture the concept of power in a patriarchal society. The area of economic empowerment focuses on the monetary gain from tourism development while social empowerment deals with equal participation in decision-making, the standard of living, reduction in poverty, skill upgrading, and knowledge building (Kumar De, 2013). Tran and Walter (2014) identified by linking the objective of women empowerment and tourism and hidden agendas there is a need to analyze the impacts from a critical point of investigation. On the other hand, policies that govern women's empowerment have been criticized for being an "instrumentalist" approach to the relationships between gender equality and development (Cotterell et al., 2020). The release of Global Report on Women and Tourism Second edition following through with the case studies and some the lessons learnt was the need include women in decision making in terms of quality participation, skill, and career development where women can reorganize for fair strategic consultations.

Tourism and Women Empowerment in the Fijian Tourism Industry Context

Tourism and development have been in a cordial relationship in Fiji as it a major contributor to the country's economy (Kumar et al., 2019; Chandra et al., 2023). Fiji has been dependent on tourism after substituting agriculture. Like other Developing countries, Fiji too saw potential benefits from tourism and began to adopt tourism as an alternative form of development community based tourism (Chilufya et al., 2019; Pratt, 2013). Community-based tourism began as the Indigenous Fijian (*I Taukei*) saw potential benefits it brings to the community (Ponting & O'Brien, 2014; Kerstetter & Bricker, 2009). One of the core problems associated with community-based tourism is the lack of support and capacity building. Scheyvens and Russell, (2012) pointed out that community members in the Yaskawa Group situated in the Western part of Fiji benefit from tourism development thus the hierarchal-based system of decision truly depends on the *Madagali*(Landowner). The development of tourism caused problems for women who were involved in the ecotourism project in Taveuni, the distress between *Mataqali*. Women were excluded from the decision-making process and saw male-oriented economic gain which resulted in even structure of ownership (Farrelly, 2011).

Women are involved directly and indirectly in community-level tourism development. Most women in the community level of tourism development are involved. Women are viewed as social structuralist in embracing identity for the community cohesiveness (Movono & Dahles, 2017). Women in rural communities are linked to the agriculture sector and are also required to fulfill their requirements at home and to the community (Pratt et al., 2015). To fulfill the Fijian culture women are involved in a cultural way of life called *solesolevaki* which is termed as members of the community to work as a group for a common purpose. As tourism development leaped in the past decades, the transformation which is derived from tourism acts as an agent of change to the host community as identified in the works of (Bakas, 2017; Butlera, 2017). Women's empowerment and the role of women in Fiji especially in the interior location were confined to limited space as men were in control of decision making (Fiji Women's Fund, 2018). In rural communities, women's economic empowerment is strongly influenced by the traditional obligation which is linked to communal land tenure (UN Women, 2014). A community-related study by (Movono & Dahles, 2017) areas reveals that women were part of a group that took part in solving issues related to the village of Vatuolalai village located along the Coral Coast. In the concentrated areas of tourism development such as Sigatoka, women are part of economic sustainability and meeting financial and cultural commitments.

Women's economic empowerment has been a success to the local women and the village as well. Through economic gain, women were recognized for collective actions and the development of small projects in villages (Movono et al., 2018). Women's entrepreneurship in tourism was also successful in bringing benefits to the local women that contributed to potential opportunities, negotiation in creating a change. However, with the changes in the role of women, there is contradicting of factors associated with the change in women's that impacted the cultural significance of the Fijian traditions as (Pratt et al., 2013) identified the "Tribe Wanted" project carried in the Northern part of Fiji where women were required to dress conservatively as one of the requirements of cultural practice. The Indigenous people take pride in their culture and strong inhabitants to preserve their culture thus with tourism development. A study by Gibson. (2015) in the village of Wayalailai on the outskirts of the Western Division in Fiji claimed that women in the community are a subject change from tourism despite a simple, economical primarily subsistence lifestyle which are controlled with strict cultural mannerisms. Finally, the Millennium Development Goal 2nd Report of Fiji 2010 highlighted that the failure of empowering women is a complex problem due to political aspects that disregard women being leaders in society because women do not possess customary entitlement and chiefly position.

RESEARCH AREA

This research focuses on Biausevu village, situated 5 km inland from Sigatoka in the western part of Fiji. A key attraction for tourists is the Savanamatey Waterfall, located 2 km from the village, renowned for its diverse flora and fauna within a natural setting. Sigatoka has been a focal point for tourism and community-based tourism studies, as discussed in previous works by Pratt et al. (2015), Movono & Dahles (2017), and Movono et al. (2018). Biausevu village takes pride in preserving its rich Indigenous Fijian culture and traditions, deeply rooted in the concept of Vanua (land). The term "vanua" holds significant cultural and ancestral value for Indigenous Fijians, as highlighted in studies by Pratt et al. (2013) and Movono & Dahles (2017).

The village comprises approximately 52 households with a total population exceeding 250, both men and women actively participating in tourism development efforts. Local guides lead visitors to the waterfall, incorporating cultural rituals like the yagona ceremony to seek permission for village visits. The kava ceremony follows, and tour guides accompany visitors during the waterfall excursion. Recognizing the economic potential of tourism, village members transitioned from nearby resort jobs to community-based tourism activities. Women and men receive compensation from tour companies through package fees, primarily generated from handicrafts and souvenirs. Visitor satisfaction is notably high, evidenced by Trip Advisor reviews and tour companies offering trips to Biausevu village.

The introduction of tourism has significantly impacted the host community, prompting the formation of the Biausevu Tourism Committee to oversee sustainable development and village enhancement. However, the rapid tourism growth posed threats to biodiversity, leading to land clearance for ecotourism initiatives. The United Nations Development Program (UNDP) supported a conservation project focusing on community-based ecotourism to mitigate environmental impacts. This initiative generated numerous employment opportunities, including tour guides, storytellers, and handicraft sellers, with an emphasis on collective decision-making involving women to achieve broader project goals.

engagement. Women also need to understand the relationships between economic gains while protecting the image of the community as a means of educating herself on entrepreneurship, the links between service provider and receiver are whether paramount to the community's social capital or women's quality of life still been unclear which is prevalent in Melanesian Society (Anderson & Eswaran, 2009; Rahman et al., 2014). Although higher education promotes entrepreneurial activities it was also evident that women did not upgrade their education level. This clearly indicates that socio empowerment of women is affected due to high commitment towards CBT women are not able to upgrade their education level.

We find that age has a significant non-linear effect under both methods and the minimum threshold age after which entrepreneurial engagement increases are in the range 45-47. One of the reasons women had to actively engage in tourism despite age restriction due to the age gap. Young women were encouraged to pursue further education away from home while the older generation continued to be part of tourism ventures. We also found out that stronger entrepreneurial engagement weakens the leadership role of women. The outcome of weak leadership also contributes ineffectively towards women's ability in decision making. Thus, ineffective outcome of economic empowerment changes the circumstances for hierarchal empowerment and women become part of the bigger picture of attaining leadership roles in the community. In other words, the difference in women taking a whole of economic benefit is one an area that needs consideration from creating the issues of "double burden" (Jimenez-Esquinas, 2017; Spenceley & Goodwin, 2007; Anderson & Eswaran, 2009). However, women in countries with a strong association with the strong patriarchal based decision making women are subject to accept enforcement which is formed through an unclear vision of tourism development (Jeffrey, 2017). The concept of high importance was given as an alternative way or direct employment where women had control over the source of funds and a sense of economic dependence on tourism at the community level (Boluk et al., 2019). Interaction terms viz. education, income, leadership, and income have a negative effect which indicates that the underlying variables are substitutes in promoting women's entrepreneurial engagement. This implies that either income from tourism, education, or leadership can be used to promote women's entrepreneurial engagement. We also note that with age there is problems associated with women's health and well-being affecting the quality of life. Women are facing health issue due to CBT, since women are at the forefront of they must undergo challengers affecting their health and livelihood. With this finding we underscore that women's socio cultural empowerment is affected since this quality of life is strongly associated with socio cultural empowerment.

Also noted the association between tourism development, and socio-cultural empowerment had effects on women in the village. The common understanding of women's socio empowerment leads to political empowerment where women are described as social structuralist of sustainable development (Movono & Dahles, 2017). It was evident that men still had dominance over resources in the village which overall contributed to the power play. Women were also seen as part of the wider community that holds a symbolic relationship with the culture and beliefs of the Indigenous Fiji culture. However due to the high demand for culture-based activities women strongly felt that they were being exploited for commercial purposes, but women did not have other options to retaliate because of the benefits of economic empowerment. Women's socio-cultural empowerment concerning their attachment to indigenous welfare was being affected as women moved away from traditional practices and more include themselves towards economic gains. Women were also affected by the visitor arrival on Sunday *Sigatabu* which is a common term for Sunday as the villages would go to church on that day and fulfill their religious requirement. When combining the two components of and socio-cultural traditions heritage protection can be debated with different interests and women are still vulnerable to exploitation (Jimenez-Esquinas, 2017. The certainty of attaining a harmonious balance between gender and socio-cultural empowerment materialized if women are given a voice that can be heard and accepted with diligence. Acceptance of women's voice is part of maintaining empowerment which can change the views regarding perpetuated inequalities (Kato, 2019). However, gender norms have created a gap between men and women to equally participating in tourism (Birendra, 2020; Kerstetter & Bricker, 2009. Such barriers are still present with strong views and limiting women to participate in tourism and access to the induced benefits. A shift in tourism in a particular community area affects social change, there is a shift in fixed gender ideologies which is accompanied by negotiating and reconstituting women's involvement.

Table 3. Logit results

Variable	Coefficient	Std. Error	z-Statistic	Prob.
Log of INCOME from tourism	81.98846***	25.43749	3.223135	0.0013
INVOLVEMENT	-122.5724**	61.10456	-2.005945	0.0449
QLF	3.089667*	1.579694	1.955865	0.0505
EDUCATION	365.6618**	124.9880	2.925575	0.0034
Log of AGE	-298.3813**	132.4823	-2.252235	0.0243
(Log of AGE)^2	39.00851**	17.74289	2.198544	0.0279
Leadership	93.65908**	43.37482	2.159296	0.0308
EDUCATION*Log of INCOME	-35.00594***	11.89351	-2.943280	0.0032
Log of INCOME*INVOLVEMENT	11.88206**	5.937061	2.001337	0.0454

continued on following page

Table 3. Continued

Variable	Coefficient	Std. Error	z-Statistic	Prob.
Leadership*Log of INCOME	-8.808867**	4.133872	-2.130900	0.0331
Intercept	-308.3139	316.8958	-0.972919	0.3306
Model Statistics				
McFadden R-squared	0.597235	Mean dependent var		0.593750
S.D. dependent var	0.498991	S.E. of regression		0.377250
Akaike info criterion	1.231607	Sum squared resid		2.988674
Schwarz criterion	1.735454	Log-likelihood		-8.705714
Hannan-Quinn criteria.	1.398618	Deviance		17.41143
Restr. Deviance	43.22973	Restr. log-likelihood		-21.61487
LR statistic	25.81831	Avg. log-likelihood		-0.272054
Prob(LR statistic)	0.003992			
Hosmer-Lemeshow test statistic	7.400	(P Value = 0.49)		
Andrews test statistic	7.366	(P Value = 0.41)		

Source: Estimated in Stata 15.

Table 4. Probit results

Variable	Coefficient	Std. Error	z-Statistic	Prob.
Log of INCOME from tourism	49.03857***	15.40205	3.183899	0.0015
INVOLVEMENT	-71.81902**	30.31684	-2.368948	0.0178
QLF	1.835985***	0.693731	2.646537	0.0081
EDUCATION	215.2893***	73.35928	2.934725	0.0033
Log of AGE	-175.6557***	60.19632	-2.918047	0.0035
(Log of AGE)^2	22.94652***	8.005883	2.866208	0.0042
Leadership	57.27974**	24.25281	2.361778	0.0182
EDUCATION*Log of INCOME	-20.61142***	6.984848	-2.950876	0.0032
Log of INCOME*INVOLVEMENT	6.962394**	2.937777	2.369953	0.0178
Leadership*Log of INCOME	-5.387073**	2.312650	-2.329393	0.0198
Intercept	-189.4828	162.7302	-1.164398	0.2443
Model Statistics				
McFadden R-squared	0.606476	Mean dependent var		0.593750
S.D. dependent var	0.498991	S.E. of regression		0.376134
Akaike info criterion	1.219123	Sum squared resid		2.971008

continued on following page

Table 4. Continued

Variable	Coefficient	Std. Error	z-Statistic	Prob.
Schwarz criterion	1.722970	Log-likelihood		-8.505966
Hannan-Quinn criteria.	1.386134	Deviance		17.01193
Restr. Deviance	43.22973	Restr. log-likelihood		-21.61487
LR statistic	26.21780	Avg. log-likelihood		-0.265811
Prob(LR statistic)	0.003458			
Hosmer-Lemeshow test statistic	7.119	(P Value = 0.52)		
Andrews test statistic	7.366	(P Value = 0.41)		

Source: Estimated in Stata 15.

CONCLUSION AND POLICY IMPLICATIONS

In this paper, we have examined community-based tourism and using economic and social-cultural aspects as indicators. The paper is also in response to SDG 5 with a critical investigation using the Logit and Probit Model to examine the relationship of the 2 indicators. The relationship of tourism development and has been unclear in establishing a potential link that looks at women's quality of life hence as required by SDG 5. Women in CBT are more vulnerable since they are bounded by the patriarchal centric communal objective that constitutes the whole village. Since the study is based in one of a rural community in Fiji there is a high level of association between the variable identified in the research. The results are seminal in commenting that women perceive economic empowerment as one an important indicator whilst socio-cultural association show an indifference relationship. The study is concerning critical thinking applied to women's livelihood and we further exaggerate the finding based on real-life scenarios. Women in Biausevu also had to change being involved in tourism. Women's economic empowerment contributed positively towards monetary gain however due to a level of dependency from tourism women had to undergo a change that affected their socio-cultural aspects of empowerment. Through the present findings, it was evident that the age of women played an important role in women's economic empowerment leading to entrepreneurial motivations. Women's education level is also a contributor to economic empowerment as those women with high education level perceived interest in tourism involvement. However, with high level of dependency women were not able to upgrade their education level. The introduction of tourism in Biausevu has opened opportunities for but has limited opportunities for socio-cultural empowerment. The leadership of women was present at homes and village level but limited to the hierarchal structure of the Indigenous culture and traditional norms. Based on the finding it is also evident that although women's economic empowerment is playing a crucial role in women life it has also insufficiently affected socio cultural empowerment. A high reliance on tourism, increasing age with health effects women are faced with hardships. There is high possibility that women are less favorable towards allowing their daughters to take part in CBT. As women do understand the negative effect CBT has contributed to their livelihood.

With the current problems associated with socio cultural empowerment there is no form of support from the stakeholders involved in CBT. In some sense women know the problems they are faced with . Yet, they cannot voice out their concerns due to the dilemma that tourism has positively contributed towards economic empowerment. Thus, tourism being least sustainable towards socio cultural empowerment has been the notable finding for the present chapter. As aligned with the Global Report SDGs it is important to understand the relationships of sustainable tourism and how well certain policy can be holistically achieved. The role of state and agencies is fundamental that facilitates women's equality in a community-based setting however there is a level of insignificance between customary law and state law in Fiji. To find a balance between sustainable tourism benefits and requires continuous training and development with a clear and developed understanding of both the negative and positive side of tourism it has on the lives of women. A society that has accepted tourism as a contributor to growth should be accepting not only the income women accumulate in the society, but the hardships and personal life constrain. In terms of training and development importance aspects such as control and distribution of tourism income and mutual based decision in planning and development in the village. Alternative forms of tourism such as Agri Tourism should have been developed through tourism partners which could saw men and women more involved and at the same time continue their traditional aspects of life and the association with the *Vanua*. As for further research could be done on other rural communities located within Fiji. Since there is a significant drop in visitors to Fiji it would be beneficial to look at the effects women face in villages who were mostly reluctant on tourist since the tourism sector in Fiji has effects on mandating potential opportunities and improving women's economic empowerment but constrains based on patriarchal structure also affects women's socio-cultural empowerment.

The authors of this publication declare there are no competing interests.

This research received no specific grant from any funding agency in the public, commercial, or not-for-profit sectors. Funding for this research was covered by the author(s) of the article.

REFERENCES

Aghazamani, Y., Kerstetter, D., & Pete Allison, P. (2020). Women's perceptions of empowerment in Ramsar, a tourism destination in northern Iran. *Women's Studies International Forum*, 79, 1–10. 10.1016/j.wsif.2020.102340

Alarcón, D. M., & Cole, S. (2019). No sustainability for tourism without gender equality. *Journal of Sustainable Tourism*, 27(7), 903–919. 10.1080/09669582.2019.1588283

Anderson, S., & Eswaran, M. (2009). What determines female autonomy? Evidence from Bangladesh. *Journal of Development Economics*, 90(2), 179–191. 10.1016/j.jdeveco.2008.10.004

Bakas, F. E. (2017). A beautiful mess': Reciprocity and positionality in gender and tourism beautiful. *Journal of Hospitality and Tourism Management*, 33, 126–133. 10.1016/j.jhtm.2017.09.009

Bakas, F. E. (2017). Community resilience through entrepreneurship: The role of gender. *Journal of Enterprising Communities: People and Places in the Global Economy*, 11(1), 61–77. 10.1108/JEC-01-2015-0008

Birendra, K. C. (2020). Ecotourism for wildlife conservation and sustainable livelihood via community-based homestay: A formula to success or a quagmire? *Current Issues in Tourism*, 1–17. 10.1080/13683500.2020.1772206

Boluk, K., & Carnicelli, S. (2015). Activism and Critical Reflection through Experiential Learning. *Journal of Teaching in Travel & Tourism*, 15(3), 242–251. 10.1080/15313220.2015.1059304

Boluk, K., Cavaliere, C., & Higgins-Desbiolles, F. (2019). A critical framework for interrogating the United Nations Sustainable Development Goals 2030 Agenda in tourism. *Journal of Sustainable Tourism*, 27(7), 847–864. 10.1080/09669582.2019.1619748

Boluk, K. A., Cavaliere, T. C., & Duffy, L. N. (2019). A pedagogical framework for the development of the critical tourism citizen. *Journal of Sustainable Tourism*, 27(7), 865–881. 10.1080/09669582.2019.1615928

Butlera, G. (2017). Fostering community empowerment and capacity building through tourism: Perspectives from Dulls room, South Africa. *Journal of Tourism and Cultural Change*, 15(3), 199–212. 10.1080/14766825.2015.1133631

Cave, P., & Kilic, S. (2010). The Role of Women in Tourism Employment with Special Reference to Antalya, Turkey. *Journal of Hospitality Marketing & Management*, 19(3), 280–292. 10.1080/19368621003591400

Chandra, R. A., Prasad, N. S., Kumar, N. N., & Stephens, M. M. (2023). Social Media and Online Marketing Implication on Family Businesses Success: A Tourism Industry Perspective. In *Family Businesses in Tourism and Hospitality: Innovative Studies and Approaches* (pp. 223–241). Springer Nature Switzerland. 10.1007/978-3-031-28053-5_13

Chilufya, A., Hughes, E., & Scheyvens, R. (2019). Tourists and community development: Corporate social responsibility or tourist social responsibility? *Journal of Sustainable Tourism*, 27(10), 1513–1529. 10.1080/09669582.2019.1643871

Cornwall, A. (2016). Women's empowerment: What works. *Journal of International Development*, 28(3), 342–359. 10.1002/jid.3210

Costa, C., Breda, Z., Bakas, F. E., Durão, M., & Pinho, I. (2016). Through the gender looking-glass: Brazilian tourism entrepreneurs. *International Journal of Gender and Entrepreneurship*, 8(3), 282–306. 10.1108/IJGE-07-2015-0023

Cotterell, D., Ferreira, J.-A., Hales, R., & Arcodia, C. (2020). Cultivating conscientious tourism caretakers: A phenomenon graphic continuum towards stronger sustainability. *Current Issues in Tourism*, 23(8), 1004–1020. 10.1080/13683500.2019.1577369

Ditta-Apichai, M., Gretzel, U., & Kattiyapornpong, U. (2024). Platform empowerment: Facebook's role in facilitating female micro-entrepreneurship in tourism. *Journal of Sustainable Tourism*, 32(3), 540–559. 10.1080/09669582.2023.2215479

Dolezal, C., & Novelli, M. (2022). Power in community-based tourism: Empowerment and partnership in Bali. *Journal of Sustainable Tourism*, 30(10), 2352–2370. 10.1080/09669582.2020.1838527

Doneys, P., Doane, D. L., & Norm, S. (2020). Seeing empowerment as relational: Lessons from women participating in development projects in Cambodia. *Development in Practice*, 30(2), 268–280. 10.1080/09614524.2019.1678570

Duffy, L., Kline, C., Mowatt, R., & Chancellor, H. (2015). Women in tourism: Shifting gender ideology in the DR. *Annals of Tourism Research*, 52, 72–86. 10.1016/j.annals.2015.02.017

Farrelly, T. A. (2011). Indigenous and democratic decision-making: Issues from community-based ecotourism in the Bouma National Heritage Park, Fiji. *Journal of Sustainable Tourism*, 19(7), 817–835. 10.1080/09669582.2011.553390

Ferguson, L. (2011). Promoting gender equality and empowering women? Tourism and the third Millennium Development Goal. *Current Issues in Tourism*, 14(3), 235–249. 10.1080/13683500.2011.555522

Ferguson, L., & Alarcón, D. M. (2015). Gender and sustainable tourism: reflections on theory and practice. *Journal of Sustainable Tourism, 23*(3), 401-416. 10.1080/09669582.2014.957208

Figueroa-Domecq, C., & Perez, M. S. (2020). Application of a gender perspective in tourism research: a theoretical and practical approach. *Journal of Tourism Analysis*. 10.1108/JTA-02-2019-0009

Figueroa-Domecq, C., Pritchard, A., Segovia-Pérez, M., Morgan, N., & Villacé-Molinero, T. (2015). Tourism gender research: A critical accounting. *Annals of Tourism Research*, 52, 87–103. 10.1016/j.annals.2015.02.001

Figueroa-Domecqa, C., Jong, A., & Williams, A. M. (2020). Gender, tourism & entrepreneurship: A critical review. *Annals of Tourism Research*, 84, 102980. 10.1016/j.annals.2020.102980

Fiji Womens Fund. (2018). *Fiji Womens Fund*. FWF. https://fijiwomensfund.org/project/talanoa-treks/

Filippopoulou, C., Galariotis, E., & Spyrou, S. (2020). An early warning system for predicting systemic banking crises in the Eurozone: A logit regression approach. *Journal of Economic Behavior & Organization*, 172, 344–363. 10.1016/j.jebo.2019.12.023

Gentry, K. M. (2007). Belizean women and tourism work: Opportunity or impediment? *Annals of Tourism Research*, 34(2), 477–496. 10.1016/j.annals.2006.11.003

Gibson, D. (2015). *Community-based tourism in Fiji: a case study of Wayalailai Ecohaven Resort, Yasawa Island Group*. Routledge.: Tourism in Pacific Islands.

Higgins-Desbiolles, F., Carnicelli, S., Krolikowski, C., Wijesinghe, G., & Boluk, K. (2019). Degrowing tourism: Rethinking tourism. *Journal of Sustainable Tourism*, 27(12), 1926–1944. 10.1080/09669582.2019.1601732

Hughes, E., & Scheyvens, R. (2016). Corporate social responsibility in tourism post-2015: A development first approach. *Tourism Geographies*, 18(5), 469–482. 10.1080/14616688.2016.1208678

Imbaya, B. O., Sitati, N. W., & Lenaiyasa, P. (2019). Capacity building for inclusive growth in community-based tourism initiatives in Kenya. *Tourism Management Perspectives*, 30, 11–18. 10.1016/j.tmp.2019.01.003

Jeffery, H. (2018). Tourism and Womens Rights in Tunisia. In Cole, S. (Ed.), *Gender Equality and Tourism: Beyond Empowerment* (pp. 96–107). CABI. 10.1079/9781786394422.0096

Jeffrey, H. (2017). Gendering the tourism curriculum whilst becoming an academic. *Anatolia*, 28(4), 530–539. 10.1080/13032917.2017.1370779

Jimenez-Esquinas, G. (2017). "This is not only about culture" on tourism, gender stereotypes and other affective fluxes. *Journal of Sustainable Tourism*, 25(3), 311–326. 10.1080/09669582.2016.1206109

Kato, K. (2019). Gender and sustainability – exploring ways of knowing – an Eco humanities perspective. *Journal of Sustainable Tourism*, 27(7), 939–956. 10.1080/09669582.2019.1614189

Kerstetter, D., & Bricker, K. (2009). Exploring Fijian's sense of place after exposure to tourism development. *Journal of Sustainable Tourism*, 17(6), 691–708. 10.1080/09669580902999196

Khoo-Lattimor, C., Ling Yang, E., & Je, J. S. (2019). Assessing gender representation in knowledge production: A critical analysis of UNWTO's planned events. *Journal of Sustainable Tourism*, 27(7), 920–938. 10.1080/09669582.2019.1566347

Kimbu, A. N., & Ngoasong, M. Z. (2016). Women as vectors of social entrepreneurship. *Annals of Tourism Research*, 60, 63–79. 10.1016/j.annals.2016.06.002

Kling, K. G., Margaryan, L., & Fuchs, M. (2020). (In) equality in the outdoors: Gender perspective on recreation and tourism media in the Swedish mountains. *Current Issues in Tourism*, 23(2), 233–247. 10.1080/13683500.2018.1495698

Kumar, N., Kumar, R. R., Patel, A., & Stauvermann, P. (2019). Exploring the Effect of Tourism and Economic Growth in Fiji: Accounting for Capital, Labor, and Structural Breaks. *Tourism Analysis*, 16(2), 115–130. 10.3727/108354218X1539 1984820468

Kumar, N. N., Chandra, R. A., & Patel, A. (2021). Mixed frequency evidence of the tourism growth relationship in small Island developing states: A case study of Tonga. *Asia Pacific Journal of Tourism Research*, 26(3), 294–307. 10.1080/10941665.2020.1862884

Kumar De, U. (2013). Sustainable Nature-based Tourism, Involvement of Indigenous Women and Development: A Case of North-East India. *Tourism Recreation Research*, 38(3), 311–324. 10.1080/02508281.2013.11081756

Ling, R. S., Wu, B., Park, J., Shu, H., & Morrison, A. M. (2013). Womens Role in Sustaining village and Rural tourism in China. *Annals of Tourism Research*, 43, 624–650. 10.1016/j.annals.2013.07.009

Liu, T., Li, M., & Lu, M.-F. (2020). Performing femininity: Women at the top (doing and undoing gender). *Tourism Management*, 80, 104–130. 10.1016/j.tourman.2020.104130

Morais, D., Yarnal, C., And, E. D., & Dowler, L. (2005). The impact of ethnic tourism on gender roles: A comparison between the Bai and the Mosuo of Yunnan province, PRC. *Asia Pacific Journal of Tourism Research*, 10(4), 361–367. 10.1080/10941660500363678

Movono, A., & Dahles, H. (2017). Female empowerment and tourism: A focus on businesses in a Fijian village. *Asia Pacific Journal of Tourism Research*, 22(6), 681–692. 10.1080/10941665.2017.1308397

Movono, A., Dahles, H., & Becken, S. (2018). Fijian culture and the environment: A focus on the ecologicaland social interconnectedness of tourism development. *Journal of Sustainable Tourism*, 26(3), 451–469. 10.1080/09669582.2017.1359280

Movono, A., & Hughes, E. (2020). Tourism partnerships: Localizing the SDG agenda in Fiji. *Journal of Sustainable Tourism*, 1–15. 10.1080/09669582.2020.1811291

Panta, S. K., & Thapa, B. (2018). Entrepreneurship and women's empowerment in gateway communities of Bardia National Park Nepal. *Journal of Ecotourism*, 17(1), 20–42. 10.1080/14724049.2017.1299743

Pécot, M., Ricaurte-Quijano, C., Khoo, C., Vázquez, M. A., Barahona-Canales, D., Yang, E. C. L., & Tan, R. (2024). From empowering women to being empowered by women: A gendered social innovation framework for tourism-led development initiatives. *Tourism Management*, 102, 104883. 10.1016/j.tourman.2024.104883

Pettersson, K., & Cassel, S. H. (2014). Women tourism entrepreneurs: Doing gender on farms in Sweden. *Gender in Management*, 29(8), 487–504. 10.1108/GM-02-2014-0016

Phommavong, S., & Sörensson, E. (2014). Ethnic tourism in Lao PDR: Gendered divisions of labour in community-based tourism for poverty reduction. *Current Issues in Tourism*, 17(4), 350–362. 10.1080/13683500.2012.721758

Ponting, J., & O'Brien, D. (2014). Liberalizing Nirvana: An analysis of the consequences of common pool resource deregulation for the sustainability of Fiji's surf tourism industry. *Journal of Sustainable Tourism*, 22(3), 384–402. 10.1080/09669582.2013.819879

Prasad Acharya, B. P., & Halpenny, E. (2013). Homestays as an Alternative Tourism Product for Sustainable Community Development: A Case Study of Women-Managed Tourism Product in Rural Nepal. *Tourism Planning & Development*, 10(4), 367–387. 10.1080/21568316.2013.779313

Pratt, S. (2013). Minimising food miles: Issues and outcomes in an eco-tourism venture in Fiji. *Journal of Sustainable Tourism*, 21(8), 1148–1165. 10.1080/09669582.2013.776060

Pratt, S., Gibson, D., & Movono, A. (2013). Tribal Tourism in Fiji: An Application and Extension of Smith's 4Hs of Indigenous Tourism. *Asia Pacific Journal of Tourism Research*, 18(8), 894–912. 10.1080/10941665.2012.717957

Pratt, S., McCabe, S., & Movono, A. (2015). Gross happiness of a 'tourism' village in Fiji. *Journal of Destination Marketing & Management*, 5(1), 26–35. 10.1016/j.jdmm.2015.11.001

Pritchard, A., & Morgan, N. (2005). Representations of 'ethnographic knowledge': Early comic postcards of Wales. *Discourse, communication and tourism*, 53-75. 10.21832/9781845410216-006

Rahman, M., Mostofa, M., & Hoque, M. (2014). Women's household decision-making autonomy and contraceptive behavior among Bangladeshi women. *Sexual & Reproductive Healthcare : Official Journal of the Swedish Association of Midwives*, 5(1), 9–15. 10.1016/j.srhc.2013.12.00324472384

Rasoolimanesh, S., Ramakrishna, S., Hall, M., Esfandiar, K., & Seyf, S. (2020). A systematic scoping review of sustainable tourism indicators in relation to the sustainable development goals. *Journal of Sustainable Tourism*, 23(1), 1–21. 10.1080/09669582.2020.1775621

Ribeiro, M. A., Adam, I., Kimbu, A. N., Afenyo-Agbe, E., Adeola, O., Figueroa-Domecq, C., & de Jong, A. (2021). Women entrepreneurship orientation, networks and firm performance in the tourism industry in resource-scarce contexts. *Tourism Management*, 86, 104343. 10.1016/j.tourman.2021.104343

Saarinen, J., & Rogerson, C. (2014). Tourism and the Millennium Development Goals: Perspectives beyond 2015. *Tourism Geographies*, 16(1), 23–30. 10.1080/14616688.2013.851269

Scheyvens, R., & Russell, M. (2012). Tourism and poverty alleviation in Fiji: Comparing the impacts of small- and large-scale tourism enterprises. *Journal of Sustainable Tourism*, 20(3), 417–436. 10.1080/09669582.2011.629049

Spenceley, A., & Goodwin, H. (2007). Nature-Based Tourism and Poverty Alleviation: Impacts of Private Sector and Parastatal Enterprises in and Around Kruger National Park, South Africa. *Current Issues in Tourism*, 10(2-3), 255–277. 10.2167/cit305.0

Surangi, H. A. K. N. S. (2018). What influences the networking behaviours of female entrepreneurs? *International Journal of Gender and Entrepreneurship*, 10(2), 116–133. 10.1108/IJGE-08-2017-0049

Tavakoli, R., Mura, P., & Devi Rajaratnam, S. D. (2017). Social capital in Malaysian homestays: Exploring hosts' social relations. *Current Issues in Tourism*, 20(10), 1028–1043. 10.1080/13683500.2017.1310189

Tran, L., & Walter, P. (2014). Ecotourism, gender, and development in northern Vietnam. *Annals of Tourism Research*, 1(44), 116–130. 10.1016/j.annals.2013.09.005

Tucker, H., & Boonabaana, B. (2012). A critical analysis of tourism, gender, and poverty reduction. *Journal of Sustainable Tourism*, 20(3), 437–455. 10.1080/09669582.2011.622769

UNWTO. (2010). *Global Report on Women in Tourism 2010*. World Tourism Organization.

Valeri, M., & Katsoni, V. (Eds.). (2021). *Gender and tourism: Challenges and entrepreneurial opportunities*. Emerald Publishing Limited. 10.1108/9781801173223

Vongvisitsin, T. B., Huang, W. J., & King, B. (2024). Urban community-based tourism development: A networked social capital model. *Annals of Tourism Research*, 106, 103759. 10.1016/j.annals.2024.103759

Vujko, A., Tretiakova, T., Petrović, M., Radovanović, M., Gajić, T., & Vuković, D. (2019). Women's empowerment through self-employment in tourism. *Annals of Tourism Research*, 76, 328–330. 10.1016/j.annals.2018.09.004

Walter, P. (2011). Gender Analysis in Community-based Ecotourism. *Tourism Recreation Research*, 36(2), 159–168. 10.1080/02508281.2011.11081316

Walters, T. (2018). Gender equality in academic tourism, hospitality, leisure, and events conferences. *Journal of Policy Research in Tourism, Leisure & Events*, 10(1), 17–32. 10.1080/19407963.2018.1403165

Wilkinson, P., & Pratiwi, W. (1995). Gender and Tourism in An Indonesian Village. *Annals of Tourism Research*, 22(2), 283-299. DOI: 10.1016/0160-7383(94)00077-8

Women, U. N. (2014). Womens Economic Empowerment. Victoria Parade, Suva, Fiji: UN Women.

World Tourism Organization. (2019). *Global Report on Women in Tourism* (2nd ed.). UNWTO.

Chapter 7
A Holistic Study on the Work–Family Conflict of Women Employees in the Indian Tourism Industry

Divya Singh

K.R. Mangalam University, India

Poonam Kumari

https://orcid.org/0000-0001-9618-1894

K.R. Mangalam University, India

Kristin Sajeev

K.R. Mangalam University, India

ABSTRACT

The purpose of this research is to perform a comprehensive study of work-family conflict among female employees in the Indian tourist business. It seeks to identify the elements that contribute to work-family conflict, investigate its influence on women's well-being and turnover intentions, and provide strategies to mitigate its effects. The study's findings emphasize the enormous impact of work-family conflict on female employees in India's tourist companies. Long working hours, high job demands, and a lack of workplace assistance are all factors that lead to work-family conflict. The study also outlines methods such as flexible work arrangements, supportive organizational policies, and training programs that might assist reduce work-family conflict, increase women's psychological safety, and reduce turnover intentions.

DOI: 10.4018/979-8-3693-3166-8.ch007

INTRODUCTION

The tourism industry stands as a dynamic sector with unique challenges, where the roles of women employees have become increasingly significant. It has emerged as a key player in the global market, attracting millions of visitors annually (Singh *et al.*, 2023). As the tourism industry expands, understanding the work-family conflict faced by women employees becomes crucial for ensuring a diverse and inclusive workforce (Khan et al., 2024). This section provides an overview of the Indian tourism industry, its growth trajectory, and the need to address work-family conflict among & turnover intentions among frontline female employees. The COVID-19 epidemic has caused these lines to become even more hazy, which has increased the conflict between work and family for women employees in the tourism sector (Frank et al., 2021). Due to the growing pressures on both work and family life in contemporary industrial cultures, it is difficult to maintain work-family balance (Mishra, 2021). Women are expected to balance several responsibilities at once, dividing their time between work and family (Demerouti & Bakker 2023). Job burnout, discontent, work stress, excessive working hours, and role conflict are the most prevalent stressors that lead to the occurrence of work-family conflict in terms of women it will elevate more in tourism sector (Anand & Vohra, 2020; Elahi et al., 2022; Kooraram & Durbarry, 2022).

Work-family conflict is a major concern for frontline female tourism employees in India. These personnel frequently struggle to balance their work and family duties, which has a detrimental impact on their well-being and job performance. Jobs in the tourism industry sometimes demand employees to work long hours, including weekends and holidays, making it difficult for women to balance their family duties. Many female professionals in the tourism industry struggle to obtain inexpensive and dependable childcare or elder care, making it difficult to manage work and family obligations. Frontline work in the tourism industry may be physically and emotionally exhausting, leaving employees with little energy and time for their families.

Societal expectations about gender roles and responsibilities might put further pressure on women to choose home obligations over employment (Islam, 2020).

Work-family conflict hampers employees' productivity and also affects employee intentions to quit the job (Medina-Garrido et al., 2021), psychological distress (Dong et al., 2022) and psychological safety (Duncan, 2023). This study's main goal is to clarify the connection between work-family conflict and its influence on women employees' intentions to quit the job in the tourism industry. Furthermore, it is still necessary to investigate how psychological safety, in the context of work-family conflict, lower the degree of intentions to leave the workforce in context of women employees in the tourism sector. The tourism industry in India may not always provide flexible work options, such as part-time or telecommuting, which might assist women better balance their work and family duties. Traditional gender norms and cultural expectations in India frequently impose a greater responsibility on women for caring and domestic tasks. This can lead to tension when women are also attempting to further their careers in the tourism business. This proposed chapter aims to conduct a comprehensive and holistic study on the work-family conflict experienced by frontline women working in the tourism industry. By delving into the multifaceted aspects of this conflict, the chapter seeks to identify contributing factors, understand the nuances of its impact, and propose viable solutions to enhance the work-life balance for women employees. This chapter also adds to the body of literature by examining mediating effects of psychological safety in an effort to clarify how turnover intentions are impacted by the interplay of the work and family domains by assessing the mediating role of psychological safety in the relationship between work-family conflict and turnover intentions. Also explore the distinctive challenges faced by frontline female employees in balancing work and family responsibilities in a sector known for its irregularities and demands and identify and examine the factors within the tourism industry that contribute to work-family conflict, such as seasonal nature, customer-driven pressures, and organizational support mechanisms. This study also proposes effective strategies and solutions, including the implementation of flexible work policies and the promotion of supportive organizational cultures, to mitigate work-family conflict for frontline women employees in the Tourism sector in India. The tourism sector, like many other industries, faces several challenges related to gender equality and the treatment of women employees.

LITERATURE REVIEW

Research on conflict between job and family conflict in the context of the Indian tourism industry is limited but growing. Women frequently have specific obstacles in managing work and family commitments, and these issues can be amplified in industries such as tourism, which may have demanding schedules and seasonal fluctuations in workload. Understanding the specific factors that contribute to job and family conflict among women in the Indian tourism industry might assist organizations in developing focused interventions to aid these employees. Relevant literature includes studies on women's employment challenges, family dynamics, and the unique aspects of the Indian work culture. Gupta et al. (2019) on gender roles in Indian families and Singh and Jain (2020) exploring work-family balance in the Indian hospitality sector. Reviewing existing literature, this section examines studies on work-family conflict, turnover intentions, and the mediating effects of work and family satisfaction. Srivastava and Singh (2017) on the relationship between work-family conflict and psychological health in India, as well as Greenhaus and Beutell (1985) on the influence of job demands on family life.

Work-Family Conflict (WFC) and Turnover Intentions (TOI)

Women have many responsibilities in their life, and conflicts between work and family might arise when these responsibilities are incompatible. According to Greenhaus and Beutell (1985, p. 77), WFC is characterised as "a form of interrole conflict in which the role pressure from the work and family domains are mutually incompatible in some respect."

This section investigates the direct relationship between WFC and TOI among women employees in the Indian tourism industry. It also explores the specific dimensions of WFC that most strongly contribute to TOI.

Baykal (2020) stated 'Women keep experiencing many career challenges in the workplace even as more of them occupy higher positions in the professional arena according to a major study by' (Derks, 2016). Even though we have legislation protecting equal opportunities and international mandates at our disposal, women encounter these barriers in the male-dominated business worlds which are subtle but very strong. Such surroundings usually involve women eschewing traditional feminine features and become masculine, which is indispensable to making senior management a success. The paradox arisen due to the conflict between societal expectations and workplace demands provides the concept called "queen bee", where female bosses choose to isolate themselves from femininity and other female workers so that they become successful in their position. This process somehow contributes to the creation of new boundaries for others. Regrettably, this problem creates a discontent solitary among workers and turnover with the aim of reflecting the importance of systemic change.

Rawat *et al.*, (2023) looked at factors that can cause WFC and FWC as well as factors related to turnover intentions. The researchers came up with that working stress influenced WFC significantly that was in line with the previous studies. Interestingly, family responsibility was not linked to FWC and probably this was because the participants are old and due to the reduced family roles as well specially for women counterparts. This thereby demands additional study on the demographic as a factor of conflict dynamics. Study reiterates the fact that several categories of organizations should be studied to have the withdrawal behaviours of employees like turnover intention, absenteeism, and tardiness better understood.

Ogakwu *et al.*, (2023) analysed into the effect of job–family conflict (JFC) on quit intentions among women doctors with stress acting as a mediator and perceived organizational support as a moderator. The correlational outcomes showed that there is a positive relation between both WFC and TI, this finding coincides with previous studies. Besides, WFC has a positive correlation with job stress. Nevertheless, the stress at work did not play the mediating role between high WFC and sleep patterns. Support at work which is the perception of organizational support weakened the relationship between the WFC-TI link, reaffirming its multiplication effect on the intentions to quit. The study outlines the role of organizational support in reducing the burden of labour issues among female doctors in Lahore.

Akinbobola (2016) emphasizes on the family-work conflict as the most vital factor, influencing the quality of work life, and impacting the retention. It implies that the intentions to quit among the youthful women is high than among the grown-up women. The implication are higher recruitment costs, absence cases, and low retention rates, which in turn result in losing a corporate talent. Establishing the government as a support unit is advised, by implementing the relevant policies aimed at the promotion of gender equality, and also women emancipation programs. Organizations are also reminded to pursue solutions such as flexible working schedules, increased maternity leave and professional development prospects to bring about changes that will bring gender in the workplace and empower women at all levels.

Tafvelin (2020) delves into intragroup conflict within women-dominated workplaces, offering valuable insights into task, relationship, and process conflicts. Drawing from their findings, the author highlights the prevalence of task conflicts across professions and the significant impact of relationship conflicts on employee well-being, particularly in increasing perceptions of depression. Additionally, the paper identifies social workers as experiencing more task conflicts, possibly reflecting the complexity of their professional work. While process conflicts have comparatively less impact on well-being, they still contribute to negative outcomes, notably depression. This comprehensive analysis underscores the importance of understanding intragroup conflict dynamics for fostering a healthy work environment and organizational productivity.

Mohanty (2018) have identified women's contribution in tourism economy, although adverse circumstances continue to hamper this involvement. Issues like gender discrimination, delegated leadership roles, and possibility of wage discrimination are a great stumbling block the empowerment of women in this area. Preventive efforts in the form of agenda setting, policy implementation, and human capital development are needed to tackle these challenges successfully. Additionally, more research and implementation initiatives need to be developed continually to achieve the gender equality objective and promote the tourism industry's sustainability.

Jayswal (2015) examined In India women faces hurdles and their position are not improved, even they are called half the population as the 2015 sex ratio, Yet, government initiatives, especially in tourism sector, are directed to adding to women employment. Tourism, a major source of income that accounts for a significant portion of the GDP and employment, is empowering female participation, illuminating their expanding place in the sector and the potential for empowerment.

Cinamon (2002) inquired it is necessary to grasp the finer shades of gender differences in the relative significance of family and personal roles, and the implications for work-family conflict are of the utmost importance. Moving forward from the research of (Cinamon, 2002), which showcased three distinct worker profiles ranked based on the priority of the work-and-family roles, the authors set to explore both inter- and intra-gender variations of this construct. The study intends to explore the distinct challenges and experiences that the individuals face in the process of managing professional and familial roles using a profile based gap analysis to determine how men and women differ in their distribution across these various roles.

Shelton (2006) highlights the venture performance of female owned businesses and it's improvement with the application of work-family strategies. Role-sharing strategies become preferable tactics and this technique brings about the assimilation of work and family affairs. Thus, inter-role conflict can be eliminated to an extent. Sharing the duties of a venture through the use of participative management methods is delineated as a critical aspect for successful female entrepreneurs to strike a balance between business commitments and family roles.

Pai (2009) addressed the current problem with diversity in corporate leadership, especially women under-representation in the very top posts. It looks into the idea of the "glass ceiling "and illustrates the research findings that paint a picture of persistent obstacles despite works to foster diversity. This paper brings out the challenges that women and the minorities face in rising to executive positions in diverse companies that have well-structured diversity strategies.

Sojo (2016) examines how women's well-being is influenced by what goes on in the workplace in a negative way. It scrutinized 88 studies with over 73,000 working women in them, and it was concluded that both the more intense and less frequent situations (i.e., sexual coercion) and the higher frequency and lower intensity situations (i.e., gender harassment) have similar damages to women's well-being. These events were as bad as the established occupational stressors. Power relations between perpetrators and victims were among the topics addressed in this essay and future research directions and organization interventions to tackle these problems are also suggested. Research on Work-Family Conflict (WFC) and Turnover Intentions (TOI) among women in the Indian tourism industry is sparse but critical. Women in India confront specific hurdles as a result of cultural expectations and conventional gender roles, which can affect their work-life balance and job satisfaction. Investigating the association between WFC and TOI among women in the tourism industry might give significant insights into the variables driving turnover intentions in this particular setting. Long working hours, the seasonal nature of the sector, and a lack of support networks can all contribute to WFC, which influences women's decisions to stay or leave their occupations.

H1 Work-to-family conflict is positively associated with turnover intentions.

H2 Family-to-work conflict is positively associated with turnover intentions.

Work to Family Conflict and Psychological Safety

A positive psychological climate at work fosters the sense of psychological safety within the organization, while a work-family relationship contributes to the growth of the psychological climate at work (Khairy et al., 2023). When an individual believes that his well-being is enhanced by his workplace, the organization is deemed to have a psychologically secure climate (Hayat & Afshari 2021). A significant psychological environment that "shapes how people inhabited their roles in the organization" is psychological safety (Kahn, 1990).

The conclusion extracted by the (Carmeli, 2009) in the referred research strongly suggests that relational theories in sociology and psychology stands as an import issue, the very topic is in agreement with the quest for deeper study of social constructs within organizations. Underlining the vitally important role of high-quality relationship in facilitating key organizational potentials especially learning the paper calls for deeper investigations into how these relationship in conjunction with other relational constructs like trust and liking contribute to fostering of success organizations as well as performance improvement. This statement stimulates further research on the interrelationship of relational factors and organizational capabilities which, in turn, may indicate links between aspiration of capability creators for competitive advantage and interest of research in behavioural scientists in interpersonal dynamics contributing to performance level in social interactions at workplace. This study explores how such relational dynamics act as the driving forces behind positive organizational change and achievement of desired outcomes, and therefore, future research questions should tackle this in order to help us better understand how organizational dynamics unfold and what strategies to employ in improving organizational performance. (Frazier, 2017) notes that in the world of today, with the fast pace and fierce competition, organizations should have continual transformation that creates learning, change, and innovations. The construct of psychological safety, understood as a belief in a work environment receptive to interpersonal risk taking, is recognized as a priority factor developing employee engagement and organizational steering. Despite its recent explosive empirical surge, questions still remain as to what the causes and consequences are. The aim of this study to carry out a meta-analysis, which seeks to clarify the relative importance of various antecedents and also to explore the individual and group level implications of psychological safety, and through this, we shall identify the place of this critical construct in our understanding of this subject, and how it could inform future researches. Smith (2018) investigated even after all the actions taken to promote firefighter safety, safety of firefighter is still a considerable problem. The research highlights that investigating the influence of psychosocial and organizational factors, such as stress and burnout, on safety outcomes is a necessary act. Burnout has a negative outcome on safety performance, inducing poor communication and carefulness to procedures. Research on work-family conflict and psychological safety among women in the Indian tourism industry is an important and understudied issue. job-family conflict arises when job expectations interfere with home duties, causing stress and bad effects for employees. Psychological safety is the belief that one's work environment is safe for interpersonal risk-taking and the expressing of ideas without fear of repercussions.

H3. *Work to family conflict (W-FC) has a significant effect on Psychological Safety (PS).*

H4. *Family to work conflict (F-WC) has a significant effect on Psychological Safety (PS).*

Psychological Safety and Employee Turnover Intentions

Edmondson (2004) highlights the subtleties regarding psychological safety and interpersonal trust. This makes clear that trust in the other person depends on the assumption of their goodwill, while psychological safety allows people to bring forth their views without any fear of getting punished. Making psychological safety a central issue, the paper explains how it facilitates learning processes in the context of teamwork, capitalizing on observations from different organizational environments. The paper concludes by recommending possible routes for practical implementation and additional research. Nu'man (2021) analyses how previous studies provide insights on the legal protection of frontline female workers in the context of informal activities, especially those found in tourism area like Dusun Bambu. This review additionally notes the studies referring to illegal safeguards, unequal negotiation power and lack of information concerning workers' rights among women. Furthermore, it also looks at interventions by the different stakeholders and points out the orphaned areas in these interventions. The paper delves into the synthesis of this context, setting the grounds and the need to put the center of its consideration on the rights and welfare of frontline female workers in Dusun Bambu. Understanding how psychological safety impacts turnover intentions is especially essential in the Indian tourism industry, where women may experience distinct obstacles in terms of work-life balance and gender conventions. Supportive leadership, inclusive work practices, and a diversity-focused culture may all help women employees feel more protected. Studying this link can assist tourism firms in identifying measures to increase psychological safety and minimize turnover intentions among frontline female employees. It may also emphasize the significance of fostering inclusive and supportive work environments that encourage gender equality and employee well-being.

H5. Physiological Safety has significant relationship with Employee turnover intentions.

Mediating Role of Psychological Safety (PS)

Pacheco (2015) highlights the vital role of workplace factors like organizational culture and psychological safety in shaping employee voice and silence, while underscoring the need to understand its impacts. Psychological safety cannot be overemphasized in organizations as a means of ensuring open communication. The different forms of silence, including acquiescent and defensive silence, forms the core issue in an attempt to achieve psychological safety. The research has revealed a link between silence on the part of employees as well as an unconscious absence of psychological safety that support the need for the organizations to create environments that foster employees' ability to share their concerns and ideas without the fear of retribution. Liu (2020) commences by stating supervisory incivility as low-grade deviant behaviour by supervisors towards employees which included calling them in public by name, slapping or even shouting at them, and this includes examples like public criticism and slander. They marked out adverse influence of leaders' insubordination on employees' attitudes, behaviour and mental health. Although previous studies centred on the dyadic relationship between supervisors and subordinates as it relates to supervisor incivility, this study offers a shift of focus to the broader perspective of women within organizations and the repercussion of such incivility on the organization as a chain of aggressive event or actions.

Research in this area can assist firms in identifying areas for change in their work practices and policies to promote greater work-life balance and psychological safety for frontline female employees. It can also help to shape strategies to promote gender equality and foster a more inclusive work environment in the tourism industry.

H6 Physiological safety mediates the relationship between work-to-family conflict and turnover intentions.

H7 Physiological safety mediates the relationship between family-to-work conflict and turnover intentions.

Conceptual Model

The conceptual foundation for this research is as follows: Figure 1: Conceptual model of work-family conflict, family-work conflict, psychological safety, and turnover Intentions.

Figure 1. Model of work-family conflict (WFC), family-work conflict (FWC), psychological safety (PS), and turnover Intentions (TOI)

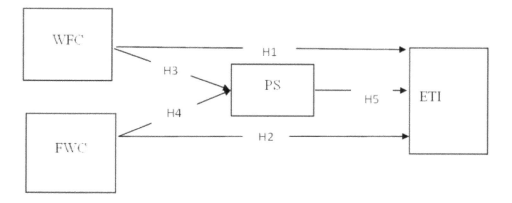

METHODOLOGY

The purpose of this study was to evaluate psychological safety as a mediating variable, work-family conflict as independent variables, and turnover intentions as a dependent variable in the estimation model. The questionnaire, which was distributed to 400 female participants who worked as a frontline employee tourism business, was created using a 7-point Likert scale. A total of 222 respondents completed the survey from Tourism industry.

Participants

The sample consisted of 222 frontline female employees from the Indian Tourism sector. These frontline female employees consist of Hotel Staff like Front desk employees, housekeeping attendants, female restaurant servers, female employees working in travel agencies and female flight attendants. Women who were married

(59.5%) or unmarried (40.5%), stated their marital status. The tenure ranged from one year to forty years, with a mean of 1.25 (SD =.58).

Measures

Work-family conflict and *Family-work conflict* were investigated using 10 items borrowed from Adams et al. (1996) and Netemeyer *et al.*, (1996). Sample item included "The demands of my work interfere with my home and family life."

Psychological safety was measured using 12-item scale developed by Hall et al., (2010). One such item is ""Management acts decisively when a concern of an employees' psychological status is raised"

Turnover intentions were measured using the four-items adapted from Bluedorn's (1982). A sample item included "I am thinking about quitting my line of work."

Analysis

Exploratory Factor Analysis (EFA)

Data was reduced using Exploratory Factor Analysis (EFA), and principal component analysis was done using Kaiser Normalization via varimax rotation. Only items with factor loadings larger than 0.4 were preserved, while the remainder were eliminated (Hair *et al.*, 2010).

Eigenvalues over one were found to account for 73.024% of the variation. Table 1 shows the results of the Bartlett's test for sphericity and the Kaiser-Meyer-Olkin (KMO) estimate of sample adequacy. As a result, a sample size of 222 was deemed appropriate for this study.

Table 1. KMO and Bartlett's Test

Kaiser-Meyer-Olkin Measure of Sampling Adequacy.		.933
Bartlett's Test of Sphericity	Approx. Chi-Square	4810.148
	df	300
	Sig.	.000

Using EFA, all five Work Family Conflict (WFC) items, all five Family Work Conflict (FWC) items, eleven out of twelve Psychological Safety (PS) items, and all four Employee Turnover Intentions (ETI) items were retained. As a consequence, twenty-five items were selected for the final analysis from a total of twenty-six. Table 2 reveals that all twenty of the retained items had factor loadings greater than 0.4.

Table 2. Exploratory factor analysis

	Component			
	1	**2**	**3**	**4**
PS11	.769			
PS12	.749			
PS9	.748			
PS10	.744			
PS5	.698			
PS6	.691			
PS7	.668			
PS2	.666			
PS8	.657			
PS4	.631			
PS3	.506			
ET11		.875		
ETI2		.836		
ETI4		.835		
ETI3		.806		
WFC2			.825	
WFC4			.818	
WFC1			.803	
WFC5			.786	
WFC3			.774	
FWC3				.845
FWC4				.821
FWC5				.782
FWC1				.778
FWC2				.766

Extraction Method: Principal Component Analysis.

Rotation Method: Varimax with Kaiser Normalization.

a. Rotation converged in 6 iterations.

Reliability Analysis

A reliability study was done to determine the degree of consistency among the numerous measurements (Hair *et al.,* 2010). Thus, the dependability of twenty kept items was assessed. According to Hair *et al.,* (2010), a Cronbach α score of 0.6 or higher indicates a credible scale.

The Cronbach α score for all constructs was more than 0.6, indicating the reliability of the twenty maintained items. The total scale dependability was likewise shown to be more than 0.6. The overall and individual construct reliabilities are presented in Table 3.

Table 3. Reliability

S. No	Construct	Individual Construct Reliability	Overall Reliability
1.	WFC	.914	
2.	FWC	.903	.938
3.	PS	.945	
4.	ETI	.933	

Figure 2. Model of work-family conflict, family-work conflict, psychological safety and employee turnover intentions

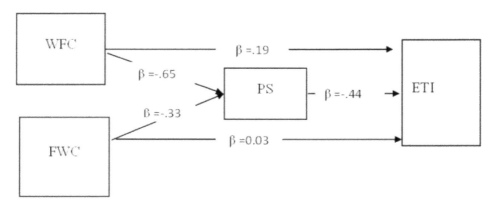

Mediating Effect

Preacher and Hayes (2008) established a bootstrapping technique with 5,000 resamples to analyze H6 and H7, which revealed that PS would mediate the relationship between WFC and ETI (H6) and FWC and ETI (H7). To establish the importance of total, direct, and indirect effects, a bootstrap technique with 5,000 resamples was used. The total, direct, and indirect impacts of WFC and ETI were found to be significant, as were the effects of FWC and ETI (Table 4).

Table 4. Results of hierarchical regression

Variables	Model 1				Model 2				Model 3			
	B	SE	B	Sig	B	SE	B	Sig.	B	SE	β	Sig.
(Constant)	3.812	.509		.000	6.357	.387		.000	6.955	.387		.000
Single	-.528	.265	-.147	-.47	-.303	.183	-.084	.100	-.298	.183	-.083	.100
Tenure	-107	.226	-.035	.636	-.016	.156	-.005	.916	-.018	.156	-.006	.908
PS					-.737**	.047	-.726**	.000	-.790	.065	-.778	.000
WFC									.101*	.057	.104*	.004
FWC									.021	.062	.019	.738

Note- Dependent Variable: Employee Turnover Intentions (ETI)

Model 1 (R^2 = .02; p< .01; F (3,218) =1.71, p<0.1); Model 2 (R^2 = .53, p< .01; F (4, 217) =62.92, p<0.1); Model 3 (R^2 = .54, p< .01; F (6,215) =42.69, p<0.1). PS= Psychological Safety; WFC= Work-Family conflict; FWC= Family-Work conflict.

Table 5. Hypotheses results

Hypotheses	Relationship	Standard β	Result
H1	WFC → ETI	0.19	Accepted
H2	FWC → ETI	0.03	Not Accepted
H3	WFC → PS	0.65	Accepted
H4	FWC → PS	0.33	Accepted
H5	PS → ETI	0.44	Accepted
H6	WFC → PS → ETI	0.10	Accepted
H7	FWC → PS → ETI	0.01	Not Accepted

Note: **p<0.05; WFC= Work Family Conflict, FWC= Family Work Conflict, OC= Psychological Safety, ETI=Employee Turnover Intentions

FINDING

Regression Analysis and Hypotheses Testing

Hierarchical multiple regression results are presented in Tables 4. Models 1 involving inclusion of demographic variables as control variables (R^2 = .02; p< .01; F (3,218) =1.71, p<0.1) made statistically significant contributions to predicting ETIs. However, none of the included demographic variables, made a statistically significant contribution on their own, in explainingETIs. Model 2 adding JE makes a significant contribution to ETIs (R^2 = .53, p< .01; F (4, 217) =62.92, p<0.1). PS significantly negatively reduces TOIs (*b*=. -72, *p*<.01). Models 3 involving addition of WFC and FWC made statistically significant contributions (R^2 = .54, p< .01; F

(6,215) =42.69, p<0.1). However, only WFC ($b= .10$, $p<.05$) makes a statistically significant positive contribution to ETIs, while FWC is not a statistically significant positive contributor to TOIs

Support from family is essential for a healthy work-life balance, and this is reflected in the work itself, which boosts job satisfaction and ultimately increases productivity (Aruldoss, et, al 2021). There is a clear correlation between both dependent and independent variables according to an analysis of way models and estimate models. The results will provide insightful information to the academic community as well as business community, promoting a positive work environment for women in the Indian tourism industry. The findings indicate that work-family conflict is not only harmful to women employees' individual well-being, but it also has larger consequences for organizational performance, productivity and employee turnover intentions in case of women employees. Addressing work-family conflict is thus not only a social responsibility issue, but also a strategic one for tourism industry. These enterprises may establish a more friendly and inclusive work environment by introducing policies such as flexible working hours, telecommuting alternatives, and employee assistance programs, which allow women to better manage their work and family commitments (Travis, *et al.*, 2019). Furthermore, establishing a culture that prioritizes work-life balance and supports gender equality can boost women's general well-being while also contributing to a more motivated, engaged, and productive workforce.

PRACTICAL IMPLICATIONS AND RECOMMENDATIONS

The paper concludes by providing practical implications for organizations in the Indian tourism industry to address work-family conflict and its consequences like psychological stress and women employee's intentions to quit the job. Recommendations will include strategies for enhancing psychological safety and overall well-being, thereby reducing turnover intentions among women employees in the tourism sector. Organizations in the Indian tourism operations should think about establishing flexible work arrangements including flexitime, telecommuting, and reduced workweeks. These agreements can assist frontline female employees in better balancing work and family commitments, decreasing work-family conflict.

Organizations should create and execute helpful policies such as paid parental leave, on-site daycare, and family-friendly workplaces which help in reducing the stress in women employees. These regulations can assist reduce the stress and burden of juggling work and family responsibilities.

Organizations should offer training and development opportunities for frontline female employees to improve their skills and talents. This can boost their job happiness and motivation, leading to improved retention rates and productivity.

Employers should provide work-life balance initiatives such as wellness programs, stress management training, and counselling services. These programs can assist frontline female employees deal with work-family conflicts and enhance their general well-being.

Managers should receive training on how to spot and help frontline female employees who are experiencing work-family conflicts. Providing management support may make employees feel appreciated and supported, resulting in increased job satisfaction and engagement.

Organizations should encourage gender equality in the workplace by giving women equal opportunity for professional progression, leadership roles, and compensation. This can help eliminate gender discrimination and increase overall job happiness.

Future study should investigate the efficacy of various treatments and techniques in minimizing work-family conflict among frontline female employees in the Indian tourism business. This can assist to identify best practices and guide policy choices in this area.

FUTURE RESEARCH AND LIMITATIONS

Longitudinal research tracking changes in work-family conflict over time might reveal significant insights into the factors that lead to conflict and how they evolve.

Comparing work-family conflict among industries within India and between nations could help in identifying industry-specific or cultural factors that impact conflict intensity. Testing the efficacy of various interventions, such as flexible work arrangements, family support programs, and management training programs, in reducing work-family conflict among frontline female tourism employees. Using qualitative approaches to investigate frontline female tourism professionals' lived experiences, such as interviews or focus groups, may give a more comprehensive knowledge of the elements that lead to work-family conflict and employee turnover intentions.

This study employs a cross-sectional design, limiting the capacity to draw causal findings or follow changes in work-family conflict over time. Existing research on this issue may have limitations, such as small sample sizes or a lack of representation of women in the Indian tourism business, limiting the generalizability of results. Addressing these constraints and focusing on future research topics may help to broaden our understanding of work-family conflict among frontline female employees in the Indian tourism sector, as well as guide the development of more effective policies and practices to promote work-life balance and address employee turnover intentions.

CONCLUSION

The chapter's goal in conducting this comprehensive study is to bring light on the nuances of work-family conflict faced by female employees in the tourism sector and, from there, offer practical suggestions to improve their general well-being and professional fulfillment.

Front line female employees encounter discrimination in employment, promotion, and salary, resulting in decreased work satisfaction. Balancing job responsibilities and family obligations may be difficult, especially in positions that require long or unpredictable hours. Frontline female employees, particularly those in customer-facing professions, may confront safety risks, such as harassment and assault. Women may have fewer prospects for job progression as a result of prejudices or limited access to training and development programs. Despite performing equivalent duties, women may be paid less than males, which can lead to financial instability. Companies are learning that a "happy" employee is a more productive one, thus they are getting more involved in helping employees resolve work-family conflicts and showing greater concern for the personal life of their employees (Devi, *et al.*, 2024). This is when it becomes important to consider factors that result in psychological fulfillment and, in turn, motivate higher levels of professional achievement. At the same time, factors that lead to doubt, unhappiness, insecurity, and conflict are responsible for a reduction in the well-being of individuals as well as organizations, and as such, require more attention. Previous research in the area of psychological well-being has the drawback of not going far enough in examining the influence of non-organizational elements on performance. In order to solve the restriction, this study highlights the importance of family as a critical component that affects people's psychological safety and general well-being. This study shed light on the complicated and diverse topic of work-family conflict among frontline female employees in India's tourism sector. A thorough examination of current literature and empirical study revealed numerous noteworthy conclusions. First and foremost, it is clear that work-family conflict is a common issue for women in this field, with variables such as excessive working hours, inconsistent scheduling, and a lack of support networks all contributing to the conflict. Second, the influence of work-family conflict on different elements of women's life, such as physical and mental health, job satisfaction, and family relationships, has been discussed. Finally, the study highlighted various techniques and interventions that firms may use to reduce work-family conflict and improve the well-being of frontline female employees.

Overall, this study adds useful insights to the current literature on work-family conflict and lays the groundwork for future research and policy development in this field.

REFERENCES

Adams, G. A., King, L. A., & King, D. W. (1996). Relationships of job and family involvement, family social support, and work–family conflict with job and life satisfaction. *The Journal of Applied Psychology*, 81(4), 411. 10.1037/0021-9010.81.4.411

Akinbobola, O. I. (2016). Appraisal of Role Conflict on Quality of Work Life and Turnover Intention among Corporate Women Workforce. *European Journal of Humanities and Social Sciences*, 35(1).

Anand, A., & Vohra, V. (2020). Alleviating employee work-family conflict: Role of organizations. *The International Journal of Organizational Analysis*, 28(2), 313–332.

Baykal, E. S. (2020). Queen bee syndrome: a modern dilemma of working women and its effects on turnover intentions. *Strategic Outlook for Innovative Work Behaviours: Interdisciplinary and Multidimensional Perspectives*, 165-178.

Bluedorn, A. C. (1982). A unified model of turnover from organizations. *Human Relations*, 35(2), 135–153. 10.1177/001872678203500204

Boyar, S. L. (2003). Work-family conflict: A model of linkages between work and family domain variables and turnover intentions. *Journal of Managerial Issues*, 175–190.

Carmeli, A. B. (2009). Learning behaviours in the workplace: The role of high-quality interpersonal relationships and psychological safety. *Systems Research and Behavioral Science: The Official Journal of the International Federation for Systems Research*, 26(1), 81–98. 10.1002/sres.932

Cinamon, R. G. (2002). Gender differences in the importance of work and family roles: Implications for work–family conflict. *Sex Roles*, 47, 531–541.

Demerouti, E., & Bakker, A. B. (2023). Job demands-resources theory in times of crises: New propositions. *Organizational Psychology Review*, 13(3), 209–236.

Dong, M., Zhang, T., Li, Y., & Ren, Z. (2022). The effect of work connectivity behavior after-hours on employee psychological distress: The role of leader workaholism and work-to-family conflict. *Frontiers in Public Health*, 10, 722679.35284392

Duncan, H. (2023). *Organizational Embeddedness and the Roles of Support and Psychological Safety for Caregiving Senior-Level Employees Experiencing Work-Family Conflict* [Doctoral dissertation, Converse University].

Edmondson, A. C. (2004). Psychological safety, trust, and learning in organizations: A group-level lens. *Trust and distrust in organizations: Dilemmas and approaches, 12*, 239-272.

Elahi, N. S., Abid, G., Contreras, F., & Fernández, I. A. (2022). Work–family and family–work conflict and stress in times of COVID-19. *Frontiers in Psychology*, 13, 951149.36304883

Frank, E., Zhao, Z., Fang, Y., Rotenstein, L. S., Sen, S., & Guille, C. (2021). Experiences of work-family conflict and mental health symptoms by gender among physician parents during the COVID-19 pandemic. *JAMA Network Open*, 4(11), e2134315–e2134315.34767022

Frazier, M. L. (2017). Psychological safety: A meta-analytic review and extension. *Personnel Psychology*, 70(1), 113–165. 10.1111/peps.12183

Gragnano, A., Simbula, S., & Miglioretti, M. (2020). Work–life balance: Weighing the importance of work–family and work–health balance. *International Journal of Environmental Research and Public Health*, 17(3), 907.32024155

Greenhaus, J. H., & Beutell, N. J. (1985). Sources of conflict between work and family roles. *Academy of Management Review*, 10(1), 76–88.

Gupta, A. (2019). Gender roles in Indian families: A contemporary review. *International Journal of Gender & Women's Studies*, 7(2), 180–195.

Hall, G. B., Dollard, M. F., & Coward, J. (2010). Psychosocial safety climate: Development of the PSC-12. *International Journal of Stress Management*, 17, 353–383.

Hayat, A., & Afshari, L. (2021). Supportive organizational climate: A moderated mediation model of workplace bullying and employee well-being. *Personnel Review*, 50(7/8), 1685–1704.

Islam, A. (2020). 'It gets really boring if you stay at home': Women, work and temporalities in urban India. *Sociology*, 54(5), 867–882.

Jayswal, D. K. (2015). Women's participation and Tourism industry: An overview. *Research Journal of Humanities and Social Sciences*, 6(4), 269–273.

Khairy, H. A., Liu, S., & Sheikhelsouk, S., EI-Sherbeeny, A. M., Alsetoohy, O., & Al-Romeedy, B. S. (2023). The Effect of benevolent leadership on job engagement through psychological safety and workplace friendship prevalence in the tourism and hospitality industry. *Sustainability*, 15(17), 13245.

Khan, N. A., Bahadur, W., Ramzan, M., & Pravdina, N. (2024). Turning the tide: An impact of leader empowering behavior on employees' work–family conflict, spillover and turnover intention in tourism. *Leadership and Organization Development Journal*.

Kooraram, S., & Durbarry, R. (2022). Impact of spousal support on Work-family/ family work conflicts: A qualitative study of married working women in Mauritius. *International Journal of Early Childhood Special Education*, 14(5).

Liu, C. E. (2020). Supervision incivility and employee psychological safety in the workplace. *International Journal of Environmental Research and Public Health*, 17(3), 840.32013097

Medina-Garrido, J. A., Biedma-Ferrer, J. M., & Rodríguez-Cornejo, M. V. (2021). I quit! Effects of work-family policies on the turnover intention. *International Journal of Environmental Research and Public Health*, 18(4), 1893.33669281

Mishra, G. (2021). *Work-Family Conflict and Family-Friendly Policies for Working Women in India*. Lulu Publication.

Mohanty, P. S. (2018). Women at work: exploring the issues and challenges of women employees in travel and tourism. *Indian Journal of Economics and Development, 6*(1), 1-5. doi: (online): 2320-9836ISSN

Netemeyer, B. a. (1996). Development and Validation of Work-Family Conflict and Family-Work Conflict Scales. *The Journal of Applied Psychology*, 81(4). Advance online publication. 10.1037/0021-9010.81.4.400

Nu'man, M. H. (2021, June). Protection of Informal Female Workers in Tourist Sector Company. In *Social and Humanities Research Symposium (SORES 2020),* (pp. 68-71). Atlantis Press.

Pacheco, D. C. (2015). *Silence in organizations and psychological safety: a literature review.European Scientific Journal,* (Special Edition), 293-308. doi: : 1857ISSN

Pai, K. (2009). Glass ceiling: Role of women in the corporate world. *Competitiveness Review*, 19(2), 106–113.

Shaukat, R. Y. (2017). Examining the linkages between relationship conflict, performance and turnover intentions: Role of job burnout as a mediator. *International Journal of Conflict Management*, 28(1), 4–23. 10.1108/IJCMA-08-2015-0051

Shelton, L. M. (2006). Female entrepreneurs, work–family conflict, and venture performance: New insights into the work–family interface. *Journal of Small Business Management*, 44(2), 285–297.

Singh, N. Y.-M. (2023). Exploring the impact of functional, symbolic, and experiential image on approach behaviors among state-park tourists from India, Korea, and the USA. *Humanities & Social Sciences Communications*, 10(14).36721793

Singh, R., & Jain, K. (2020). Work-family balance in the Indian hospitality sector. *International Journal of Hospitality Management*, 88, 102503.

Smith, T. D. (2018). Assessment of relationships between work stress, work-family conflict, burnout and firefighter safety behavior outcomes. *Safety Science*, 103, 287–292. 10.1016/j.ssci.2017.12.005

Sojo, V. E. (2016). Harmful workplace experiences and women's occupational well-being: A meta-analysis. *Psychology of Women Quarterly*, 40(1), 10–40. 10.1177/0361684315599346

Srivastava, N., & Singh, A. K. (2017). Impact of work-family conflict on psychological well-being of Indian women employees. *Vikalpa*, 42(1), 50–66.

Syed, A. A. (2018). Work-family conflict and turnover intentions: Moderated mediation model. *Human Resource Research*, 2(1), 95–106. 10.5296/hrr.v2i1.13925

Tafvelin, S. K. (2020). The prevalence and consequences of intragroup conflicts for employee well-being in women-dominated work. *Human Service Organizations, Management, Leadership & Governance*, 44(1), 47–62. 10.1080/23303131.2019.1661321

Chapter 8
Innovative Measures to Promote Social Responsibility in Tourism:
The Role of Tourism in Facing the Prostitution Exploitation

Érica Simão

School of Management, Hospitality, and Tourism, University of Algarve, Portugal

Rui Manuel Mendonça-Pedro
https://orcid.org/0000-0002-3240-2528

School of Management, Hospitality, and Tourism & CinTurs, University of Algarve, Portugal

ABSTRACT

The chapter intends to reflect on the theoretical role of tourism in reducing inequalities in society (SDG 1 and 16), the supply chain innovations and innovative products in tourism (SDG 8), employment opportunities for marginalised social sectors in tourism (SDG 1 and 8) and the challenges faced by women in tourism (SDG 5). This research aims to analyse the theoretical impacts that the legalisation of prostitution would have on a tourism destination, on the individuals involved, and on contributing to the diversity of tourism products (supply chain innovations). The result of this NLR of the responsibility in tourism in the face of prostitution resulted in the analysis of the impact felt by residents with prostitution. The understanding of the distinction between formal employment and informal employment, thus framing the best position for prostitution. The ethical concerns associated with prostitution are

DOI: 10.4018/979-8-3693-3166-8.ch008

exploitation, trafficking, and prejudgment. The regulation of the demand for sexual services marketed in different political contexts.

INTRODUCTION

The subject of prostitution legalisation is very complex, being the subject of public debate. There are several opinions about your function, a way of working to exploit vulnerabilities and the revelation of social inequalities (Søntvedt, 2009).

The legality of prostitution varies throughout the world. In some countries, it is legal and regulated, while in others, it is prohibited. There are five legal models regarding prostitution: the regulator, the abolitionist, the prohibitionist, the neo-abolitionist, and the legislators (Cho et al., 2013; Ribeiro & Silva, 2019). In Europe, legislators show a neo-abolitionist tendency, which includes criminalisation as another means to achieve the end of eradicating it (Ribeiro & Silva, 2019). Prostitution is an activity that exposes the worker to physical and mental risks. Not being a recognised profession makes it extremely stigmatised and viewed with prejudice (Hung, 2024). Furthermore, not being recognised, it is leading to the exploitation of this trade in marginalised, controlled, and regulated areas, leading to a greater risk of exploitation and violence (Cho et al., 2013; Hung, 2024; Ribeiro & Silva, 2019).

In the tourist context, sexuality has been an object of commodified study, practised using prostitution, being seen only as a risk factor for health and controversial practices for human dignity (Bhadra, 2022; Wen et al., 2020). However, these factors happen mainly in regions where gender inequality and socio-economic asymmetries are more established, and it is possible to observe a significant difference between the power of the client and sex workers (Matheson & Finkel, 2013; Omondi & Ryan, 2017). It is necessary to be aware that not all sexual relations that are practised in a tourist context involve negative characteristics, namely exploitation and trafficking (Marques & Lança, 2016).

The chapter intends to reflect on the theoretical role of tourism in reducing inequalities in society (SDG 1 and 16), the supply chain innovations and innovative products in tourism (SDG 8), employment opportunities for marginalised social sectors in tourism (SDG 1 and 8) and the challenges faced by women in tourism (SDG 5). Therefore, to accomplish the theoretical and holistic approach to an "old social issue", this research aims to analyse the theoretical impacts that the legalisation of prostitution would have on a tourism destination, on the individuals involved, and on contributing to the diversity of tourism products (supply chain innovations). First, to examine the impacts of prostitution, legal/regulated and non-legal/non-regulated, in tourism destinations. Second, to provide a critical review of the social responsibility of tourism facing prostitution. Third, to investigate innovative measures to prevent and reduce prostitution exploitation in the tourism context.

This chapter is divided into six main sections. The first section introduces the topic of prostitution, research objectives and chapter structure. The background, in the second section, includes a conceptualisation of prostitution issues. The third part consists of the methodology, i.e., a literature review method supported by the PRISMA framework. The following section, the fourth part, consists of the results and discussion according to a) the impacts of prostitution legal/regulated and non-legal/non-regulated in tourism destinations; b) a critical review of the social responsibility of tourism facing prostitution; and c) innovative measures to prevent and reduce prostitution exploitation in the tourism context. Moreover, the authors mention lines for future research in the fifth part. The paper closes with a conclusion that focuses on the study's aims.

BACKGROUND

Prostitution definition is a complex issue. Moreover, according to Escot et al. (2022), prostitution refers to the act of selling sexual services – which involves the transaction of sexual services for money. Similarly, Jenkins (2023, p. 1) argues that "[…] prostitution is the practice of engaging in relatively indiscriminate sexual activity, in general with someone who is not a spouse or a friend, in exchange for immediate payment in money or other valuables." Sexual services and prostitution were always focused on women's involvement, however, recently, attention has shifted to male and supply also (Johansson & Hansen, 2023; Matthews, 2018). The sex workers involved in this trade are predominantly women, although men and transgender individuals also participate (Boels, 2015; Johansson & Hansen, 2023; Matthews, 2018). "[…] prostitutes may be female, male or transgender, and prostitution may entail heterosexual or homosexual activity […]" (Jenkins, 2023, p. 1).

In the context of tourism, the word prostitution is abolished in contrast to the recognition of the term sex tourism (Marques & Lança, 2016; Mawby, 2017; Omondi & Ryan, 2017). The argument's core revolves around the act's morality and legality. Various countries approach this issue differently, with laws ranging from complete criminalisation to decriminalisation and legalisation (Boels, 2015; Boels & Verhage, 2016; Matheson & Finkel, 2013; Matthews, 2018; Williams & Lansky, 2013).

It is necessary to highlight the distinction between forced prostitution and voluntary prostitution. The volunteer is exercised by individuals over 18 years of age who, in exchange for money or some material good, decide to practice sexual activities. The forced is the one that someone exercises under violence, fear, coercion, or other type of domination, being forced to exercise sexual practices (Ribeiro & Silva,

2019). The consent of the prostitute in the practice of sexual acts makes it possible to distinguish prostitution from other situations in which the practice of sexual acts is a crime, such as situations of trafficking in human beings for sexual exploitation (Marques & Lança, 2016; Ribeiro & Silva, 2019).

The specific effects of the legalisation of prostitution may vary according to the policies adopted, local conditions and cultural attitudes. The debate on this subject involves a wide range of perspectives, however, it will have more significant repercussions on demand, supply and the amount of prostitution (Cho et al., 2013).

Starting from the demand effect, some customers will be dissuaded from consuming commercial sexual services if prostitution is illegal because there is a probability of being processed, increasing the costs of getting involved in the activity. The legalisation of prostitution would increase the demand for prostitution (Cho et al., 2013).

As for the offer, the legalisation of prostitution will induce potential sex workers to enter the market. Those who were dissuaded from offering sexual services for fear of the illegality of the function. On the other hand, the offer may also decrease since the State will require the payment of taxes on legalised prostitution, while illegal prostitution does not imply the payment of them (Cho et al., 2013; Søntvedt, 2009). With the increase in demand and supply, the balance of prostitution will be more outstanding in the legalised regime through approaches to regulating prostitution to ensure safer working conditions and the protection of their rights.

Sex and its entire industry are constantly expanding, although with many taboos and prejudices. Retrograde ideas are still very present today, which take advantage of the sector's fragility to feed prejudices. Therefore, sex tourism has a very negative connotation because it is usually associated with problems such as paedophilia, human trafficking, the spread of diseases, violence, and discrimination, among others (Ballester-Brage et al., 2014).

In short, the legalisation of prostitution would contribute to tourism in terms of the diversity of the tourist offer of the regions, such as the creation of specific packages for the segment, the creation of legalised spaces suitable for the trade of sexual activity and even the economy, due to the exploitation of a new trend, providing the creation of new jobs/employment and better working conditions (Ballester-Brage et al., 2014; Williams, 2013).

METHODOLOGY

Narrative Literature Review: The Method

The study intends to analyse the theoretical impacts that the legalisation of prostitution would have on a tourism destination, on the individuals involved, and on contributing to the diversity of tourism products (supply chain innovations). To achieve this aim, a narrative literature review (NLR) supported by the PRISMA framework was carried out (Kim & So, 2022; Page et al., 2021). NLR is a methodology widely used by scholars to systematise data, screening results, and theorise outputs (Greenhalgh et al., 2016; Moher et al., 2016; Sukhera, 2022). This methodology has been employed in many tourism studies and other fields of study (Fleuret, 2024; Vada et al., 2023). NLR is considered an accurate method as it is transparent when searching, collecting, and selecting articles. Reporting the number of excluded and included articles at different stages increases its rigour and allows the comparison of results when replicated (Moher et al., 2016; Sukhera, 2022).

Narrative Literature Review: The Process

The chapter's methodology was an NLR The authors selected relevant articles from Scopus, ScienceDirect and Google Scholar databases; published in social science journals; peer-reviewed articles, review papers and book chapters; English language only; between January 1st, 2013, December 1st, 2023; and documents that are included in conclusions section relevant material regarding the topics: prostitution legalisation and its impacts, prostitution and destination effects and sex tourism and social responsibility.

These databases were selected due to their being among the leading research databases with diverse interdisciplinary areas, as suggested by Fleuret (2024), Zhang et al. (2023) and Greenhalgh et al. (2016).

The search terms utilised (i.e., terms included in the article's title, abstract, and/ or keywords) were related to "Tourism" OR "Destination" AND "Prostitution" OR "Sexual" OR "Sex" AND "Legalization" AND "Exploitation" AND "Social Responsibility".

The selection process begins with the first screening of inclusion and exclusion papers. This search showed 38 results from both databases (Scopus – 15, Science-Direct – 21 and Google Scholar – 2). The Prisma flowchart framework (Figure 1) shows in detail the number of articles screened and excluded at the different steps of this review process (Moher et al., 2016; Page et al., 2021).

The following section presents the findings, including the NLR outcomes (i.e., the research methods used in the final sample of 20 articles), text mining and visualisation using VOSviewer software – version 1.6.20 (Bukar et al., 2023; Jan van Eck & Waltman, 2011), the macro-perspective results (e.g., the impacts of prostitution, legal/regulated and non-legal/non-regulated, in tourism destinations as a social responsibility obligation of the tourism sector/industry), and the micro-perspective outcomes (e.g., the innovative measures to prevent and reduce prostitution exploitation in the tourism context, contributing to the diversity of tourism supply/products)

Figure 1. Prisma flowchart

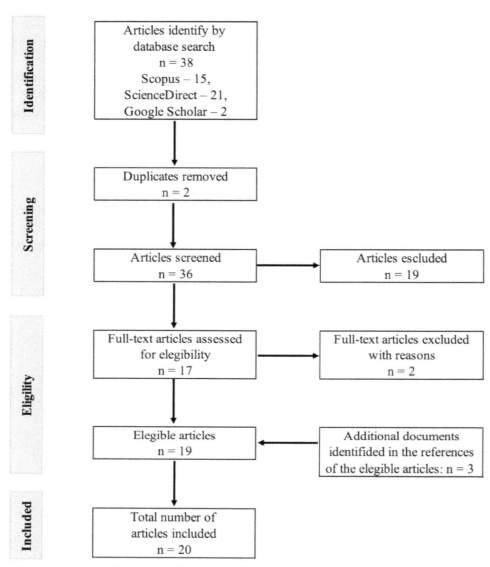

Source: Adapted from (Moher et al., 2016; Page et al., 2021).

RESULTS AND DISCUSSION

The results were presented and systematised according to the three major themes. The NLR outcomes – articles by year, articles by journal, geographical distribution, and articles allocation by theme, through text mining and visualisation techniques using VOSviewer software (Bukar et al., 2023; Jan van Eck & Waltman, 2011). Moreover, the outcomes were presented and according to the macro-perspective results – the impacts of prostitution, legal/regulated and non-legal/non-regulated, in tourism destinations as a social responsibility obligation of the tourism sector/ industry and to the micro-perspective – the innovative measures to prevent and reduce prostitution exploitation in the tourism context, contributing to the diversity of tourism supply/products.

Narrative Literature Review Outcomes

The final corpus of articles for analysis consisted of 20 documents indexed in Scopus, ScienceDirect and Google Scholar. Although it is an emergent area of research because it is an actual and fundamental issue that societies still debate, studies following an integrated social approach and a holistic understanding of the prostitution issue, even in the tourism context, are scarce.

Distribution of Paper by Year

The final corpus of articles for analysis comprised 20 documents. The text figure shows the evolution of the publication related to the topic study between January 2013 and December 2023 (Figure 2).

Figure 2. Publications evolution around the theme in the tourism context

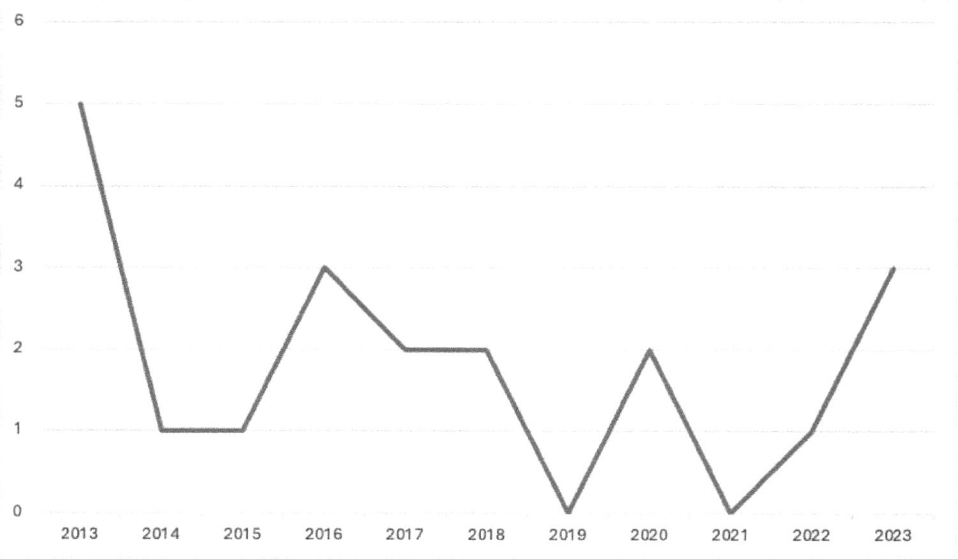

Source: Authors elaboration.

It can be observed that there was a decrease in publications from 2013 to 2021 and 5 to 0 documents, respectively. Furthermore, between 2021 and 2023, the interest in the topic increases again. The data shows a social, health, cultural, and economic problem that needs to be explained and solved (Allwood, 2018; Boels, 2015; Williams & Lansky, 2013).

Distribution of Papers Geographically and by Journal/Book

Figure 3 shows that the publications under review were developed in different geographical locations, according to the corresponding author affiliation. Therefore, the geographical areas represented were Europe (12), Asia (3), North America (3), Africa (1), and Australia (1). The geographical areas of South America and the Middle East did not have any publications around the theme from January 2013 to December 2023.

Figure 3. Publications evolution around the theme per geographical location

Source: Authors elaboration.

According to the data (Figure 3), the countries that produced the most documents and debated the prostitution topic were the United Kingdom (6), followed
by the United States of America (3), Belgium (2), Portugal (2), India (2), Sweden
(1), Germany (1), Australia (1), South Korea (1), and Kenya (1). Additionally, the
countries from the European continent have more publications than other continents
during the study date established. Perhaps it is in response to the increase in problems related to prostitution or possibly to the growing initiative to solve the issue.

The following figure (Figure 4) comprehends the publications around the theme
per journal. As a preliminary analysis, 75% of the journals were more specialised in
social sciences (i.e., Women's Studies International Forum, Sexualities, Sexuality
& Culture, Sexuality Research and Social Policy, etc.) and 25% in the tourism context (e.g., Tourism Management, Journal of Hospitality and Tourism Management,
International Journal of Tourism Policy and Brazilian Annals of Tourism Studies).

Figure 4. Publications evolution around the theme per journal

Source: Authors elaboration.

The above data show a few percentages of the studies conducted by tourism experts (Figure 4). Possibly, the development of more studies around the prostitution theme can contribute to increasing awareness of the social responsibility of tourism in society, minorities, and excluded communities to develop social consciousness of sexual rights, sexual violence, and prostitution (Bhadra, 2022; Omondi & Ryan, 2017).

The following figure illustrates the lexical network distribution and relation around the prostitution topic in the selected publications (Figure 5).

According to the data (Figure 5), prostitution is the central keyword (in orange colour) that is connected to *human trafficking, sex trafficking, sex work, sex buyers, domestic violence, parenting, global, crime,* […] *strategies, political attitudes, policy,* […]. This illustration could advocate a cause-effect relationship on the topic; perhaps reducing illegal prostitution, the cause, will reduce all the other effects. Moreover, several publications have previously linked prostitution with human trafficking, sex trafficking, violence, etc. (Johansson & Hansen, 2023; Mann, 2023; Matheson & Finkel, 2013; Ornelas et al., 2023; Wen et al., 2020).

Figure 5. Lexical network around the prostitution topic

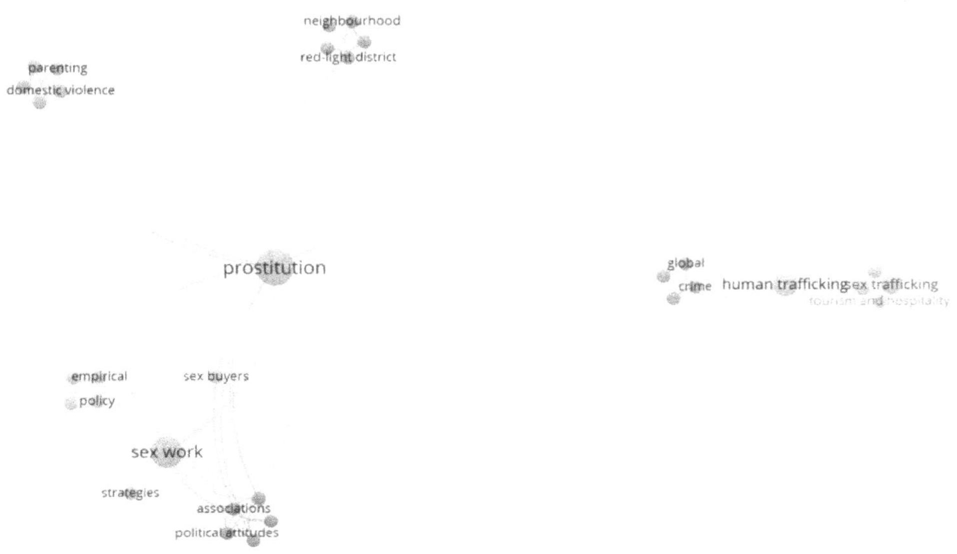

Source: Authors' elaboration based on VOSviewer software.

As a preliminary analysis, the documents were organised into two themes following the issues presented and the principal conclusions (Table 1). Of the documents analysed, 65% were related to the "strategies and policies for prostitution regulation" theme and 35% were associated with the "social, moral, and economic impacts of prostitution and human trafficking" theme.

Table 1. Themes around the prostitution topic in the dataset

Theme	Document title	Author(s)/Year	Conclusions / Key outcomes
Social and economic impacts of prostitution and human trafficking.	Exploring the complex relationship between prostitution and human trafficking	(Mann, 2023)	• Reveals the profound impact of economic theory on the relationship between prostitution and human trafficking. • Ethnicity's influence on the demand for prostitution and its link to human trafficking is also explored. • A real interconnectedness of prostitution and human trafficking. • The role played by demand, economics, and societal dynamics contribute to the supply.

continued on following page

Table 1. Continued

Theme	Document title	Author(s)/Year	Conclusions / Key outcomes
Social and moral impacts of prostitution. Strategies and policies for prostitution regulation.	From empowerment to exploitation: predicting positive and negative associations with the exchange of sexual services for payment	(Johansson & Hansen, 2023)	• Predicting attitudes towards the exchange of sexual services for payment, the women exhibit a stronger association with the negative concepts than men. • The acceptability of exchanging sexual services for payment has no discernible impact on association with the negative concepts.
Strategies and policies for prostitution regulation.	Social schemas about human trafficking involving grills and women: a systematic review	(Ornelas et al., 2023)	• Differences were found in social schemas between different social groups, namely victims, professionals, and media, namely on beliefs, attributions, awareness, and knowledge. • Media social schemas mainly were focused on human trafficking for sexual exploitation. • Victims and youth at risk of human trafficking showed awareness about the risk factors and recruitment strategies but showed a lack of knowledge regarding local resources to help them in case of need. • Professionals presented the most incongruent schemas, suggesting that their knowledge depends on the type of organization they belong to and their personal attitudes and perceptions about human trafficking involving girls and women.
Strategies and policies for prostitution regulation.	Exploring dimensions of sexual issues in disasters and conflicts: need to bridge the gaps between policy and practice	(Bhadra, 2022)	• Protection of sexual rights and preventing the survivors from experiencing sexual violence are essential for their rehabilitation and recovery.
Strategies and policies for prostitution regulation.	Perceptions of provider power among sex buyers	(Monto & Milrod, 2020)	• Cultural and economic factors that affect the experience of female sex providers, we examine how those processes also shape perceptions of power among buyers. • The diversity of individuals who buy and sell sex means that power relationships between buyers and providers vary substantially.
Social and economic impacts of prostitution and human trafficking.	A systematic review of the sex trafficking-related literature: lessons for tourism and hospitality research	(Wen et al., 2020)	• The results reveal three clusters: (1) sex commercialization, migration, and modern slavery; (2) child exploitation, sexual abuse, and health; and (3) human trafficking and institutional environments.

continued on following page

Table 1. Continued

Theme	Document title	Author(s)/Year	Conclusions / Key outcomes
Strategies and policies for prostitution regulation.	Agenda setting, agenda blocking and policy silence: why is there no EU policy on prostitution?	(Allwood, 2018)	• Prostitution some issues become defined as problems requiring public policy responses and others do not; how they appear on …, or are excluded from …, the policy agenda at the member state and EU level; and how issues, frames and proposals are ignored or actively silenced within policymaking structures and processes.
Social and moral impacts of prostitution.	Regulating the demand for commercialized sexual services	(Matheson & Finkel, 2013)	• In recent years, attention has increasingly shifted towards the buyers rather than those who provide sexual services. • Women involved in prostitution are increasingly coming to be seen as victims in need of support rather than offenders deserving punishment.
Strategies and policies for prostitution regulation.	Crime and tourism: what the available statistics do or do not tell us	(Mawby, 2017)	• Tourism has long been recognised as a crime generator. • Create better measures that can more appropriately inform policy for both criminal justice agencies and destination management organisations (DMOs).
Social and economic impacts of prostitution.	Sex tourism: romantic safaris, prayers and witchcraft at the Kenyan coast	(Omondi & Ryan, 2017)	• Local women compete to engage tourists on romantic safaris. • They have to employ different skills and, at times, seek the help of witchcraft and their supernatural powers to succeed. • Women run a number of risks that include becoming addicted to the easy life that, in turn, compromises their ability to do something else for a living.
Strategies and policies for prostitution regulation.	Prostitution in Europe between regulation and prohibition. Comparing legal situations and effects	(Reinschmidt, 2016)	• Experts in Austria and Switzerland are calling for harmonisation of regulations by means of a federal law. • Netherlands and Germany have implemented a new national law for the regulation of prostitution. • Research shows that: personal mandatory registration of individuals in street and window prostitution and regulations range from no mandatory consultation to a weekly requirement to be examined for sexually transmitted diseases. • The prostitution law (ProstG) in Germany shows that the decision has been made to the effect that prostitution is permitted and regulated.

continued on following page

Table 1. Continued

Theme	Document title	Author(s)/Year	Conclusions / Key outcomes
Social impacts.	Beyond everyday life. Love and sexuality during tourism: preliminary results of an exploratory research in the Algarve (Portugal)	(Marques & Lança, 2016)	• The relationship between the holidays and the availability for romance and sex and, on the other hand, a strong erotic and sexual potential of the tourism destination, even for married tourists.
Strategies and policies for prostitution regulation.	Prostitution in the neighbourhood: impact on residents and implications for municipal regulation	(Boels & Verhage, 2016)	• Not all residents experience adverse impacts of prostitution. • The regulation incorporates particular residents' concerns regarding nuisance, which conforms to the ongoing regeneration and gentrification of the broader area, which can be framed within the 'urban renaissance' discourse. • Maintain prostitution in the area and improve sex workers' safety and working conditions.
Strategies and policies for prostitution regulation.	The challenges of Belgian prostitution markets as legal informal economics: an empirical look behind the scenes at the older profession in the world	(Boels, 2015)	• Prostitution can certainly not, by definition, be equated with exploitation, coercion or male domination. • No complete consensus was found regarding the legalisation and regularisation of prostitution and its related activities.
Social and moral impacts of prostitution.	Participation in prostitution: associated outcomes within familial relationships	(Zeglin, 2014)	• Prostitution participation is not a predictor of parenting satisfaction, relationship satisfaction, or reporting being the victim of domestic violence. • However, prostitution is associated with a significantly increased chance of perpetrating domestic violence.
Strategies and policies for prostitution regulation.	Does legalized prostitution increase human trafficking	(Cho et al., 2013)	• Countries where prostitution is legal experience larger reported human trafficking inflows.
Strategies and policies for prostitution regulation.	Organizations working on behalf of prostitutes: an analysis of goals, practices, and strategies	(Oselin & Weitzer, 2013)	• The organizations facing prostitution are categorized in terms of their core perspective on sex work: Radical Feminist – Maintain criminalisation and abolish social condemnation. Sex Work – End criminalisation and social condemnation. Youth Oriented – Abolish punitive laws regarding youth. Neutral - Promote harm reduction.

continued on following page

Table 1. Continued

Theme	Document title	Author(s)/Year	Conclusions / Key outcomes
Social and economic impacts of prostitution.	Paradoxes of gendering strategy in prostitution policies: South Korea's "toleration-regulation regime," 1961-1979	(Park, 2013)	• The prostitution policies of the Park regime functioned as a matrix that established the boundaries of the virtuous community by building sexual and civil hierarchies between men and women as well as between chaste and fallen women.
Strategies and policies for prostitution regulation.	Sex trafficking and the Vancouver Winter Olympic Games: Perceptions and preventative measures	(Matheson & Finkel, 2013)	• The Vancouver Winter Olympic Games can be a catalyst for trafficking – in terms of specific preventative measures – the provision of awareness campaigns.
Strategies and policies for prostitution regulation.	Informal employment in developed and developing economies: Perspectives and policy responses	(Williams & Lansky, 2013)	• Prostitution is a diversity of the informal economy. • Policy implications of the perspective it explores.

Source: Authors elaboration.

Figure 6. WordCloud significant critical outcomes of the publications around the theme

Source: Authors elaboration.

The analysis of Figure 6 once again highlights the complex intersection between prostitution, human trafficking, social exploitation, sexual experiences, women's rights and policies. Addressing these interconnected issues requires a multi-faceted approach that combines legal, social, economic, and educational interventions aimed at protecting the rights and dignity of all individuals, especially those most vulnerable to exploitation and abuse. This often involves collaboration between governments, law enforcement agencies, Non-Governmental Organizations (NGOs), and communities to implement comprehensive prevention, intervention and support strategies. The tourism industry is essential for integration, support, and addressing global issues. Furthermore, tourism is a significant economic driver for many countries, providing employment opportunities, fostering cultural exchange, generating revenue, promoting social justice, safeguarding public health, and achieving sustainable development goals in the Global Village.

The Impacts of Prostitution Legal/Regulated in Tourism Context

There is an extensive and permanent discussion about sex work and prostitution, contributing empirically to its current policy. From the European point of view, the total consensus on the legalisation and regularisation of prostitution and related activities did not happen (Boels, 2015; Boels & Verhage, 2016). The regulation of prostitution is a complex task, and it is necessary to consider a wide range of life situations and concerns in this area. It is required to give a uniform legislative response to the different requirements of the sector with a bill for the protection of prostitutes (Reinschmidt, 2016).

According to the same author, a typology often used in the literature divides political approaches in the area of prostitution into models of criminalisation, legalisation and discrimination (Reinschmidt, 2016). The distinction between the models is based on two political strategies, first on the abolition of prostitution and reduction of adverse effects, and second, the recognition of prostitution as a profession like any other. The social and political approach to prostitution is strongly influenced by value judgments and moral beliefs reflected in the political objectives (Allwood, 2018; Oselin & Weitzer, 2013; Reinschmidt, 2016).

First, the prohibition of prostitution – the sale of sexual services is prohibited; second, prohibition of the purchase of sexual services – it is legal to provide sexual services, however, there can be no exchange of material goods, at least because the purchase of them is a criminal offence; third, prostitution is legal, but not regulated – the prostitution itself is allowed, this means that prostitutes and customers are not punished for the exchange of paid sexual services (e.g., prostitution itself is permitted, however, subject to any other legal requirements, such as registrations or authorisations); and fourth, the prostitution is legal and regulated – the prostitution is allowed and regulated by directives supported in health, commercial law and involve licensing systems for brothels and mandatory registration for prostitutes. (Allwood, 2018; Oselin & Weitzer, 2013; Reinschmidt, 2016).

In Europe Continent the third model is the most frequent, prostitution is legal, but not regulated, included in the following countries: Belgium, Czech Republic, Denmark, Estonia; Finland, France, Great Britain, Ireland, Italy, Luxembourg, Portugal and Spain. The first model is the least frequent, the prohibition of prostitution, which includes the following countries: Croatia, Lithuania and Russia (Reinschmidt, 2016).

A new prostitution bill has been discussed, providing for a licensing system for companies, vehicles and prostitution events. According to this model, only individuals with a license from the competent authorities will be authorised to exploit prostitution companies (Johansson & Hansen, 2023; Reinschmidt, 2016). Furthermore, the assignment of the license is linked to specific local and technical criteria, such as workplace facilities, which ensure the protection of workers and customers, and the age minimum for prostitution employed (Johansson & Hansen, 2023; Reinschmidt, 2016). Therefore, operators must ensure the health and safety of the people present (e.g., the obligation to provide condoms, hygiene products, …), and the structure of the service can only be imposed by the prostitute and the customer instead of the operator (Reinschmidt, 2016).

Other European countries where prostitution is legal and regulated by other directives are Austria, Switzerland, Netherlands and Germany, they strive to manage commercial prostitution through provisions actively. These countries have laws relating to prostitution that are distinct from each other, and countries do not show a lack of uniformity on the subject. This lack of regulatory uniformity has contributed to adverse effects. First, like the lack of communication on the part of prostitutes, who often must move to different places to be able to work, this case applies particularly to migrant prostitutes, who suffer from a lack of linguistic skills and knowledge about their legal situation (Johansson & Hansen, 2023; Reinschmidt, 2016). Second, the fragmentation of prostitution legislation leads to displacement problems, because prostitution legislation changes according to the countries, which results in difficulty in controlling the markets and preventing illegalities; this problem results from the lack of room for manoeuvre in the regulation of the sexual market (Johansson & Hansen, 2023; Reinschmidt, 2016).

The continuous political debate about the regulation of prostitution shows that the question of the best way to manage prostitution, socially and politically, is characterised by moral value judgments (Reinschmidt, 2016). However, the fundamental decisions of how society deals with prostitution in general transcend all types of legislation.

The Impacts of Prostitution Non-Legal/ Non-Regulated in Tourism Context

Analysing the characteristics and effects of prostitution policies in countries where prostitution is non-legal/non-regulated was quite strict. Some governments adopted a zero-tolerance approach to prostitution, considering it as a socially harmful and morally acceptable activity (Allwood, 2018; Oselin & Weitzer, 2013; Park, 2013; Reinschmidt, 2016).

According to Park (2013), for example, in South Korea, scholars claim that the regime is associated with highly gender-specific dynamics, however, it has failed to contain the growth of the sex industry in Korea. The sex industry is for foreigners only, nevertheless, this prostitution policy controlled at the local level was unsuccessful, leading them to examine the international dimensions of prostitution policies and their internal effects (Park, 2013). This type of prostitution policy defines, classifies and evaluates what constitutes the sex trade and once defined, it is also up to the government to apply policies with punishments, thus controlling active criminals, compressing their dangers and optimising their utilities (Park, 2013).

In the legal discourse of non-legal and non-regulated, the prostitute produces differences and hierarchies between prostitutes versus women, but also between men and women. In some cases, the policy of prostitution affects other positions, i.e., many feminists agree that punishing prostitutes reinforces the segregation between them and other women, functioning as a warning to other women to adapt to patriarchal norms (Boels & Verhage, 2016; Park, 2013; Zeglin, 2014). This behaviour originated the thought that "[…] sexuality of women is dangerous and vulnerable, while that of men is natural" (Park, 2013, p. 75).

Some countries face prostitution with elements of criminal law and social security law (prohibition versus regulation) because the entertainment industry, specifically that aimed at tourists, and especially in the form of sex tourism, promotes economic growth (Marques & Lança, 2016; Omondi & Ryan, 2017; Park, 2013). The sex industry was a particularly profitable sector of economic activity (Omondi & Ryan, 2017; Park, 2013; Williams & Lansky, 2013). However, in some countries where prostitution is forbidden, prostitutes are seen in two ways, on the one hand, they are considered perverse offenders who threaten society, having to be controlled and repressed, on the other hand, they are considered poor women abandoned by their families and exploited by the owners of brothels, being protected and rehabilitated. These two distinct views of prostitution create a negligence point of view, misunderstandings, social segregation, social exclusion, and a marginalised activity (Park, 2013; Williams & Lansky, 2013).

Consequently, prohibition and regulation of prostitution at the same time can collide with each other. If the government opts for a prohibitive regime of thorough policy, prostitution tends to go underground, making it difficult to track, license, register and examine prostitutes (Matheson & Finkel, 2013; Williams & Lansky, 2013). In addition, ideologically, prohibition considers it an absolute criminal activity to be eradicated, while the regulation finds it a necessary evil to be managed (Omondi & Ryan, 2017; Park, 2013). According to Park (2013), prostitution prohibition and regulation coexist.

A Critical Review of the Social Responsibility of Tourism Facing Prostitution

The sex industry has become increasingly visible, accessible, and socially acceptable in the community in recent times. Still, prostitution continues to be stigmatised; the areas characterised by the concentration of sexual business are associated with disturbances, public disorder, deterioration, and crime (Boels & Verhage, 2016). The disturbances related to prostitution have been the subject of allegations. Given the private character of companion and private prostitution, it is assumed that these types of prostitution cause less public disorder. The discomfort from street prostitution comes from three factors: first, customers can disturb public order, for example, by throwing garbage, urinating in public, and producing noise (screams, car horns); prostitutes can induce inconvenience by directly offering services to customers in an obvious way; and, finally, the degraded nature of neighbourhoods where window and brothel prostitution is often housed, the poor state of the facilities (lack of basic sanitation, minimum health conditions, pollution), paving the way for degeneration and impoverishment of the neighbourhood, which may attract nuisances (Boels & Verhage, 2016).

The regulation of prostitution in a country and a tourism context could have a significant influence on the spatial regulation of sex work. In shaping the regulation, the government is challenged by divergent pressures and objectives that are difficult to align (gentrification versus protection of sex workers and acceptance of prostitution) (Mawby, 2017; Monto & Milrod, 2020; Oselin & Weitzer, 2013). The regulation brings advantages in reducing the inconveniences related to prostitution. Criminal law can be beneficial in reducing crimes associated with prostitution, such as exploitation, forced prostitution, human trafficking and making profits from prostitutes (Allwood, 2018; S. Y. Cho et al., 2013; Mann, 2023; Mawby, 2017). It is crucial to fight against these phenomena to be able to transform the prostitution sector into a healthy industry in which prostitutes work in decent conditions and can make demands on customers, and it is possible to reduce the inconvenience caused to residents (Boels & Verhage, 2016).

Sexuality is inserted in the basis of society, and sexual development happens throughout the life cycle of the human being (Bhadra, 2022). Through Freud's theory of psychosexual development, it was established that pleasure and experiences play a fundamental role in human development and sexuality, feelings, thoughts, behaviours, expressions, and expectations are an essential part of a person in a person's life cycle through intimacy and activity (Bhadra, 2022; Oselin & Weitzer, 2013). Sensuality deals with consciousness, acceptance and comfort with one's body as physiological and psychological pleasures that are satisfactory and pleasurable. Intimacy is the ability and need to experience and feel emotions and sexual intimacy with other human beings. These are three fundamental aspects of healthy and consensual sexual relations. The term sexualisation refers to the use of sexual power to influence, control and manipulate others, this behaviour may include sexual violence, exploitation, abduction, forced marriage, among others (Bhadra, 2022).

Being able to define and distinguish informal employment from formal employment has been the subject of an ongoing debate about prostitution. Most definitions outline informal employment in terms of what is missing or insufficient concerning formal employment (Williams & Lansky, 2013). Starting from the 15th International Conference on Labour Statistics definition, efforts were made to solve the ambiguities relating to informal employment statistics. For this purpose, the definition of employment in the informal sector covered all jobs of companies in the informal sector or all individuals who, during a particular reference, are or have been employed by at least one company in the informal sector, regardless of their employment status (Williams & Lansky, 2013). A policy aimed at reducing informality aims to bring informal workers and companies into the sphere of formality. This has led to the growth of the formal economy, decent work, and increased tax revenues in support of social objectives. Hence, the importance of facilitating formalisation, transferring informal workers to formal jobs, registering and taxing formalised companies, and providing informal workers and operators with social benefits (Johansson & Hansen, 2023; Oselin & Weitzer, 2013; Williams & Lansky, 2013).

The intersection between tourism and prostitution raises ethical concerns, arguing that tourism often increases the flow of demand for commercial sex, contributing to the exploitation of vulnerable individuals, such as human trafficking (Mann, 2023; Wen et al., 2020). To be able to understand the relationship between prostitution and human trafficking, it is essential to base the respective concepts. The United Nations defines the concept of human trafficking as covers three components (United Nations, 2008): a) an action in which the person is recruited, transported, transferred, sheltered or received; b) the use of means through which the action is carried out, such as threats, forces, coercion, kidnapping, fraud, deception, abuse of power or a position of vulnerability; and c) an objective of exploitation (such as sexual exploitation).

According to Mann (2023), prostitution refers to the exchange of consensual sexual services in exchange for material goods. However, several times are related to human trafficking. Furthermore, human trafficking is a severe problem in the sex industry, presenting a vast number of victims, especially women and children (Cho et al., 2013; Mann, 2023; Wen et al., 2020). Based on the available data, we have identified that countries where prostitution is legal have a higher number of registered cases of human beings, however, it is necessary to analyse this factor further to be able to understand if prostitution influences cases of human trafficking (Mann, 2023). Human trafficking is a modern form of slavery; this clandestine business has reached pandemic dimensions, affecting more than 40 million victims worldwide, and the industry earns more than 150 billion dollars per year (Wen et al., 2020).

According to the principle of economics, the legalisation of prostitution can have two effects. The first is the effect of scale, in which there is an increase in the prostitution market and, consequently, an increase in cases of human trafficking; and the second is the substitution effect, in which the demand for trafficked prostitutes decreases as legalised prostitutes become preferential (Mann, 2023). Countries where prostitution is legal tend to have larger prostitution markets, where the majority of victims of human trafficking are exploited, for example, the rate of human trafficking in Germany, where prostitution is legal, is 60 times higher than in Sweden, where prostitution is considered a criminal offence, although Germany has a population ten times larger than Sweden (Mann, 2023).

Several authors state that a weak economic structure of a country creates an environment conducive to exploitation, leaving people at a disadvantage due to violence, poverty and ethnicity; this type of structure is more common in developing countries (Cho et al., 2013; Mann, 2023; Wen et al., 2020). To combat human trafficking, it is essential to have solid legislation with efficient judicial processes and systems to support victims (Cho et al., 2013; Wen et al., 2020).

The continuous and growing focus on sex trafficking raised the issue of men buying sexual services from women who have been coerced or subjected to forms of oppression, deception or intimidation. Consequently, prostitution has come to be seen as a toxic mixture of economic pressures, physical coercion and emotional tensions in which women are increasingly identified as victims (Matthews, 2018). Perhaps the reasons why men pay for sexual services have been exploited tend to involve claims that they are looking for sexual variety, attracted by the prospect of illicit encounters, or desire for impersonal and uncomplicated sex.

The legalisation of prostitution in some countries has taken a different direction. The scale of prostitution and the level of demand have decreased, conversely, the increased involvement of criminal networks, along with reports of abuse, sex trafficking and the worsening of conditions for some women, caused them to refuse licenses to a large part of operators (Mann, 2023; Matthews, 2018). There are regular operations aimed at combating sex trafficking, while buyers of sexual services have an obligation to show identification and are encouraged to report situations in which they suspect that the women they encounter have been trafficked (Matthews, 2018). This development raised questions about the issue of legalisation, although in the Netherlands, for example, it has led to a decrease in demand through the strict licensing applied and complied with by companies, which is combined with anti-trafficking ethics and stricter surveillance of buyers (Matthews, 2018). There has also been a negative change in local residents regarding the impacts of prostitution, particularly when it involves prostitutes exposed to levels of coercion (Matthews, 2018). Thus, in terms of the initial objectives, prostitution legalisation can be seen as a failure in terms of the expansion of the sex trade, the increase in exploitation and the inability to provide adequate health care (Cho et al., 2013; Mann, 2023; Matthews, 2018; Mawby, 2017; Reinschmidt, 2016). Moreover, in other situations, it was found that the legalisation of prostitution failed because it encouraged the involvement of criminal networks, fuelling the expansion of the illegal sector while reducing demand and supply in the licensed sector (Cho et al., 2013; Mann, 2023; Matthews, 2018; Mawby, 2017; Reinschmidt, 2016).

This result suggests the need to examine the different effects of the legislation concerning broader governance and control strategies. The nature of the sex industry and its various sectors are simultaneously subject to varying forms of organisation and regulation. Thus, street and off-street activities should be treated differently, while companions and those who work in brothels, clubs or private apartments may be subject to different forms of regulation regarding the sex marketed (Allwood, 2018; Cho et al., 2013; Matthews, 2018; Mawby, 2017; Reinschmidt, 2016).

Innovative Measures to Prevent and Reduce Prostitution Exploitation

Sex tourism is defined as tourism whose primary motivation is to consummate commercial sexual relations (Matheson & Finkel, 2013). This type of tourism states that tourist flows are characterised in most cases by tourists from developed countries participating in sexual services; however, the opposite situation also happens (Matheson & Finkel, 2013; Omondi & Ryan, 2017).

The characteristics of sex tourism were outlined from its geographies, relationships, motivations and aspects of gender, analysing the exploitative characteristics of sex tourism, the imbalances of power in relationships due to social inequalities and the exploitative working conditions of sex workers (Matheson & Finkel, 2013). It is important to emphasise that human trafficking is distinct from sex work, if sexual services are provided consensually, then the acts do not fall under trafficking – the label only applies when individuals are arrested against their will and forced to participate in prostitution (Matthews, 2018; Ornelas et al., 2023; Wen et al., 2020).

As for sex tourism, abolitionists suggest that prostitution is not a choice, so it constitutes sexual exploitation and oppression. They assume that prostitution is a violation of people's human rights within the research on tourism and its industry (Matheson & Finkel, 2013; Wen et al., 2020). An alternative perspective states that sex work is a voluntary choice and that greater attention should be paid to the protection of the health and safety of the sex worker, as well as the improvement of their working conditions and granting the regulation and legalisation of the profession (Matheson & Finkel, 2013).

A new perspective has emerged that suggests that sex tourism could be implicated at a much higher level, as sports mega-events, romantic holidays, sex tourism, ... and contribute to tourists increasing the demand for sexual services provided by sex workers (Marques & Lança, 2016; Matheson & Finkel, 2013; Omondi & Ryan, 2017). Unfortunately, hotel and tourism companies play a supporting role in trafficking activities indirectly. Considering the legal point of view, the United Nations and other regional organisations seek to eradicate sex trafficking through provisions such as the Council of Europe and the Convention on Combating Trafficking in Personnel, in Particular Women and Children (Matheson & Finkel, 2013). Despite international efforts to achieve the goal of eradicating sex trafficking, international law is partial, the conventions generate minimal changes, and the national competencies underlying the efforts to combat sex trafficking are neither uniform nor universal (Matheson & Finkel, 2013; Wen et al., 2020). The lack of political will exacerbates these discrepancies in responding to the problem, including the framing of prostitution legislation (Wen et al., 2020).

Studies on prostitution have long emphasised the power differentials between buyers and suppliers, as well as the way prostitution contributed to gender inequality. Prostitution is based on the existence of a particular set of relationships. In some studies, these relationships present people with a choice between poverty, violence or prostitution. It can be understood as a monotonous job (Matthews, 2018; Wen et al., 2020). In addition, buyers of sexual services usually occupy higher social positions than workers and are overwhelmingly men. Just emphasising exploitation, abuse, trafficking, oppression, and structural differences in the positions of buyers and suppliers simplifies the nature of transactional exchange and implies a static power relationship in which buyers have greater power (Wen et al., 2020). The assumptions about power are implicit in contemporary dialogues about the degree to which prostitution is consensual. The choice to buy or sell sexual services can be more or less consensual, depending on constraints such as material limitations, age, skill, and social contexts ... On the other hand, reports of sex workers include providers who have chosen sex work despite other employment opportunities, seeing prostitution as an essential and desirable profession (Matthews, 2018; Monto & Milrod, 2020; Wen et al., 2020). Unlike sexual service providers, buyers are often motivated by desires, not being forced to participate in prostitution by financial requirements or forced by other individuals to seek paid sexual services; thus, their power in paid sexual exchanges is shaped by various social constraints, as well as the physical proximity to the markets of prostitution, therefore, satisfying their sexual and emotional desires (Wen et al., 2020).

In some countries, sex tourism is actively promoted but rarely openly tolerated. Sex tourism represents a significant part of the Gross National Product (Matheson & Finkel, 2013). This is a strong relationship and knowledge between trips and travel brochures that present erotic images in their promotional materials. The high availability and visibility of the sexual entertainment industries in different locations are designed to contribute to equalising the tourist experience (Matthews, 2018). Although sexual entertainment is an encouraging factor in shaping demand, some travel abroad with the specific objective of buying sexual services. In addition to organised trips abroad to certain countries to buy sexual services, it is a phenomenon that is attracting a considerable number of tourists, especially at sports events and other organised trips (Marques & Lança, 2016; Matheson & Finkel, 2013; Omondi & Ryan, 2017). However, the relationship between prostitution and events has focused mainly on sex trafficking and the increase in the number of women involved in prostitution during significant events. For example, not only men who travel to watch these sporting events but also construction workers; many stay away from home for long periods, and these individuals help to increase demand (Matheson & Finkel, 2013; Matthews, 2018).

In general, the emphasis on sex tourism showed that the world is increasingly globalised due to migration and tourism and that demand patterns are constantly changing and intensifying. Typically, in the poorest countries with limited employment and low wages, without the sex trade being poorly regulated or unregulated, they cause problems such as coercion and trafficking. Consequently, buyers of sexual services abroad tend to choose destinations where anonymity and distancing are essential factors for buyers who have selected the destination they intend to travel (Marques & Lança, 2016; Matthews, 2018; Mawby, 2017).

Policies and interventions aimed at regulating the demand for sex tourism should be taken considering the different political and cultural contexts; these variations should not mean that it is necessary to adopt a position of cultural relativism or accept the existing political situation (Matthews, 2018; Mawby, 2017; Omondi & Ryan, 2017).

FUTURE RESEARCH DIRECTIONS

Research on prostitution's impacts in the tourism context is a complex and sensitive issue that requires careful consideration of ethical, social, and legal dimensions. These subjects need further qualitative and quantitative research. Some potential future research directions should be addressed to the impact of prostitution activity on the local community (i.e., investigate the social, cultural, and economic effects of prostitution on local communities in tourist destinations); examine the legal frameworks prostitution in different tourist destinations and their implications for sex workers, tourists, and local communities; investigate the prostitution value chain, explore the factors driving demand for prostitution among tourists and investigate tourist motivations.

Moreover, future studies may consider exploring the role of prostitution in shaping the sustainability of tourism destinations (social inclusion) and developing frameworks for sustainable tourism that take into account the complexities of sex work, investigating the integration of prostitution into tourism policy and planning processes, including considerations of zoning, licensing, and regulation; and developing research on sociology, social stigma and discrimination faced by sex workers in tourist destinations, as well to promote the rights and dignity of sex workers.

Finally, develop longitudinal studies to track changes in the impacts of prostitution over time, allowing for the evaluation of policy interventions, social trends and the role of the tourism industry facing prostitution for interdisciplinary collaboration, ethical sensitivity, and a focus on promoting the well-being and rights of all individuals involved.

CONCLUSION

This article includes a broad view of innovative social responsibility measures in tourism to understand tourism's role in the face of prostitution.

The article proposed to identify two types of political regimes in the face of prostitution, legal/regulated and non-legal/non-regulated, and to interpret their effects. We thus understand that the political approaches chosen to manage prostitution are different from country to country, creating a climate of instability and uncertainty for prostitutes, resulting in displacement effects preventing the control of the market, there is a more significant lack of information and stimulating prejudices.

The result of this NLR of the responsibility in tourism in the face of prostitution resulted in the analysis of the impact felt by residents with prostitution. The understanding of the distinction between formal and informal employment, thus framing the best position for prostitution. The ethical concerns associated with prostitution are exploitation, trafficking, and prejudgment – the regulation of the demand for sexual services marketed in different political contexts.

This study also helps in the understanding of measures to prevent exploitation in prostitution in a tourist context, addressing the typology and motivation of sex tourism and the relationship between sport and sexual services.

ACKNOWLEDGMENT

The authors are thankful for the support from the CinTurs - Research Centre for Tourism, Sustainability and Well-being and FCT - Foundation for Science and Technology.

REFERENCES

Allwood, G. (2018). Agenda setting, agenda blocking and policy silence: Why is there no EU policy on prostitution? *Women's Studies International Forum*, 69, 126–134. 10.1016/j.wsif.2018.06.004

Ballester-Brage, L., Pozo-Gordaliza, R., & Orte-Socías, C. (2014). Delocalized Prostitution: Occultation of the New Modalities of Violence. *Procedia: Social and Behavioral Sciences*, 161, 90–95. 10.1016/j.sbspro.2014.12.015

Bhadra, S. (2022). Exploring dimensions of sexual issues in disasters and conflicts: Need to bridge the gaps between policy and practice. *Sexologies*, 31(3), 277–290. 10.1016/j.sexol.2021.11.006

Boels, D. (2015). The Challenges of Belgian Prostitution Markets as Legal Informal Economies: An Empirical Look Behind the Scenes at the Oldest Profession in the World. *European Journal on Criminal Policy and Research*, 21(4), 485–507. 10.1007/s10610-014-9260-8

Boels, D., & Verhage, A. (2016). Prostitution in the neighbourhood: Impact on residents and implications for municipal regulation. *International Journal of Law, Crime and Justice*, 46, 43–56. 10.1016/j.ijlcj.2016.01.002

Bukar, U. A., Sayeed, M. S., Razak, S. F. A., Yogarayan, S., Amodu, O. A., & Mahmood, R. A. R. (2023). A method for analyzing text using VOSviewer. *MethodsX*, 11, 102339. Advance online publication. 10.1016/j.mex.2023.10233937693657

Cho, S. Y., Dreher, A., & Neumayer, E. (2013). Does Legalized Prostitution Increase Human Trafficking? *World Development*, 41(1), 67–82. 10.1016/j.worlddev.2012.05.023

Cho, S.-Y., Dreher, A., & Neumayer, E. (2013). Does Legalized Prostitution Increase Human Trafficking? *World Development*, 41(1), 67–82. https://ssrn.com/abstract=1986065Electroniccopyavailableat:https://ssrn.com/abstract=1986065Electroniccopyavailableat:http://ssrn.com/abstract=1986065Electroniccopyavailableat:https://ssrn.com/abstract=1986065. 10.1016/j.worlddev.2012.05.023

Escot, L., Belope-Nguema, S., Fernández-Cornejo, J. A., Del Pozo-García, E., Castellanos-Serrano, C., & Cruz-Calderón, S. F. (2022). Can the legal framework for prostitution influence the acceptability of buying sex? *Journal of Experimental Criminology*, 18(4), 885–909. 10.1007/s11292-021-09465-y

Fleuret, S. (2024). Backpackers' Tourism and Health: A Narrative Literature Review. *Geographies*, 4(1), 40–51. 10.3390/geographies4010003

Greenhalgh, T., Raftery, J., Hanney, S., & Glover, M. (2016). Research impact: A narrative review. In *BMC Medicine* (*Vol. 14*, Issue 1). BioMed Central Ltd. 10.1186/s12916-016-0620-8

Hung, J. (2024). *Legalising Prostitution in Thailand: A Policy-Oriented Examination of the (De-) Construction of Commercial Sex*. Springer. 10.1007/978-981-99-8448-0

Jan van Eck, N., & Waltman, L. (2011). Text mining and visualization using VOSviewer. *ISSI Newsletter, 7*(3), 50–54. www.vosviewer.com

Jenkins, J. (2023, December 1). *Prostitution*. Encyclopedia Britannica. https://www.britannica.com/topic/prostitution

Johansson, I., & Hansen, M. A. (2023). From Empowerment to Exploitation: Predicting Positive and Negative Associations with the Exchange of Sexual Services for Payment. *Sexuality & Culture*. 10.1007/s12119-023-10174-z

Kim, H., & So, K. K. F. (2022). Two decades of customer experience research in hospitality and tourism: A bibliometric analysis and thematic content analysis. *International Journal of Hospitality Management*, 100, 103082. 10.1016/j.ijhm.2021.103082

Mann, P. (2023). Exploring the Complex Relationship Between Prostitution and Human Trafficking. *Asian Journal of Multidisciplinary Research & Review*, 4(5), 57–72. 10.55662/AJMRR.2023.4501

Marques, J., & Lança, M. (2016). Beyond Everyday Life. Love and Sexuality during Tourism: Preliminary Results of an Exploratory Research in the Algarve (Portugal). *Revista Anais Brasileira de Estudos Turísticos*, 6(2), 7–22.

Matheson, C. M., & Finkel, R. (2013). Sex trafficking and the Vancouver Winter Olympic Games: Perceptions and preventative measures. *Tourism Management*, 36, 613–628. 10.1016/j.tourman.2012.08.004

Matthews, R. (2018). Regulating the demand for commercialized sexual services. In *Women's Studies International Forum, 69*, 1–8. Elsevier Ltd. 10.1016/j.wsif.2018.03.007

Mawby, R. I. (2017). Crime and tourism: What the available statistics do or do not tell us. *International Journal of Tourism Policy*, 7(2), 81–92. 10.1504/IJTP.2017.085292

Moher, D., Shamseer, L., Clarke, M., Ghersi, D., Liberati, A., Petticrew, M., Shekelle, P., Stewart, L. A., Estarli, M., Barrera, E. S. A., Martínez-Rodríguez, R., Baladia, E., Agüero, S. D., Camacho, S., Buhring, K., Herrero-López, A., Gil-González, D. M., Altman, D. G., Booth, A., & Whitlock, E. (2016). Preferred reporting items for systematic review and meta-analysis protocols (PRISMA-P) 2015 statement. *Revista Espanola de Nutricion Humana y Dietetica*, 20(2), 148–160. 10.1186/2046-4053-4-125554246

Monto, M., & Milrod, C. (2020). Perceptions of provider power among sex buyers. *Sexualities*, 23(4), 630–644. 10.1177/1363460719831977

Omondi, R. K., & Ryan, C. (2017). Sex tourism: Romantic safaris, prayers and witchcraft at the Kenyan coast. *Tourism Management*, 58, 217–227. 10.1016/j.tourman.2015.11.003

Ornelas, S., Camilo, C., Csalog, R. A., Hatzinikolaou, K., & Calheiros, M. M. (2023). Social schemas about human trafficking involving girls and women: A systematic review. *Aggression and Violent Behavior*, 73, 101873. 10.1016/j.avb.2023.101873

Oselin, S. S., & Weitzer, R. (2013). Organizations working on behalf of prostitutes: An analysis of goals, practices, and strategies. *Sexualities*, 16(3–4), 445–466. 10.1177/1363460713481741

Page, M. J., McKenzie, J. E., Bossuyt, P. M., Boutron, I., Hoffmann, T. C., Mulrow, C. D., Shamseer, L., Tetzlaff, J. M., Akl, E. A., Brennan, S. E., Chou, R., Glanville, J., Grimshaw, J. M., Hróbjartsson, A., Lalu, M. M., Li, T., Loder, E. W., Mayo-Wilson, E., McDonald, S., & Moher, D. (2021). The PRISMA 2020 statement: An updated guideline for reporting systematic reviews. *Journal of Clinical Epidemiology*, 134, 178–189. 10.1016/j.jclinepi.2021.03.00133789819

Park, J. M. (2013). Paradoxes of gendering strategy in prostitution policies: South Korea's "toleration-regulation regime," 1961-1979. *Women's Studies International Forum*, 37, 73–84. 10.1016/j.wsif.2012.10.008

Ribeiro, F. B., & Silva, M. C. (2019). Persecution or Recognition? Abolitionism, self-determination and recognition of rights of sex workers. *A Gazeta de Antropología, 35*(1), 1–16. www.gazeta-antropologia.es/?p=5132

Søntvedt, M. (2009). *Making sense of sex tourism through the accounts of sex tourists: A Foucauldian discourse analysis of sex tourists' online communication* [Martes Thesis]. University of Oslo.

Sukhera, J. (2022). Narrative Reviews in Medical Education: Key Steps for Researchers. In *Journal of graduate medical education, 14*(4), 418–419. NLM (Medline). 10.4300/JGME-D-22-00481.1

United Nations. (2008). *An Introduction to Human Trafficking: Vulnerability, Impact and Action*. UN. www.ungift.org

Vada, S., Dupre, K., & Zhang, Y. (2023). Route tourism: a narrative literature review. In *Current Issues in Tourism, 26*(6). Routledge. 10.1080/13683500.2022.2151420

Wen, J., Klarin, A., Goh, E., & Aston, J. (2020). A systematic review of the sex trafficking-related literature: Lessons for tourism and hospitality research. *Journal of Hospitality and Tourism Management*, 45, 370–376. 10.1016/j.jhtm.2020.06.001

Williams, C. C., & Lansky, M. A. (2013). Informal employment in developed and developing economies: Perspectives and policy responses. In *International Labour Review* (Vol. 152, Issue 4). https://ssrn.com/abstract=2706621

Williams, E. (2013). *Sex Tourism in Bahia - Ambiguous Entanglements*. University of Illinois - Board of Trustees. https://www.ebsco.com/terms-of-use

Zeglin, R. J. (2014). Participation in prostitution: Associated outcomes within familial relationships. *Sexuality Research & Social Policy*, 11(1), 50–62. 10.1007/s13178-013-0143-4

Zhang, Y., Moyle, B., Dupré, K., Lohmann, G., Desha, C., & MacKenzie, I. (2023). Tourism and natural disaster management: A systematic narrative review. *Tourism Review*, 78(6), 1466–1483. 10.1108/TR-08-2022-0377

ADDITIONAL READING

Hung, J. (2024). *Legalising Prostitution in Thailand: A Policy-Oriented Examination of the (De-) Construction of Commercial Sex*. Springer. 10.1007/978-981-99-8448-0

Lança, M. (2021). *Sun, Sand, Sea and (of course) Sex*. [PhD Thesis, Faculty of Economics, University of Algarve].

Lança, M., Marques, J., & Pinto, P. (2014). *Structural Equation Modelling Applied to Sex, Romance and Liminal Behaviour in Tourism Context – The Case of Faro International Bike Meeting*. CIEO-Research Centre for Spatial and Organizational Dynamics, University of Algarve, 2014-6.

Sontvedt, M. (2009). *Making sense of sex tourism through the accounts of sex tourists: A Foucauldian discourse analysis of sex tourists' online communication.* [MSc Thesis, Department of Psychology, University of Oslo].

Williams, E. (2013). *Sex Tourism in Bahia - Ambiguous Entanglements.* University of Illinois - Board of Trustees. 10.5406/illinois/9780252037931.001.0001

KEY TERMS AND DEFINITIONS

Intimacy: This is the ability and need to experience and feel emotions and sexual intimacy with other human beings.

Prostitution: The practice of engaging in relatively indiscriminate sexual activity, in general, with someone who is not a spouse or a friend in exchange for immediate payment in money or other valuables. Prostitutes may be female, male, or transgender, and prostitution may entail heterosexual or homosexual activity, but historically, most prostitutes have been women, and most clients are men.

Sensuality: Deals with consciousness, acceptance, and comfort with one's own body, as well as physiological and psychological pleasures that are satisfactory and pleasurable.

Sex Tourism: This is a type of tourism activity in which the visitor's essential motivation is to have sexual participation with prostitutes and residents.

Sexualisation: This refers to the use of sexual power to influence, control and manipulate others; this behaviour may include sexual violence, exploitation, abduction, and forced marriage, among others.

Tourism: Tourism is a social, cultural and economic phenomenon that entails people moving to countries or places outside their usual environment for personal or business/professional purposes. These people are called visitors (tourists or excursionists, residents or non-residents), and tourism has to do with their activities, some of which involve tourism expenditure.

Chapter 9
Community–Based Tourism as a Sustainable Direction for the Tourism Industry:
Evidence From the Indian Sundarbans

Arnab Gantait
https://orcid.org/0000-0002-1664-2193
Independent Researcher, India

Ravish Mathew
Sri Sri University, Odisha, India

Prama Chatterjee
Central Tribal University of Andhra Pradesh, India

Kuldeep Singh
https://orcid.org/0000-0002-7999-1585
Amity University, Gurugram, India

ABSTRACT

The evolving global tourism industry increasingly emphasizes sustainable practices benefiting both the environment and local communities. Community-Based tourism (CBT) in the Indian Sundarbans exemplifies this approach, preserving cultural and natural heritage while fostering grassroots socio-economic development. Through qualitative research methods including in-depth interviews, participant observations,

DOI: 10.4018/979-8-3693-3166-8.ch009

and document analysis, this study reveals CBT's positive impact. It showcases successful cultural heritage preservation, community engagement in conservation, local empowerment, and economic diversification through tourism activities. Furthermore, CBT facilitates cultural exchange, education, and responsible tourism practices. This research provides nuanced insights into CBT's multifaceted benefits, offering valuable lessons for sustainable tourism development in ecologically sensitive areas worldwide. By raising awareness among communities, tourism planners, and policymakers, this study aims to support successful implementation of CBT initiatives in diverse tourist destinations.

INTRODUCTION

In recent years, the paradigm of global tourism has shifted towards a more sustainable and community-centric approach, marking a shift from traditional mass tourism models. At the forefront of this transformation is the concept of Community-Based Tourism (CBT), recognized for its potential to foster sustainable development while preserving the cultural and environmental integrity of destinations. This research endeavors to delve into the role of CBT as a sustainable direction for the tourism industry, with a specific focus on its application and impact in the Indian Sundarbans. The Indian Sundarbans, a sprawling mangrove delta recognized as a UNESCO World Heritage Site, represents a unique blend of rich biodiversity, indigenous cultures, and delicate ecosystems. As tourism increasingly becomes a potent force shaping the destinies of such regions, it becomes imperative to assess and advocate for models that not only cater to the economic aspirations of local communities but also ensure the long-term well-being of the environment. Here it is to be noted that, every tourism site must strike a balance between environmental preservation, economic growth, and genuine travel experiences if it is to remain viable over the long run. The current study situates itself at the nexus of sustainable tourism practices, community empowerment, and environmental conservation, aiming to illuminate how CBT initiatives in the Sundarbans exemplify a holistic and responsible approach to tourism. By adopting a qualitative research methodology, this investigation seeks to capture the nuanced experiences, perspectives, and outcomes associated with CBT, offering a more comprehensive understanding of its implications for both the local communities and the broader tourism industry. As the global call for sustainable practices gains momentum, it is imperative to critically examine and document the successes, challenges, and transformative potential of community-based tourism. By offering evidence-based insights focusing on the Indian Sundarbans, this research contributes to a deeper understanding of the transformative potential of CBT, advocating for its adoption as a sustainable direction for the broader tourism industry. The findings hold implications for policymakers, practitioners, and researchers, providing a foundation for informed decision-making in the pursuit of a more sustainable and equitable trajectory for the tourism industry.

RESEARCH METHODOLOGY

The research methodology employed in this paper adopts a qualitative approach to comprehensively explore the concept of Community-Based Tourism (CBT) and its associated benefits. The study involves an extensive review and analysis of relevant literature, encompassing media reports, published articles, government documents, and various working papers. To ensure a thorough understanding of the subject, the authors have engaged with a diverse range of sources, including academics, non-governmental organizations (NGOs), and practitioners involved in Community-Based Tourism initiatives. The insights gathered from these consultations contribute valuable perspectives to the research. The research methodology incorporates a meticulous examination of the data derived from reports, reviews, and experts' responses. Thematic and content analysis techniques are applied to scrutinize the acquired information. By triangulating data from multiple sources and employing rigorous analysis methods, this study aims to provide a comprehensive and well-informed exploration of the dynamics surrounding Community-Based Tourism.

UNVEILING THE POTENTIAL OF COMMUNITY-BASED TOURISM: A REVIEW

In recent decades, sustainable development has emerged as a crucial concern in all tourism destinations. Developing nations worldwide are actively working to leverage their diverse sectors for the benefit of socially and economically marginalized populations (Gantait, Singh, Bhowmik, & Swamy, 2022). In this pursuit, numerous destinations and tourism enterprises have formulated policies aimed at providing immediate advantages to impoverished and underdeveloped communities. Through a range of initiatives, they seek to address the pressing needs of these communities, fostering socio-economic progress and inclusivity (Nilnoppakun & Ampavat, 2016; Boley, McGehee & Hammett, 2017). The focus is on delivering tangible and prompt benefits to uplift disadvantaged populations, reflecting a commitment to addressing social inequalities and promoting overall development. In this context, Community-based Tourism (CBT) has emerged as a significant form of sustainable tourism that prioritizes community involvement, fostering economic well-being, and enhancing sustainability at the grassroots level, thereby contributing to the preservation of local culture and the environment (Dodds, Ali, & Galaski, 2018).

Community-Based Tourism (CBT) stands out as a remarkable initiative gaining widespread recognition. This approach is increasingly embraced due to its purported ability to invigorate rural economies by delivering tangible economic benefits to residents (Mehmetoglu, 2001). The essence of CBT lies in empowering local communities by expanding the scope of their livelihoods, thereby fostering economic resilience (Shikida et al., 2010; Zapata et al., 2011). It plays a pivotal role in supporting struggling economies through the strategic optimization of linkages and the reduction of resource leakages, as highlighted by Lapeyre (2010). Moreover, CBT contributes to enhanced stakeholder cooperation, fostering collaboration and mutual benefit (Lopez-Guzman et al., 2011). One of the distinctive features of CBT is its recognized potential as a valuable tool for promoting tourist destinations. CBT encapsulates a diverse array of elements integral to the essence of local culture. Encompassing facets such as entertainment, interpersonal interactions, the natural environment, superstructure, culinary experiences, locally crafted products, and accommodations, CBT goes beyond conventional tourism paradigms (Mayaka, Croy, & Cox, 2019; Simpson, 2008; Lee, & Jan, 2019). A good number of studies affirm that these components collectively constitute essential attributes of a tourism destination (Lee, & Jan, 2019; Mtapuri & Giampiccoli, 2013; Simpson, 2008).

The authenticity of local entertainment, the warmth of community interactions, the preservation of the natural environment, the charm of local architecture, the richness of indigenous cuisine, the uniqueness of handmade products, and the character of accommodations collectively define the distinctive appeal of a destination. Embracing these aspects in community-based tourism not only enriches the visitor experience but also ensures that the cultural tapestry of the locale remains vibrant and authentic, thereby contributing to the overall allure and sustainability of the tourism destination. In this context, CBT emerges as a holistic approach with multifaceted benefits. It not only addresses economic concerns by providing local communities with a means of financial upliftment but also contributes to the preservation of cultural authenticity and environmental integrity. By diversifying livelihoods, CBT empowers communities to chart a sustainable course for their future. Its impact extends beyond economic realms, fostering stakeholder collaboration and promoting a responsible approach to tourism. In the larger context, CBT is not merely a model for economic sustainability but a pathway to harmonizing tourism with the values of environmental consciousness. It is a worthwhile choice for destinations seeking greater visibility and a commitment to delivering high-quality, responsible tourism experiences. As global interest in sustainable practices continues to rise, CBT stands as a beacon for those aiming to create a positive and lasting impact on both local communities and the broader tourism landscape.

TIDAL TRANSFORMATION: THE JOURNEY OF COMMUNTY DRIVEN TOURISM INITIATIVES IN THE INDIAN SUNDARBANS

The Indian Sundarbans, renowned for its unique mangrove ecosystem and rich biodiversity, have become a focal point for redefining tourism through a sustainable lens. In this context, Community-led ecotourism initiatives emerge as a transformative pathway, steering the tourism industry in this region toward a more sustainable and inclusive future. The following section explores the narrative of community-driven tourism initiatives amidst the unique tidal landscapes of the Indian Sundarbans, highlighting the transformative journey undertaken by the local tourism stakeholders in fostering sustainable tourism practices and socio-economic development within this region.

THE SUNDARBANS ECOTOURISM PROJECT: PROMOTING SUSTAINABLE TOURISM PRACTICES

The ecotourism project, supported by the West Bengal Forest Development Corporation and the Sundarban Tiger Reserve (STR) authority aims to involve local communities in sustainable tourism. It includes various initiatives such as (1) guided nature tours, (2) boat tours, and (3) cultural performances.

Into the Wild: Sundarbans Nature Tours With the Local Eco-Guides

Local villagers participate as guides and hosts, providing tourists with insights into the Sundarbans' ecology and traditional way of life. The Sundarban National Park Authority has recruited a total number of 40 permanent registered eco-guides from different forest fringe villages of the Sundarban National Park. Apart from these eco-guides, every year, in the peak tourist seasons, the forest authority hires 20 more eco-guides from the forest-adjacent villages. Before entering this reserve forest area, every tourist boat has to take one of these eco-guides with them unless and until there is any shortage at the forest controlling offices of STR at Sajnekhali, Jharkhali, Jhingekhali, and Bagna. While accompanying the tourists, these eco-guides perform a wide range of duties such as interpreting the natural and cultural history of the Sundarbans, enhancing tourists' awareness and concern for ecotourism, deterring the tourists from annoying the wild animals or throwing litter on the river and so on. These registered eco-guides play a crucial role in enhancing the satisfaction of tourists through various means. They enhance the satisfaction of tourists by providing them with a well-rounded, educational, and safe experience.

Their expertise, cultural insights, and commitment to responsible tourism contribute significantly to the overall quality of the tourist experience in this unique and ecologically sensitive region. The following Table 1 displays the current strength of the registered eco-guides at the Sundarban National Park (India).

Table 1. Registered eco-guides of Sundarban National Park (India)

Registered Eco-Guides of Sundarban Tiger Reserve			
Sl. No.	**Name**	**Reg. No.**	**Village**
1	Subhendubikash Jodder	02/STR	Dayapur
2	Mrityunjay Mandal	03/STR	Dayapur
3	Mrinal Kanti Mandal	23/STR	Dayapur
4	Monoranjan Mandal	19/STR	Dayapur
5	Krishnapada Baidya	29/STR	Dayapur
6	Subrata Baidya	37/STR	Dayapur
7	Anirudha Roy	44/STR	Dayapur
8	Dharanimohan Mistry	22/STR	Dayapur
9	Arun Sarkar	27/STR	Dayapur
10	Saptoshi Mondal	26/STR	Dayapur
11	Bikash Ranjan Mistry	24 /STR	Dayapur
12	Animesh Mridha	39/STR	Dayapur
13	Amar Kanti Mandal	01/STR	-
14	Ashok Mandal	06/STR	Jamespur
15	Kritiprosad Mondal	05/STR	Jamespur
16	Tarunkanti Baidya	04/STR	Jamespur
17	Himanshu Mandal	07/STR	Jamespur
18	Susanta Sarkar	25 /STR	Jamespur
19	Ajit Mandal	20/STR	Aanpur
20	Pravas Raptan	15/STR	Aanpur
21	Sadhan Biswas	17/STR	Kumirmari
22	Ratan Jana	38/STR	Sonaga
23	Mrinmay Mandal	42/STR	Sonaga
24	Santosh Barman	40/STR	Sonaga
25	Ramkrishna Mandal	31/STR	Bali
26	Haripada Ggharami	32/STR	Bali
27	Nirmal Mandal	33/STR	Bali
28	Bhabatosh Mandal	34/STR	Bali

continued on following page

Table 1. Continued

Registered Eco-Guides of Sundarban Tiger Reserve			
Sl. No.	Name	Reg. No.	Village
29	Krishnapada Mandal	35/STR	Bali
30	SantirajanJoddar	43/STR	Pakhirala
31	Sujit Raptan	08/STR	Pakhirala
32	Amar Raptan	21/STR	Pakhirala
33	Monoranjan Raptan	10/STR	Pakhirala
34	Mrinal Raptan	37/STR	Pakhirala
35	Samar Joddar	13/STR	Pakhirala
36	Nityananda Chowkidar	30/STR	Pakhirala
37	Tapas Khatua	11/STR	Pakhirala
38	Dipak Giri	12/STR	Pakhirala
39	Manas Mandal	09/STR	Pakhirala
40	Anup Mandal	41/STR	Pakhirala

Source: Primary Data

Waterway Wanderlust: Local-Led Boat Tours in the Sundarbans

To travel in the remote expanse of the Sundarban National Park to explore its dense mangrove forests and wildlife, the only way is the waterway. Hence, the sole mode of transport here is the mechanized boats. These boats are of three distinct categories: (1) Ferry Boat, (2) Passenger Boat, and (3) Tourist Boat/Vessel - cater to different needs within this unique ecosystem. The Ferry Boats help tourists and local people to cross the rivers between two nearby village islands. On the other hand, the Passenger Boats carry people from one island to another at a long distance. Meanwhile, Tourist Boats/Vessels are specifically tailored for the enjoyment of tourists, providing them with immersive experiences to admire the mesmerizing sights of the Sundarbans jungles from the water. Unlike other conventional National Parks in India, where the jungle safari is typically organized by the Forest Authorities, in the Sunderban National Park, the entire tour system is operated by the Tour Operators and the Local Boat Owner's Association with taking necessary permission from the Forest Authority. Therefore, the tourists visiting the Sundarban National Park are to avail of the boats, supplied by them only. Moreover, the adventure aboard tourist's vessels in the Sundarban National Park typically begins at dawn and concludes by nightfall, enabling visitors to delve deeply into exploration throughout the day. To enhance the tourists' experience, the tour operators generally enlist the culinary expertise of local villagers, who serve as boatmen, adeptly preparing breakfast and lunch during the journey. This collaborative effort not only ensures seamless logistics but also puts light on the integral role of the local community people in tourism activities. Beyond mere sightseeing, this mode of exploration offers a gateway to the Sundarbans' cultural and ecological tapestry, providing visitors with an authentic glimpse into the region's vibrant heritage. Through this immersive journey, travelers not only witness the wildlife and the natural beauty of the park but also forge connections with the communities that call it a "home", fostering a deeper appreciation for the interplay between humans and the environment.

Mangrove Melodies: Cultural Expressions by Sundarbans Artisans

Besides the Jungle Safari, the diverse array of fairs and festivals such as Baishakhi Mela, Charak Mela, Manasa Mela, Baruni Mela, Bono Bibi Utsav, Sundarban Kristi Mela O Loksanskriti Utsav, Sundarban Hilsa Festival, Ganga Sagar Mela, etc. in the Indian Sundarbans region also offers the visitors a unique window into the community life. Various indigenous tribal groups, such as Santal, Munda, Oraon, etc. were brought to this region during the British colonial era to clear the forest areas as well as, barricading the rivers. Their descendants now speak in Bengali. Among these groups, music holds significant cultural importance as they use songs and dance to preserve their age-old cultural heritages. Various groups such as "Tiplighiri Adibasi Tusu Sampradaya" showcase their cultural heritage through performances, providing tourists with an enriching experience while supporting the Adivasi community's livelihoods and cultural preservation efforts. Moreover, "Bonbibi-r Palagaan", a revered dramatic tradition in the Indian Sundarbans, also reflects the cultural richness and syncretic heritages of this region. Despite its historical significance, it remained largely marginalized until recent efforts by Palagaan artists and the West Bengal government-sponsored initiatives elevated its prominence. Recognized as a cultural asset for tourism, "Bonbibi-r Palagaan" now features prominently in almost every tourist itinerary.

The Ecotourism project within the Sundarban National Park aligns with Sustainable Development Goals (SDGs) through its emphasis on responsible travel, fostering environmental preservation, community involvement, and economic growth. Focusing on the conservation and sustainable use of terrestrial and marine ecosystems, the ecotourism project in the Indian Sundarbans supports the Sustainable Development Goals related to responsible management, utilization, and preservation of biodiversity (SDG 15), poverty eradication (SDG 1), and inclusive economic growth (SDG 8). Additionally, it contributes to sustainable consumption and production (SDG 12) by encouraging resource management. Through partnerships with local communities, ecotourism bolsters social inclusion (SDG 10) and empowers marginalized groups. Overall, ecotourism in the Indian Sundarbans catalyzes achieving a harmonious balance between environmental protection, socio-economic development, and cultural preservation.

Here, the following Table 2 demonstrates a continual rise in the revenue derived from ecotourism within the Sundarban National Park across successive years. This data indicates the consistent growth in the park's financial gains from the eco-friendly community-led tourism endeavours.

Table 2. Conservation fund raised from ecotourism (From 2005 – 06 to 2016 – 17)

Tourism Revenue (INR) Earned from Each Entry Point of the Sundarban National Park						
Year	Canning Range	Sonakhali (N.P. East) Range	Sajnekhali Range	Bashirhat Range	Gosaba Range	Total
2005-06	7,47,365	2,57,705	12,74,461	1,53,635	0	24,33,166
2006-07	6,65,170	3,56,045	17,80,235	1,77,535	0	29,78,985
2007-08	9,94,006	4,36,860	18,02,470	1,16,902	0	33,50,238
2008-09	8,07,945	6,86,625	25,71,320	73,425	0	41,39,315
2009-10	5,15,145	5,30,345	20,25,895	1,08,170	2,53,295	34,32,850
2010-11	2,41,934	9,65,130	22,78,905	1,09,400	2,18,685	38,14,054
2011-12	5,10,085	19,86,715	51,95,290	3,49,785	3,19,009	83,60,884
2012-13	5,71,590	27,03,545	77,67,004	7,30,000	0	1,17,72,139
2013-14	3,23,890	32,03,800	95,15,090	10,32,790	0	1,40,75,570
2014-15	3,51,660	34,16,300	1,30,19,060	15,00,680	0	1,82,87,700
2015-16	2,16,120	31,60,730	1,46,29,050	14,95,560	0	1,95,01,460
2016-17	1,47,180	12,83,550	1,72,67,010	19,29,200	0	2,06,26,940
2017-18	1,36,250	2,005,580	17,382,450	2,099,800	0	2,16,24,080
Total	**62,28,340**	**2,09,92,230**	**9,65,08,240**	**9,76,882**	**7.90,989**	**13,43,97,381**

Source: Annual Report 2017-18, STR

The economic sustenance of a large section of residents inhabiting various forest fringe revenue villages in the Indian Sundarbans is now intricately intertwined with the influx of tourism revenue. Presently, the livelihoods of thousands of individuals in this remote coastal region are directly or indirectly linked to the inflow of tourism revenue. The following Table 3 briefly explains the different avenues, through which local community people participate in tourism in the Sundarban National Park region. This data stems from interviews conducted with tourism stakeholders and residents during comprehensive field studies.

Table 3. Avenues of community participation in tourism

Direct Involvement in Tourism	Indirect Involvement in Tourism
1. Running hotel / homestay business. 2. Running tour and travel business. 3. Running transport business. 4. Working as hotel staff, tour guide, etc. 5. Running small businesses such as food and tea stalls and selling snacks, mineral water, local cuisines, and different FMCG products. 6. Performing in local acts and plays - Banabibi Pal, Seetala Pala, Manasha Pala, Tusu Dance, Jhumur Dance, Baulgan etc. 7. Selling Non-Wood Forest Products such as: Bael, Sapodilla, Green Coconut etc.; Mangrove products such as Chakkera mangrove fruit; forest procured crude honey; pisciculture products such as Crab, Fish etc. in tourist seasons.	1. Work as labour in tourist boats in a daily wage basis 2. Work as labour in hotel construction in the fringe villages 3. Lease own land to the outside investors for commercial purposes 4. Work as middle man between the tourist and the hoteliers 5. Tourist boat repairing works 6. Work as casual labour in tourist hotels in peak tourist seasons

Source: Primary Data

COMMUNITY-BASED TOURISM PROGRAMS: ENGAGING COMMUNITIES FOR SHARED PROSPERITY

By following the "Principles of Sustainable Tourism" and "Guidelines of Responsible Tourism", a few community-driven projects in the Indian Sundarbans are contributing significantly towards achieving economic prosperity, social equity, and environmental quality – the three main pillars of the sustainable tourism development. Among these, the two most prominent CBT initiatives are: (1) The Sundarban Jungle Camp, and (2) the TORA Eco-Resort and Life Experience Centre.

The Sunderban Jungle Camp

The Sunderban Jungle Camp is located at the largest forest fringe revenue village in the Sundarban Tiger Reserve region – Bali village, next to the Vidya range. This CBT project has a long history behind its initiation. There was a time when the people of Bali village in Gosaba Block were mostly involved in agriculture for their livelihoods. However, as agriculture was not producing that much benefit, a large section of villagers became dependent on the forest resources; which resulted in heavy biotic pressure on the forest ecosystem. Moreover, the lack of job scope forced these people to be involved in various kinds of illegal activities like poaching inside the reserve forest areas. During 2000-2001, the growing number of poaching incidents became a headache for the National Park Authority. Another prime concern was the sustainable use of the water bodies in the STR region, as this is the breeding ground of various types of aquatic species; but, due to unscientific and illegal fishing activities by many of the community people, the threats to the marine ecosystem were looming large. In this scenario, the STR authority was eagerly looking for an alternative way that could help the local economy flow uninterruptedly and serious issues like poverty, hunger, over-dependence on forest resources, illegal fishing, animal poaching, man-animal conflict etc. could also be mitigated. Collaborating with WWF India (West Bengal), the STR authority started various conservation programmes in the forest fringe villages to offer the local villagers some sort of economic relief by involving them in these activities. The STR authority invited "Help Tourism" to start a CBT Project, in which local people can participate. In 2002, 'Help Tourism' started a project - "Sundarban Jungle Camp". Later other tourism stakeholders like NGO – ACT (Association for Conservation and Tourism), WWF (West Bengal), Bali Nature & Wildlife Conservation Society (BNWCS), Wildlife Protection Society of India (WPSI), and Bali Eco Development Committee also joined in this initiative. The Sundarban Jungle Camp (SJC) has now emerged as a successful CBT model in the Indian Sunderbans. It combines ecotourism with community involvement and emphasizes responsible tourism practices. By taking different socio-economic and environmental responsibilities like creating jobs for local people, purchasing products from local suppliers, developing new tourism products based on local resources, supporting local Self Help Groups, reintroducing local culture i.e. Banabibi Palagan, supporting local education, spending a portion of net profit in conservation, making people aware of the adverse effect of plastic by conducting no plastic campaign, using non-conventional energy i.e. solar power for energy management etc. this CBT project is playing a crucial role in the sustainable tourism development of the Bali village in the Indian Sundarbans.

Figure 1. Contribution of SJC towards Sustainable Development

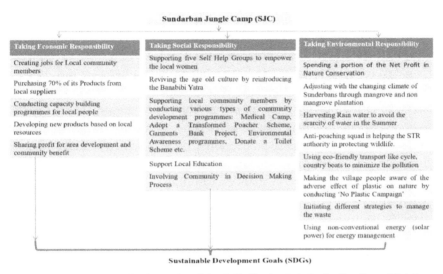

The above-mentioned Figure 1 shows the contribution of "The Sunderban Jungle Camp" towards the sustainable development of Bali village and its people.

Tora Eco-Resort and Life Experience Centre: Painting a Sustainable Tomorrow

In the heart of the Indian Sundarbans, the TORA Eco-Resort and Life Experience Centre stands as a beacon of sustainable development, embodying the spirit of community-based initiatives. By intertwining economic empowerment, environmental stewardship, and cultural preservation, TORA contributes substantially to the sustainable development of Bali village. During 2000 - 2001, issues like school dropout, illegal trade, and lack of employment opportunities became a serious problem in the STR region, the World Wildlife Fund (WWF), India, along with the STR Authority and Wildlife Protection Society of India (WPSI) came forward to offer the local community members an alternative source of income through Community Based Tourism (CBT) Projects and conservation activities. Mr. Anil Mistry, the Chief promoter of the Bali Nature and Wildlife Conservation Society (BNWCS), and a conservationist donated his land for this project. Later, in 2013, BNWCS collaborated with VIVADA Inland Waterways Ltd. to take this CBT initiative to a new height. This project has won many accolades including the "Runner Up" trophy of the "TOFTigers Wildlife Tourism Award" in 2018. Like Sunderbans Jungle Camp, this CBT project also has emerged as a successful responsible tourism model in the STR region. The multifaceted contributions of this CBT project in the sustainable tourism development in the Bali village, Indian Sundarbans are as follows:

[1] TORA involves the residents of Bali village in its day-to-day operations. By training and employing locals in various capacities, the project ensures economic empowerment, fostering a sense of ownership and pride within the community.

[2] TORA serves as a platform for economic diversification in Bali village. Beyond traditional livelihoods, community members engage in hospitality services, guiding, and cultural performances, resulting in improved income streams and enhanced economic resilience.

[3] TORA prioritizes environmental sustainability, implementing eco-friendly practices within the resort and surrounding areas. From waste management initiatives to nature-friendly construction, the project showcases a commitment to preserving the delicate mangrove ecosystem of the Sundarbans.

[4] TORA has become a hub for cultural exchange, allowing tourists to immerse themselves in the rich heritage of the Sundarbans. Local artisans showcase traditional crafts, and cultural performances breathe life into ancient traditions, fostering cultural preservation and awareness.

[5] TORA goes beyond tourism, integrating educational programs that enlighten both tourists and locals about the importance of mangrove conservation and sustainable living practices. The project acts as an educational catalyst, instilling environmental stewardship values in all its stakeholders.

[6] TORA exemplifies a community-driven decision-making process. Local input is actively sought in matters ranging from tourism activities to conservation efforts, ensuring that the Bali village community has a say in shaping the trajectory of the project and its impact on their lives.

Here. Figure 2 has briefly described the contribution of the Tora Eco Resort and Life Experience Centre in achieving the Sustainable Development Goals (SDGs) in the context of Bali village in the STR (Sundarban Tiger Reserve) region.

Figure 2. Contribution of Tora Eco Resort and life experience centre towards sustainable development

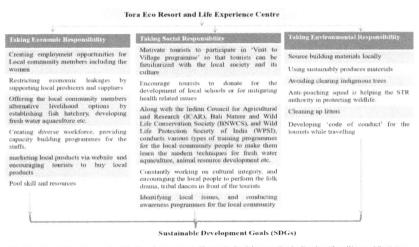

Like another prominent community-based tourism initiative i.e., The Sundarban Jungle Camp; Tora Eco Resort and Life Experience Centre has also emerged as a successful responsible tourism model in the Indian Sundarbans.

JFMCS IN THE INDIAN SUNDARBANS: THE GREEN GUARDIANS

The Joint Forest Management Committees (JFMCs) in the Indian Sundarbans stand at the forefront of a holistic approach to sustainable development, where community-based tourism becomes a vehicle for both environmental conservation and economic empowerment. Through their collaborative efforts, the Sundarbans JFMCs showcase a model where responsible forest management and thriving tourism coexist, ensuring a harmonious future for the Sundarbans and its communities. Through JFMCs, local communities are empowered to actively participate in decision-making processes related to forest management. This empowerment extends to tourism initiatives, where community members become stewards of their environment, fostering a sense of ownership crucial for the success of community-based tourism. These JFMCs also play a key role in preserving the cultural heritage of the local communities. By intertwining cultural preservation with forest management practices, they create a unique environment that becomes a draw for culturally inclined tourists, contributing to the success of community-based tourism endeavors. Moreover, these JFMCs act as facilitators for collaborative tourism planning. By bringing together community representatives, environmental experts, and tourism professionals, they ensure that tourism initiatives align with both conservation goals and community aspirations, creating a sustainable model for tourism development. In collaboration with community-based tourism operators, these JFMCs pave the way for economic diversification. Through training programs and partnerships, JFMCs enable local communities to participate in tourism-related activities, thereby enhancing livelihoods and creating economic resilience. In the Sundarban National Park region, the Joint Forest Management Committees (JFMCs) play an important role in collaborating with park authorities to address violations of forest regulations. The effectiveness of the JFMCs is pivotal in enhancing the condition of the forest and its surrounding areas, underscoring their significance in sustainable forest management and conservation efforts.

SUNDARBANS HOMESTAY NETWORK: DUAL DELIGHT FOR LOCALS AND TRAVELLERS

The Sundarbans Homestay Network represents a dual delight – a source of economic empowerment for the local community people and an avenue for travelers to immerse themselves in the authenticity of the Sundarbans. This model not only transforms tourism into a mutually beneficial exchange but also lays the foundation for a sustainable and harmonious coexistence between the Sundarbans and those who seek to explore its wonders. For travelers such initiatives unfold an authentic journey into the heart of local life. The experience goes beyond the conventional tourist trails, providing an immersive encounter with the culture, traditions, and daily lives of the Sundarbans residents. Visitors are welcomed into the warm embrace of homestays, creating memories that extend far beyond typical travel experiences. The homestay model facilitates meaningful cultural exchange. Travelers gain insights into the rich cultural heritage of the Sundarbans, sharing moments with their hosts and partaking in local customs. This cultural dialogue fosters mutual understanding, breaking down barriers between guests and hosts and creating a tapestry of shared experiences. Many homestays adopt eco-friendly practices, contributing to the conservation of the delicate ecosystem. Travelers are educated about the importance of preserving the natural beauty of the Sundarbans, and promoting responsible and sustainable tourism. exemplifies the power of community-led tourism. Local people actively participate in decision-making processes, ensuring that tourism aligns with their values and aspirations. This inclusive approach fosters a sense of ownership and pride among the community members, making tourism a tool for positive change.

LOCAL LUMINANCE: SUNDARBAN'S HOMEGROWN HOSPITALITY VENTURES

While visiting the Indian Sundarbans, one can also experience the authentic charm and the warm hospitality at the locally-owned hotels. Run by a few passionate locals of Gosaba, Basanti, Canning, etc. these accommodation units offer a unique glimpse into the region's culture while providing comfortable accommodations. From cozy guesthouses to eco-friendly resorts, indulge in the essence of Sundarbans' hospitality with personalized service and unforgettable experiences. The majority of the staff in these hotels are hired from the forest fringe villages for various roles such as cooking, cleaning, housekeeping, etc.

SUSTAINABLE SOUVENIRS: COMMUNITY-DRIVEN ECO SHOP VENTURES

In recent times, tourists' attitudes towards consuming products during their visit to any ecotourism destination have undergone drastic changes due to the high level of awareness towards the conservation of nature. Tourists wish to buy a couple of products made of local raw materials not as a souvenir but as a token of love and responsibility. Being more conscious about health and hygiene, nowadays consumers have started preferring eco-products. Consequently, several eco shops have emerged within the Indian Sundarban region to cater to this demand, providing visitors with sustainable options that align with their values and ethos. These Eco-shops have offered the local artisans with new avenues for showcasing their crafts, fostering a sense of pride and economic opportunity within the community. A few of the best examples of such sustainable Souvenirs in the Sundarban National Park region are:

[1] The Rangabelia Mahila Industrial Co-operative Society Limited, under the "Rangabelia Project" is running a community-driven eco-shop venture - "PASORA" inside the Sajnekhali Interpretation Centre as well as in the village Pakhiralaya, located just opposite to the Sajnekhali Wildlife Sanctuary (WLS). Here, visitors can explore and purchase a diverse array of handicrafts skillfully crafted by local women.

[2] The Jamespur JFMC runs a National Jute Board-authorized souvenir shop - "Sundarban Eco-friendly Handicraft Products', where visitors can buy different kinds of eco-friendly handicrafts made by the locals.

[3] In Jhingekhali Beat (Bashirhat Range of STR), the local JFMC (Joint Forest Management Committee) members run one Eco-shop, where local products are sold during the tourist season.

Here, the following Table 4 provides a concise overview of the Eco-shops operated by the local people of the forest fringe villages in the Sundarban National Park area and the locally crafted products available in these shops made by local community people.

Table 4. Eco Shops in the Sundarban National Park region and the products available

Eco Shops in the STR Region	Available Products for Sale
PASORA - Run by the Rangabelia Mahila Industrial Co-operative Society Limited	Hand Batik (Tulis), Weaving products, Tailoring, Garments, Bon Madhu (crude honey), Jute products, Bamboo crafts, etc.
Sundarban Eco-friendly Handicraft Products Run by Jamespur JFMC	Carry bag, Ladies bag, Tourist hat, cap, etc. made of jute.
Eco-shop run by the JFMC of Jhingekhali	Local hand made products

Source: Primary Data

All these above-stated examples illustrate how community-based tourism initiatives in the Indian Sundarbans are playing a vital role in creating opportunities for both local community people and tourists. These initiatives go beyond traditional tourism models, emphasizing sustainability, community engagement, and the preservation of local culture and environment.

LESSONS LEARNT

Community-based tourism (CBT) has emerged as a sustainable direction for the tourism industry, and evidence from the Indian Sundarbans supports this notion. The following points highlight how CBT initiatives in the Indian Sundarbans pave the way towards sustainability in the tourism sector:

1. Community-based tourism in the Sundarbans emphasizes the preservation of local cultures and traditions. Visitors have the opportunity to engage with indigenous communities, participate in cultural activities, and experience the unique way of life in the region. This not only ensures the conservation of cultural heritage but also provides a source of pride and income for local people.

2. The Sundarbans is a delicate and ecologically significant mangrove ecosystem. CBT initiatives in the region often incorporate environmental conservation efforts. Local communities actively participate in mangrove reforestation projects, wildlife conservation, and the promotion of eco-friendly practices, contributing to the long-term health of the ecosystem.

3. CBT empowers local communities by involving them directly in tourism activities. Through homestays, guided tours, and other services, community members become active participants in the tourism value chain. This not only generates income but also fosters a sense of ownership and responsibility for the sustainable development of their resources.

4. Tourism has the potential to alleviate poverty by providing alternative sources of income. In the Sundarbans, where traditional livelihoods may be vulnerable to environmental changes, CBT offers a means of economic diversification. Local people can engage in hospitality services, handicraft production, and cultural performances, reducing dependence on single-sector incomes.

5. CBT facilitates cultural exchange between visitors and local communities. Tourists gain insights into the Sundarbans' ecology, cultural practices, and challenges faced by the residents. This exchange fosters mutual understanding and promotes responsible tourism behavior. Additionally, educational initiatives within CBT projects educate tourists about the importance of environmental conservation.

6. Unlike mass tourism, which often has a significant environmental footprint, CBT in the Sundarbans tends to be more sustainable. Initiatives focus on responsible tourism practices, minimizing negative impacts on the fragile ecosystem. This includes controlled visitor numbers, waste management strategies, and the use of eco-friendly technologies.

7. Sustainable tourism involves local communities in decision-making processes. In the Sundarbans, CBT initiatives often collaborate with residents to determine the types of tourism activities, infrastructure development, and conservation measures that align with community needs and aspirations.

8. Community-based tourism can enhance the resilience of communities to external shocks, such as environmental disasters or economic downturns. By diversifying income sources and promoting self-sufficiency, CBT initiatives in the Sundarbans contribute to the overall resilience of local communities.

The evidences taken from the Indian Sundarbans supports the idea that community-based tourism can be a sustainable direction for the tourism industry. By integrating social, cultural, and environmental considerations, CBT not only benefits local communities but also ensures the long-term viability of tourism in ecologically sensitive areas like Indian Sundarbans. This model serves as a positive example for other regions seeking to balance tourism development with environmental and cultural preservation.

CONCLUSION

In conclusion, the exploration of Community-Based Tourism (CBT) as a sustainable direction for the tourism industry, with a specific focus on the Indian Sundarbans, reveals a promising and transformative paradigm. The evidence gathered through this study underscores the multifaceted benefits and potential that CBT holds for fostering sustainable tourism development in ecologically sensitive regions. The Indian Sundarbans, known for its rich biodiversity and delicate ecosystems, face the dual challenge of conservation and economic development. The evidence presented demonstrates that CBT initiatives offer a viable and harmonious solution by actively involving local communities in tourism endeavors. This approach not only empowers residents economically but also catalyzes for the preservation of cultural heritage and the delicate mangrove ecosystem. The success stories emerging from CBT initiatives in the Sundarbans echo the positive impact on both tourists and local communities. Tourists, seeking authentic and responsible travel experiences, find themselves immersed in the vibrant culture of the Sundarbans while actively participating in conservation efforts. Simultaneously, local people, through community-led decision-making and economic participation, become stewards of their environment. In the case of the Indian Sundarbans, all the evidences highlight that CBT is not merely a niche concept but a viable and holistic model for steering the tourism industry in a sustainable direction. It reflects a harmonious integration of economic empowerment, cultural preservation, environmental conservation, and community engagement. As the global tourism landscape evolves, the evidence from the Indian Sundarbans serves as a beacon, guiding the tourism industry toward practices that respect and enhance the natural and cultural treasures of destinations. The evidence-based insights presented in this study advocate for the wider adoption of Community-Based Tourism as a sustainable and responsible direction, not only in other parts of India but also as a global imperative for the future of tourism. However, the journey toward sustainable tourism through CBT is not without its challenges. Issues such as infrastructure development, capacity building, and balancing the influx of tourists with environmental preservation require careful consideration. There is also a need for continued collaboration among stakeholders, including local communities, governmental bodies, NGOs, and the private sector, to address these challenges effectively.

REFERENCES

Boley, B. B., McGehee, N. G., & Hammett, A. T. (2017). Importance-performance analysis (IPA) of sustainable tourism initiatives: The resident perspective. *Tourism Management*, 58, 66–77. 10.1016/j.tourman.2016.10.002

Dodds, R., Ali, A., & Galaski, K. (2018). Mobilizing knowledge: Determining key elements for success and pitfalls in developing community-based tourism. *Current Issues in Tourism*, 21(13), 1547–1568. 10.1080/13683500.2016.1150257

Gantait, A., Singh, K., Bhowmik, S., & Swamy, G. A. (2022). Can Community Based Tourism Be a Sustainable Solution for a Better Community Life? Discussing the Concept, Benefits, and Challenges. In Kour, R. (Ed.), *Rani, R., Vaishali* (1st ed., pp. 63–79). Emerging Trends in Social Science Research.

Lapeyre, R. (2010). Community-based tourism as a sustainable solution to maximise impacts locally? The Tsiseb Conservancy case,Namibia. *Development Southern Africa*, 27(5), 757–772. 10.1080/0376835X.2010.522837

Lee, T. H., & Jan, F. H. (2019). Can community-based tourism contribute to sustainable development? Evidence from residents' perceptions of the sustainability. *Tourism Management*, 70, 368–380. 10.1016/j.tourman.2018.09.003

López-Guzmán, T., Sánchez-Cañizares, S., & Pavón, V. (2011). Community-based tourism in developing countries: A case study. *Tourismos*, 6(1), 69–84.

Mayaka, M., Croy, W. G., & Cox, J. W. (2019). A dimensional approach to community-based tourism: Recognising and differentiating form and context. *Annals of Tourism Research*, 74, 177–190. 10.1016/j.annals.2018.12.002

Mehmetoglu, M. (2001). Economic scale of community-run festivals: A Case study. *Event Management*, 7(2), 93–102. 10.3727/152599501108751506

. Mtapuri, O., & Giampiccoli, A. (2013). Interrogating the role of the state and nonstate actors in community-based tourism ventures: Toward a model for spreading the benefits to the wider community. *South African Geographical Journal= Suid-Afrikaanse Geografiese Tydskrif, 95*(1), 1-15.

Nilnoppakun, A., & Ampavat, K. (2016). Is pai a sustainable tourism destination? *Procedia Economics and Finance*, 39, 262–269. 10.1016/S2212-5671(16)30322-7

Shikida, A., Yoda, M., Kino, A., & Morishige, M. (2010). Tourism relationship model and intermediary for sustainable tourism management: Case study of the Kiritappu Wetland Trust in Hamanaka, Hokkaido. *Tourism and Hospitality Research*, 10(2), 105–115. 10.1057/thr.2009.29

Simpson, M. C. (2008). Community benefit tourism initiatives—A conceptual oxymoron? *Tourism Management*, 29(1), 1–18. 10.1016/j.tourman.2007.06.005

Zapata, M. J., Hall, C. M., Lindo, P., & Vanderschaeghe, M. (2011). Can community-based tourism contribute to development and poverty alleviation? Lessons from Nicaragua. *Current Issues in Tourism*, 14(8), 725–749. 10.1080/13683500.2011.559200

Chapter 10
From Temples to Tranquillity:
The Role of Religious and Wellness Tourism in India's Sustainable Future

Natasha
Amity University, Noida, India

Kavita Indapurkar
https://orcid.org/0000-0003-4388-2915
Amity University, Noida, India

ABSTRACT

Global tourism is becoming progressively acknowledged for its link to the sustainable development goals (SDGs). This study aims to explore how India can meet its sustainable development objectives through religious and wellness tourism. The study explores the effect of push and pull factors on travelers' motivation to travel. The study uses a quantitative and exploratory design, incorporating data gathered from 142 questionnaire responses. Results indicate that independent variables accounted for 38% of the variance in travel motivation, with a R Square value of 0.331. While gender and the cultural significance of the destination are important determinants, other factors may not have as much of an impact on motivation. The study emphasizes how tourism can support sustainable development, especially when it comes to promoting social inclusion, economic growth, and environmental preservation. The research's insights can help location managers, tourist authorities, and legislators create sustainable tourism experiences and regulations that support all-encompassing growth.

DOI: 10.4018/979-8-3693-3166-8.ch010

INTRODUCTION

In the realm of contemporary travel, the intertwining of spirituality, well-being, and cultural immersion is gradually constructing a novel standard and modern-day travellers are now in pursuit of reflective and meaningful experiences that establish a deep connection with the spirit of a place, its customs, and its inhabitants. This turn has driven religious, wellness and cultural tourism to the forefront, particularly in a vibrant and diverse country such as India. This expanding tourism industry plays a significant role in aiding to sustainable development, in addition it is a catalyst for economic growth, job creation and cultural exchange. India with its rich background of religious, wellness, cultural and rural tourism stands as a vibrant scenery that captivates the imagination of travellers from around the world.

India, a land where ancient temples softly whisper tales of faith and tranquil landscapes cradle traditions, naturally captivate religious and wellness tourists who are yearning for transformative experiences. For travellers, embarking on pilgrimages it allows them to catch a glimpse of India's diverse faiths, ranging from the vivacious Holi celebrations in Vrindavan to the serene Buddhist monasteries located in the Himalayas. These journeys foster cultural understanding and spiritual connection, effectively eradicating barriers and building profound bonds with local communities. Beyond the experiential and cultural engagement, India offers a safe haven for those seeking peace and rejuvenation. Whether it is to indulge in Ayurvedic spa treatments in Kerala or doing yoga in the peaceful ashrams of Rishikesh, India provides a widespread approach to well-being that nurtures the body and the soul. India can encourage responsible tourism, protect its natural and cultural resources, and assist local communities by utilizing its rich cultural and spiritual legacy (Chandra & Kumar, 2021).

Religious tourism has been a major driver of tourist inflow to India. It involves travellers motivated by faith and the pursuit of spiritual experiences. It includes diverse forms of engagement, such as journeys undertaken to visit sacred sites for religious purposes, which are often associated with seeking blessings, fulfilling vows, or celebrating special occasions (Smith, 1992). Religious tourism has a strong potential to draw both cultural and commercial travellers to India. It encompasses a wide range of religious minorities, rituals and the traditional rites, touristic religious locations, and religious tourism (Budovich, 2023). Well-being, a relatively new trend in tourism, is growing at an impressive rate. The Global Wellness Institute has defined wellness tourism as a travel activity associated with the pursuit of sustaining and improving one's personal wellbeing. There has been an increase in the growing number of people that are visiting locations with wellness services all around the world. There are two reasons for the 'wellness' concept's emergence. The first is that the World Health Organisation (WHO) has long promoted the integration of "wellbeing" and "fitness" into its global health plans and the second being that as a result of increase in education, the people are now becoming more aware of their health and ways to stay healthy (Koncul, 2012). Religious and wellness tourism in India are closely related with cultural and rural tourism. Many religious and wellness destinations hold significant cultural value. They often feature historical landmarks, sacred sites, traditional practices, and cultural festivals that attract tourists interested in exploring the cultural heritage of a region. Destinations for religious and wellness tourism are frequently found outside of major cities, in rural areas. Learning about the people and customs of many nations and areas can be greatly aided by cultural travel (Šťastná et al, 2020). A retreat to nature is sometimes associated with rural tourism. Comparably, going back to one's historical roots—personal, ethnic, or entire civilizations can be viewed as cultural tourism (Matei, 2015).

The World Tourism Organization (UNWTO, 2021) has recognized that "tourism is one of the driving forces of global economic growth and is currently responsible for the creation of 1 in 11 jobs. By giving access to decent work opportunities in the tourism sector, society, in particular, young people and women, can benefit from improved skills and professional development. The sector's contribution to job creation is recognized in target 8.9: by 2030, devise and implement policies to promote sustainable tourism that creates jobs and promotes local culture and products." In recent years, the significance of tourism for the local economy in terms of wealth creation, job creation, and economic stimulus has been recognized and, in this regard, tourism is viewed as an agent of economic change and a catalyst for development. One of the most important goals of the tourism industry is the economic development of local communities (Pourtaheri et al., 2012). This sector also plays a major role in the economic growth of both urban and rural communities (Mandych et al., 2022; Mróz, 2021; Rad et al., 2017). The economic development of the host society is promoted by tourists and their purchases (Jamalpour, 2022), and the best approach to create this environment is to combine natural and cultural heritage-related attractions (Patwardhan et al., 2020)

Travel motivation are the start of tourism activities, additionally they are the outcome of a coordinated activity between internal and external tourism environment factors as well as the behaviour of the visitors themselves. The primary factors influencing travel motivations are the surroundings, travel patterns etc. Diverse visitor types are motivated to travel in different ways and have various reasons for engaging in tourism activities. Prior to a trip, visitors have psychological expectations that shape their desires and requirements and have a significant impact on their motivation to travel. Travelers' psychological expectations and experiences, as well as cultural norms, health, and economic conditions, are all influenced by a variety of elements, including the destination's social and economic climate and outside influences like the public security environment. Philip Kotler (2008) argues that motivation, perception, beliefs, and attitudes are the primary psychological elements that impact human behaviour when it comes to making decisions as consumers or tourists.

For many developing nations, tourism is a significant economic sector (Mitchell & Ashley, 2009). Additionally, sustainability is driven by focus on the future and it makes deliberate attempts to preserve the natural resources, and the social and cultural heritage to protect the environmental ecosystems, along with promoting economic richness and a better human health. Clean and green natural landscaping, a healthy biodiversity, and sociocultural elements that represent the level of motivation of tourists have to visit a location and the openness of the local population to receive them are all examples of sustainability. Since tourism growth and sustainability are viewed as interrelated concepts, the level of sustained and environmentally friendly travel is strongly impacted by increases in tourism development and visitor arrivals (Azam et al., 2018; Hassan et al., 2020).

This study is divided into several sections in order to thoroughly explore the variables influencing traveller's motivation to travel. The first section includes a survey of the literature that explores the theoretical underpinnings of tourism motivation. It uses the push and pull concept to clarify the several elements that influence travelers' decisions to travel to particular locations. The research aims & objectives are outlined in the next section, with a particular emphasis on examining the impact of tourist's preference, demographic characteristics, and monthly income on their motivation to travel. The third section presents the study hypotheses, which establish a connection between independent variables - trip profile, cultural heritage, infrastructure and facilities, monthly individual income, demographic characteristics, and the dependent variable - visitors' motivation. The quantitative technique of the study, which uses IBM SPSS for data analysis, is described in the fourth section. The research tool, data collecting procedure, and analytical methods—such as regression analysis, exploratory factor analysis, and reliability statistics—are also explained in this section. Section five in detail presents the analysis of data including reliability tests, exploratory factor analysis results, model specifications, regression analysis, and interpretation of findings. In the final section the research findings are discussed, along with the implications and limitations of the research. The section also offers further readings in the field.

LITERATURE REVIEW

Religious and wellness tourism have emerged as significant segments of the global tourism industry, attracting a large number of tourists each year. These forms of tourism have gained popularity due to the growing need for relaxation, rejuvenation, and spiritual experiences in a fast-paced and stressful world (Csirmaz & Pető, 2015). Planning and growing the tourist industry with a purpose and sustainability is crucial, requiring compromises between the goals of the economy, society, and the environment. The allure of religious sites and pursuit of spiritual experience resonates deeply with the travellers, offering opportunities for mental and spiritual wellbeing, thus supporting SDG 3's objective of good health and well-being . Religious tourism often involves visiting sacred sites and participating in religious rituals and practices, which can have a positive impact on mental and spiritual well-being. Participating in wellness tourism activities, such as yoga retreats, meditation workshops, and spa treatments, can contribute to improving mental and physical health. Moreover, religious and wellness tourism can also contribute to achieving SDG 11 by promoting sustainable cities and communities (Alexis-Thomas, 2020).

Religious tourism can foster peace, interfaith dialogue, and cultural understanding, aligning with the goal of promoting peaceful and inclusive societies for sustainable development (Kuoyan, 2022). Additionally, in line with SDG 12 Responsible Consumption and Production, wellness tourism encourages environmentally friendly travel behaviours that lessen negative impacts on the local population and environment (Pratt, 2022). Wellness retreats in India emphasize organic, locally sourced, and sustainable food options. Particularly in hilly regions, these retreats frequently give priority to energy efficiency and renewable energy sources for powering their facilities. They employ solar panels, LED lighting, and other devices that lower energy use and greenhouse gas emissions, supporting the development of clean, affordable energy (SDG 7). The achievement of Sustainable Development Goals can be facilitated by travellers' motivation for religious and wellness travel (Ottenbacher et al., 2015; Paniccia et al., 2017).

Motivation plays a pivotal role in travellers' decisions to engage in religious and wellness tourism. Comprehending the variables influencing traveller's motivation to visit locations is essential for efficient administration and promotion. People with strong religious links are drawn to each other for pilgrimages and spiritual fulfilment, which makes religious motivation stand out (Michaels et al., 2021). Motivation is heavily influenced by perceptions of a destination's cleanliness, safety, and friendliness as well as by infrastructure and accessibility. Successful marketing strategies that highlight distinctive experiences and social influences—such as word-of-mouth and internet reviews—also have an impact on traveller's motivation and decision to travel (Aqmal & Setiawan, 2022). Motivation and destination image sits at the core of every travel decision. Finding out how tourists choose a site based on their perception of it as well as other factors is crucial (López-Sanz et al., 2021). Destination image is crucial to the establishment of a successful tourism industry (Tasci & Gartner, 2007). Travellers' motivation processes heavily rely on this image (Ejarque, 2017).

Additionally, a visitor's motive plays a significant role in the construction of their perception of a location (Mimi et al., 2010; Álvarez & Esper, 2010).

Numerous writers have extensively researched motivation in a variety of fields, including marketing, sociology, and psychology. Motivation is the process's main driver. From the standpoint of tourism, motivation is among the most significant and thoroughly investigated factors. Wong et al. (2018) draw attention to the impact that motives have on the tourism process, particularly for the traveller. A pioneering study was conducted by Dann (1977). He tried to shed light on why individuals travel and what factors influence their decision. Cultural intentions, also known as "pull" motivations explain the choice of destination or type of destination, whereas socio-psychological motives, sometimes known as "push" motives, explain the desire to take vacations. Together with this author, Crandall (1980), drawing from Crompton's study, adds to the discussion of the importance of motivation in tourist behaviour by enumerating seventeen distinct personal motivations. These are undoubtedly an expansion of Crompton's nine reasons. Other writers, including Line et al. (2018), emphasize the significance of motives in visitor behaviour. They discuss the significance of motivation and draw a particular connection between sustainability initiatives and motivation. The notion of push and pull forces is a prominent theory utilized to explain the motivation of visitors.

The theory of push and pull motivations distinguishes two main factors: Push factors are defined as internal causes that inspire or generate a desire to fulfil a need to travel and pull factors are acknowledged as destination features and can be categorized into three kinds:1) main pull factors, such as landscape, cities, climate, wildlife, historical sites, and local cultural attractions (Lubbe, 2003); 2) secondary, such as lodging, catering, entertainment, and sports; and 3) tertiary, such as marketing and costs. According to Heung et al., (2001) and Sangpikul, (2008), pull motivation factors react to and enhance natural push motivation factors. Push and pull factors explain how people are drawn to a destination by its features and how they are pushed by incentive variables into making travel decisions (Uysal & Jurowski, (1993) in (Yoon & Uysal, 2005)). According to a study on wellness tourism by Gan et al., (2023) traveller's behavioural intentions is influenced by factors such as life stress and involvement in health and wellness. Religion, as a motivator for travel, has been studied extensively (Kim et al., 2016). This study investigated the effect of psychological factors, including motivation, perception, learning, and belief, on the decision to visit religious tourism destinations. The study further identified that perception and belief had a significant and dominant influence on the decision and motivation to visit religious tourism destinations (Filmi et al., 2022).

Push and pull incentives were used by Correia et al. (2004) and Money & Crotts (2003) to try to explain why Portuguese travelers go to exotic locations. To evaluate the reasons behind tourists' travels, push and pull variables have been used widely

(Kanagaraj and Bindu, 2013; Michael et al., 2017; Wijaya et al., 2018). Collin and Tisdell (2002) discovered that travelers' choices of holiday destinations and their involvement in tourism-related activities are influenced by demographic characteristics. The push and pull theories underpin this study. The push factors are an individual's age, gender, and monthly income; the pull factors are the infrastructure and amenities (such as the standard of the transportation system, the variety and quality of lodging, the facilities, and services they want, like restaurants and shops), recommendations and reviews, value for money, historical and cultural significance, distinctive customs and practices, and the local language.

The decision and incentive of visitors to visit a location are influenced by a variety of elements, in addition to those related to religion and well-being. Various studies have looked at different facets of decision-making and customer behaviour in the tourist industry (Horner & Swarbrooke, 2020; Ulker-Demirel & Çiftci, 2020; Han, 2021; Santos et al., 2022; Gordan et al., 2023). A destination's demand for tourism may also be influenced by other factors, such as climate change (Rosselló-Nadal, 2014), weather conditions (Muñoz et al., 2023), climate variation (Goh, 2012), transport options, variety of tourism industry products, image destination (overall cognitive, image, and conative image) (Afshardoost & Eshaghi, 2020), tourists' safety sense (safety concerns and information, facilities and services for the tourists, as well as environment, regional culture, and safety information) (Zou & Meng, 2020). When travellers are choosing a destination, they consider a number of issues, including safety and security, specifically if they are visiting a foreign country (Mavondo & Reisinger, 2005). Scholars that have studied and are studying tourism have put up a number of reasons for why safety is an element of a destination's image. The existence of public security systems, a stable environment, a steady social order, the friendliness of the residents, and the availability of facilities and tools are a few examples (Chauhan, 2007; George, 2003; Xie et al., 2021).

A number of studies have emphasized the economic role that tourism plays in reducing poverty and the ways in which it may foster community development and economic prosperity. Governments, non-governmental groups, and international institutions including the United Nations, World Bank, and United Nations Conference on Trade and Development (UNCTAD) have made reducing poverty a priority worldwide (Vanegas et al., 2015). The UNWTO (2002) integrated the positive findings of four research in its 2002 Report on Tourism and Poverty Alleviation, which shows how tourism may support and execute programs aimed at reducing poverty, raise incomes, and strengthen the impact of tourism development on poverty alleviation. While some tourism proponents claim that tourism can be a magic bullet for ending poverty and inequality (Croes & Vanegas, 2008), other research (Pluss and Backes, 2002 cited in Scheyvens, 2007; Mbaiwa, 2005) demonstrates that tourism has little impact on reducing extreme poverty. According to Ashley et al., (2000), the creation of tourism-related goods and services could provide economically disadvantaged members of society with employment opportunities, hence reducing poverty. Similar research indicates that foreign exchange profits from tourism contribute significantly to increases in employment, family income, tax revenues, and economic growth (Croes & Vanegas, 2008); Durbarry, 2002; Hazari & Sgro, 1995); Kim et al., 2006; Sugiyarto et al., 2003). Using the AGE model, Saayman et al. (2012) demonstrate how rising tourism in South Africa contributes to the growth of the real gross domestic product (GDP) of the nation. Marzo-Navarro (2017) also said that rural tourism helps destination regions develop and grow economically, so achieving the goals of economic, sociocultural, and sustainability is crucial.

The extant body of literature pertaining to "religious tourism" and "wellness tourism" is noticeably sparse, despite its noteworthy influence on the welfare of tourists and the sustainable growth of the tourism sector. Numerous academics and industry professionals suggested that different types of tourism, such ecotourism, soft tourism, green tourism, and responsible tourism, among others, should be promoted as means of promoting sustainable tourist growth. There aren't many studies that look at how demographic characteristics affect Indian travelers' willingness to travel. The majority of work on India till date has focused on case for the North-Indian hilly states of Himachal Pradesh and Uttarakhand (Gambhir et al., 2021), sustainable ecotourism development in Rameswaram, Tamil Nadu (Mallick et al., 2020) and other state specific religious sites. There are also very few studies on wellness tourism in India. Thus, by looking at demographic and destination preference elements that influence traveller's willingness to visit a place for religious and wellness purposes in India, this study aims to close the gap in knowledge. Additionally, this study is significant because it sheds light on how variables like age, gender, monthly individual income and preference factors like Infrastructure and Amenities, Cultural Heritage and Trip Profile affect traveller's motivation to visit Indian destinations.

RESEARCH OBJECTIVES

1. To study and analyse the influence of Push Factors on tourists' motivation to travel to a destination.

The study's primary goal is to investigate and evaluate how the push factors - demographic variables like age & gender, and monthly income impact travellers' motivation to visit a certain location.

2. To analyse the influence of Pull Factors (preference factors) on tourist motivation to travel to a destination.

The aim is to research and evaluate how tourists are motivated to travel to a destination based on their preference of destination factors. The destination factors are pull factors - the historical and cultural significance, distinctive customs and practices, high-quality transportation infrastructure, high-quality and variety of lodging, recommendations and reviews, value for money and language.

RESEARCH HYPOTHESIS

Numerous writers have extensively researched motivation in a variety of fields, including psychology, sociology, and marketing. Motivation is the process's main engine. From the perspective of tourism, motivation is among the most significant and well-researched factors.

Motivations play a significant role in the tourism process, particularly for the traveller (Wong et al., 2018). Dann (1977) conducted one of the earliest studies. He tried to clarify why individuals travel and what factors influence their decision. This was the first discussion of push and pull factors. Many others have elaborated on how this motivation is affected by various attributes of a person and the destination. Therefore, in this study we observe the influence of these attributes on the motivation of a tourist to visit a destination and propose the following hypothesis:

H1: The Push Factors have an impact on tourists' motivation to travel to a destination.
H1-1: The demographic factor gender has an impact on tourists' motivation to travel to a destination.
H1-2: The demographic factor age has an impact on tourists' motivation to travel to a destination.
H1-3: The monthly individual income has an impact on tourists' motivation to travel to a destination.

and

H2: The Pull Factors (preference factors) have an impact on tourists' motivation to travel to a destination.
H2-1: The Cultural Heritage has an impact on tourists' motivation to travel to a destination.
H2-2: The Infrastructure and Amenities has an impact on tourists' motivation to travel to a destination.
H2-3: The Trip Profile has an impact on tourists' motivation to travel to a destination.

RESEARCH METHODOLOGY

1. Methodology

The research is exploratory and quantitative in nature. The requirement to examine the complex interactions between trip profile, infrastructure, facilities, cultural heritage, individual income, and demographic characteristics on travelers' willingness to visit to a location justifies the use of an exploratory study design. Exploratory and quantitative research allows the freedom to discover new patterns and insights within the data while still facilitating methodical data gathering and analysis. This method makes it easier to identify important variables and how they could affect travelers' motivation by using statistical tools to examine quantitative data, such as regression analysis. Travelers' motivation to travel is influenced by a complex interaction of circumstances, and the approach chosen to investigate this interplay and get a greater knowledge of the phenomena is therefore in line with the goal of the study.

2. Research Instrument

Two main sections made up the research questionnaire. General information on the respondents – age, gender, employment status, and monthly individual income was addressed in the first section. There were six questions in this section. Information on tourists' travel and destination preference was included in the second section. On a Likert scale ranging from 1 (strongly disagree) to 5 (strongly agree), respondents were asked to rate the list of preference statements in order of agreement or disagreement, indicating if those statements described their preference. The Likert scale was utilized in this study, and Kozak (2002) noted that it is ideal for use in studies centered on tourists.

3. Data Collection

This research is grounded on an exploratory study and has employed a quantitative approach that utilizes primary data sourced from a questionnaire specifically a Google form administered to a representative sample of population aged 18 and above, in order to ensure a level of maturity and understanding while filling the questionnaire. The selection process employed in determining the various components of the constructs relied on a comprehensive review of existing literature. This ensured that all the relevant factors were included in the study. To have an adequate amount of data for analysis, a total of 142 valid questionnaires were successfully completed between the months of February 2024 and March 2024. The data collection process was facilitated through the administration of the questionnaire, which ensured collection of accurate and reliable data. All the items in the questionnaire adhered to a uniform 5-point Likert scale, wherein a rating of 1 indicates strong disagreement and a rating of 5 indicates strong agreement. However, for items such as Age, Gender, and Monthly individual income, a multiple-choice option was used.

For the actual data collection, a pretest of the questionnaire was conducted on a sample of 20 individuals to assess the effectiveness of the scales and the clarity of the multiple questions in the questionnaire.

4. Data Analysis

Following the confirmation of the questionnaire's accuracy, the data collection phase commenced. IBM Social Science Statistical Package (SPSS) Statistic software was used to analyse the obtained data. The analysis served to provide insights into the research objectives. To guarantee data consistency, the first stage involves evaluating the measurement scales' reliability using Cronbach's alpha. The next step is exploratory factor analysis, which assesses if the data are suitable for factor analysis by using Bartlett's test of sphericity and the Kaiser-Meyer-Olkin (KMO) measure of sample adequacy. The sufficiency of the data is shown by a substantial Bartlett's test and a high KMO score (usually above 0.6). The amount of variation explained by the extracted components is then determined by looking at the overall variance explained; a cumulative explained variance of at least 60% is deemed adequate. In order to optimize the variation explained by the components, the study use the principal component factor analysis approach to extract factors. In order to determine the underlying dimensions of the constructs, factor loadings in the rotating component matrix are evaluated. Loadings greater than 0.50 are regarded as statistically and practically significant, suggesting strong relationships between variables and factors. Total variance explained is analyzed to estimate the percentage of variation explained by the extracted factors. Lastly, regression analysis is used to determine the strength and direction of the correlations between the predictor variables and travelers' motivation to visit to a place. ANOVA is used to assess for the significance of the regression model and coefficients.

ANALYSIS

1. Reliability Test

Among the most popular dependability metrics in the social and organizational sciences is Cronbach's alpha reliability and it is a measure of "internal consistency" dependability is Cronbach's alpha (Cronbach, 1951).

Table 1. Reliability statistics

Cronbach's Alpha	N of Items
.850	18

Table 1 presents the value of Cronbach's Alpha for variables D1 to D15 and Age, Gener and monthly individual income is greater than 0.5 which indicates that the variables have a good level of consistency. Cronbach's Alpha value of 0.850 suggests that 17 variables are measuring the destination preference with good reliability.

2.   Exploratory Factor Analysis

A factor analysis was carried out to make analysis of certain variables easier. Principal Component Analysis (PCA) was the method of choice since it is a factor analysis technique that may be used to identify the underlying dimensions or factors in the interactions between the values of the variables under study (Harman, 1976). It is a statistical technique that lowers the number of variables in a data matrix by organizing and summarizing the information (Lozares & Lopez, 1991). By obtaining linear combinations with maximum variance that are uncorrelated to the original variables, this strategy seeks to reduce the number of dimensions (Aguilera et al., 1996). In this study we have used factor analysis to reduce the number of variables for Preference. Earlier Preference had 14 variables, however after the factor analysis only 8 variables were retained which were categorised into "Cultural Heritage", "Infrastructure and Amenities" and "Trip Profile". Having retained these factors, the research aims to find the influence of demographic factors and Preference factors on Motivation of tourists to visit a destination.

2.1 KMO and Bartlett's Test

Table 2. KMO and Bartlett's Test

Kaiser-Meyer-Olkin Measure of Sampling Adequacy.		**.850**
Bartlett's Test of Sphericity	Approx. Chi-Square	1215.183
	df	105
	Sig.	.000

For factors of Destination Preference (D1 to D14) the KMO value is 0.850 which is close to 1, indicates that the sample is adequate for PCA, and it is acceptable. The Barlett's Test assesses the degree of connectivity between the variables observed in the data set. The computed chi-square value of 1215.183 and significance result (Sig. = .000) indicates a good correlation between the variables. These are good conditions for PCA.

2.2 Total Variance Explained

Table 3. Total variance explained

Component	Initial Eigenvalues			Rotation Sums of Squared Loadings		
	Total	% of Variance	Cumulative %	Total	% of Variance	Cumulative %
1	6.468	43.118	43.118	3.718	24.785	24.785
2	1.882	12.548	55.666	3.364	22.430	47.214
3	1.374	9.161	64.826	2.642	17.612	64.826
4	.936	6.241	71.067			
5	.828	5.517	76.584			
6	.647	4.311	80.895			
7	.544	3.629	84.523			
8	.474	3.159	87.682			
9	.388	2.590	90.272			
10	.358	2.385	92.657			
11	.325	2.164	94.821			
12	.229	1.529	96.350			
13	.204	1.363	97.712			
14	.154	1.028	100.000			

Extraction Method: Principal Component Analysis.

Eigen values and variance explained are presented in the above table as a result of applying Principal Component Analysis (PCA) for extraction. Rotation Sums of Squared Loadings shows you only those factors that met the cut-off criterion (extraction method). In this case, there were three factors with eigenvalues greater than 1. The data set initially consisted of 14 components. Upon extraction it is now segmented into three distinct linear components. These three factors collectively explain 64.826% of variance. Consequently, these three factors can explain 64.826% of the common variance shared amongst the 14 variables (Indapurkar, 2017).

2.3 Factor Loading - Rotated Component Matrix

A statistical technique called factor analysis finds common patterns among variables in a dataset, thereby reducing the number of variables in it. Another name for it is "dimension reduction". The process determines the unseen variables that lead to these fluctuations by first using the observable variables as linear combinations of components plus "error" terms.

Table 4. Rotated Component Matrix

	Component		
	1	**2**	**3**
D1 (Historical and cultural significance)			.870
D2 (Unique traditions and Practices)			.867
D3 (Ease of travel and accessibility)	.586		
D4 (Quality of transportation infrastructure)	.735		
D5 (Importance of feeling safe and secure)	.642		
D6 (Unique and authentic cultural immersion)			.667
D7 (Variety of adventure activities)			
D8 (Quality and variety of accommodation)	.747		
D9 {desired facilities and services (e.g., restaurants, shops)}	.702		
D10 (climate and weather)	.558	.608	
D11 (Recommendations and reviews)		.705	
D12 (Affordability of travel and accommodation)	.614	.610	
D13 (Value for money)		.700	
D14 (Language)		.832	

Extraction Method: Principal Component Analysis.

The Rotated Component Matrix shows the correlation between the variables and the principal components as a result of which variables under each component can be grouped into one variable head. Based on these results D1 & D2 are grouped into "Cultural Heritage", D4, D8 & D9 into "Infrastructure and Amenities" and D11, D13, & D14 into "Trip Profile". Other variables were excluded as their factor loading values were less than 0.7.

Table 5. New category of variables

Factors		
Demographic Factors	**Age**	
	Gender	
Monthly individual income	Monthly individual income from all sources	

continued on following page

Table 5. Continued

Factors		
Demographic Factors	**Age**	
	Gender	
Preference Factors	Quality of transportation infrastructure	Infrastructure and Amenities (P1)
	Quality and variety of accommodation	
	Desired facilities and services (e.g., restaurants, shops)	
	Recommendations and reviews	Trip Profile (P2)
	Value for money	
	Language	
	Historical and cultural significance	Cultural Heritage (P3)
	Unique traditions and Practices	

The above table presents the new variable categories after the Factor Analysis.

3. Regression

Equation: $M = \beta0 + \beta1 \cdot P1 + \beta2 \cdot P2 + \beta3 \cdot P3 + \beta4 \cdot Age + \beta5 \cdot Gender + \beta6 \cdot Monthly\ Income + \epsilon$

Independent Variables: $P1$, $P2$, $P3$, Age, Gender, and Monthly Income.

Dependent Variable: Motivation (M)

Table 6. Regression: Model summary

Model	R	R Square	Adjusted R Square	Std. Error of the Estimate	R Square Change	F Change			Sig. F Change	
						Change Statistics				
1		.380	.353	.47395	.380	13.887	6		.000	2.203

The multiple correlation coefficient, also known as the coefficient of multiple determination, illustrates the relationship between the observed and anticipated values of the explanatory variable. The R in this case is 0.616, indicating a moderate direct positive relationship between the explained variable (motivation) and the explanatory variable (Demographics and Preference). From the above analysis results we can see that the coefficient of variable, R Square value is 0.380 which implies that the independent variables explains 38% variance in the dependent variable that is Motivation. The independent variables – age, gender, monthly individual income, P1, P2 and P3, have statistically significant effects on dependent variable Motivation (M) as suggested by P-vale < 0.05. The 0.353 value of adjusted R square suggests that the model explains a moderate proportion of variation in dependent variable Motivation. The standard error of estimates is 0.47395, which indicates that the model's predictions are closer to the actual values of Motivation. To examine this model's overall importance, the F statistic is employed. Durbin Watson examines the regression model for mistakes or residual autocorrelation (Maxwell & David, 1995). When the value approaches 2, the autocorrelation becomes negligible. Given this situation's Durbin-Watson rating of 2.203, positive autocorrelation may occur.

Table 7. Regression: ANOVA

Model		Sum of Squares	df	Mean Square	F	Sig.
1	Regression	18.717	6	3.119	13.887	.000[a]
	Residual	30.550	136	.225		
	Total	49.267	142			

From Table 8. The F- Value of 13.887 (P < 0.05) indicates the statistical significance of ANOVA results for the proposed regression model. This implies that Demographic variables, monthly income and Preference variables have a significant relationship with dependent variable motivation. The F calculated value 13.887 is greater than the approximate F critical value 2.166, which also indicates that result is statistically significant. The significance level of 0.000 is less than 0.05 which means the independent variables Demographics, Monthly income and Preference have a significant effect on dependent variable motivation. The residual sum of squares value is 30.550 which represents the error term of the sample. The regression model's significance is further strengthened by ANOVA results.

Table 8. Regression: Coefficients

Model	Unstandardized Coefficients		Standardized Coefficients	t	Sig.	Correlations			Collinearity Statistics	
	B	Std. Error	Beta				Partial		Tolerance	VIF
(Constant)	1.019	.197		5.162						
Age	-.030	.053	-.045	-.563		-.001	-.048		.711	1.406
Gender	.156	.079	.140	1.989		.239	.168	.134	.920	1.087
Monthly individual income from all sources	-.004	.038	-.009	-.107		-.040	-.009		.722	1.386
P1	.099	.082	.105	1.207		.338	.103	.081	.601	1.665
P2	.021	.061	.027	.339		.253	.029	.023	.703	1.422
P3	.320	.048	.515	6.668		.590	.496	.450	.765	1.308

From Table 9 we get the values of β's. When all the independent variables are 0 the estimated motivation score is obtained by the intercept, or constant β0. The intercept is relevant in the model with a significant t-value and a low p- value. P1 and P2 have a positive but not statistically significant relationship with motivation.

Thus, P1 and P2 do not have an impact on motivation, therefore we reject H2-2 and H2-3. With p value 0.000 (less than 0.05), P3 has a positive and statistically significant relationship with motivation. This implies that if there is a 1% increase in P3, motivation tends to increase by 0.320 units. Thus, P3 has an impact on motivation, therefore we accept H2-1. Gender has an impact on motivation; therefore, we accept H1-1. Gender has a positive and significant relationship with motivation and males have a higher average value indicating that they are much more motivated than women to travel. The reason for this might be the safety and security concerns of a destination due to which women are reluctant to travel. Age does not significantly affect the motivation of a person to travel. Monthly individual income has a negative, but non-significant relationship with motivation. Thus, we reject H1-2 and H1-3.

RESULTS DISCUSSION

This study examined the relationship between demographic factors (age and gender), monthly income and preference factors (historical and cultural significance, unique traditions, lodging, transit, recommendations, value, travel style, and language etc.) in terms of the motivation of passengers to travel. Significant and non-significant effects are shown in the findings, providing important details regarding these interactions. The data analysis's conclusions highlight a number of important facts about the factors being studied and how they affect travelers' desire to visit a certain location. To begin with, the reliability test using Cronbach's Alpha indicates that the destination preference variables show a strong degree of consistency; a Cronbach's Alpha value of 0.850 indicates excellent reliability. This suggests that the variables measure destination choice internally and effectively. Second, preference variables were reduced from 15 to 9 using the exploratory factor analysis (EFA), and these 9 components were divided into three categories: "Cultural Heritage," "Infrastructure and Amenities," and "Trip Profile." The sample size is good enough for principal component analysis (PCA), as indicated by the significant Bartlett's Test and the KMO value of 0.850. Furthermore, the three extracted components explain 64.826% of the variation when taken as a whole, offering important new information about the fundamental aspects of traveler preferences. The factor loading findings, which classify variables under each component according to their correlation, provide more insight into the link between variables and main components. In order to guarantee robustness, variables with factor loading values less than 0.7 were not included in the study.

The study's findings indicated that there was a somewhat positive correlation between the independent factors (demographics, monthly income, and preferences) and the dependent variable (motivation). The R-squared value of 0.380 indicates that 38% of the variance in tourist motivation is explained by the factors that were chosen. This indicates a somewhat robust model, implying that variables other than those evaluated also influence tourists' motivation. The adjusted R-squared value (0.353), which accounts for the number of independent variables, supports this conclusion even more. Furthermore, the significance of the entire model is validated by the statistically significant F-value (13.887, $p < 0.05$). The analysis revealed a considerable positive link between age and motivation. This suggests that older tourists could be motivated differently than younger ones. Further research may explore these age-specific discussion in more detail. Fascinatingly, motivation was not statistically significantly impacted by wealth or gender. These variables may affect travel choices, although they may have less of an effect on motivation in general. Larger or more varied sample sizes in future research may clarify any interactions or mediating effects. P3 i.e. cultural heritage and tourist motivation were shown to have a favourable and statistically significant association, according to the research. This implies that individuals who embark on journeys are more likely to be drawn to destinations they perceive as having greater cultural importance and distinct traditional customs. Within the confines of this investigation, it was observed that there was a lack of statistically significant correlation between the motivation of travellers and the quality of infrastructure and amenities, as well as the characteristics of their travel profile.

While the literature review provides valuable insights into various factors influencing tourists' motivation and destination choices, some findings contrast with the results of the current study. According to some findings, factors, such as climate change (Rosselló-Nadal, 2014), transport options, variety of tourism industry products, image destination (overall cognitive, image, and conative image) (Afshardoost & Eshaghi, 2020), tourists' safety sense (safety concerns and information, facilities and services for the tourists, as well as environment, regional culture, and safety information) (Zou & Meng, 2020) affect the tourism motivation and demand. However, in this study we see that it is the gender and the cultural significance of the destination that has a significant effect, while the other factors are found insignificant.

This outcome could be attributed to a variety of factors, encompassing diverse possibilities. While these aspects may rank highly in the considerations of travellers during the selection of a travel location, they may not necessarily serve as the principal driving forces behind their decision to travel. Furthermore, it is plausible that these factors are subjective and subject to fluctuations based on the particular preferences of each individual. The current study focuses on the effects of demographic traits and particular destination preferences on tourists' motivation in the Indian context, narrowing the scope of earlier research that emphasized the influence of broad factors like climate change, transportation options, and overall destination image on motivation for travel. This change in emphasis enables a more thorough examination of elements that could be especially important or distinctive to Indian tourists. Furthermore, cultural influences have a big influence on travel selections since the current study indicated that motivation is significantly impacted by cultural heritage and destination importance. These results imply that, although more general factors like destination perception and climate change still matter, Indian tourists' willingness to visit particular places may be more strongly influenced by their cultural background and personal preferences.

CONCLUSION

Tourism holds the potential to contribute to all the 17 SDGs (Trupp & Dolezal, 2020; UNWTO & UNDP, 2017). Tourism has direct and strong links with SDGs 8, 12 and 17, on 'Decent Work and Economic Growth', 'Responsible Consumption and Production', and 'Partnerships for the Goals', respectively. Though tourism has a direct citation in the above three SDGs, it also is a significant driver for accomplishing the remaining 14 SDGs as well (International Institute of Sustainable Development, 2015; UNWTO & UNDP, 2017). India's economy has benefited greatly from religious tourism, which makes money via a variety of channels including transportation, lodging, religious item and souvenir sales, and admission fees to sacred sites. Religious tourism brings individuals from different backgrounds together, which fosters inclusion and social cohesion. Religious places are frequently found in regions like woods, mountains, and riverbanks that are delicate to the environment. In order to maintain these places' biodiversity and natural beauty, sustainable management is essential. India's wellness travel destinations frequently place a high priority on sustainability and environmental protection by putting policies in place that limit carbon emissions, use renewable energy sources, and protect natural ecosystems. In India, wellness tourism encourages partnerships and cooperation between many stakeholders, such as governmental organizations, commercial businesses, and local communities.

Travelers who are in search of cultural encounters tend to gravitate towards destinations that not only contribute positively to the local economy but also make efforts to safeguard and promote the indigenous culture while ensuring that fair wages are paid to all involved parties. By actively endorsing regional products and lending support to small-scale enterprises, these travellers play a crucial role in fostering economic stability within the region, aligning with the Sustainable Development Goal 8 which focuses on promoting decent work and sustainable economic growth. This emphasis on ethical tourism practices not only benefits the local communities and businesses but also enhances the overall travel experience for those seeking a deeper connection with the destinations they visit (Haid, 2024).

Moreover, travellers who seek authentic cultural experiences highly appreciate their interactions with indigenous communities, promoting social integration and fostering mutual understanding between different cultures (SDG 10: Reduced Inequalities) (Patching-Bunch, 2015). In order to promote social cohesion and empowerment, tourists who are driven by volunteerism and community engagement take part in sustainable tourism initiatives like beach clean-ups, wildlife conservation projects, or community development programs (SDG 1: No Poverty, SDG 2: Zero Hunger, SDG 4: Quality Education) (Speer PW, 2001); (S. Nima Orazani, 2023). These findings demonstrate that tourism can help achieve sustainability and sustainable development goals.

Tourism assumes a critical and central role in addressing and making contributions towards multiple Sustainable Development Goals (SDGs). By creating job opportunities across various sectors such as guiding, handicrafts, and local businesses, tourism significantly assists in the achievement of Goal 1: No Poverty, specifically by generating income for individuals located at the base of the economic pyramid (BoP). Moreover, the introduction of programs like homestay initiatives not only offers supplementary income sources for rural households but also plays a vital role in supporting efforts to alleviate poverty. Additionally, the introduction of educational schemes focusing on hospitality and cultural awareness serves to empower individuals belonging to marginalized communities, thereby improving their chances of securing employment and ultimately making a positive impact on Goal 8: Decent Work and Economic Growth. The emphasis placed on ensuring the involvement of local residents in the development of tourism projects is crucial as it guarantees that the advantages stemming from such programs are distributed fairly, directly addressing Goal 10: Reduced Inequalities. Furthermore, the enhancement of tourism-related infrastructure, encompassing improvements in waste management and sanitation, not only enriches the overall visitor experience but also contributes to raising living standards in rural areas, aligning with the principles delineated in Goal 11: Sustainable Cities and Communities. Finally, the advocacy for responsible consumption and production behaviours through the establishment of ecotourism initiatives plays a substantial role in contributing to Goal 12, as it advocates for sustainable management of resources that benefits both tourists and local communities alike. Through its rich cultural heritage and commitment to holistic wellness, India emerges as a beacon of sustainable tourism, offering transformative experiences that resonate with both the individual soul and the collective mission for a better world.

IMPLICATIONS

The study's insights may be used by tourism authorities and destination managers to create sustainable tourism experiences that address tourists' objectives, especially with regard to gender-specific preferences and cultural importance. Destinations may build sustainable development results and draw tourists by providing genuine and culturally immersing experiences. The findings are considered valuable for marketers, tourism city managers, tourism planning organisations etc, as they are for researchers and academics, by providing insight on how to motivate and entice tourists to visit a destination. Strategies can be build using the push and pull factors identified in the study. To achieve Sustainable Development effectively, it is essential to make informed decisions utilizing the findings of this study, especially relating to the formulation of sustainable tourism policies at the local, regional, and national levels. These policies play a pivotal role in promoting sustainable development in rural areas and fostering local economic prosperity through job creation. Economic progress directly contributes to achieving sustainable social development, which stands as a fundamental element in eradicating poverty and reducing inequalities in rural communities. This study underscores the interconnectedness between economic growth, social well-being, and environmental sustainability, emphasizing the symbiotic relationship between these factors for holistic and enduring rural development. By incorporating these insights into policymaking and strategic planning, stakeholders can pave the way for a more sustainable and equitable future for rural populations.

LIMITATIONS AND FUTURE RESEARCH DIRECTIONS

The study's sample size could not adequately reflect the wide range of visitors visiting India who engage in wellness and religious tourism activities. Larger and more representative sample sizes may be used in future studies to gain a deeper comprehension of the reasons behind visitors' actions. The study has restricted itself to specific variables because of which the study cannot be generalised. Future studies can also include more variables such as tourists' motivation for sustainable travel, .Research comparing the motives and actions of travellers at various Indian religious and wellness tourism locations might provide insight into the elements influencing the growth of sustainable tourism in certain areas. Cross-country comparisons can also be undertaken in further studies.

REFERENCES

Alexis-Thomas, C. (2020). An examination of issues related to tourism and health and well-being as a sustainable development goal by tourism providers in Tobago. *Worldwide Hospitality and Tourism Themes*, 12(3), 293–303. 10.1108/WHATT-02-2020-0006

Álvarez, F. S. (2010). Tourism Destination Image and Motivations: The Spanish Perspective of Mexico. *Journal of Travel & Tourism Marketing*, 27(4), 349–360. 10.1080/10548408.2010.481567

Aqmal, N., & Setiawan, A. B. (2022). Analysis of Factors Affecting the Decision to Visit Tourists to Religious Tourism. *Indonesian Journal of Development Economics*, 5(3), 319–331. 10.15294/efficient.v5i3.54045

Ashley, C. G. H. (2000). *Pro-poor tourism: Putting poverty at the heart of the tourism agenda*. Overseas Development Institute.

Ashley, J. M. (2009). Tourism and Poverty Reduction: Pathways to Prosperity. *Tourism and Poverty Reduction: Pathways to Prosperity*, 1-157. Taylor and Francis. 10.4324/9781849774635

Azam, M. A. M., Mahmudul Alam, M., & Haroon Hafeez, M. (2018). Effect of tourism on environmental pollution: Further evidence from Malaysia, Singapore and Thailand. *Journal of Cleaner Production*, 190, 330–338. 10.1016/j.jclepro.2018.04.168

Budovich, L. (2023). The impact of religious tourism on the economy and tourism industry. *Hervormde Teologiese Studies*, 79(1). 10.4102/hts.v79i1.8607

César Muñoz, A. Á. (2023). Modelling the effect of weather on tourism: Does it vary across seasons? *Tourism Geographies*, 25(1), 265–286. 10.1080/14616688.2020.1868019

Chauhan, V. (2007). *Safety and security perceptions of tourists visiting Kashmir*. Advances in Hospitality and Leisure. 10.1016/S1745-3542(06)03001-3

Collins, D., & Tisdell, C. (2002). Gender and differences in travel life cycles. *Journal of Travel Research*, 41(2), 133–143. 10.1177/004728702237413

Correia, A., & Pimpão, A. (2004). 10). Decision-making processes of Portuguese tourist travelling to South America and Africa. *International Journal of Culture, Tourism and Hospitality Research*, 2(4), 330–373. 10.1108/17506180810908989

Crandall, R. (1980). Motivations for Leisure. *Journal of Leisure Research*, 12(1), 45–54. 10.1080/00222216.1980.11969418

Cronbach, L. (1951). Coefficient alpha and the internal structure of tests. *Psychometrika*, 16(3), 297–334. 10.1007/BF02310555

Crotts, R. B. (2003). The effect of uncertainty avoidance on information search, planning, and purchases of international travel vacations. *Tourism Management*, 24(2), 191–202. 10.1016/S0261-5177(02)00057-2

Daniela Matušíková, K. Š. (2021). The Impact of the COVID-19 Pandemic on Holiday Preferences at the Example of Z Generation Within the Youth Tourism. In A. D. Mahmut Demir, *Handbook of Research on the Impacts and Implications of COVID-19 on the Tourism Industry.*10.4018/978-1-7998-8231-2

Dann, G. (1977). Anomie, ego-enhancement and tourism. *Annals of Tourism Research*, 4(4), 184–194. 10.1016/0160-7383(77)90037-8

Dann, G. M. (1977). Anomie, ego-enhancement and tourism. *Annals of Tourism Research*, 4(4), 184–194. 10.1016/0160-7383(77)90037-8

Dolezal, C. T. &. (2020). Tourism and the Sustainable Development Goals in Southeast Asia. *Advances in Southeast Asian Studies.*, *13*. https://doi.org/ doi:10.14764/10.ASEAS-0026

Durbarry, R. (2002). The economic contribution of tourism in Mauritius. *Annals of Tourism Research*, 29(3), 862–865. 10.1016/S0160-7383(02)00008-7

Ejarque, J. (2017). *Marketing and Management of Tourist Destinations: New Models and Strategies 2.0.*

Eshaghi, M. A. (2020). Destination image and tourist behavioural intentions: A meta-analysis. *Tourism Management*, 81, 104154. 10.1016/j.tourman.2020.104154

Éva Csirmaz, K. P. (2015). International Trends in Recreational and Wellness Tourism. *Procedia Economics and Finance*, 32, 755–762. 10.1016/S2212-5671(15)01458-6

Filmi, B. a. (2022). Psychological Factors of Religion Traveler and Decision to Visit. *Jurnal Ilmiah Syi'ar*, 103-113.

Gambhir, D. K. (2021). Religious Tourism and Sustainable Development: Perspectives from Hill States in India. In *Handbook of Sustainable Development and Leisure Services* (pp. 273-287). Springer. 10.1007/978-3-030-59820-4_18

Gan, T. Z., Zheng, J., Li, W., Li, J., & Shen, J. (2023). Health and Wellness Tourists' Motivation and Behavior Intention: The Role of Perceived Value. *International Journal of Environmental Research and Public Health*, 20(5), 4339. 10.3390/ ijerph2005433936901356

George, R. (2003). Tourist's perceptions of safety and security while visiting Cape Town. *Tourism Management*, 24(5), 575–585. https://www.sciencedirect.com/science/article/pii/S0261517703000037. 10.1016/S0261-5177(03)00003-7

Goh, C. (2012). Exploring impact of climate on tourism demand. *Annals of Tourism Research*, 39(4), 1859–1883. 10.1016/j.annals.2012.05.027

Gordan, M.-I., Pe , E., Popescu, G., Brad, I., Milin, A. I., Adamov, T. C., Ciolac, R., Pascariu, A. R., & Iancu, T. (2023). Factors Influencing the Accommodation Prices of Romanian Rural Tourism. *Sustainability (Basel)*, 15(1), 191. 10.3390/su15010191

Haid, M., Albrecht, J. N., Tangl, P., & Plaikner, A. (2024). Regional Products and Sustainability. *Sustainability (Basel)*, 16(2), 628. 10.3390/su16020628

Han, H. (2021). Consumer behavior and environmental sustainability in tourism and hospitality: A review of theories, concepts, and latest research. *Journal of Sustainable Tourism*, 29(7), 1021–1042. 10.1080/09669582.2021.1903019

Harman, H. H. (1976). *Modern Factor Analysis*. University of Chicago Press.

Harsanti, K. F. (2013). The Influence of Marketing Mix, Psychology. *Diponegoro Journal of Social and Politic*, 1-9.

Hassan, A. K. J., Kennell, J., & Chaperon, S. (2020). Rhetoric and reality in Bangladesh: Elite stakeholder perceptions of the implementation of tourism policy. *Tourism Recreation Research*, 45(3), 307–322. 10.1080/02508281.2019.1703286

Heung, V. C., Qu, H., & Chu, R. (2001). The relationship between vacation factors and socio-demographic and travelling characteristics: The case of Japanese leisure travellers. *Tourism Management*, 22(3), 259–269. 10.1016/S0261-5177(00)00057-1

Horner, S. a. (2020). *Consumer Behaviour in Tourism* (4th ed.). Routledge. 10.4324/9781003046721

Indapurkar, K. (2017). Financial Literacy Among Educated Urban Youth: Issues and Challenges. *International Journal of Economic Research*.

Jamalpour, H. a.-D. (2022). Cultural memory and neuro-critical reading of Ian McEwan's atonement. *Revista de Investigaciones Universidad del Quindío*, 436-442. 10.33975/riuq.vol34nS2.1142

Jay, L., & Michaels, J. P.-Z. (2021). Individual Differences in Religious Motivation Influence How People Think. *Journal for the Scientific Study of Religion*, 60(1), 64–82. 10.1111/jssr.12696

Kanagaraj, C. a. (2013). An Analysis of push and pull travel motivations of domestic tourists to Kerala. *International Journal of Management and Business Studies*, 3, 112–118.

Kim, H. J., Chen, M.-H., & Jang, S. C. S. (2006). Tourism expansion and economic development: The case of Taiwan. *Tourism Management*, 27(5), 925–933. 10.1016/j. tourman.2005.05.01132287716

Koncul, N. (2012). Wellness: A New Mode of tourism. *Economic Research-Ekonomska Istraživanja*, 525-534. 10.1080/1331677X.2012.11517521

Kozak, M. (2002). Comparative analysis of tourist motivations by nationality and destinations. *Tourism Management*, 23(3), 221–232. 10.1016/S0261-5177(01)00090-5

Kuoyan, W. (2022). Sustainable Tourism Development Based upon Visitors' Brand Trust: A Case of "100 Religious Attractions". *Sustainability (Basel)*, 14(4), 1977. 10.3390/su14041977

Line, N. H., Hanks, L., & Miao, L. (2018). Image matters: Incentivizing green tourism behaviour. *Journal of Travel Research*, 57(3), 296–309. 10.1177/0047287517697848

López-Sanz, J. M., Penelas-Leguía, A., Gutiérrez-Rodríguez, P., & Cuesta-Valiño, P. (2021, July 23). P.-L. A.-R.-V. (2021). Rural Tourism and the Sustainable Development Goals. A Study of the Variables That Most Influence the Behavior of the Tourist. *Frontiers in Psychology*, 12, 722973. 10.3389/fpsyg.2021.72297334367040

Lozares, C. (1991). El análisis de componentes principales. *Papers Rev. Sociol.*, 37, 31–63. 10.5565/rev/papers/v37n0.1595

Lubbe, B. A. (2003). *Tourism Management in Southern Africa*. Pearson Education South Africa.

M., A. A., Ocaña, F. A., & and Valderrama, M. J. (1996). Análisis de componentes principales de un proceso estocástico con funciones muestrales escalonadas. *QÜESTIIÓ*, 7 - 28.

Mandych I.A., B. A. (2022). Features of assessing the investment attractiveness of high-tech projects. *Russian Technological Journal.*, 75-86. 10.32362/2500-316 X-2022-10-2-75-86

Marzo-Navarro, M. (2017). Development of integrated rural tourism from the perspective of residents: Proposed model. *Journal of Tourism and Cultural Heritage. Pasos (El Sauzal)*, 15, 841–859. 10.25145/j.pasos.2017.15.057

Matei, F. D. (2015). Cultural Tourism Potential, as Part of Rural Tourism Development in the North-East of Romania. *Procedia Economics and Finance*, 453–460. 10.1016/S2212-5671(15)00584-5

Maxwell, L. K., & David, C. H. (1995). The application of the durbin-watson test to the dynamic regression model under normal and non-normal errors. *Econometric Reviews*, 14(4), 487–510. 10.1080/07474939508800333

Mbaiwa, J. (2005). The problems and prospects of sustainable tourism development in the Okavango Delta, Botswana. *Journal of Sustainable Tourism*, 13, 203–227. 10.1080/01434630508668554

Meng, Y. Z. (2020). Chinese tourists' sense of safety: Perceptions of expected and experienced destination safety. *Current Issues in Tourism*, 23(15), 1886–1899. 10.1080/13683500.2019.1681382

Michael, N. W., Wien, C., & Reisinger, Y. (2017). Push and pull escape travel motivations of Emirati nationals to Australia. *International Journal of Culture, Tourism and Hospitality Research*, 11(3), 274–296. 10.1108/IJCTHR-04-2016-0039

Mimi Li, L. A. (2010). A Missing Link in Understanding Revisit Intention—The Role of Motivation and Image. *Journal of Travel & Tourism Marketing*, 27(4), 335–348. 10.1080/10548408.2010.481559

Mróz, F. (2021). The impact of COVID-19 on pilgrimages and religious tourism in Europe during the first six months of pandemic. *Journal of Religion and Health*, 60(2), 625–645. 10.1007/s10943-021-01201-033611686

Nima, S., & Orazani, K. J. (2023). What works and why in interventions to strengthen social cohesion: A systematic review. *Journal of Applied Social Psychology*, 53(10), 938–995. 10.1111/jasp.12990

Ottenbacher, M. C., Schwebler, S., Metzler, D., & Harrington, R. J. (2015). Sustainability Criteria for Tourism Attractions: A Case Study of Germany. [IJSESD]. *International Journal of Social Ecology and Sustainable Development*, 6(2), 20–39. 10.4018/ijsesd.2015040102

P, H. B. (1995). Tourism and growth in a dynamic model of trade. *The Journal of International Trade and Economic Development*, 4, 243-252. 10.1080/09638199500000019

Paniccia, P. M., Leoni, L., & Baiocco, S. (2017). Interpreting Sustainability through Co-Evolution: Evidence from Religious Accommodations in Rome. *Sustainability (Basel)*, 9(12), 2301. https://www.mdpi.com/2071-1050/9/12/2301. 10.3390/su9122301

Patching-Bunch, J. (2015). Learning Intercultural Competency through International Immersion Travel. *University Honors Theses.*, 305. Advance online publication. 10.15760/honors.274

Patwardhan, V. R., Ribeiro, M. A., Woosnam, K. M., Payini, V., & Mallya, J. (2020). Visitors' loyalty to religious tourism destinations: Considering place attachment, emotional experience and religious affiliation. *Tourism Management Perspectives*, 36, 100737. 10.1016/j.tmp.2020.100737

Pearce, P., & Morrison, A. a. (1998). *Tourism: Bridges across continents.* McGraw-Hill.

Philip Kotler, K. L. (2008). *Marketing Management.* Pearson Education.

Pourtaheri, M. R., Rahmani, K., & Ahmadi, H. (2012). Impacts of religious and pilgrimage tourism in rural areas: The case of Iran. *Journal of Geography and Geology*, 4(3), 122. 10.5539/jgg.v4n3p122

Rad, M. S. (2017). Psychological capital and academic burnout in students of clinical majors in Iran. *Acta Facultatis Medicae Naissensisthis*, 311-319. 10.1515/afmnai-2017-0035

Reisinger, Y., & Mavondo, F. (2005). Travel anxiety and intentions to travel internationally: Implications of travel risk perception. *Journal of Travel Research*, 43(3), 212–225. 10.1177/0047287504272017

Rosselló-Nadal, J. (2014). How to evaluate the effects of climate change on tourism. *Tourism Management*, 42, 334–340. 10.1016/j.tourman.2013.11.006

Royanty, I. S. (2017). Visiting the Museum (Survey of East Java Stone Transport Museum Tourists). *Journal of Business Administration*, 84-92.

Saayman, M. R. R., Rossouw, R., & Krugell, W. (2012). The impact of tourism on poverty in South Africa. *Development Southern Africa*, 10(3), 231–254. 10.1080/0376835X.2012.706041

Sangpikul, A. (2008). A factor-cluster analysis of tourist motivations: A case of U.S. senior travellers. *Tourism (Zagreb)*, 56, 23–40.

Santos, V. R., Ramos, P., Sousa, B., Almeida, N., & Valeri, M. (2022). Factors influencing touristic consumer behaviour. *Journal of Organizational Change Management*, 35(3), 409–429. 10.1108/JOCM-02-2021-0032

Scheyvens, R. (2007). Exploring the tourism-poverty nexus. *Current Issues in Tourism*, 10(2-3), 231–254. 10.2167/cit318.0

Smith, V. L. (1992). Hosts and Guests Revisited. *The American Behavioral Scientist*, 36(2), 187–199. 10.1177/0002764292036002006

Speer, P. W., Jackson, C. B., & Peterson, N. A. (2001). The Relationship between Social Cohesion and Empowerment: Support and New Implications for Theory. *Health Education & Behavior*, 28(6), 716–732. 10.1177/109019810102800605 11720274

Šťastná, M., Vaishar, A., Brychta, J., Tuzová, K., Zloch, J., & Stodolová, V. (2020). Cultural Tourism as a Driver of Rural Development. Case Study: Southern Moravia. *Sustainability (Basel)*, 12(21), 9064. https://www.mdpi.com/2071-1050/12/21/9064. 10.3390/su12219064

Sugiyarto, G. B. A., Blake, A., & Sinclair, M. T. (2003). Tourism and globalization: Economic impact in Indonesia. *Annals of Tourism Research*, 30(3), 683–701. 10.1016/S0160-7383(03)00048-3

Suraj Kumar Mallick, S. R. (2020). Sustainable ecotourism development using SWOT and QSPM approach: A study on Rameswaram, Tamil Nadu. *International Journal of Geoheritage and Parks*, 8(3), 185–193. Advance online publication. 10.1016/j.ijgeop.2020.06.001

Tasci, A. D., & Gartner, W. C. (2007). Destination Image and Its Functional Relationships. *Journal of Travel Research*, 45(4), 413–425. 10.1177/0047287507299569

Ulker-Demirel, E., & Ciftci, G. (2020). A systematic literature review of the theory of planned behavior in tourism, leisure and hospitality management research. *Journal of Hospitality and Tourism Management*, 43, 209–219. 10.1016/j.jhtm.2020.04.003

United Nations Development Programme. (2017). *Tourism and the Sustainable Development Goals – Journey to 2030*. UN. https://www.e-unwto.org/doi/pdf/10.18111/9789284419401

United Nations World Tourism Organization (UNWTO). (2021). *Tourism and the Sustainable Development Goals – Journey to 2030*. UNWTO. https://www.e-unwto.org/doi/epdf/10.18111/9789284419401

UNWTO Highlights Tourism's Role for SDGs. (2015). International Institute of Sustainable Development. http://sdg.iisd.org/news/unwto-highlights-tourisms-role-for-sdgs/

Uysal, M. J. (1993). An Empirical Testing of the Push and Pull factors of Tourist Motivations. *CHRIE Conference*, (pp. 162-63). Research Gate.

Vanegas, M. G. W.Sr, Gartner, W., & Senauer, B. (2015). Tourism and poverty reduction: An economic sector analysis for Costa Rica and Nicaragua. *Tourism Economics*, 21(1), 159–182. 10.5367/te.2014.0442

Vanegas, R. C. (2008). Cointegration and causality between tourism and poverty reduction. *Journal of Travel Research*, 47(1), 94–103. 10.1177/0047287507312429

Wijaya, S. W., Wahyudi, W., Kusuma, C. B., & Sugianto, E. (2018). Travel motivation of Indonesian seniors in choosing destination overseas. *International Journal of Culture, Tourism and Hospitality Research*, 12(2), 185–197. 10.1108/IJCTHR-09-2017-0095

Wong, I. A., Law, R., & Zhao, X. R. (2018). Time-Variant Pleasure Travel Motivations and Behaviors. *Journal of Travel Research*, 57(4), 437–452. 10.1177/0047287517705226

Xie, C. Z., Zhang, J., & Morrison, A. M. (2021). Developing a Scale to Measure Tourist Perceived Safety. *Journal of Travel Research*, 60(6), 1232–1251. 10.1177/0047287520946103

Yoon, Y. U., & Uysal, M. (2005). An examination of the effects of motivation and satisfaction on destination loyalty: A structural model. *Tourism Management*, 26(1), 45–56. 10.1016/j.tourman.2003.08.016

Zhou, Z. (2020). Religious Tourism in Zimbabwe: A Stakeholders` Perspective. In M. W. Emilia Alaverdov, *Global Development of Religious Tourism.* 10.4018/978-1-7998-5792-1

Compilation of References

. Mtapuri, O., & Giampiccoli, A. (2013). Interrogating the role of the state and nonstate actors in community-based tourism ventures: Toward a model for spreading the benefits to the wider community. *South African Geographical Journal= Suid-Afrikaanse Geografiese Tydskrif, 95*(1), 1-15.

Acker, J. (1998). The future of "gender and organizations": Connections and boundaries. *Gender, Work and Organization*, 5(4), 195–206. 10.1111/1468-0432.00057

Adams, G. A., King, L. A., & King, D. W. (1996). Relationships of job and family involvement, family social support, and work–family conflict with job and life satisfaction. *The Journal of Applied Psychology*, 81(4), 411. 10.1037/0021-9010.81.4.411

Adie, B. A., Amore, A., & Hall, M. C. (2020). Just Because It Seems Impossible, Doesn't Mean We Shouldn't At Least Try: The Need for Longitudinal Perspectives on Tourism Partnerships and the SDGs. *Journal of Sustainable Tourism*, 30(10), 2282–2297. 10.1080/09669582.2020.1860071

Aghazamani, Y., Kerstetter, D., & Pete Allison, P. (2020). Women's perceptions of empowerment in Ramsar, a tourism destination in northern Iran. *Women's Studies International Forum*, 79, 1–10. 10.1016/j.wsif.2020.102340

Ahamad, T., & Narayana, A. (2020). Eradicating Poverty & Approach to Sustainable Development with Special Emphasis to Millennium Development Goal-1: An Indian Perspective. *International Journal of Scientific & Technology Research*, 9(1), 51–57.

Ahmed, F., Azam, M., & Bose, T. K. (2010). Factors affecting the selection of tour destination in Bangladesh: An empirical analysis. *International Journal of Business and Management*, 5(3), 52.

Airey, D. (2020). Education for tourism: A perspective article. *Tourism Review*, 75(1), 260–262. 10.1108/TR-02-2019-0074

Airways office. (2019). *Top 10 Travel Agency in Bangladesh*. Airways Office. https://airwaysoffice. com/top-10-travel-agency-in-bangladesh/

Akhy, A. A., & Roy, M. (2020). Socio-economic impacts of accommodation on tourism development: Bangladesh perspective. In *Tourism marketing in Bangladesh* (pp. 51–71). Routledge. 10.4324/9781003007241-7

Akinbobola, O. I. (2016). Appraisal of Role Conflict on Quality of Work Life and Turnover Intention among Corporate Women Workforce. *European Journal of Humanities and Social Sciences*, 35(1).

Akinwale, Y. O. (2021). Energy consumption, trade openness and economic growth: Empirical evidence from Nigeria. *International Journal of Energy Economics and Policy*, 11(6), 373–380. 10.32479/ijeep.11617

Alarcón, D. M., & Cole, S. (2019). No sustainability for tourism without gender equality. *Journal of Sustainable Tourism*, 27(7), 903–919. 10.1080/09669582.2019.1588283

Alauddin, M., Shah, M. F., & Ullah, H. (2014). Tourism in Bangladesh: A prospects analysis. *Information and Knowledge Management*, 4(5), 67–73.

Alexis-Thomas, C. (2020). An examination of issues related to tourism and health and well-being as a sustainable development goal by tourism providers in Tobago. *Worldwide Hospitality and Tourism Themes*, 12(3), 293–303. 10.1108/WHATT-02-2020-0006

Alkire, S., & Deneulin, S. (2009). The human development and capability approach. In *An introduction to the human development and capability approach* (pp. 22–48). Routledge.

Allwood, G. (2018). Agenda setting, agenda blocking and policy silence: Why is there no EU policy on prostitution? *Women's Studies International Forum*, 69, 126–134. 10.1016/j.wsif.2018.06.004

Álvarez, F. S. (2010). Tourism Destination Image and Motivations: The Spanish Perspective of Mexico. *Journal of Travel & Tourism Marketing*, 27(4), 349–360. 10.1080/10548408.2010.481567

Al-Yousif, Y. K. (2008). Education expenditure and economic growth: Some empirical evidence from the GCC countries. *Journal of Developing Areas*, 42(1), 69–80. https://www.jstor.org/stable/40376194. 10.1353/jda.0.0025

Amin, M., & Islam, A. (2014). Are There More Female Managers in the Retail Sector? Evidence from Survey Data in Developing Countries. *Journal of Applied Econometrics*, 17(2), 213–228.

Anand, A., & Vohra, V. (2020). Alleviating employee work-family conflict: Role of organizations. *The International Journal of Organizational Analysis*, 28(2), 313–332.

Anderson, S., & Eswaran, M. (2009). What determines female autonomy? Evidence from Bangladesh. *Journal of Development Economics*, 90(2), 179–191. 10.1016/j.jdeveco.2008.10.004

Aqmal, N., & Setiawan, A. B. (2022). Analysis of Factors Affecting the Decision to Visit Tourists to Religious Tourism. *Indonesian Journal of Development Economics*, 5(3), 319–331. 10.15294/efficient.v5i3.54045

Ara, A., Hussain, M. E., & Sardar, S. (2020). An exploratory Approach to Pro-Poor Tourism and Poverty Alleviation in some Selective Tourism Destinations of Bangladesh. *Journal of Business Studies*, 13(1), 1–17.

Compilation of References

Arora, R., & Sarker, T. (2022). Financing for sustainable development goals (SDGs) in the era of COVID-19 and beyond. *European Journal of Development Research*, 35(1), 1–19. 10.1057/s41287-022-00571-936620200

Ashley, C., Roe, D., & Goodwin, H. (2001). *Pro-poor tourism strategies: Making tourism work for the poor: A review of experience* (Pro-poor Tourism Rep. No. 1). Nottingham: The Russell Press.

Ashley, J. M. (2009). Tourism and Poverty Reduction: Pathways to Prosperity. *Tourism and Poverty Reduction: Pathways to Prosperity*, 1-157. Taylor and Francis. 10.4324/9781849774635

Ashley, C. G. H. (2000). *Pro-poor tourism: Putting poverty at the heart of the tourism agenda*. Overseas Development Institute.

Ashraf, M., Ullah, L., Shuvro, M. A., & Salma, U. (2019). Transition from millennium development goals to sustainable development goals: Blueprint of Bangladesh for implementing the sustainable development goals 2030. *Medicine Today*, 31(1), 46–59. 10.3329/medtoday.v31i1.40323

Asian Development Bank. (1999). *Fighting Poverty in Asia and the Pacific: The Poverty Reduction Strategy*. ADB.

Aslam, M. S. M., Awang, K. W., & Othman, N. B. H. (2014). Issues and Challenges in Nurturing Sustainable Rural Tourism Development. *Tourism. Leisure and Global Change*, 1, 75–89.

Aytug, H. K., & Mikaeili, M. (2017). Evaluation of Hopa's Rural Tourism Potential in the Context of European Union Tourism Policy. *Procedia Environmental Sciences*, 37, 234–245. 10.1016/j.proenv.2017.03.039

Azam, M. A. M., Mahmudul Alam, M., & Haroon Hafeez, M. (2018). Effect of tourism on environmental pollution: Further evidence from Malaysia, Singapore and Thailand. *Journal of Cleaner Production*, 190, 330–338. 10.1016/j.jclepro.2018.04.168

Azam, M., & Awan, A. M. (2022). Health is wealth: A dynamic sur approach of examining a link between climate changes and human health expenditures. *Social Indicators Research*, 163(2), 505–528. 10.1007/s11205-022-02904-x

Bakas, F. E. (2017). A beautiful mess': Reciprocity and positionality in gender and tourism beautiful. *Journal of Hospitality and Tourism Management*, 33, 126–133. 10.1016/j.jhtm.2017.09.009

Bakas, F. E. (2017). Community resilience through entrepreneurship: The role of gender. *Journal of Enterprising Communities: People and Places in the Global Economy*, 11(1), 61–77. 10.1108/JEC-01-2015-0008

Balaji, B. (2011). Causal nexus between public health expenditure and economic growth in four southern Indian states. *The IUP Journal of Public Finance, IX*(3), 7–22. https://ideas.repec.org//a/icf/icfjpf/v09y2011i3p7-22.html

Ballester-Brage, L., Pozo-Gordaliza, R., & Orte-Socías, C. (2014). Delocalized Prostitution: Occultation of the New Modalities of Violence. *Procedia: Social and Behavioral Sciences*, 161, 90–95. 10.1016/j.sbspro.2014.12.015

Bangladesh Bureau of Statistics. (2023). *Household Income and Expenditure Survey, Bangladesh.* BBS. https://bbs.portal.gov.bd/sites/default/files/files/bbs.portal.gov.bd/page/57def76a_aa3c_46e3_9f80_53732eb94a83/2023-04-13-09-35-ee41d2a35dcc47a94a595c88328458f4.pdf

Bardasi, E., Sabarwal, S., & Terrell, K. (2011). How Do Female Entrepreneurs Perform? Evidence from Three Developing Regions. *Small Business Economics*, 37(4), 417–441. 10.1007/s11187-011-9374-z

Barro, R. J., & Lee, J. W. (2013). A new data set of educational attainment in the world, 1950–2010. *Journal of Development Economics*, 104, 184–198. 10.1016/j.jdeveco.2012.10.001

Baykal, E. S. (2020). Queen bee syndrome: a modern dilemma of working women and its effects on turnover intentions. *Strategic Outlook for Innovative Work Behaviours: Interdisciplinary and Multidimensional Perspectives*, 165-178.

Bedir, S. (2016). Healthcare expenditure and economic growth in developing countries. *Advances in Economics and Business*, 4(2), 76–86. 10.13189/aeb.2016.040202

Bekele, M., Sassi, M., Jemal, K., & Ahmed, B. (2024). Human capital development and economic sustainability linkage in Sub-Saharan African countries: Novel evidence from augmented mean group approach. *Heliyon*, 10(2), 1–14. 10.1016/j.heliyon.2024.e2432338293427

Bhadra, S. (2022). Exploring dimensions of sexual issues in disasters and conflicts: Need to bridge the gaps between policy and practice. *Sexologies*, 31(3), 277–290. 10.1016/j.sexol.2021.11.006

Bharati, N. K., Chancel, L., Piketty, T., & Somanchi, A. (2024). *Income and wealth Inequality in India, 1922-2023: The Rise of the Billionaire Raj.* (Working paper No. 2024/09). World Inequality Lab, Paris.

Bhargava, A., Jamison, D. T., Lau, L. J., & Murray, C. J. L. (2001). Modeling the effects of health on economic growth. *Journal of Health Economics*, 20(3), 423–440. 10.1016/S0167-6296(01)00073-X11373839

Bhat, R., & Jain, N. (2004). *Time series analysis of private health care expenditures and GDP: Co-integration results with structural breaks* [Working Paper]. https://vslir.iima.ac.in:8443/xmlui/handle/11718/1954

Birendra, K. C. (2020). Ecotourism for wildlife conservation and sustainable livelihood via community-based homestay: A formula to success or a quagmire? *Current Issues in Tourism*, 1–17. 10.1080/13683500.2020.1772206

Biswas, C., Omar, H., & Rashid-Radha, J. R. R. (2020). The Impact of Tourist Attractions and Accessibility on Tourists' satisfaction: The Moderating Role of Tourists' age. *Geo Journal of Tourism and Geosites*, 32(4), 1202–1208. 10.30892/gtg.32402-558

Biswas, S., Dandapat, B., Alam, A., & Satpati, L. (2022). India's achievement towards sustainable Development Goal 6 (Ensure availability and sustainable management of water and sanitation for all) in the 2030 Agenda. *BMC Public Health*, 22(1), 2142. 10.1186/s12889-022-14316-036414936

Bloom, D. E., Canning, D., & Sevilla, J. (2004). The effect of health on economic growth: A production function approach. *World Development*, 32(1), 1–13. 10.1016/j.worlddev.2003.07.002

Bluedorn, A. C. (1982). A unified model of turnover from organizations. *Human Relations*, 35(2), 135–153. 10.1177/001872678203500204

Boels, D. (2015). The Challenges of Belgian Prostitution Markets as Legal Informal Economies: An Empirical Look Behind the Scenes at the Oldest Profession in the World. *European Journal on Criminal Policy and Research*, 21(4), 485–507. 10.1007/s10610-014-9260-8

Boels, D., & Verhage, A. (2016). Prostitution in the neighbourhood: Impact on residents and implications for municipal regulation. *International Journal of Law, Crime and Justice*, 46, 43–56. 10.1016/j.ijlcj.2016.01.002

Boley, B. B., McGehee, N. G., & Hammett, A. T. (2017). Importance-performance analysis (IPA) of sustainable tourism initiatives: The resident perspective. *Tourism Management*, 58, 66–77. 10.1016/j.tourman.2016.10.002

Boluk, K. A., Cavaliere, C. T., & Duffy, L. N. (2019). A pedagogical framework for the development of the critical tourism citizen. *Journal of Sustainable Tourism*, 27(7), 865–881. 10.1080/09669582.2019.1615928

Boluk, K. A., Cavaliere, C. T., & Higgins-Desbiolles, F. (2019). A critical framework for interrogating the United Nations Sustainable Development Goals 2030 Agenda in tourism. *Journal of Sustainable Tourism*, 27(7), 847–864. 10.1080/09669582.2019.1619748

Boluk, K., & Carnicelli, S. (2015). Activism and Critical Reflection through Experiential Learning. *Journal of Teaching in Travel & Tourism*, 15(3), 242–251. 10.1080/15313220.2015.1059304

Boonsiritomachai, W., & Phonthanukitithaworn, C. (2019). Residents' support for sports events tourism development in beach city: The role of community's participation and tourism impacts. *SAGE Open*, 9(2), 2158244019843417. 10.1177/2158244019843417

Boyar, S. L. (2003). Work-family conflict: A model of linkages between work and family domain variables and turnover intentions. *Journal of Managerial Issues*, 175–190.

Bradley, M., Fraioli, C., & Osusky, D. (2021). *SDG Insights Report*.

Bruni, A., Gherardi, S., & Poggio, B. (2004). Entrepreneur-mentality, gender and the study of women entrepreneurs. *Journal of Organizational Change Management*, 17(3), 256–268. 10.1108/09534810410538315

Buckley, R. (2012). Sustainable tourism: Research and reality. *Annals of Tourism Research*, 39(2), 528–546. 10.1016/j.annals.2012.02.003

Budovich, L. (2023). The impact of religious tourism on the economy and tourism industry. *Hervormde Teologiese Studies*, 79(1). 10.4102/hts.v79i1.8607

Buhalis, D., Leung, X. Y., Fan, D., Darcy, S., Chen, G., Xu, F., Wei-Han Tan, G., Nunkoo, R., & Farmaki, A. (2023). Tourism 2030 and the contribution to the sustainable development goals: The tourism review viewpoint. *Tourism Review*, 78(2), 293–313. 10.1108/TR-04-2023-620

Bukar, U. A., Sayeed, M. S., Razak, S. F. A., Yogarayan, S., Amodu, O. A., & Mahmood, R. A. R. (2023). A method for analyzing text using VOSviewer. *MethodsX*, 11, 102339. Advance online publication. 10.1016/j.mex.2023.10233937693657

Butlera, G. (2017). Fostering community empowerment and capacity building through tourism: Perspectives from Dulls room, South Africa. *Journal of Tourism and Cultural Change*, 15(3), 199–212. 10.1080/14766825.2015.1133631

Cabezas, A. L. (2006). The Eroticization of Labor in Cuba's All-Inclusive Resorts: Performing Race, Class and Gender in the New Tourist Economy. *Social Identities*, 12(5), 507–521. 10.1080/13504630600920092

Camargo, B. A., & Gretzel, U. (2017). What do tourism students know about sustainability and sustainable tourism? An exploratory study of Latin American students. *Journal of Teaching in Travel & Tourism*, 17(2), 101–117. 10.1080/15313220.2017.1294038

Campos-Soria, J., Marchante-Mera, A., & Ropero-García, M. (2011). Patterns of occupational segregation by gender in the hospitality industry. *International Journal of Hospitality Management*, 30(1), 91–102. 10.1016/j.ijhm.2010.07.001

Carmeli, A. B. (2009). Learning behaviours in the workplace: The role of high-quality interpersonal relationships and psychological safety. *Systems Research and Behavioral Science: The Official Journal of the International Federation for Systems Research*, 26(1), 81–98. 10.1002/sres.932

Carvalho, I., Costa, C., Lykke, N., & Torres, A. (2019). Beyond the Glass Ceiling: Genderism Tourism Management. *Annals of Tourism Research*, 75, 79–91. 10.1016/j.annals.2018.12.022

Cave, P., & Kilic, S. (2010). The Role of Women in Tourism Employment with Special Reference to Antalya, Turkey. *Journal of Hospitality Marketing & Management*, 19(3), 280–292. 10.1080/19368621003591400

César Muñoz, A. Á. (2023). Modelling the effect of weather on tourism: Does it vary across seasons? *Tourism Geographies*, 25(1), 265–286. 10.1080/14616688.2020.1868019

Chandra, R. A., Prasad, N. S., Kumar, N. N., & Stephens, M. M. (2023). Social Media and Online Marketing Implication on Family Businesses Success: A Tourism Industry Perspective. In *Family Businesses in Tourism and Hospitality: Innovative Studies and Approaches* (pp. 223–241). Springer Nature Switzerland. 10.1007/978-3-031-28053-5_13

Chauhan, V. (2007). *Safety and security perceptions of tourists visiting Kashmir*. Advances in Hospitality and Leisure. 10.1016/S1745-3542(06)03001-3

Chelliah, R. J., & Shanmugam, K. R. (2007). Strategy for poverty reduction and narrowing regional disparities. *Economic and Political Weekly*, 42(34), 3475–3481. https://www.jstor.org/stable/4419942

Chilufya, A., Hughes, E., & Scheyvens, R. (2019). Tourists and community development: Corporate social responsibility or tourist social responsibility? *Journal of Sustainable Tourism*, 27(10), 1513–1529. 10.1080/09669582.2019.1643871

Chok, S., Macbeth, J., & Warren, C. (2007). Tourism as a tool for poverty alleviation: A critical analysis of "pro-poor tourism" and implications for sustainability. *Current Issues in Tourism*, 10(2-3), 144–165. 10.2167/cit303

Cho, M. (2002). An Analysis of Sexual Harassment in Korean Hotels from the Perspective of Female Employees. *Journal of Human Resources in Hospitality & Tourism*, 1(3), 11–29. 10.1300/J171v01n03_02

Cho, S. Y., Dreher, A., & Neumayer, E. (2013). Does Legalized Prostitution Increase Human Trafficking? *World Development*, 41(1), 67–82. 10.1016/j.worlddev.2012.05.023

Chung, T. W. (2016). A Study on Logistics Cluster Competitiveness among Asia Main Countries using the Porter's Diamond Model. *The Asian Journal of Shipping and Logistics*, 32(4), 257–264. 10.1016/j.ajsl.2016.12.010

Cinamon, R. G. (2002). Gender differences in the importance of work and family roles: Implications for work–family conflict. *Sex Roles*, 47, 531–541.

Cini, F., Van der Merwe, P., & Saayman, M. (2015). Tourism students' knowledge and tenets towards ecotourism. *Journal of Teaching in Travel & Tourism*, 15(1), 74–91. 10.1080/15313220.2014.999737

Clark, D. (2005). Sen's capability approach and the many spaces of human well-being. *The Journal of Development Studies*, 41(8), 1339–1368. 10.1080/00220380500186853

Collins, D., & Tisdell, C. (2002). Gender and differences in travel life cycles. *Journal of Travel Research*, 41(2), 133–143. 10.1177/004728702237413

Cornwall, A. (2016). Women's empowerment: What works. *Journal of International Development*, 28(3), 342–359. 10.1002/jid.3210

Correia, A., & Pimpão, A. (2004). 10). Decision-making processes of Portuguese tourist travelling to South America and Africa. *International Journal of Culture, Tourism and Hospitality Research*, 2(4), 330–373. 10.1108/17506180810908989

Costa, C., Breda, Z., Bakas, F. E., Durão, M., & Pinho, I. (2016). Through the gender looking-glass: Brazilian tourism entrepreneurs. *International Journal of Gender and Entrepreneurship*, 8(3), 282–306. 10.1108/IJGE-07-2015-0023

Cotter, D. A., Hermsen, J. M., Ovadia, S., & Vanneman, R. (2001). The glass ceiling effect. *Social Forces, 80*(2), 655–682.

Cotterell, D., Ferreira, J.-A., Hales, R., & Arcodia, C. (2020). Cultivating conscientious tourism caretakers: A phenomenon graphic continuum towards stronger sustainability. *Current Issues in Tourism*, 23(8), 1004–1020. 10.1080/13683500.2019.1577369

Cotterell, D., Hales, R., Arcodia, C., & Ferreira, J.-A. (2019). Overcommitted to tourism and under committed to sustainability: The urgency of teaching "strong sustainability" in tourism courses. *Journal of Sustainable Tourism*, 27(7), 882–902. 10.1080/09669582.2018.1545777

Crandall, R. (1980). Motivations for Leisure. *Journal of Leisure Research*, 12(1), 45–54. 10.1080/00222216.1980.11969418

Cronbach, L. (1951). Coefficient alpha and the internal structure of tests. *Psychometrika*, 16(3), 297–334. 10.1007/BF02310555

Crotts, R. B. (2003). The effect of uncertainty avoidance on information search, planning, and purchases of international travel vacations. *Tourism Management*, 24(2), 191–202. 10.1016/S0261-5177(02)00057-2

Currie, J., & Moretti, E. (2003). Mother's education and the intergenerational transmission of human capital: Evidence from college openings. *The Quarterly Journal of Economics*, 118(4), 1495–1532. 10.1162/003355303322552856

Daniela Matušíková, K. Š. (2021). The Impact of the COVID-19 Pandemic on Holiday Preferences at the Example of Z Generation Within the Youth Tourism. In A. D. Mahmut Demir, *Handbook of Research on the Impacts and Implications of COVID-19 on the Tourism Industry*. 10.4018/978-1-7998-8231-2

Dann, G. (1977). Anomie, ego-enhancement and tourism. *Annals of Tourism Research*, 4(4), 184–194. 10.1016/0160-7383(77)90037-8

de Lange, D. E. (2013). How do universities make progress? Stakeholder-related mechanisms affecting adoption of sustainability in university curricula. *Journal of Business Ethics*, 118(1), 103–116. 10.1007/s10551-012-1577-y

Demerouti, E., & Bakker, A. B. (2023). Job demands-resources theory in times of crises: New propositions. *Organizational Psychology Review*, 13(3), 209–236.

Deneulin, S., & Shahani, L. (Eds.). (2009). *An introduction to the human development and capability approach: Freedom and agency*. IDRC. 10.4324/9781849770026

Dias, J., & Tebaldi, E. (2012). Institutions, human capital, and growth: The institutional mechanism. *Structural Change and Economic Dynamics*, 23(3), 300–312. 10.1016/j.strueco.2012.04.003

Ditta-Apichai, M., Gretzel, U., & Kattiyapornpong, U. (2024). Platform empowerment: Facebook's role in facilitating female micro-entrepreneurship in tourism. *Journal of Sustainable Tourism*, 32(3), 540–559. 10.1080/09669582.2023.2215479

Dodds, R., Ali, A., & Galaski, K. (2018). Mobilizing knowledge: Determining key elements for success and pitfalls in developing community-based tourism. *Current Issues in Tourism*, 21(13), 1547–1568. 10.1080/13683500.2016.1150257

Dolezal, C. T. &. (2020). Tourism and the Sustainable Development Goals in Southeast Asia. *Advances in Southeast Asian Studies., 13*. https://doi.org/ doi:10.14764/10.ASEAS-0026

Dolezal, C., & Novelli, M. (2022). Power in community-based tourism: Empowerment and partnership in Bali. *Journal of Sustainable Tourism*, 30(10), 2352–2370. 10.1080/09669582.2020.1838527

Dolnicar, S., Grün, B., & Leisch, F. (2018). Market Segmentation. Springer. 10.1007/978-981-10-8818-6

Doneys, P., Doane, D. L., & Norm, S. (2020). Seeing empowerment as relational: Lessons from women participating in development projects in Cambodia. *Development in Practice*, 30(2), 268–280. 10.1080/09614524.2019.1678570

Dong, M., Zhang, T., Li, Y., & Ren, Z. (2022). The effect of work connectivity behavior after-hours on employee psychological distress: The role of leader workaholism and work-to-family conflict. *Frontiers in Public Health*, 10, 722679.35284392

Duffy, L., Kline, C., Mowatt, R., & Chancellor, H. (2015). Women in tourism: Shifting gender ideology in the DR. *Annals of Tourism Research*, 52, 72–86. 10.1016/j.annals.2015.02.017

Duncan, H. (2023). *Organizational Embeddedness and the Roles of Support and Psychological Safety for Caregiving Senior-Level Employees Experiencing Work-Family Conflict* [Doctoral dissertation, Converse University].

Durbarry, R. (2002). The economic contribution of tourism in Mauritius. *Annals of Tourism Research*, 29(3), 862–865. 10.1016/S0160-7383(02)00008-7

Dyer, S., McDowell, L., & Batnitzk, A. (2010). The impact of migration on the gendering of service work: The case of a west London hotel. *Gender, Work and Organization*, 17(6), 635–657. 10.1111/j.1468-0432.2009.00480.x

Edmondson, A. C. (2004). Psychological safety, trust, and learning in organizations: A group-level lens. *Trust and distrust in organizations: Dilemmas and approaches, 12*, 239-272.

Ejarque, J. (2017). *Marketing and Management of Tourist Destinations: New Models and Strategies 2.0.*

Elahi, N. S., Abid, G., Contreras, F., & Fernández, I. A. (2022). Work–family and family–work conflict and stress in times of COVID-19. *Frontiers in Psychology*, 13, 951149.36304883

Eluwole, K., Bekun, F. V., & Lasisi, T. T. (2022). Fresh insights into tourism-led economic growth nexus: A systematic literature network analysis approach. *Asia Pacific Journal of Tourism Research*, 27(4), 374–410. 10.1080/10941665.2022.2075775

Escot, L., Belope-Nguema, S., Fernández-Cornejo, J. A., Del Pozo-García, E., Castellanos-Serrano, C., & Cruz-Calderón, S. F. (2022). Can the legal framework for prostitution influence the acceptability of buying sex? *Journal of Experimental Criminology*, 18(4), 885–909. 10.1007/s11292-021-09465-y

Eshaghi, M. A. (2020). Destination image and tourist behavioural intentions: A meta-analysis. *Tourism Management*, 81, 104154. 10.1016/j.tourman.2020.104154

Éva Csirmaz, K. P. (2015). International Trends in Recreational and Wellness Tourism. *Procedia Economics and Finance*, 32, 755–762. 10.1016/S2212-5671(15)01458-6

Fainshmidt, S., Smith, A., & Judge, W. Q. (2016). National Competitiveness and Porter's Diamond Model: The Role of MNE Penetration and Governance Quality. *Global Strategy Journal*, 6(2), 81–104. 10.1002/gsj.1116

Farrelly, T. A. (2011). Indigenous and democratic decision-making: Issues from community-based ecotourism in the Bouma National Heritage Park, Fiji. *Journal of Sustainable Tourism*, 19(7), 817–835. 10.1080/09669582.2011.553390

Ferguson, L., & Alarcón, D. M. (2015). Gender and sustainable tourism: reflections on theory and practice. *Journal of Sustainable Tourism, 23*(3), 401-416. 10.1080/09669582.2014.957208

Ferguson, L. (2010). Promoting gender equality and empowering women? Tourism and the third Millennium Development Goal. *Current Issues in Tourism*, 14(3), 235–249. 10.1080/13683500.2011.555522

Figueroa-Domecq, C., & Perez, M. S. (2020). Application of a gender perspective in tourism research: a theoretical and practical approach. *Journal of Tourism Analysis*. 10.1108/JTA-02-2019-0009

Figueroa-Domecqa, C., Jong, A., & Williams, A. M. (2020). Gender, tourism & entrepreneurship: A critical review. *Annals of Tourism Research*, 84, 102980. 10.1016/j.annals.2020.102980

Figueroa-Domecq, C., Pritchard, A., Segovia-Pérez, M., Morgan, N., & Villacé-Molinero, T. (2015). Tourism gender research: A critical accounting. *Annals of Tourism Research*, 52, 87–103. 10.1016/j.annals.2015.02.001

Fiji Womens Fund. (2018). *Fiji Womens Fund*. FWF. https://fijiwomensfund.org/project/talanoa-treks/

Filippopoulou, C., Galariotis, E., & Spyrou, S. (2020). An early warning system for predicting systemic banking crises in the Eurozone: A logit regression approach. *Journal of Economic Behavior & Organization*, 172, 344–363. 10.1016/j.jebo.2019.12.023

Filmi, B. a. (2022). Psychological Factors of Religion Traveler and Decision to Visit. *Jurnal Ilmiah Syi'ar*, 103-113.

Fleuret, S. (2024). Backpackers' Tourism and Health: A Narrative Literature Review. *Geographies*, 4(1), 40–51. 10.3390/geographies4010003

Fong, B. Y. F., & Law, V. T. S. (2021). *Sustainable Development Goal 3*. Routledge. 10.4324/9781003220169

Frank, E., Zhao, Z., Fang, Y., Rotenstein, L. S., Sen, S., & Guille, C. (2021). Experiences of work-family conflict and mental health symptoms by gender among physician parents during the COVID-19 pandemic. *JAMA Network Open*, 4(11), e2134315–e2134315.34767022

Frazier, M. L. (2017). Psychological safety: A meta-analytic review and extension. *Personnel Psychology*, 70(1), 113–165. 10.1111/peps.12183

Frick, J., Kaiser, F. G., & Wilson, M. (2004). Environmental knowledge and conservation behavior: Exploring prevalence and structure in a representative sample. *Personality and Individual Differences*, 37(8), 1597–1613. 10.1016/j.paid.2004.02.015

Fried, L.I. (1989). *A new breed of entrepreneur-women.*

Gambhir, D. K. (2021). Religious Tourism and Sustainable Development: Perspectives from Hill States in India. In *Handbook of Sustainable Development and Leisure Services* (pp. 273-287). Springer. 10.1007/978-3-030-59820-4_18

Gan, T. Z., Zheng, J., Li, W., Li, J., & Shen, J. (2023). Health and Wellness Tourists' Motivation and Behavior Intention: The Role of Perceived Value. *International Journal of Environmental Research and Public Health*, 20(5), 4339. 10.3390/ijerph2005433936901356

Gantait, A., Mohanty, P., Singh, K., & Sinha, R. (2021). Pro-Poor Tourism Development in India: Reality or Hyperbole! *Psychology and Education*, 58(2), 9672–9682.

Gantait, A., Singh, K., Bhowmik, S., & Swamy, G. A. (2022). Can Community Based Tourism Be a Sustainable Solution for a Better Community Life? Discussing the Concept, Benefits, and Challenges. In Kour, R. (Ed.), *Rani, R., Vaishali* (1st ed., pp. 63–79). Emerging Trends in Social Science Research.

Garrod, B. (2003). Local participation in the planning and management of ecotourism: A revised model approach. *Journal of Ecotourism*, 2(1), 33–53. 10.1080/14724040308668132

Gaspar, V., Amaglobeli, D., Garcia-Escribano, D., Prady, D., & Soto, M. (2019). *Fiscal policy and development: human, social, physical investment for SDGs*. IMF Staff Discussion Note. https://www.imf.org/en/Publications/Staff-Discussion-Notes/Issues/2019/01/18/Fiscal-Policy -and-Development-Human-Social-and-Physical-Investments-for-the-SDGs-46444

Gasper, D., Shah, A., & Tankha, S. (2019). The Framing of Sustainable Consumption and Production in <scp>SDG</scp> 12. *Global Policy*, 10(S1), 83–95. 10.1111/1758-5899.12592

Gaur, V. S., & Koltru, R. (2018). *Sustainable Tourism in the Indian Himalayan Region. NITI Aayog Report-II*. Government of India.

Gebrehiwo, K. G. (2016). The impact of human capital development on economic growth in Ethiopia: Evidence from ARDL approach to co-integration. *Bahir Dar Journal of Education*, 16(1), 1–23. https://www.ajol.info/index.php/bdje/article/view/249033

Gentry, K. M. (2007). Belizean women and tourism work: Opportunity or impediment? *Annals of Tourism Research*, 34(2), 477–496. 10.1016/j.annals.2006.11.003

George, R. (2003). Tourist's perceptions of safety and security while visiting Cape Town. *Tourism Management*, 24(5), 575–585. https://www.sciencedirect.com/science/article/pii/ S0261517703000037. 10.1016/S0261-5177(03)00003-7

Getz, D., Carlsen, J., & Morrison, A. (2004). *The family Business in Tourism and Hospitality. Trowbridge*. Cromwell Press. 10.1079/9780851998084.0000

Ghosh, J. (2010). *Poverty reduction in China and India: policy implication and trends.* (DESA Working Paper No. 92, ST/ESA/2010/DWP/92).

Ghosh, P. K., Shariff, A., & Mondal, S. K. (2002). *Indian public expenditure on social sector and poverty alleviation programmes during the 1990s.* (Working Paper 169). National Council of Applied Economic Research Human Development Division, Overseas Development Institute, Westminster, London, UK.

Ghosh, P., & Cheruvalath, R. (2007). Indian female entrepreneurs as catalysis for economic growth and development. *International Journal of Entrepreneurship and Innovation*, 8(2), 139–147. 10.5367/000000007780808048

Gibson, D. (2015). *Community-based tourism in Fiji: a case study of Wayalailai Ecohaven Resort, Yasawa Island Group.* Routledge.: Tourism in Pacific Islands.

Gil, J. D. B., Reidsma, P., Giller, K., Todman, L., Whitmore, A., & van Ittersum, M. (2019). Sustainable development goal 2: Improved targets and indicators for agriculture and food security. *Ambio*, 48(7), 685–698. 10.1007/s13280-018-1101-430267284

Globalsurvey-SDGs. (2020). *Report of results global survey on sustainability and the SDGs - awareness, priorities, need for action. Hamburg.* Global Survey. https://www.globalsurvey-sdgs.com/wp-content/uploads/2020/01/20200205_SC_Global_Survey_Result-Report_english_final.pdf

Globescan. (2023). *Growing awareness of the SDGs.* Globescan. https://globescan.com/2023/11/22/growing-awareness-of-the-sdgs/

Glyptou, K., Amore, A., & Adie, B. A. (2022). From aspirations to applications: The SDGs and the role of indicators in the measurement of sustainable tourism. In A. Farmaki, L. Altinay, & X. Font (Eds.), *Planning and Managing Sustainability in Tourism, Hospitality and Events* (pp. 13-25). (Tourism, Hospitality & Event Management). Springer. 10.1007/978-3-030-92208-5_2

Goh, C. (2012). Exploring impact of climate on tourism demand. *Annals of Tourism Research*, 39(4), 1859–1883. 10.1016/j.annals.2012.05.027

Gomes, B. (2021). *The tourism value chain and the prospect of pro-poor tourism in Cox's Bazar, Bangladesh.* [Unpublished Thesis]. https://eprints.bournemouth.ac.uk/35140/

Goodwin, H. (2006). *Measuring and reporting the impact of tourism on poverty.* University of Surry, UK. Chrome. https://www.haroldgoodwin.info/resources/measuring.pdf

Gordan, M.-I., Pe , E., Popescu, G., Brad, I., Milin, A. I., Adamov, T. C., Ciolac, R., Pascariu, A. R., & Iancu, T. (2023). Factors Influencing the Accommodation Prices of Romanian Rural Tourism. *Sustainability (Basel)*, 15(1), 191. 10.3390/su15010191

Gossling, S., & Michael Hall, C. (2019). Sharing versus collaborative economy: How to align ICT developments and the SDGs in tourism? *Journal of Sustainable Tourism*, 27(1), 74–96. 10.1080/09669582.2018.1560455

Government of Bangladesh. (2016). *Tourism Master Plan of Bangladesh*. Seventh Five-Year Plan 2016-2020, Ministry of Civil Aviation & Tourism, Planning Commission, Dhaka. https://file.portal.gov.bd/uploads/8ef2a505-c131-4a8f-b6d0-2ac4760cc936//631/6c4/06a/63 16c406a9807875210649.pdf

Government of India. (2012). *12th Five Year Plan (2012-2017) Report on Tourism*. Government of India. https://tourism.gov.in/sites/default/files/2019-10/020220120146055.pdf

Gragnano, A., Simbula, S., & Miglioretti, M. (2020). Work–life balance: Weighing the importance of work–family and work–health balance. *International Journal of Environmental Research and Public Health*, 17(3), 907.32024155

Greenhalgh, T., Raftery, J., Hanney, S., & Glover, M. (2016). Research impact: A narrative review. In *BMC Medicine* (*Vol. 14*, Issue 1). BioMed Central Ltd. 10.1186/s12916-016-0620-8

Greenhaus, J. H., & Beutell, N. J. (1985). Sources of conflict between work and family roles. *Academy of Management Review*, 10(1), 76–88.

Guijarro, F., & Poyatos, J. A. (2018). Designing a sustainable development goal index through a Goal programming model: The case of EU-28 countries. *Sustainability*, 10, 1-17.

Gupta, A. (2019). Gender roles in Indian families: A contemporary review. *International Journal of Gender & Women's Studies*, 7(2), 180–195.

Haas, B. (2023). Achieving SDG 14 in an equitable and just way. *International Environmental Agreement: Politics, Law and Economics*, 23(2), 199–205. 10.1007/s10784-023-09603-z

Hafci, B. (2018). Could Rural Tourism be a Good Generator of Women Workforce?: The Case of Kirazli Town. *International Rural Tourism and Development Journal*, 2(2).

Hafsa, S. (2020). Economic contribution of tourism industry in Bangladesh: At a glance. *Global Journal of Management and Business Research*, 20(1), 29–38. 10.34257/GJMBRFVOL20IS1PG29

Haid, M., Albrecht, J. N., Tangl, P., & Plaikner, A. (2024). Regional Products and Sustainability. *Sustainability (Basel)*, 16(2), 628. 10.3390/su16020628

Halkos, G., & Gkampoura, E.-C. (2021). Where do we stand on the 17 Sustainable Development Goals? An overview on progress. *Economic Analysis and Policy*, 70, 94–122. 10.1016/j. eap.2021.02.001

Hall, C. M. (2019). Constructing sustainable tourism development: The 2030 agenda and the managerial ecology of sustainable tourism. *Journal of Sustainable Tourism*, 27(7), 1044–1060. 10.1080/09669582.2018.1560456

Hall, C. M., Seyfi, S., & Koupaei, S. N. (2023). Politics and the sustainable development goals: Tourism Agenda 2030 perspective article. *Tourism Review*, 78(2), 314–320. 10.1108/TR-10-2022-0498

Hall, G. B., Dollard, M. F., & Coward, J. (2010). Psychosocial safety climate: Development of the PSC-12. *International Journal of Stress Management*, 17, 353–383.

Han, H. (2021). Consumer behavior and environmental sustainability in tourism and hospitality: A review of theories, concepts, and latest research. *Journal of Sustainable Tourism*, 29(7), 1021–1042. 10.1080/09669582.2021.1903019

Hansen, H., & Rand, J. (2014). Estimates of Gender Differences in Firm's Access to Credit in Sub-Saharan Africa. *Economics Letters*, 123(3), 374–377. 10.1016/j.econlet.2014.04.001

Hanushek, E. A., & Woessmann, L. (2007). *The role of education quality for economic growth* (SSRN Scholarly Paper 960379). https://papers.ssrn.com/abstract=96037910.1596/1813-9450-4122

Haq, F., & Medhekar, A. (2019). Challenges for 'innovative transformation' in heritage tourism development in India and Pakistan. In Srivastava, S. (Ed.), *Conservation and Promotion of Heritage Tourism* (pp. 127–154). IGI Global. 10.4018/978-1-5225-6283-2.ch006

Harman, H. H. (1976). *Modern Factor Analysis*. University of Chicago Press.

Harsanti, K. F. (2013). The Influence of Marketing Mix, Psychology. *Diponegoro Journal of Social and Politic*, 1-9.

Hasell, J. (2022). *From $1.90 to $2.15 a day: the updated International Poverty Line.* Our World in Data. https://ourworldindata.org/from-1-90-to-2-15-a-day-the-updated-international-poverty-line

Hassan, A. K. J., Kennell, J., & Chaperon, S. (2020). Rhetoric and reality in Bangladesh: Elite stakeholder perceptions of the implementation of tourism policy. *Tourism Recreation Research*, 45(3), 307–322. 10.1080/02508281.2019.1703286

Hayat, A., & Afshari, L. (2021). Supportive organizational climate: A moderated mediation model of workplace bullying and employee well-being. *Personnel Review*, 50(7/8), 1685–1704.

Heung, V. C., Qu, H., & Chu, R. (2001). The relationship between vacation factors and socio-demographic and travelling characteristics: The case of Japanese leisure travellers. *Tourism Management*, 22(3), 259–269. 10.1016/S0261-5177(00)00057-1

Higgins-Desbiolles, F., Carnicelli, S., Krolikowski, C., Wijesinghe, G., & Boluk, K. (2019). Degrowing tourism: Rethinking tourism. *Journal of Sustainable Tourism*, 27(12), 1926–1944. 10.1080/09669582.2019.1601732

Horner, S. a. (2020). *Consumer Behaviour in Tourism* (4th ed.). Routledge. 10.4324/9781003046721

Howitt, P. (2005). Health, human capital, and economic growth: A schumpeterian perspective. In López-Casasnovas, G., Rivera, B., & Currais, L. (Eds.), *Health and Economic Growth* (pp. 19–40). The MIT Press., 10.7551/mitpress/3451.003.0005

Hughes, E., & Scheyvens, R. (2016). Corporate social responsibility in tourism post-2015: A development first approach. *Tourism Geographies*, 18(5), 469–482. 10.1080/14616688.2016.1208678

Hung, J. (2024). *Legalising Prostitution in Thailand: A Policy-Oriented Examination of the (De-) Construction of Commercial Sex.* Springer. 10.1007/978-981-99-8448-0

Ighodalo, A. (2012). Poverty and sustainable socio-economic development in Africa: The Nigeria experience. *European Scientific Journal, 8*(26), 51-65. chrome-extension://efaidnbmnnnibpca-jpcglclefindmkaj/https://core.ac.uk/download/pdf/236412432.pdf

Imbaya, B. O., Sitati, N. W., & Lenaiyasa, P. (2019). Capacity building for inclusive growth in community-based tourism initiatives in Kenya. *Tourism Management Perspectives*, 30, 11–18. 10.1016/j.tmp.2019.01.003

Indapurkar, K. (2017). Financial Literacy Among Educated Urban Youth: Issues and Challenges. *International Journal of Economic Research.*

International Finance Corporation (2011). *Strengthening Access to Finance for Women-Owned SMEs in Developing Countries.* IFC.

Islam, A. (2020). 'It gets really boring if you stay at home': Women, work and temporalities in urban India. *Sociology*, 54(5), 867–882.

Islam, A., Muzi, S., & Amin, M. (2019). Unequal Laws and the Disempowerment of Women in the Labour Market: Evidence from Firm-Level Data. *The Journal of Development Studies*, 55(5), 822–844. 10.1080/00220388.2018.1487055

Izurieta, G., Torres, A., Pati, J., Vasco, C., Vasseur, L., Reyes, H., & Torres, B. (2021). Exploring community and key stakeholders' perception of scientific tourism as a strategy to achieve SDGs in the Ecuadorian Amazon. *Tourism Management Perspectives*, 39, 100830. 10.1016/j. tmp.2021.100830

Jamalpour, H. a.-D. (2022). Cultural memory and neuro-critical reading of Ian McEwan's atonement. *Revista de Investigaciones Universidad del Quindío*, 436-442. 10.33975/riuq.vol34nS2.1142

Jan van Eck, N., & Waltman, L. (2011). Text mining and visualization using VOSviewer. *ISSI Newsletter, 7*(3), 50–54. www.vosviewer.com

Jay, L., & Michaels, J. P.-Z. (2021). Individual Differences in Religious Motivation Influence How People Think. *Journal for the Scientific Study of Religion*, 60(1), 64–82. 10.1111/jssr.12696

Jayswal, D. K. (2015). Women's participation and Tourism industry: An overview. *Research Journal of Humanities and Social Sciences*, 6(4), 269–273.

Jeffery, H. (2018). Tourism and Womens Rights in Tunisia. In Cole, S. (Ed.), *Gender Equality and Tourism: Beyond Empowerment* (pp. 96–107). CABI. 10.1079/9781786394422.0096

Jeffrey, H. (2017). Gendering the tourism curriculum whilst becoming an academic. *Anatolia*, 28(4), 530–539. 10.1080/13032917.2017.1370779

Jenkins, J. (2023, December 1). *Prostitution*. Encyclopedia Britannica. https://www.britannica.com/topic/prostitution

Jeyacheya, J., & Hampton, M. P. (2020). Wishful thinking or wise policy? Theorising tourism-led inclusive growth: Supply chains and host communities. *World Development*, 131, 104960. 10.1016/j.worlddev.2020.104960

Jimenez-Esquinas, G. (2017). "This is not only about culture" on tourism, gender stereotypes and other affective fluxes. *Journal of Sustainable Tourism*, 25(3), 311–326. 10.1080/09669582.2016.1206109

Jin, H., Qian, X., Chin, T., & Zhang, H. (2020). A global assessment of sustainable development based on modification of the human development index via the Entropy method. *Sustainability (Basel)*, 12(8), 1–20. 10.3390/su12083251

Johansson, I., & Hansen, M. A. (2023). From Empowerment to Exploitation: Predicting Positive and Negative Associations with the Exchange of Sexual Services for Payment. *Sexuality & Culture*. 10.1007/s12119-023-10174-z

Jones, P., Hillier, D., & Comfort, D. (2017). The sustainable development goals and the tourism and hospitality industry. *Athens Journal of Tourism*, 4(1), 7–18. 10.30958/ajt.4.1.1

Joseph, S. (2017). Sustainable Medical Tourism Model - A Case Study of Kerala, India. *Asia-Pacific Journal of Innovation in Hospitality and Tourism*, 6(1), 77–98.

Kanagaraj, C. a. (2013). An Analysis of push and pull travel motivations of domestic tourists to Kerala. *International Journal of Management and Business Studies*, 3, 112–118.

Kato, K. (2019). Gender and sustainability – exploring ways of knowing – an Eco humanities perspective. *Journal of Sustainable Tourism*, 27(7), 939–956. 10.1080/09669582.2019.1614189

Kaushal, V., & Yadav, R. (2021). Understanding customer experience of culinary tourism through food tours of Delhi. *International Journal of Tourism Cities*, 7(3), 683–701. 10.1108/IJTC-08-2019-0135

Kc, B., Dhungana, A., & Dangi, T. B. (2021). Tourism and the sustainable development goals: Stakeholders' perspectives from Nepal. *Tourism Management Perspectives*, 38(1), 1–13. 10.1016/j.tmp.2021.100822

Kc, B.KC. (2024). Pedagogy in operationalizing sustainable development goals. *Journal of Hospitality, Leisure, Sport and Tourism Education*, 34, 100476. 10.1016/j.jhlste.2023.100476

Kerstetter, D., & Bricker, K. (2009). Exploring Fijian's sense of place after exposure to tourism development. *Journal of Sustainable Tourism*, 17(6), 691–708. 10.1080/09669580902999196

Khairy, H. A., Liu, S., & Sheikhelsouk, S., EI-Sherbeeny, A. M., Alsetoohy, O., & Al-Romeedy, B. S. (2023). The Effect of benevolent leadership on job engagement through psychological safety and workplace friendship prevalence in the tourism and hospitality industry. *Sustainability*, 15(17), 13245.

Khan, N. A., Bahadur, W., Ramzan, M., & Pravdina, N. (2024). Turning the tide: An impact of leader empowering behavior on employees' work–family conflict, spillover and turnover intention in tourism. *Leadership and Organization Development Journal*.

Kharub, M., & Sharma, R. (2017). Comparative analyses of competitive advantage using Porter diamond model (the case of MSMEs in Himachal Pradesh). *Competitiveness Review*, 27(2), 132–160. 10.1108/CR-02-2016-0007

Khizar, H. M. U., Younas, A., Kumari, S., Akbar, A., & Poulova, P. (2023). The progression of sustainable development goals in tourism: A systematic literature review of past achievements and future promises. *Journal of Innovation & Knowledge*, 8(4), 12–23. 10.1016/j.jik.2023.100442

Khoo-Lattimor, C., Ling Yang, E., & Je, J. S. (2019). Assessing gender representation in knowledge production: A critical analysis of UNWTO's planned events. *Journal of Sustainable Tourism*, 27(7), 920–938. 10.1080/09669582.2019.1566347

Kimbu, A. N., & Ngoasong, M. Z. (2016). Women as vectors of social entrepreneurship. *Annals of Tourism Research*, 60, 63–79. 10.1016/j.annals.2016.06.002

Kim, H. J., Chen, M.-H., & Jang, S. C. S. (2006). Tourism expansion and economic development: The case of Taiwan. *Tourism Management*, 27(5), 925–933. 10.1016/j.tourman.2005.05.01132287716

Kim, H., & So, K. K. F. (2022). Two decades of customer experience research in hospitality and tourism: A bibliometric analysis and thematic content analysis. *International Journal of Hospitality Management*, 100, 103082. 10.1016/j.ijhm.2021.103082

Kling, K. G., Margaryan, L., & Fuchs, M. (2020). (In)equality in the outdoors: Gender perspective on recreation and tourism media in the Swedish mountains. *Current Issues in Tourism*, 23(2), 233–247. 10.1080/13683500.2018.1495698

Koch, F., & Krellenberg, K. (2018). How to Contextualize SDG 11? Looking at Indicators for Sustainable Urban Development in Germany. *ISPRS International Journal of Geo-Information*, 7(12), 464. 10.3390/ijgi7120464

Kogovsek, M., & Kogovsek, M. (2012). Hospitality and Tourism Gender Issues Remain Unsolved: A Call for Research. *Quaestus*, 6, 194–203.

Koirala, B. S., & Pradhan, G. (2019). Determinants of sustainable development: Evidence from 12 Asian countries. *Sustainable Development (Bradford)*, 28(3), 1–7. 10.1002/sd.1963

Koncul, N. (2012). Wellness: A New Mode of tourism. *Economic Research-Ekonomska Istraživanja*, 525-534. 10.1080/1331677X.2012.11517521

Kooraram, S., & Durbarry, R. (2022). Impact of spousal support on Work-family/family work conflicts: A qualitative study of married working women in Mauritius. *International Journal of Early Childhood Special Education*, 14(5).

Kozak, M. (2002). Comparative analysis of tourist motivations by nationality and destinations. *Tourism Management*, 23(3), 221–232. 10.1016/S0261-5177(01)00090-5

Krauss, J. E. (2022). Unpacking SDG 15, its targets and indicators: Tracing ideas of conservation. *Globalizations*, 19(8), 1179–1194. 10.1080/14747731.2022.2035480

Kreinin, H., & Aigner, E. (2022). From "Decent work and economic growth" to "Sustainable work and economic degrowth": A new framework for SDG 8. *Empirica*, 49(2), 281–311. 10.1007/s10663-021-09526-5

Küfeoğlu, S. (2022). SDG-1 No Poverty. In *Emerging Technologies* (pp. 191–208). Springer. 10.1007/978-3-031-07127-0_3

Kumar De, U. (2013). Sustainable Nature-based Tourism, Involvement of Indigenous Women and Development: A Case of North-East India. *Tourism Recreation Research*, 38(3), 311–324. 10.1080/02508281.2013.11081756

Kumar, N. N., Chandra, R. A., & Patel, A. (2021). Mixed frequency evidence of the tourism growth relationship in small Island developing states: A case study of Tonga. *Asia Pacific Journal of Tourism Research*, 26(3), 294–307. 10.1080/10941665.2020.1862884

Kumar, N., Kumar, R. R., Patel, A., & Stauvermann, P. (2019). Exploring the Effect of Tourism and Economic Growth in Fiji: Accounting for Capital, Labor, and Structural Breaks. *Tourism Analysis*, 16(2), 115–130. 10.3727/108354218X15391984820468

Kumar, P., Ahmed, F., Singh, R. K., & Sinha, P. (2018). Determination of hierarchical relationships among sustainable development goals using interpretive structural modeling. *Environment, Development and Sustainability*, 20(5), 2119–2137. 10.1007/s10668-017-9981-1

Kumar, S., Kumar, N., & Vivekadhish, S. (2016). Millennium development goals (MDGs) to sustainable development goals (SDGs): Addressing unfinished agenda and strengthening sustainable development and partnership. *Indian Journal of Community Medicine*, 41(1), 1–4. 10.4103/0970-0218.17095526917865

Kuoyan, W. (2022). Sustainable Tourism Development Based upon Visitors' Brand Trust: A Case of "100 Religious Attractions". *Sustainability (Basel)*, 14(4), 1977. 10.3390/su14041977

Lacitignola, D., Petrosillo, I., Cataldi, M., & Zurlini, G. (2007). Modelling socio-ecological tourismbased systems for sustainability. *Ecological Modelling*, 206(1), 191–204. 10.1016/j.ecolmodel.2007.03.034

Lampert, M., & Papadongonas, P. (2016). *Towards 2030 without poverty*. Amsterdam: Glocalities. https://www.glocalities.com/reports/towards-2030-without-poverty.html

Lapeyre, R. (2010). Community-based tourism as a sustainable solution to maximise impacts locally? The Tsiseb Conservancy case,Namibia. *Development Southern Africa*, 27(5), 757–772. 10.1080/0376835X.2010.522837

Latifi, M.-A., Nikou, S., & Bouwman, H. (2021). Business model innovation and firm performance: Exploring causal mechanisms in SMEs. *Technovation*, 107, 102274. 10.1016/j.technovation.2021.102274

Leal Filho, W., Kovaleva, M., Tsani, S., îrcă, D.-M., Shiel, C., Dinis, M. A. P., Nicolau, M., Sima, M., Fritzen, B., Lange Salvia, A., Minhas, A., Kozlova, V., Doni, F., Spiteri, J., Gupta, T., Wakunuma, K., Sharma, M., Barbir, J., Shulla, K., & Tripathi, S. (2023). Promoting gender equality across the sustainable development goals. *Environment, Development and Sustainability*, 25(12), 14177–14198. 10.1007/s10668-022-02656-136124160

Lee, J., & Barro, R. J. (2001). Schooling quality in a cross-section of countries. *Economica*, 68(272), 465–488. https://www.jstor.org/stable/3549114. 10.1111/1468-0335.00257

Lee, T. H., & Jan, F. H. (2019). Can community-based tourism contribute to sustainable development? Evidence from residents' perceptions of the sustainability. *Tourism Management*, 70, 368–380. 10.1016/j.tourman.2018.09.003

Lenao, M. (2015). Challenges facing community-based cultural tourism development at Lekhubu Island, Botswana: A comparative analysis. *Current Issues in Tourism*, 18(6), 579–594. 10.1080/13683500.2013.827158

León-Gómez, A., Forero, J. A. M., & Santos-Jaén, J. M. (2023). A bibliometric analysis of sustainability education in tourism universities. *SAGE Open*, 13(3), 1–20. 10.1177/21582440231193215

Li, C., Zhao, G., Koh, K. P., Xu, Z., Yue, M., Wang, W., Tan, Y., & Wu, L. (2024). Impact of China's financial development on the sustainable development goals of the Belt and Road Initiative participating countries. *Humanities & Social Sciences Communications*, 11(294), 1–12. 10.1057/s41599-024-02791-2

Line, N. H., Hanks, L., & Miao, L. (2018). Image matters: Incentivizing green tourism behaviour. *Journal of Travel Research*, 57(3), 296–309. 10.1177/0047287517697848

Ling, R. S., Wu, B., Park, J., Shu, H., & Morrison, A. M. (2013). Womens Role in Sustaining village and Rural tourism in China. *Annals of Tourism Research*, 43, 624–650. 10.1016/j.annals.2013.07.009

Liu, C. E. (2020). Supervision incivility and employee psychological safety in the workplace. *International Journal of Environmental Research and Public Health*, 17(3), 840.32013097

Liu, T., Li, M., & Lu, M.-F. (2020). Performing femininity: Women at the top (doing and undoing gender). *Tourism Management*, 80, 104–130. 10.1016/j.tourman.2020.104130

López-Guzmán, T., Sánchez-Cañizares, S., & Pavón, V. (2011). Community-based tourism in developing countries: A case study. *Tourismos*, 6(1), 69–84.

López-Sanz, J. M., Penelas-Leguía, A., Gutiérrez-Rodríguez, P., & Cuesta-Valiño, P. (2021, July 23). P.-L. A.-R.-V. (2021). Rural Tourism and the Sustainable Development Goals. A Study of the Variables That Most Influence the Behavior of the Tourist. *Frontiers in Psychology*, 12, 722973. 10.3389/fpsyg.2021.72297334367040

Lozares, C. (1991). El análisis de componentes principales. *Papers Rev. Sociol.*, 37, 31–63. 10.5565/rev/papers/v37n0.1595

Lubbe, B. A. (2003). *Tourism Management in Southern Africa*. Pearson Education South Africa.

Luo, X., & Bao, J. (2019). Exploring the impacts of tourism on the livelihoods of local poor: The role of local government and major investors. *Journal of Sustainable Tourism*, 27(3), 344–359. 10.1080/09669582.2019.1578362

M., A. A., Ocaña, F. A., & and Valderrama, M. J. (1996). Análisis de componentes principales de un proceso estocástico con funciones muestrales escalonadas. *QÜESTIIÓ*, 7 - 28.

Mallick, S. (2009). Macroeconomic policy and poverty reduction in India. *IGIDR Proceeding/ Project Report Series*.

Mandych I.A., B. A. (2022). Features of assessing the investment attractiveness of high-tech projects. *Russian Technological Journal.*, 75-86. 10.32362/2500-316X-2022-10-2-75-86

Mann, P. (2023). Exploring the Complex Relationship Between Prostitution and Human Trafficking. *Asian Journal of Multidisciplinary Research & Review*, 4(5), 57–72. 10.55662/AJMRR.2023.4501

Manolis, E. N., & Manoli, E. N. (2021). Raising awareness of the Sustainable Development Goals through Ecological Projects in Higher Education. *Journal of Cleaner Production*, 279, 123614. 10.1016/j.jclepro.2020.123614

Manomaivibool, P. (2015). Wasteful tourism in developing economy? A present situation and sustainable scenarios. *Resources, Conservation and Recycling*, 103, 69–76. 10.1016/j.resconrec.2015.07.020

Marques, J., & Lança, M. (2016). Beyond Everyday Life. Love and Sexuality during Tourism: Preliminary Results of an Exploratory Research in the Algarve (Portugal). *Revista Anais Brasileira de Estudos Turísticos*, 6(2), 7–22.

Marzo-Navarro, M. (2017). Development of integrated rural tourism from the perspective of residents: Proposed model. *Journal of Tourism and Cultural Heritage. Pasos (El Sauzal)*, 15, 841–859. 10.25145/j.pasos.2017.15.057

Matei, F. D. (2015). Cultural Tourism Potential, as Part of Rural Tourism Development in the North-East of Romania. *Procedia Economics and Finance*, 453–460. 10.1016/S2212-5671(15)00584-5

Matheson, C. M., & Finkel, R. (2013). Sex trafficking and the Vancouver Winter Olympic Games: Perceptions and preventative measures. *Tourism Management*, 36, 613–628. 10.1016/j.tourman.2012.08.004

Matthews, R. (2018). Regulating the demand for commercialized sexual services. In *Women's Studies International Forum, 69*, 1–8. Elsevier Ltd. 10.1016/j.wsif.2018.03.007

Mawby, R. I. (2017). Crime and tourism: What the available statistics do or do not tell us. *International Journal of Tourism Policy*, 7(2), 81–92. 10.1504/IJTP.2017.085292

Mawla, M. R., & Rahman Khan, M. Z. (2020). A Study on Sustainable Development Goal 7: Future Plan to Achieve the Affordable and Clean Energy-Bangladesh Perspective. *2020 IEEE Region 10 Symposium (TENSYMP)*, (pp. 421–426). IEEE. 10.1109/TENSYMP50017.2020.9230795

Maxwell, L. K., & David, C. H. (1995). The application of the durbin-watson test to the dynamic regression model under normal and non-normal errors. *Econometric Reviews*, 14(4), 487–510. 10.1080/07474939508800333

Mayaka, M., Croy, W. G., & Cox, J. W. (2019). A dimensional approach to community-based tourism: Recognising and differentiating form and context. *Annals of Tourism Research*, 74, 177–190. 10.1016/j.annals.2018.12.002

Mbaiwa, J. (2005). The problems and prospects of sustainable tourism development in the Okavango Delta, Botswana. *Journal of Sustainable Tourism*, 13, 203–227. 10.1080/01434630508668554

Medhekar, A. (2022). Australia's Bilateral and Multilateral Health Sector Partnership with South Asian Nations: Opportunities and Challenges. In Medhekar, A., Saha, S., & Haq, F. (Eds.), *Strategic Cooperation and Partnerships Between Australia and South Asia: Economic Development, Trade, and Investment Opportunities Post-COVID-19*. (pp. 1-21). Pennsylvania USA: IGI Global.

Medhekar, A. (2023). The Economic Dimensions of Indian Railways 'Bharat Gaurav' Pilgrimage Routes. In V.J.P. Domingues Martinho *et al.,* (Eds.), *Experiences, Advantages, and Economic Dimensions of Pilgrimage Routes,* (pp. 306- 327). Pennsylvania USA: IGI Global.

Medhekar, A., & Haq, F. (2020). Cross-Border Cooperation for Bilateral Trade, Travel and Tourism: A Challenge for India and Pakistan. In Castanho, R. A. (Ed.), *Cross-Border Cooperation Strategies for Sustainable Development.Chapter10* (pp. 168–191). IGI Global. 10.4018/978-1-7998-2513-5.ch010

Medhekar, A., & Roy, K. (2010). Public and private sector partnerships for correcting infrastructure bottleneck in India. In Roy, K. C., Medhekar, A., & Chittoo, H. (Eds.), *Globalization and Development: Country Experiences* (pp. 15–30). Nova Science.

Medina-Garrido, J. A., Biedma-Ferrer, J. M., & Rodríguez-Cornejo, M. V. (2021). I quit! Effects of work-family policies on the turnover intention. *International Journal of Environmental Research and Public Health*, 18(4), 1893.33669281

Mehmetoglu, M. (2001). Economic scale of community-run festivals: A Case study. *Event Management*, 7(2), 93–102. 10.3727/152599501108751506

Mehrara, M. (2011). Health expenditure and economic growth: An ardl approach for the case of Iran. *Journal of Economics and Behavioral Studies*, 3(4), 249–256. https://ideas.repec.org//a/rnd/arjebs/v3y2011i4p249-256.html. 10.22610/jebs.v3i4.277

Meng, Y. Z. (2020). Chinese tourists' sense of safety: Perceptions of expected and experienced destination safety. *Current Issues in Tourism*, 23(15), 1886–1899. 10.1080/13683500.2019.1681382

Michael, N. W., Wien, C., & Reisinger, Y. (2017). Push and pull escape travel motivations of Emirati nationals to Australia. *International Journal of Culture, Tourism and Hospitality Research*, 11(3), 274–296. 10.1108/IJCTHR-04-2016-0039

Milton, S. (2021). Higher education and sustainable development goal 16 in fragile and conflict-affected contexts. *Higher Education*, 81(1), 89–108. 10.1007/s10734-020-00617-z

Mimi Li, L. A. (2010). A Missing Link in Understanding Revisit Intention—The Role of Motivation and Image. *Journal of Travel & Tourism Marketing*, 27(4), 335–348. 10.1080/10548408.2010.481559

Mishra, G. (2021). *Work-Family Conflict and Family-Friendly Policies for Working Women in India*. Lulu Publication.

Mishra, P. K., Rout, H. B., & Mohapatra, S. S. (2011). Causality between tourism and economic growth: Empirical evidence from India. *European Journal of Soil Science*, 18(4), 518–527.

Mohanty, P. S. (2018). Women at work: exploring the issues and challenges of women employees in travel and tourism. *Indian Journal of Economics and Development, 6*(1), 1-5. doi: (online): 2320-9836ISSN

Moher, D., Shamseer, L., Clarke, M., Ghersi, D., Liberati, A., Petticrew, M., Shekelle, P., Stewart, L. A., Estarli, M., Barrera, E. S. A., Martínez-Rodríguez, R., Baladia, E., Agüero, S. D., Camacho, S., Buhring, K., Herrero-López, A., Gil-González, D. M., Altman, D. G., Booth, A., & Whitlock, E. (2016). Preferred reporting items for systematic review and meta-analysis protocols (PRISMA-P) 2015 statement. *Revista Espanola de Nutricion Humana y Dietetica*, 20(2), 148–160. 10.1186/2046-4053-4-125554246

Monto, M., & Milrod, C. (2020). Perceptions of provider power among sex buyers. *Sexualities*, 23(4), 630–644. 10.1177/1363460719831977

Morais, D., Yarnal, C., And, E. D., & Dowler, L. (2005). The impact of ethnic tourism on gender roles: A comparison between the Bai and the Mosuo of Yunnan province, PRC. *Asia Pacific Journal of Tourism Research*, 10(4), 361–367. 10.1080/10941660500363678

Moreno, N., Moncada, S., Llorens, C., & Carrasquer, P. (2010). Double presence, paid work, and domestic-family work. *New Solutions*, 20(4), 511–526. 10.2190/NS.20.4.h21342873

Moslehpour, M., Firman, A., & Lin, C. H. (2023). The moderating impact of government support on the relationship between tourism development and growth, natural resources depletion, sociocultural degradation, economic environment, and pollution reduction: case of Indonesian economy. *Environmental Science and Pollution Research, 30*(1), 56863–56878. 10.1007/s11356-023-26231-x

Movono, A., & Dahles, H. (2017). Female empowerment and tourism: A focus on businesses in a Fijian village. *Asia Pacific Journal of Tourism Research*, 22(6), 681–692. 10.1080/10941665.2017.1308397

Movono, A., Dahles, H., & Becken, S. (2018). Fijian culture and the environment: A focus on the ecologicaland social interconnectedness of tourism development. *Journal of Sustainable Tourism*, 26(3), 451–469. 10.1080/09669582.2017.1359280

Movono, A., & Hughes, E. (2020). Tourism partnerships: Localizing the SDG agenda in Fiji. *Journal of Sustainable Tourism*, 1–15. 10.1080/09669582.2020.1811291

Moyo, C., Mishi, S., & Ncwadi, R. (2022). Human capital development, poverty and income inequality in Eastern cape province. *Development Studies Research*, 9(1), 36–47. 10.1080/21665095.2022.2032236

Mróz, F. (2021). The impact of COVID-19 on pilgrimages and religious tourism in Europe during the first six months of pandemic. *Journal of Religion and Health*, 60(2), 625–645. 10.1007/s10943-021-01201-033611686

Munar, A. M., Biran, A., Budeanu, A., Caton, K., Chambers, D., Dredge, D., Gyimothy, S., Jamal, T., Larson, M., Nilsson Lindstrom, K., Nygaard, L., & Ram, Y. (2015). The Gender Gap in the Tourism Academy: Statistics and Indicators of Gender Equality. Copenhagen: While Waiting for the Dawn.

National Tourism Policy. (2010). Ministry of Civil Aviation and Tourism. Peoples Republic of Bangladesh. In *National Tourism Policy Report* (pp. 1-17). National Tourism Policy. http://parjatan.portal.gov.bd/sites/default/files/files/parjatan.portal.gov.bd/policies/401cea95_b71f_4591_a77d_81eb95e689f6/2020-06-21-12-42-ab744be9913f6906fce79ecee1354d9a.pdf

Netemeyer, B. a. (1996). Development and Validation of Work-Family Conflict and Family-Work Conflict Scales. *The Journal of Applied Psychology*, 81(4). Advance online publication. 10.1037/0021-9010.81.4.400

Niäiä, M., Ivanovic, S., & Drpic, D. (2010). Challenges to sustainable development in Island tourism. *South East European Journal of Economic Business*, 5(2), 43–53. 10.2478/v10033-010-0014-3

Nilnoppakun, A., & Ampavat, K. (2016). Is pai a sustainable tourism destination? *Procedia Economics and Finance*, 39, 262–269. 10.1016/S2212-5671(16)30322-7

Nima, S., & Orazani, K. J. (2023). What works and why in interventions to strengthen social cohesion: A systematic review. *Journal of Applied Social Psychology*, 53(10), 938–995. 10.1111/jasp.12990

Nu'man, M. H. (2021, June). Protection of Informal Female Workers in Tourist Sector Company. In *Social and Humanities Research Symposium (SORES 2020),* (pp. 68-71). Atlantis Press.

Nurudeen, A., & Usman, A. (2010). Government expenditure and economic growth in Nigeria, 1970-2008: A disaggregated analysis. *Business and Economics Journal*, 4(1), 11. https://www.hilarispublisher.com/abstract/government-expenditure-and-economic-growth-in-nigeria-19702008-a-disaggregated-analysis-29819.html

Ogungbenle, S., Olawumi, O. R., & Obasuyi, F. O. T. (2013). *Life expectancy, public health spending and economic growth in nigeria: A vector autoregressive (Var) model.* CORE. https://core.ac.uk/display/236408152?utm_source=pdf&utm_medium=banner&utm_campaign=pdf-decoration-v1

Omondi, R. K., & Ryan, C. (2017). Sex tourism: Romantic safaris, prayers and witchcraft at the Kenyan coast. *Tourism Management*, 58, 217–227. 10.1016/j.tourman.2015.11.003

Ornelas, S., Camilo, C., Csalog, R. A., Hatzinikolaou, K., & Calheiros, M. M. (2023). Social schemas about human trafficking involving girls and women: A systematic review. *Aggression and Violent Behavior*, 73, 101873. 10.1016/j.avb.2023.101873

Oselin, S. S., & Weitzer, R. (2013). Organizations working on behalf of prostitutes: An analysis of goals, practices, and strategies. *Sexualities*, 16(3–4), 445–466. 10.1177/1363460713481741

Ottenbacher, M. C., Schwebler, S., Metzler, D., & Harrington, R. J. (2015). Sustainability Criteria for Tourism Attractions: A Case Study of Germany. [IJSESD]. *International Journal of Social Ecology and Sustainable Development*, 6(2), 20–39. 10.4018/ijsesd.2015040102

Our world in data. (2023). Our World in Data. [Online]. https://ourworldindata.org

Özgit, H., & Zhandildina, D. (2021). Investigating stakeholder awareness of the sustainable development goals and tourism stakeholder collaboration: The case of North Cyprus. *Worldwide Hospitality and Tourism Themes*, 13(4), 498–509. 10.1108/WHATT-02-2021-0027

Öz, Ö. (2002). Assessing Porter's framework for national advantage: The case of Turkey. *Journal of Business Research*, 55(6), 509–515. 10.1016/S0148-2963(00)00167-3

P, H. B. (1995). Tourism and growth in a dynamic model of trade. *The Journal of International Trade and Economic Development, 4*, 243-252. 10.1080/09638199500000019

Pachot, A., & Patissier, C. (2023). *Towards Sustainable Artificial Intelligence: An Overview of Environmental Protection Uses and Issues.* Green and Low-Carbon Economy., 10.47852/bonviewGLCE3202608

Page, M. J., McKenzie, J. E., Bossuyt, P. M., Boutron, I., Hoffmann, T. C., Mulrow, C. D., Shamseer, L., Tetzlaff, J. M., Akl, E. A., Brennan, S. E., Chou, R., Glanville, J., Grimshaw, J. M., Hróbjartsson, A., Lalu, M. M., Li, T., Loder, E. W., Mayo-Wilson, E., McDonald, S., & Moher, D. (2021). The PRISMA 2020 statement: An updated guideline for reporting systematic reviews. *Journal of Clinical Epidemiology*, 134, 178–189. 10.1016/j.jclinepi.2021.03.00133789819

Pai, K. (2009). Glass ceiling: Role of women in the corporate world. *Competitiveness Review*, 19(2), 106–113.

Paniccia, P. M., Leoni, L., & Baiocco, S. (2017). Interpreting Sustainability through Co-Evolution: Evidence from Religious Accommodations in Rome. *Sustainability (Basel)*, 9(12), 2301. https://www.mdpi.com/2071-1050/9/12/2301. 10.3390/su9122301

Panta, S. K., & Thapa, B. (2018). Entrepreneurship and women's empowerment in gateway communities of Bardia National Park Nepal. *Journal of Ecotourism*, 17(1), 20–42. 10.1080/14724049.2017.1299743

Park, J. M. (2013). Paradoxes of gendering strategy in prostitution policies: South Korea's "toleration-regulation regime," 1961-1979. *Women's Studies International Forum*, 37, 73–84. 10.1016/j.wsif.2012.10.008

Patching-Bunch, J. (2015). Learning Intercultural Competency through International Immersion Travel. *University Honors Theses.*, 305. Advance online publication. 10.15760/honors.274

Patterson, N., Mavin, S., & Turner, J. (2012). Envisioning female entrepreneur: Leaders anew from a gender perspective. *Gender in Management*, 27(9), 395–416. 10.1108/17542411211269338

Patwardhan, V. R., Ribeiro, M. A., Woosnam, K. M., Payini, V., & Mallya, J. (2020). Visitors' loyalty to religious tourism destinations: Considering place attachment, emotional experience and religious affiliation. *Tourism Management Perspectives*, 36, 100737. 10.1016/j.tmp.2020.100737

Pearce, P., & Morrison, A. a. (1998). *Tourism: Bridges across continents*. McGraw-Hill.

Pécot, M., Ricaurte-Quijano, C., Khoo, C., Vázquez, M. A., Barahona-Canales, D., Yang, E. C. L., & Tan, R. (2024). From empowering women to being empowered by women: A gendered social innovation framework for tourism-led development initiatives. *Tourism Management*, 102, 104883. 10.1016/j.tourman.2024.104883

Pena-Sanchez, A. R., Ruiz-Chico, J., Jimenez-García, M., & Lopez-Sanchez, J. A. (2020). Tourism and the SDGs: An analysis of economic growth, decent employment, and gender equality in the European Union (2009–2018). *Sustainability (Basel)*, 12(13), 5480. 10.3390/su12135480

Pérez-Rodríguez, J. V., Rachinger, H., & Santana-Gallego, M. (2021). Testing the validity of the tourism-led growth hypothesis under long-range dependence. *Current Issues in Tourism*, 24(6), 768–793. 10.1080/13683500.2020.1744537

Pesaran, M. H., & Shin, Y. (1995). *Autoregressive distributed lag modelling approach to cointegration analysis.* (DAE Working Paper Series No. 9514). Department of Economics, University of Cambridge, Cambridge.

Pettersson, K., & Cassel, S. H. (2014). Women tourism entrepreneurs: Doing gender on farms in Sweden. *Gender in Management*, 29(8), 487–504. 10.1108/GM-02-2014-0016

Philip Kotler, K. L. (2008). *Marketing Management*. Pearson Education.

Phommavong, S., & Sörensson, E. (2014). Ethnic tourism in Lao PDR: Gendered divisions of labour in community-based tourism for poverty reduction. *Current Issues in Tourism*, 17(4), 350–362. 10.1080/13683500.2012.721758

Planning Commission. (2015). *Seventh Five Year Plan FY 2016- FY 2020, Accelerating Growth, Empowering Citizens*. Dhaka: Bangladesh.

Polash, A. K., & Habeb, A. (2020). Ecotourism: A new door to possibilities for Bangladesh. *International Journal of Advances in Engineering and Management*, 2(8), 121–132.

Ponting, J., & O'Brien, D. (2014). Liberalizing Nirvana: An analysis of the consequences of common pool resource deregulation for the sustainability of Fiji's surf tourism industry. *Journal of Sustainable Tourism*, 22(3), 384–402. 10.1080/09669582.2013.819879

Porter, M. E. (1990). The Competitive Advantage of Nations. *Harvard Business Review*, 68(2), 73–93.

Pourtaheri, M. R., Rahmani, K., & Ahmadi, H. (2012). Impacts of religious and pilgrimage tourism in rural areas: The case of Iran. *Journal of Geography and Geology*, 4(3), 122. 10.5539/jgg.v4n3p122

Pradhan, B., Yadav, S., Ghosh, J., & Prashad, A. (2023). Achieving the sustainable development goals (SDGs) in the Indian states of Odisha: Challenges and opportunities. *World Development Sustainability*, 3(1), 43–52. 10.1016/j.wds.2023.100078

Prasad Acharya, B. P., & Halpenny, E. (2013). Homestays as an Alternative Tourism Product for Sustainable Community Development: A Case Study of Women-Managed Tourism Product in Rural Nepal. *Tourism Planning & Development*, 10(4), 367–387. 10.1080/21568316.2013.779313

Prasetyanto, P. K., & Sari, F. (2021). Environmental Kuznets curve: Economic growth with environmental degradation in Indonesia. *International Journal of Energy Economics and Policy*, 11(5), 622–628. 10.32479/ijeep.11609

Pratt, S. (2013). Minimising food miles: Issues and outcomes in an ecotourism venture in Fiji. *Journal of Sustainable Tourism*, 21(8), 1148–1165. 10.1080/09669582.2013.776060

Pratt, S., Gibson, D., & Movono, A. (2013). Tribal Tourism in Fiji: An Application and Extension of Smith's 4Hs of Indigenous Tourism. *Asia Pacific Journal of Tourism Research*, 18(8), 894–912. 10.1080/10941665.2012.717957

Pratt, S., McCabe, S., & Movono, A. (2015). Gross happiness of a 'tourism' village in Fiji. *Journal of Destination Marketing & Management*, 5(1), 26–35. 10.1016/j.jdmm.2015.11.001

Pritchard, A., & Morgan, N. (2005). Representations of 'ethnographic knowledge': Early comic postcards of Wales. *Discourse, communication and tourism*, 53-75. 10.21832/9781845410216-006

Pritchard, A., & Morgan, N. (2017). Tourism's lost leaders: Analysing gender and performance. *Annals of Tourism Research*, 63, 34–47. 10.1016/j.annals.2016.12.011

Pritchard, A., Morgan, N., & Ateljevic, I. (2011). Hopeful tourism: A new transformative perspective. *Annals of Tourism Research*, 38(3), 941–963. 10.1016/j.annals.2011.01.004

Psacharopoulos, G., & Patrinos, H. A. (2004). Returns to investment in education: A further update. *Education Economics*, 12(2), 111–134. 10.1080/0964529042000239140

Purcell, K. (1997). Women's employment in UK tourism: Gender roles and labour markets. In Sinclair, M. (Ed.), *Gender, work and tourism* (pp. 33–56). Routledge.

Purnell, P. J. (2022). A comparison of different methods of identifying publications related to the United Nations Sustainable Development Goals: Case study of SDG 13—Climate Action. *Quantitative Science Studies*, 3(4), 976–1002. 10.1162/qss_a_00215

Rad, M. S. (2017). Psychological capital and academic burnout in students of clinical majors in Iran. *Acta Facultatis Medicae Naissensisthis*, 311-319. 10.1515/afmnai-2017-0035

Rahman, M., Mostofa, M., & Hoque, M. (2014). Women's household decision-making autonomy and contraceptive behavior among Bangladeshi women. *Sexual & Reproductive Healthcare: Official Journal of the Swedish Association of Midwives*, 5(1), 9–15. 10.1016/j.srhc.2013.12.00324472384

Rasoolimanesh, S. M., Ramakrishna, S., Hall, C. M., Esfandiar, K., & Seyfi, S. (2023). A systematic scoping review of sustainable tourism indicators in relation to the sustainable development goals. *Journal of Sustainable Tourism*, 31(7), 1497–1517. 10.1080/09669582.2020.1775621

Raub, S. P., & Martin-Rios, C. (2019). "Think sustainable, act local" – a stakeholder-filter-model for translating SDGs into sustainability initiatives with local impact. *International Journal of Contemporary Hospitality Management*, 31(6), 2428–2447. 10.1108/IJCHM-06-2018-0453

Rauniyar, G., & Kanbur, R. (2006). *Inclusive Growth and Inclusive Development: A Review & Synthesis of Asian Development Bank Literature*. (Occasional Paper, No.8).

Reisinger, Y., & Mavondo, F. (2005). Travel anxiety and intentions to travel internationally: Implications of travel risk perception. *Journal of Travel Research*, 43(3), 212–225. 10.1177/0047287504272017

Rendon, M. L., & Bidwell, S. (2015). Success in progress? Tourism as a tool for inclusive development in Peru's Colca Valley. In Panosso Netto, A., & Trigo, L. (Eds.), *Tourism in Latin America* (pp. 207–233). Springer. 10.1007/978-3-319-05735-4_12

Ribeiro, F. B., & Silva, M. C. (2019). Persecution or Recognition? Abolitionism, self-determination and recognition of rights of sex workers. *A Gazeta de Antropología, 35*(1), 1–16. www.gazeta-antropologia.es/?p=5132

Ribeiro, M. A., Adam, I., Kimbu, A. N., Afenyo-Agbe, E., Adeola, O., Figueroa-Domecq, C., & de Jong, A. (2021). Women entrepreneurship orientation, networks and firm performance in the tourism industry in resource-scarce contexts. *Tourism Management*, 86, 104343. 10.1016/j.tourman.2021.104343

Rinaldi, A., & Salerno, I. (2020). The tourism gender gap and its potential impact on the development of the emerging countries. *Quality & Quantity*, 54(5-6), 1465–1477. 10.1007/s11135-019-00881-x

Robert, K. W., Parris, T. M., & Leiserowitz, A. A. (2005). What is sustainable development? Goals, indicators, values, and practice. *Environment*, 47(3), 8–21. 10.1080/00139157.2005.10524444

Romer, P. M. (1990). Endogenous technological change. *Journal of Political Economy*, 98(5), 71–102. 10.1086/261725

Rosato, P. F., Caputo, A., Valente, D., & Pizzi, S. (2021). 2030 Agenda and sustainable business models in tourism: A bibliometric analysis. *Ecological Indicators*, 121, 106978. 10.1016/j.ecolind.2020.106978

Rose, C. (2007). Does Female Board Representation Influence Firm Performance? The Danish Evidence. *Corporate Governance*, 15(2), 404–413. 10.1111/j.1467-8683.2007.00570.x

Rosselló-Nadal, J. (2014). How to evaluate the effects of climate change on tourism. *Tourism Management*, 42, 334–340. 10.1016/j.tourman.2013.11.006

Roxas, F. M. Y., Rivera, J. P. R., & Gutierrez, E. L. M. (2020). Framework for creating sustainable tourism using systems thinking. *Current Issues in Tourism*, 23(3), 280–296. 10.1080/13683500.2018.1534805

Roy, R. P., & Sinha Roy, S. (2019). SDG 10—A Probe into the Factors Underlying Differences in Inequality: Evidence at the Sub-national Level in India. In *2030 Agenda and India: Moving from Quantity to Quality* (1st ed., pp. 149–164). Springer. 10.1007/978-981-32-9091-4_7

Royanty, I. S. (2017). Visiting the Museum (Survey of East Java Stone Transport Museum Tourists). *Journal of Business Administration*, 84-92.

Roy, B., & Saxena, A. K. (2020). Destination competitiveness, tourism facilities and problems in promoting Uttarakhand as a tourism destination. *Journal of Tourism. Hospitality & Culinary Arts*, 12(2), 1–20.

Roy, D., Dhir, M. G. M., & Ahsan, M. K. (2016). Factors affecting tourist satisfaction: A study in Sylhet Region. *ABC Research Alert*, 4(3), 9–20. 10.18034/abcra.v4i3.307

Roy, H. (2010). The Role of Tourism to Poverty Alleviation. 10.2139/ssrn.1599971

Roy, M. (2021). Tourism Industry in Bangladesh: An Assessment of advanced SWOT Model and TOWS Matrix. In Hasan, A. (Ed.), *Tourism in Bangladesh Investment and Development Perspectives* (pp. 279–310). Springer. 10.1007/978-981-16-1858-1_18

Roy, M., Yajing, F., & Biswas, B. (2020). Economic contribution of tourism in Bangladesh: Capital investment perspective. In *Tourism Marketing in Bangladesh* (pp. 223–237). Routledge. 10.4324/9781003007241-22

Roy, P. B., Roy, T. B., & Saha, S. (2010). Pro-Poor Tourism as an Approach towards Community Development: A Case Study. *South Asian Journal of Tourism and Heritage*, 3(2), 90–98.

Roy, S. C., & Roy, M. (2015). Tourism in Bangladesh: Present status and future prospects. International. *Journal of Management Science and Business Administration*, 1(8), 53–61.

Rydzik, A., & Anitha, S. (2019). Conceptualising the Agency of Migrant Women Workers: Resilience, Reworking and Resistance. *Work, Employment and Society*, ●●●, 1–17.

Saad, S. (2021). *Culture and Handicraft Tourism in India: Tourism supporting sustainable development goals. Master's Dissertations*. Auckland University of Technology.

Saarinen, J., & Rogerson, C. (2014). Tourism and the Millennium Development Goals: Perspectives beyond 2015. *Tourism Geographies*, 16(1), 23–30. 10.1080/14616688.2013.851269

Saayman, M. R. R., Rossouw, R., & Krugell, W. (2012). The impact of tourism on poverty in South Africa. *Development Southern Africa*, 10(3), 231–254. 10.1080/0376835X.2012.706041

Sachs, J. D., Lafortune, G., Kroll, C., Fuller, G., & Woelm, F. (2022). *Sustainable Development Report 2022 - From Crisis to Sustainable Development: the SDGs as Roadmap to 2030 and Beyond*. Cambridge University Press., 10.1017/9781009210058

Saini, M., Sengupta, E., Singh, M., Singh, H., & Singh, J. (2023). Sustainable Development Goal for Quality Education (SDG 4): A study on SDG 4 to extract the pattern of association among the indicators of SDG 4 employing a genetic algorithm. *Education and Information Technologies*, 28(2), 2031–2069. 10.1007/s10639-022-11265-435975216

Sangpikul, A. (2008). A factor-cluster analysis of tourist motivations: A case of U.S. senior travellers. *Tourism (Zagreb)*, 56, 23–40.

Santero-Sanchez, R., Segovia-Perez, B., Castro-Nunez, C., Figueroa-Domecq, P., & Talón-Ballestero, P. (2015). Gender Differences in the Hospitality Industry. *Tourism Management*, 51, 234–246. 10.1016/j.tourman.2015.05.025

Santos, V. R., Ramos, P., Sousa, B., Almeida, N., & Valeri, M. (2022). Factors influencing touristic consumer behaviour. *Journal of Organizational Change Management*, 35(3), 409–429. 10.1108/JOCM-02-2021-0032

Saqib, N., & Satar, M. S. (2021). Exploring business model innovation for competitive advantage: A lesson from an emerging market. *International Journal of Innovation Science*, 13(4), 477–491. 10.1108/IJIS-05-2020-0072

Scheyvens, R. (2007). Exploring the tourism-poverty nexus. *Current Issues in Tourism*, 10(2-3), 231–254. 10.2167/cit318.0

Scheyvens, R., & Cheer, J. M. (2022). Tourism, the SDGs and partnerships. *Journal of Sustainable Tourism*, 30(10), 2271–2281. 10.1080/09669582.2021.1982953

Scheyvens, R., & Hughes, E. (2019). Can tourism help to "end poverty in all its forms everywhere"? The challenge of tourism addressing SDG1. *Journal of Sustainable Tourism*, 27(7), 1061–1079. 10.1080/09669582.2018.1551404

Scheyvens, R., & Russell, M. (2012). Tourism and poverty alleviation in Fiji: Comparing the impacts of small- and large-scale tourism enterprises. *Journal of Sustainable Tourism*, 20(3), 417–436. 10.1080/09669582.2011.629049

Seidman, G. (2017). Does SDG 3 have an adequate theory of change for improving health systems performance? *Journal of Global Health*, 7(1), 010302. 10.7189/jogh.07.01030228567275

Sen, A. (1999). *Development as Freedom*. Harvard University Press.

Shafer, S. M., Smith, H. J., & Linder, J. C. (2005). The power of business models. *Business Horizons*, 48(3), 199–207. 10.1016/j.bushor.2004.10.014

Shaukat, R. Y. (2017). Examining the linkages between relationship conflict, performance and turnover intentions: Role of job burnout as a mediator. *International Journal of Conflict Management*, 28(1), 4–23. 10.1108/IJCMA-08-2015-0051

Shelton, L. M. (2006). Female entrepreneurs, work–family conflict, and venture performance: New insights into the work–family interface. *Journal of Small Business Management*, 44(2), 285–297.

Shikida, A., Yoda, M., Kino, A., & Morishige, M. (2010). Tourism relationship model and intermediary for sustainable tourism management: Case study of the Kiritappu Wetland Trust in Hamanaka, Hokkaido. *Tourism and Hospitality Research*, 10(2), 105–115. 10.1057/thr.2009.29

Siakwah, P., Musavengane, R., & Leonard, L. (2020). Tourism governance and attainment of the sustainable development goals in Africa. *Tourism Planning & Development*, 17(4), 355–383. 10.1080/21568316.2019.1600160

Simpson, M. C. (2008). Community benefit tourism initiatives—A conceptual oxymoron? *Tourism Management*, 29(1), 1–18. 10.1016/j.tourman.2007.06.005

Singh, A. K., Kumar, S., & Jyoti, B. (2022b). Impact of the COVID-19 on food security and sustainable development goals in India: Evidence from existing literature. GNOSI: An *Interdisciplinary Journal of Human Theory and Praxis*, 5(2), 94-109. http://gnosijournal.com/index.php/gnosi/article/view/196/225

Singh, S. (2022). Do indexes assess poverty? Is tourism truly pro-poor? *Journal of Ekonomi*, 07, 06-13 https://dergipark.org.tr/ekonomi

Singh, A. K., Issac, J., & Narayanan, K. G. S. (2019). Measurement of environmental sustainability index and its association with socio-economic indicators in selected Asian economies: An empirical investigation. *International Journal of Environment and Sustainable Development*, 18(1), 57–100. 10.1504/IJESD.2019.098641

Singh, A. K., & Jyoti, B. (2023). *Impact of digitalization on global sustainable development across countries*. Green and Low-carbon Economy., 10.47852/bonviewGLCE32021482

Singh, A. K., Jyoti, B., Kumar, S., & Lenka, S. K. (2021). Assessment of global sustainable development, environmental sustainability, economic development and social development index in selected economies. *International Journal of Sustainable Development and Planning*, 16(1), 123–138. 10.18280/ijsdp.160113

Singh, A. K., & Kumar, S. (2022). Exploring the impact of sustainable development on social-economic, and science and technological development in selected countries: A panel data analysis. *Society & Sustainability*, 4(1), 55–83. 10.38157/ss.v4i1.405

Singh, A. K., Kumar, S., Sharma, A. K., & Sinha, S. (2022a). Does green entrepreneurship have an association with sustainable development and its components? Evidence from a country-wise panel data investigation. In Magd, M., Singh, D., Spicer, D., & Syed, R. T. (Eds.), *International Perspectives on Value Creation and Sustainability Through Social Entrepreneurship* (pp. 132–172). IGI Global. https://www.igi-global.com/gateway/chapter/30982910.4018/978-1-6684-4666-9.ch008

Singh, A. K., Sharma, A. K., & Jyoti, B. (2023a). Does economic development have a causal relationship with environmental degradation? Experience from different income group countries. In Sart, G. (Ed.), *Considerations on Education for Economic, Social, and Environmental Sustainability* (pp. 300–333). IGI Global. 10.4018/978-1-6684-8356-5.ch015

Singh, A. K., & Sharma, P. (2018). Implications of climatic and non-climatic variables on food security in developing economies: A conceptual review. *MOJ Food Processing & Technology*, 6(1), 1–12. 10.15406/mojfpt.2018.06.00138

Singh, A. K., Sharma, S. K., & Lenka, S. K. (2023b). Causality between green entrepreneurship and sustainable development: A cross-country analysis using ARDL model. *The IUP Journal of Applied Economics*, 22(1), 5–38.

Singh, A. K., Singh, B. J., & Negi, V. (2020). Does sustainable development have a causal relationship with environmental development? Evidence from a country-wise panel data analysis. *International Journal of Technology Management & Sustainable Development*, 19(2), 147–171. 10.1386/tmsd_00020_1

Singh, N. Y.-M. (2023). Exploring the impact of functional, symbolic, and experiential image on approach behaviors among state-park tourists from India, Korea, and the USA. *Humanities & Social Sciences Communications*, 10(14).36721793

Singh, R., & Jain, K. (2020). Work-family balance in the Indian hospitality sector. *International Journal of Hospitality Management*, 88, 102503.

Singh, S., & Jayaram, R. (2020). Attainment of the sustainable development goal of poverty eradication: A review, critique, and research agenda. *Journal of Public Affairs*, 22(1), 1–10. 10.1002/pa.2294

Singh, S., & Ru, J. (2023). Goals of sustainable infrastructure, industry, and innovation: A review and future agenda for research. *Environmental Science and Pollution Research International*, 30(11), 28446–28458. 10.1007/s11356-023-25281-536670221

Smith, T. D. (2018). Assessment of relationships between work stress, work-family conflict, burnout and firefighter safety behavior outcomes. *Safety Science*, 103, 287–292. 10.1016/j. ssci.2017.12.005

Smith, V. L. (1992). Hosts and Guests Revisited. *The American Behavioral Scientist*, 36(2), 187–199. 10.1177/0002764292036002006

Sojo, V. E. (2016). Harmful workplace experiences and women's occupational well-being: A meta-analysis. *Psychology of Women Quarterly*, 40(1), 10–40. 10.1177/0361684315599346

Soliman, M. S. (2015). Pro-poor tourism in protected areas– opportunities and challenges: "The case of Fayoum, Egypt.". *Anatolia*, 26(1), 61–72. 10.1080/13032917.2014.906353

Søntvedt, M. (2009). *Making sense of sex tourism through the accounts of sex tourists: A Foucauldian discourse analysis of sex tourists' online communication* [Martes Thesis]. University of Oslo.

Speer, P. W., Jackson, C. B., & Peterson, N. A. (2001). The Relationship between Social Cohesion and Empowerment: Support and New Implications for Theory. *Health Education & Behavior*, 28(6), 716–732. 10.1177/109019810102800060511720274

Spenceley, A. (2022). Pro-Poor Tourism's Evolution and Implications Arising from the COVID-19 Pandemic. *Tourism Planning & Development*, 19(1), 13–25. 10.1080/21568316.2021.2021470

Spenceley, A., & Goodwin, H. (2007). Nature-Based Tourism and Poverty Alleviation: Impacts of Private Sector and Parastatal Enterprises in and Around Kruger National Park, South Africa. *Current Issues in Tourism*, 10(2-3), 255–277. 10.2167/cit305.0

Spenceley, A., & Meyer, D. (2012). Tourism and poverty reduction: Theory and practice in less economically developed countries. *Journal of Sustainable Tourism*, 20(3), 297–317. 10.1080/09669582.2012.668909

Srivastava, N., & Singh, A. K. (2017). Impact of work-family conflict on psychological well-being of Indian women employees. *Vikalpa*, 42(1), 50–66.

Šťastná, M., Vaishar, A., Brychta, J., Tuzová, K., Zloch, J., & Stodolová, V. (2020). Cultural Tourism as a Driver of Rural Development. Case Study: Southern Moravia. *Sustainability (Basel)*, 12(21), 9064. https://www.mdpi.com/2071-1050/12/21/9064. 10.3390/su12219064

Subramanian, S. (2005). *Headcount poverty comparisons*. International Poverty Centre (United Nations Development Programmes) (IPC) SBS – Ed. BNDES, Brasilia, Brazil. http://www.ipc -undp.org/pub/IPCOnePager18.pdf

Sugiyarto, G. B. A., Blake, A., & Sinclair, M. T. (2003). Tourism and globalization: Economic impact in Indonesia. *Annals of Tourism Research*, 30(3), 683–701. 10.1016/S0160-7383(03)00048-3

Sukhera, J. (2022). Narrative Reviews in Medical Education: Key Steps for Researchers. In *Journal of graduate medical education, 14*(4), 418–419. NLM (Medline). 10.4300/JGME-D-22-00481.1

Sultana, R., Pala, S. S., Mohammad, A., & Tasnim, T. (2023). Achieving SDGs in Bangladesh: A meta-analysis on challenges and opportunities. *Journal of Bangladesh Institute of Planners*, 16, 77–104.

Sultana, S. (2016). Economic contribution of tourism industry in Bangladesh. *Journal of Tourism. Hospitality and Sports*, 22(2), 55–54.

Suntikul, W., Bauer, T., & Song, H. (2009). Pro-poor Tourism Development in Viengxay, Laos: Current State and Future Prospects. *Asia Pacific Journal of Tourism Research*, 14(2), 153–168. 10.1080/10941660902847203

Suraj Kumar Mallick, S. R. (2020). Sustainable ecotourism development using SWOT and QSPM approach: A study on Rameswaram, Tamil Nadu. *International Journal of Geoheritage and Parks*, 8(3), 185–193. Advance online publication. 10.1016/j.ijgeop.2020.06.001

Surangi, H. A. K. N. S. (2018). What influences the networking behaviours of female entrepreneurs? *International Journal of Gender and Entrepreneurship*, 10(2), 116–133. 10.1108/IJGE-08-2017-0049

Syed, A. A. (2018). Work-family conflict and turnover intentions: Moderated mediation model. *Human Resource Research*, 2(1), 95–106. 10.5296/hrr.v2i1.13925

Tafvelin, S. K. (2020). The prevalence and consequences of intragroup conflicts for employee well-being in women-dominated work. *Human Service Organizations, Management, Leadership & Governance*, 44(1), 47–62. 10.1080/23303131.2019.1661321

Tasci, A. D., & Gartner, W. C. (2007). Destination Image and Its Functional Relationships. *Journal of Travel Research*, 45(4), 413–425. 10.1177/0047287507299569

Tavakoli, R., Mura, P., & Devi Rajaratnam, S. D. (2017). Social capital in Malaysian homestays: Exploring hosts' social relations. *Current Issues in Tourism*, 20(10), 1028–1043. 10.1080/13683500.2017.1310189

Tedeneke, A. (2019). *Global survey shows 74% are aware of the Sustainable Development Goals*. WeForum. https://www.weforum.org/press/2019/09/global-survey-shows-74-are-aware-of-the -sustainable-development-goals/

Theocharous, A., & Philaretou, A. G. (2009). Sexual Harassment in the Hospitality Industry in the Republic of Cyprus: Theory and Prevention. *Journal of Teaching in Travel & Tourism*, 9(3-4), 288–304. 10.1080/15313220903445306

Timothy, D. J. (2007). Empowerment and stakeholder participation in tourism destination communities. In Church, A., & Coles, V. T. (Eds.), *Tourism, power, and space* (pp. 203–216). Routledge.

Tiwari, S., Mohanty, P. P., Fernando, I. N., Cifci, I., & Kuruva, M. B. (2023). Bridging tea with tourism: Empirical evidence from India and Sri Lanka. *Tourism Review*, 78(1), 177–202. 10.1108/TR-06-2022-0280

Tran, L., & Walter, P. (2014). Ecotourism, gender, and development in northern Vietnam. *Annals of Tourism Research*, 1(44), 116–130. 10.1016/j.annals.2013.09.005

Tsai, P.-H., Chen, C.-J., & Yang, H.-C. (2021). Using Porter's Diamond Model to Assess the Competitiveness of Taiwan's Solar Photovoltaic Industry. *SAGE Open*, 11(1), 215824402098828. 10.1177/2158244020988286

Tucker, H., & Boonabaana, B. (2012). A critical analysis of tourism, gender, and poverty reduction. *Journal of Sustainable Tourism*, 20(3), 437–455. 10.1080/09669582.2011.622769

Ulker-Demirel, E., & Ciftci, G. (2020). A systematic literature review of the theory of planned behavior in tourism, leisure and hospitality management research. *Journal of Hospitality and Tourism Management*, 43, 209–219. 10.1016/j.jhtm.2020.04.003

Ullah, A., Pinglu, C., Ullah, S., & Hashmi, S. H. (2021). Nexus of regional integration, socio-economic determinants and sustainable development in belt and road initiative countries. *PLoS One*, 16(7), 1–29. 10.1371/journal.pone.025429834242342

UN DESA. (2019). *The Sustainable Development Goals Report 2019*.

UN. (2015). *Transforming our world: The 2030 agenda for sustainable development*. UN. https://sustainabledevelopment.un.org/content/documents/21252030%20Agenda%20for%20Sustainable%20Development%20web.pdf?_gl=1*1l9w1zc*_ga*NDQzNTgyMjEwLjE3MTcxOTY1OTTg.*_ga_TK9BQL5X7Z*MTcxNzE5NjU5Ny4xLjEuMTcxNzE5NzUxMy4wLjAuMA

UNESCO. (2017). *Measurement strategy for SDG Target 4.7*. UNESCO. https://uis.unesco.org/sites/default/files/documents/gaml4-measurement-strategy-sdg-target4.7.pdf

United Nations Development Programme. (2017). *Tourism and the Sustainable Development Goals – Journey to 2030*. UN. https://www.e-unwto.org/doi/pdf/10.18111/9789284419401

United Nations World Tourism Organization (UNWTO). (2021). *Tourism and the Sustainable Development Goals – Journey to 2030*. UNWTO. https://www.e-unwto.org/doi/epdf/10.18111/9789284419401

United Nations. (2008). *An Introduction to Human Trafficking: Vulnerability, Impact and Action*. UN. www.ungift.org

UNWTO Highlights Tourism's Role for SDGs. (2015). International Institute of Sustainable Development. http://sdg.iisd.org/news/unwto-highlights-tourisms-role-for-sdgs/

UNWTO. (2010). *Global Report on Women in Tourism 2010*. World Tourism Organization.

UNWTO. (2017). *Discussion paper on the occasion of the international year of sustainable tourism for development*. UNWTO.

UNWTO. (2017). *Tourism and the sustainable development goals – journey to 2030*. UNWTO. https://www.e-unwto.org/doi/epdf/10.18111/9789284419401

UNWTO. (2023). *Achieving the sustainable development goals through tourism*. UNWTO. https://tourism4sdgs.org/tips_indicators/

Uysal, M. J. (1993). An Empirical Testing of the Push and Pull factors of Tourist Motivations. *CHRIE Conference*, (pp. 162-63). Research Gate.

Vada, S., Dupre, K., & Zhang, Y. (2023). Route tourism: a narrative literature review. In *Current Issues in Tourism, 26*(6). Routledge. 10.1080/13683500.2022.2151420

Valeri, M., & Katsoni, V. (Eds.). (2021). *Gender and tourism: Challenges and entrepreneurial opportunities*. Emerald Publishing Limited. 10.1108/9781801173223

Van der Merwe, M. (2003). *Women Entrepreneurs in South Africa*.

Van Tulder, R., Rodrigues, S. B., Mirza, H., & Sexsmith, K. (2021). The UN's Sustainable Development Goals: Can multinational enterprises lead the Decade of Action? *Journal of International Business Policy*, 4(1), 1–21. 10.1057/s42214-020-00095-1

Vanegas, M. G. W.Sr, Gartner, W., & Senauer, B. (2015). Tourism and poverty reduction: An economic sector analysis for Costa Rica and Nicaragua. *Tourism Economics*, 21(1), 159–182. 10.5367/te.2014.0442

Vanegas, R. C. (2008). Cointegration and causality between tourism and poverty reduction. *Journal of Travel Research*, 47(1), 94–103. 10.1177/0047287507312429

Varah, F., Mahongnao, M., Pani, B., & Khamrang, S. (2021). Exploring young consumers' intention toward green products: Applying an extended theory of planned behavior. *Environment, Development and Sustainability*, 23(6), 9181–9195. 10.1007/s10668-020-01018-z

Venugopalan, T., & Kumar, D. (2017). Sustainable development through sustainable tourism in India-A case study of Kerala tourism. *Asian Journal of Research in Business Economics and Management*, 7(12), 10–27. 10.5958/2249-7307.2017.00189.X

Vinodan, A., Sethumadhavan, M., & Manalel, J. (2022). Exploring sustainability facets of pro-poor tourism programs in India. *Enlightening Tourism: A Pathmaking Journal*, 12(2), 732-766. https://doi.org/10.33776/et.v12i2.7235

Vongvisitsin, T. B., Huang, W. J., & King, B. (2024). Urban community-based tourism development: A networked social capital model. *Annals of Tourism Research*, 106, 103759. 10.1016/j.annals.2024.103759

Vrontis, D., Christofi, M., Giacosa, E., & Serravalle, F. (2022). Sustainable development in tourism: A stakeholder analysis of the Langhe Region. *Journal of Hospitality & Tourism Research (Washington, D.C.)*, 46(5), 846–878. 10.1177/1096348020982353

Vujko, A., Tretiakova, T., Petrović, M., Radovanović, M., Gajić, T., & Vuković, D. (2019). Women's empowerment through self-employment in tourism. *Annals of Tourism Research*, 76, 328–330. 10.1016/j.annals.2018.09.004

Wahab, A. A. A. O., Kefeli, Z., & Hashim, N. (2018). *Investigating the dynamic effect of healthcare expenditure and education expenditure on economic growth in organisation of Islamic countries (Oic)* [MPRA Paper]. https://mpra.ub.uni-muenchen.de/90338/

Walter, P. (2011). Gender Analysis in Community-based Ecotourism. *Tourism Recreation Research*, 36(2), 159–168. 10.1080/02508281.2011.11081316

Walters, T. (2018). Gender equality in academic tourism, hospitality, leisure, and events conferences. *Journal of Policy Research in Tourism, Leisure & Events*, 10(1), 17–32. 10.1080/19407963.2018.1403165

Waverman, L. (1995). A critical analysis of Porter's framework on the competitive advantage of nations. In *Beyond The Diamond* (pp. 67–95). Elsevier. 10.1016/S1064-4857(95)05004-3

Wen, J., Klarin, A., Goh, E., & Aston, J. (2020). A systematic review of the sex trafficking-related literature: Lessons for tourism and hospitality research. *Journal of Hospitality and Tourism Management*, 45, 370–376. 10.1016/j.jhtm.2020.06.001

Wijaya, S. W., Wahyudi, W., Kusuma, C. B., & Sugianto, E. (2018). Travel motivation of Indonesian seniors in choosing destination overseas. *International Journal of Culture, Tourism and Hospitality Research*, 12(2), 185–197. 10.1108/IJCTHR-09-2017-0095

Wilkinson, P., & Pratiwi, W. (1995). Gender and Tourism in An Indonesian Village. *Annals of Tourism Research, 22*(2), 283-299. DOI: 10.1016/0160-7383(94)00077-8

Williams, E. (2013). *Sex Tourism in Bahia - Ambiguous Entanglements*. University of Illinois - Board of Trustees. https://www.ebsco.com/terms-of-use

Williams, C. C., & Lansky, M. A. (2013). Informal employment in developed and developing economies: Perspectives and policy responses. In *International Labour Review* (Vol. 152, Issue 4). https://ssrn.com/abstract=2706621

Wirth, L. (2001). *Breaking through the glass ceiling: Woman in management*. International Labour Office.

Women, U. N. (2014). Womens Economic Empowerment. Victoria Parade, Suva, Fiji: UN Women.

Wong, I. A., Law, R., & Zhao, X. R. (2018). Time-Variant Pleasure Travel Motivations and Behaviors. *Journal of Travel Research*, 57(4), 437–452. 10.1177/0047287517705226

World Bank (2019). *Bangladesh Poverty Assessment. Bangladesh Poverty Assessment*. World Bank.

World Bank. (2024). *Gini Index*. World Bank. https://data.worldbank.org/indicator/SI.POV.GINI

World Tourism Organisation. (2019). *International Tourism Expenditure. Statistical Yearbook 1995-2019*. WTO. https://data.worldbank.org/indicator/ST.INT.XPND.CD

World Tourism Organisation. (2019). International Tourism Number of Arrivals. *Statistical Yearbook 1995-2019*. WTO. https://data.worldbank.org/indicator/ST.INT.ARVL

World Tourism Organization. (2019). *Global Report on Women in Tourism* (2nd ed.). UNWTO. 10.18111/9789284420384

Worldslargestlesson (2023). *World's largest lesson*. World's Largest Lesson. https://worldslargestlesson.globalgoals.org/about-us/

Xie, C. Z., Zhang, J., & Morrison, A. M. (2021). Developing a Scale to Measure Tourist Perceived Safety. *Journal of Travel Research*, 60(6), 1232–1251. 10.1177/0047287520946103

Yadav, N., Gupta, M., Sharma, V., Yadav, D. K., & Sharma, A. K. (2024). How can the G-20 enhance its accountability and effectiveness? a comparative analysis of existing and proposed mechanisms. *Academy of Marketing Studies Journal*, *28*(S3), 1-11. chrome-extension://efaidnbmnnnibpcajpc-glclefindmkaj/https://www.abacademies.org/articles/how-can-the-g20-enhance-its-accountability-and-effectiveness-a-comparative-analysis-of-existing-and-proposed-mechanisms.pdf

Yang, S., Zhao, W., Liu, Y., Cherubini, F., Fu, B., & Pereira, P. (2020). Prioritizing sustainable development goals and linking them to ecosystem services: A global expert's knowledge evaluation. *Geography and Sustainability*, 1(4), 321–330. 10.1016/j.geosus.2020.09.004

Yoon, Y. U., & Uysal, M. (2005). An examination of the effects of motivation and satisfaction on destination loyalty: A structural model. *Tourism Management*, 26(1), 45–56. 10.1016/j.tourman.2003.08.016

Yuan, X., Yu, L., & Wu, H. (2021). Awareness of sustainable development goals among students from a Chinese senior high school. *Education Sciences*, 11(9), 458. 10.3390/educsci11090458

Yunis, E. (2004). *Tourism and poverty alleviation, Chief Sustainable Development of Tourism*. World Tourism Organization. www.rete.toscana.it/sett/turismo/euromeeting_2004/eng_yunis.pdf

Zapata, M. J., Hall, C. M., Lindo, P., & Vanderschaeghe, M. (2011). Can community-based tourism contribute to development and poverty alleviation? Lessons from Nicaragua. *Current Issues in Tourism*, 14(8), 725–749. 10.1080/13683500.2011.559200

Zeglin, R. J. (2014). Participation in prostitution: Associated outcomes within familial relationships. *Sexuality Research & Social Policy*, 11(1), 50–62. 10.1007/s13178-013-0143-4

Zeng, B. (2018). How can social enterprises contribute to sustainable pro-poor tourism development? *Zhongguo Renkou Ziyuan Yu Huanjing*, 16(2), 159–170. 10.1080/10042857.2018.1466955

Zhang, Y., Moyle, B., Dupré, K., Lohmann, G., Desha, C., & MacKenzie, I. (2023). Tourism and natural disaster management: A systematic narrative review. *Tourism Review*, 78(6), 1466–1483. 10.1108/TR-08-2022-0377

Zhou, Z. (2020). Religious Tourism in Zimbabwe: A Stakeholders` Perspective. In M. W. Emilia Alaverdov, *Global Development of Religious Tourism*. 10.4018/978-1-7998-5792-1

Zile, S. (2016). Sustainable development goals challenges and opportunities. *Indian Journal of Public Health*, 60(4), 247–250. 10.4103/0019-557X.19586227976644

About the Contributors

Marco Valeri is Associate Professor of Organizational Behavior, Faculty of Economics, NiccolÃ² Cusano University, Italy. He is Lecture in Applied Organizational Behaviour, Xenophon College, UK. He is Visiting Professor at University of Information Science and Technology (UIST) St. Paul The Apostle, Macedonia. He is Adjunct Professor at Faculty of Social Sciences and Leisure Management, School of Hospitality, Tourism and Events, Taylorâs University, Malaysia. He is Adjunct Professor at Faculty of Economics, Lovely Professional University (LPU), Phagwara, India. He is Associate Researcher in Strategy, Magellan Research Center, School of Management, Iaelyon Business School, Jean Monet University, France. He is Honorary Associate Professor, University of Pannonia, Hungary. Ranked #7 worldwide the most productive family economics scholars according to the ranking published by Texas State University. Heâs teaching and consultancy fields include strategic management, leadership development, cross-cultural management, international hospitality management. He is member of several Editorial Boards of international tourism journals, reviewer and editor of several handbooks on entrepreneurship, tourism and hospitality management (Emerald Publishing, Springer Publishing, Routledge Publishing, Edward Publishing and IGI Global Publishing).

Shekhar is a Research Scholar at the Faculty of Management Studies, University of Delhi. Having four years of teaching and research experience, he has published several research papers in international journals of repute. He is also serving as a reviewer for several research journals. His area of interest includes tourism development, value chain, strategy, and methodological interest include structural equation modelling, bibliometrics, and total-interpretive structural modelling. He is guest editing a special issue on Tourism Diplomacy and Global Peace for Tourism: An international interdisciplinary journal.

Natasha is currently pursuing a Bachelor's Degree in Economics at Amity School of Economics, Amity University, Noida. Her research interests lie in exploring the intersection of economics, tourism industry, labour market and sustainability.

Hulisi Binbasioglu is an associate professor of tourism and hotel management at Malatya Turgut Özal University in Türkiye and international visiting researcher at Cardiff Business School in UK. He received his BSc in Tourism and Hotel Management at Anadolu University, Eskisehir, and MSc and PhD in Marketing from İnönü University, Malatya. His teaching and research related to tourism marketing, sustainable tourism, and digital marketing. He has many articles indexed in SCI-E/ESCI/Scopus journals and international book chapters and proceedings in congresses.

Manisha Chand is an assistant lecturer at the Fiji National University.

About the Contributors

Prama Chatterjee is an Assistant Professor of Sociology at Central Tribal University of Andhra Pradesh, specializing in tribal research, technology, and society. She earned her PhD from Indira Gandhi National Tribal University, Amarkantak, M.P. Dr. Chatterjee focuses on tribal society, addressing various issues and promoting sustainable practices. With a few years of teaching experience, she has provided valuable knowledge and insights to her students. She has published articles and contributed chapters to edited books. Her work reflects a deep commitment to understanding contemporary society, the impact of technology on society, advancing the study of tribal Society and sustainable development.

Pritika Chand is an assistant instructor with the Fiji National University.

Arnab Gantait, a former UGC Project Fellow, is an independent independent researcher in tourism with a PGDM in Tourism & Travel from Indian Institute of Tourism and Travel Management (2012-2014) and UGC-NET (2014) qualification. With over three years in the industry, he has published 17 research articles, with 110+ citations. His work encompasses Responsible Tourism, Rural Tourism, Pro-poor Tourism, Heritage and Cultural Tourism, Community participation in tourism, Community based conservation, ICT in Education, etc.. Honored with the "IRSD Prominent Researcher Award" in 2023, Mr. Gantait's contributions are widely recognized on platforms like Google Scholar, SSRN, and ResearchGate.

Meenakshi Gupta is working as an Assistant Professor in the School of Economics, at Shri Mata Vaishno Devi University, Katra. She has teaching and research experience of almost 16 years. She has been a part of many academic and non- academic committees of the university since 2007. Her main areas of interest are Agricultural Economics, Environmental Economics and Development Economics. Her research work has been published in various national and international journals. She has contributed to various books also. She has also presented various articles at National and International Conferences. She is also awarded with many prestigious national and international awards. She is a life Member of Indian Economic Association, Indian Society of Agri- business and Management, Indian Society of Agricultural Economics, TIES, AERA, etc.

Kavita Indapurkar, with an experience of teaching in higher education institutions in India for over 25 years, has held several academic leadership positions and is presently Professor and is heading the School of Economics at Amity University, Uttar Pradesh, Noida Campus. A PhD in Economics and an MBA in finance, qualified at National level test for teaching in higher education in India, Prof. Dr. Kavita Indapurkar finds her research interests at the crossroads of behavioural aspects of people as consumers of various goods and or services or how do they make decisions.

Nikeel Kumar is a PHD scholar at the Royal Melbourne Institute Of Technology.

Isha Kumari is working as research scholar in the department of economics, Faculty of Management, Shri Mata Vaishno Devi University, Katra, J&K, (India).

Ravish Mathew, an esteemed scholar with dual Master's degrees in History and Tourism Administration, earned his Ph.D. in Tourism Studies from Pondicherry Central University. Currently an Assistant Professor at Sri Sri University, Cuttack, Odisha, he has over a decade of teaching experience and significant Post Doctoral experience. A recipient of the prestigious "Dr. Sarvepalli Radhakrishnan Post-Doctoral Fellowship", Dr. Mathew has authored over twenty publications in reputed tourism Scopus and UGC-Care journals and books. and presented research at more than 35 national and international conferences. His research area are ecotourism, responsible tourism, and wildlife conservation, with notable contributions to e-learning and administrative roles. His passions include visiting ecotourism and heritage sites, camping, and gastronomical tourism.

Anita Medhekar is a senior lecturer in economics and holds a PhD from Deakin University, Australia. She has completed her double Masters in pure Economics as well as in Education. She has taught at undergraduate and post graduate levels in India, Indonesia, and Australia and has nearly 30 years of teaching experience. Currently, she is teaching at Central Queensland University, Australia. Her research interests are in applied Health Economics, International Trade, Tourism Economics, Development Economics, Asia-Pacific Economies, Public Finance, South-Asia, Australian Economy, Bilateral Trade and Development for Peace, Supply Chains, Public Policy, and Public-Private Partnerships. She has presented papers at numerous international conferences and received best research paper awards. She has numerous refereed publications in journals, conference proceedings, edited books, and book chapters to her credit.

Rui Mendonça-Pedro holds a PhD in Tourism with a major in Management and Marketing from the Faculty of Economics of the University of Algarve. He is an Invited Adjunct Professor at the School of Management, Hospitality and Tourism, University of Algarve, Portimão Campus, Portugal. Rui is a collaborator research member of the Research Centre for Tourism, Sustainability and Well-being (CinTurs), University of Algarve, Faro, Portugal. In 2024, he joined the KIPT CoLab - a collaborative laboratory as a Tourism Researcher at the Lab for Sustainability. Rui's doctoral thesis developed a SEMs model (Senses, Emotions, and Memories) in the context of Tourism – Neurosciences – Psychology. The SEMs model allowed the reinforcement of the understanding, design, management, and implementation of the tourism experience more effectively, in terms of experiential stage planning and acting, namely, the sensory attributes that allow a tourist to feel and perceive an experience, to activate and evoke emotions and inscribe memories. His main research areas are: Sensory, Emotional and Memorable Consumer Experience; Tourist Experience Modelling and Design; Tourist Behaviours Trends; Tourism Sustainability.

Ankit Pathania working as an Assistant Professor in the Department of Management, Akal College of Economics, Commerce & Management, Eternal University, Baru Sahib, Distt.-Sirmaur (HP), India. He did his MBA and Doctorate in the discipline of Agri-Business Management from Dr YS Parmar University of Horticulture and Forestry, Nauni, Solan, HP, India.

Mallika Roy is an associate professor (study leave) at the Department of Economics, University of Chittagong, Bangladesh. Currently, she is a research student (PhD scholar) at Central Queensland University Australia. She was a research fellow and teaching assistant at the Department of Economics and Finance of the City University of Hong Kong. She achieved the Prestigious 'Prime Minister Gold Medal' Award in Bangladesh for her scholastic academic results. Her research interests include Macroeconomics, Economic Growth and Development. She has a teaching experience of above 12 years. She has worked in Islamia University College and BGC Trust University Bangladesh as a lecturer. After joining the University of Chittagong, she worked at the University of Professional (BUP) Bangladesh, Premier University and BGC Trust University Bangladesh as an adjunct faculty. She published many of her research papers in national and international journals. She also published several newspaper articles.

Karishma Sharma is an Assistant Lecturer at the Fiji National University Ba Campus.

Érica Simão is an Undergraduate Degree student in Tourism at the School of Management, Hospitality and Tourism at the University of Algarve (ESGHT – UAlg), Faro, Portugal. Her main research areas are Sociology of Tourism, Tourism and Social Responsibility, Social Inclusion and Social Innovation.

Ajay K. Singh is working as an Associate Professor (Research) in the Department of Humanities and Social Science, Graphic Era (Deemed to be University) Dehradun. He has worked as Assistant Professor (Economics) in the School of Liberal Arts & Management, DIT University Dehradun for 6 years. He did Post-Doctorate Research with EDI of India, Ahmedabad, Gujarat (India). He received MPhil (Economics) from DAVV Indore (India), and PhD (Economics) from IIT Indore (India. He has published several research papers in the diversified area such as climate change, agricultural productivity, assessment of food security; estimation of GFSI, development of environmental sustainability index (ESI) and its association with socio-economic indicators; measurement and determinants of entrepreneurship ecosystem, and dimension of sustainable development and its interlinkages with economic development.

About the Contributors

Kuldeep Singh currently serves as Assistant Professor in Amity School of Hospitality, amity university, Manesar, India. He completed his Ph.D. in tourism from Maharishi Dayanand University (Rohtak) in India in the year 2020. He is also a UGC (Net- JRF qualified). Dr. Singh has also served the tourism industry for couple of years and more than three years in academics. Dr. Singh has so far published more than 30 research articles in both international and national referred journals as well as in edited books in the field of Tourism. Currently, He is serving as an editor of book series in various reputed publications (Emerald, IIP series). Dr. Singh is passionate about the academic areas of Service Quality Management, Rural tourism, Ecotourism, and Sustainable tourism. He also won aspiring researchers welcome award from Indian Hospitality Congress. His credential may be verified on various research platforms like Google Scholar, SSRN, LinkedIn, Academia, and Research Gate.

Ambar Srivastava is a faculty in School of Commerce, Finance & Accountancy at Christ (Deemed to be University), Delhi NCR, Ghaziabad, India. He has qualified for the UGC-NET in commerce and completed a CA (Inter) from the Institute of Chartered Accountant of India (ICAI). Mr. Srivastava is amongst the top 5 in Master of Commerce (M. Com) from Jai Narain Vyas University, Jodhpur, Rajasthan. Besides these, he has taught at the Mohanlal Sukhadia University, Udaipur, Rajasthan. His teaching interests include financial accounting, corporate accounting, financial management, e-accounting, direct & indirect taxation, etc. He has published three textbook titled "Goods & Service Tax", "Income Tax" & "Cost Accounting" published by Choudhary Prakashan, Jaipur. He also published good research papers in reputed journals. His research interests include sustainability reporting, financial performance, corporate governance, taxation issues, etc.

Jone Toua is an Assistant lecturer at the Fiji National University.

Index

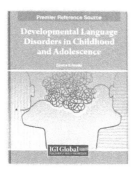

Ensure Quality Research is Introduced to the Academic Community

Become a Reviewer for IGI Global Authored Book Projects

 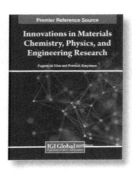 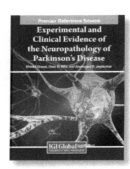 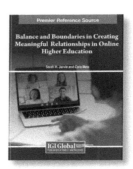

The overall success of an authored book project is dependent on quality and timely manuscript evaluations.

Applications and Inquiries may be sent to:
development@igi-global.com

Applicants must have a doctorate (or equivalent degree) as well as publishing, research, and reviewing experience. Authored Book Evaluators are appointed for one-year terms and are expected to complete at least three evaluations per term. Upon successful completion of this term, evaluators can be considered for an additional term.

If you have a colleague that may be interested in this opportunity, we encourage you to share this information with them.

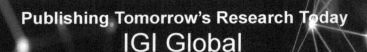

Milton Keynes UK
Ingram Content Group UK Ltd.
UKHW051043050824
446508UK00005B/120